The Heritage of
RUSSIAN VERSE

THE HERITAGE OF
RUSSIAN VERSE

INTRODUCED AND EDITED BY
Dimitri Obolensky

*

WITH PLAIN PROSE TRANSLATIONS
OF EACH POEM

Previously available as
The Penguin Book of Russian Verse

INDIANA UNIVERSITY PRESS
Bloomington   London

Published in Canada by Fitzhenry & Whiteside Limited, Don Mills, Ontario

Manufactured in the United States of America

Library of Congress Cataloging in Publication Data

Obolensky, Dimitri, 1918–   ed.
    The heritage of Russian verse.

    Reprint of the rev. ed. published in 1965 by Penguin Books, Harmondsworth, Eng., under title: The Penguin book of Russian verse.
    Includes index.
    1. Russian poetry—Translations into English.
2. English literature—Translations from Russian.
3. Russian poetry. I. Title.
PG3237.E502 1976   891.7′1′008   75–23893
ISBN 0–253–32735–0
ISBN 0–253–32736–9 pbk.

1 2 3 4 5 80 79 78 77 76

To the memory of
BORIS PASTERNAK

TABLE OF CONTENTS

INTRODUCTION xxxi

NOTE ON RUSSIAN VERSIFICATION liii

ACKNOWLEDGMENTS lxi

SLÓVO O POLKŬ ÍGOREVE (*c.* 1185), an anonymous heroic poem about the contemporary campaign of the Russian prince Igor against the Turkic Polovtsy of the steppe. The only known manuscript, discovered *c.* 1791, perished in 1812 in the fire of Moscow, after an edition had been published in 1800 and a second copy made. The text is faulty in places, which accounts for the obscurity of several passages. Some scholars have impugned the authenticity of the *Lay of Igor's Campaign*, but today it is almost universally considered genuine. It is the greatest work of Russian literature before Pushkin. It provided the subject for Borodin's opera *Prince Igor*. 1

BYLÍNY. These oral heroic poems of medieval Russia, originally sung by courtly minstrels, have in recent centuries been recited only by peasant bards, or *skaziteli*, who have modified them in accordance with their own less sophisticated outlook. Their original form is unknown, and they are all anonymous. The *bylina* relating the encounter between Il'ya of Murom – the most widely popular of the epic heroes – and Nightingale the Robber, a fantastic creature, half bird, half man, probably goes back in substance to the twelfth or eleventh century. The *bylina* of Sadko, the minstrel and rich merchant of Novgorod, is also medieval in origin. It generally comprises three separate episodes, of which the third – which is often recited independently – is given below. It provided the subject of an opera by Rimsky-Korsakov.

Первая Поездка Ильи Муромца. Илья и Соловей-Разбойник 23

Садко и Морской Царь 32

DUKHÓVNYE STIKHÍ. These oral religious poems are thought to have been composed between the fifteenth and the seventeenth centuries. Like the *byliny*, they are still recited today, though this is a rapidly dying art. The poem about Prince Josaphat, with its praise of the ascetic life, is based on the medieval romance of Barlaam and Josaphat which was translated into Russian from Greek. The *Saturday of St Dimitri* refers to the battle of Kulikovo (1380) in which the Russians, led by Prince Dimitri of Moscow, defeated the Tatars. It has been described as 'a perfect short story in verse'.

Плач Иосифа   43
Царевич Иосаф, Пустынник   44
Дмитровская Суббота   46
Сон Пресвятыя Богородицы   49

MIKHAÍL LOMONÓSOV (1711–65), the son of a fisherman of the White Sea coast, became one of the leading scientists of his time and a scholar of European reputation. A Professor of Chemistry in the Russian Academy of Sciences, he took a leading part in the foundation of Moscow University. As a legislator in the field of grammar, style, and prosody, he may be regarded as the founder of modern literary Russian. His reputation as a poet, which stood high in his own generation, has only recently begun to recover from the disdain with which his solemn odes were treated by the nineteenth-century Romantics. His *Evening Meditation* is an effective example of his philosophical poetry, scientific curiosity, and deistic outlook.

Вечернее размышление о Божием величестве при случае великого северного сияния   52

ALEKSÁNDR SUMARÓKOV (1718–77), the founder of Russian classical drama, is chiefly appreciated today for his love lyrics which, though conventional in treatment, are distinguished by their melodiousness and metrical ingenuity.

«Тщетно я скрываю сердца скорби люты»   55

GAVRIÍL DERZHÁVIN (1743–1816) combined a grand classical manner with several new features – such as the emphasis on emotional subjectivity and on the world of nature – which were further developed by poets of the early nineteenth century. His poem *The*

Monument, an adaptation of Horace's ode 'Exegi monumentum', has been unjustly eclipsed by Pushkin's celebrated piece on the same theme, which is partly modelled on Derzhavin's. *A Nightingale in a Dream* is one of the poems which Derzhavin wrote to illustrate the euphonic resources of the Russian language: it deliberately avoids the use of the letter *r*.

Властителям и судиям	57
Памятник	58
Соловей во сне	60
Цыганская пляска	61
«Река времён в своём стремленьи» (1816)	63

IVÁN KRYLÓV (*c.* 1769–1844) wrote several hundred fables, many of which have become classics. Written in a racy, robust, and somewhat archaic vernacular, they satirize incompetence, pretentiousness, and other vices from the standpoint of shrewd common sense. Many of his maxims have become popular proverbs.

Гуси	64
Квартет	65

VASÍLY ZHUKÓVSKY (1783–1852), tutor to the future emperor Alexander II, was in his lifetime chiefly famous for his patriotic poems and for his highly successful poetic translations; among the latter are renderings of Gray's *Elegy*, of ballads by Schiller, and of the *Odyssey*. To the modern reader his appeal lies in his short elegiac lyrics, simple and melodious.

К ней	68
Песня	69
19-го марта 1823 г.	70
Ночь	71
«Я Музу юную, бывало» (1824)	71

KONSTANTÍN BÁTYUSHKOV (1787–1855), an elegiac poet who learnt much from French, Italian, and Greek classical models. His verses reflect an epicurean eroticism, combined with a powerful streak of melancholy. He strongly influenced Pushkin's early poetry. He became permanently insane in 1821.

Тень друга	74
Мой гений	76
Пробуждение (1815)	77

TABLE OF CONTENTS

PRINCE PĔTR* VYÁZEMSKY (1792–1878), a close friend of Pushkin, remained, for all his close connexions with the Romantic movement, a classicist in style. His later poetry, two examples of which are given below, treats universal themes with quiet charm.

Вечер — 79

«Жизнь наша в старости – изношенный халат» — 80

BARON ANTÓN DÉL'VIG (1798–1831), Pushkin's closest friend, a poet of sensuous pleasures with a natural affinity with the Greek classics. He was an accomplished craftsman, a master of the epigram, and the first Russian poet to experiment successfully with the sonnet.

«В Испании Амур не чужестранец» — 83

ALEKSÁNDR PÚSHKIN (1799–1837) is, by common agreement – at least among his own compatriots – the greatest of all Russian writers. The major part of his lyrical poetry was written between 1820 and 1830, but some of his poetical masterpieces were composed in the last seven years of his life, when he was turning his attention to prose. A development can be traced from the sparkling ebullience of his early verse – the crowning achievement of which is the first chapter of *Evgeny Onegin*, written in 1823 – to the concentrated expressiveness and restrained power of his later poetry. By effecting a new synthesis between the three main ingredients of the Russian literary idiom – the Church Slavonic, the Western European borrowings, and the spoken vernacular – Pushkin created the language of modern Russian poetry. His personal life was made difficult by his conflicts with the authorities who disapproved of his liberal views. He was killed in a duel.

Виноград — 84

Евгений Онегин (*extract*) — 84

Борис Годунов (*extract*) — 88

К * * * — 89

Зимний вечер — 90

Пророк — 92

* The reader aiming at correct pronunciation of poets' names should note that here and elsewhere in the table of contents the sound represented by Ĕ approximates to the English *yo*, as in *yonder*.

TABLE OF CONTENTS

Поэт
Талисман 94
Руслан и Людмила (*extract*) 96
Воспоминание 98
Анчар 98
«Я вас любил : любовь ещё, быть может» 100
Бесы 101
«Для берегов отчизны дальной» 104
Осень 105
Медный Всадник (*extract*) 111
«Пора, мой друг, пора! покоя сердце просит» 115

EVGÉNY BARATÝNSKY (1800–44) was, next to Pushkin, the outstanding poet of his age. His mature verse has an intellectual acumen, a precision of style, and an astringent clarity that have been fully appreciated only in the present century.

Две доли 116
Любовь 117
Подражателям 118
Муза 119
«Болящий дух врачует песнопенье» 120
«На что вы, дни! Юдольный мир явленья» 120
Скульптор 121
«Люблю я вас, богини пенья» 122

NIKOLÁY YAZÝKOV (1803–46) was, after Pushkin and Baratynsky, the third major poet of the Golden Age. His verse, much of it concerned with nature and the physical pleasures of life, has a verbal brilliance and a sustained rhythm that are impressive.

Элегия 124
К Рейну 125

FËDOR TYÚTCHEV (1803–73) served as a diplomat in Munich and Turin, living abroad for twenty-two years. A love-affair with his daughter's governess elicited from him a group of love poems whose passionate and tragic intensity is unrivalled in the Russian language. *The Last Love* and *On the eve of the anniversary of 4 August 1864* belong to this cycle. His dualistic cosmology is expressed with characteristic lucidity in *Day and Night*. In his later years he wrote political poetry of a strongly nationalistic and Slavophile bent. *Silentium* and *A Dream at Sea* are given here in Tyutchev's own versions of 1836, and not in the 'corrected' form in which they appeared in Turgenev's edition of 1854.

Видение	129
Весенняя гроза	129
Сон на море	130
Цицерон	131
Silentium	132
«О чём ты воешь, ветр ночной?»	133
«Люблю глаза твои, мой друг»	134
День и Ночь	135
Предопределение	135
«Я очи знал – о, эти очи»	136
Последняя любовь	137
«Эти бедные селенья»	138
«О вещая душа моя»	138
«Как хорошо ты, о море ночное»	139
«Певучесть есть в морских волнах»	140
Накануне годовщины 4-го августа 1864 г.	141

DMÍTRI VENEVÍTINOV (1805–27), a friend and a distant cousin of Pushkin, was a philosophical poet and one of the first Russian adherents of Schelling's idealist philosophy. He died at the age of twenty-one, after writing some forty poems of unusual maturity.

Три розы	143
«Я чувствую, во мне горит»	144

KAROLÍNA PÁVLOVA (1807–93), of German descent, was the outstanding Russian woman poet of the nineteenth century. Her lyric verse, somewhat poor in ideas and abstract in style, is distinguished by its restrained emotional power and accomplished craftsmanship.

«О былом, о погибшем, о старом»	147
Рим (1857)	148

ALEKSÉY KOL'TSÓV (1809–42) is chiefly known for his somewhat stylized imitations of folk songs, which have caused him to be compared to Burns.

Горькая доля	150
Песня	151

TABLE OF CONTENTS

MIKHAÍL LÉRMONTOV (1814–41) was descended from George Learmont, a Scottish officer who entered the Russian service in the early seventeenth century. His literary fame began with a poem on the death of Pushkin, full of angry invective against the court circles; for this Lermontov, a Guards officer, was court-martialled and temporarily transferred to the Caucasus. With the conspicuous exception of *The Angel* (1831), the best of his poetry was written during the last five years of his life. *The Last House-warming* (1840), in which he protests against the transfer of Napoleon's body from St Helena to the Invalides, is an example of his rhetorical power. He was killed in a duel at the age of twenty-seven.

Ангел	154
«Когда волнуется желтеющая нива»	155
Демон (*extract*)	156
Первое января	159
Казачья колыбельная песня	161
«И скучно, и грустно, и некому руку подать»	163
Последнее новоселье	164
Отчизна	168
Сон	169
«Выхожу один я на дорогу»	170

COUNT ALEKSÉY TOLSTÓY (1817–75), a distant cousin of the novelist and a childhood friend of Alexander II, was a resolute champion of the freedom of art in a utilitarian age. His poetry is idealistic and full of joyful vitality. He excelled in the short sentimental lyric, in the historical ballad, and especially in humorous verse – a field in which he has no peer among Russian poets. The *Troparion* from his long poem *John Damascene* is a paraphrase of parts of the burial service of the Orthodox Church. The *Ballad of the Chamberlain Delarue* satirizes the advocates of non-resistance to evil.

Князь Михайло Репнин	172
«По гребле неровной и тряской»	175
Иоанн Дамаскин (*extract*)	177
«То было раннею весной»	181
Баллада о камергере Деларю	181

xvii

YÁKOV POLÓNSKY (1819–98) was a Romantic with
an eclectic style and an unaffected lyrical grace.

Колокольчик   186
Лебедь   188

AFANÁSY FET (1820–92) was the illegitimate son of a
Russian squire, Shenshin, and a German woman
named Fet (Foeth). His short lyrics, outstanding for
their technique, have a melodiousness unsurpassed
in Russian nineteenth-century poetry; they are mostly
concerned with nature and love.

«Я пришёл к тебе с приветом» (1843)   190
Ивы и берёзы   191
«Буря на небе вечернем»   191
«Ещё весны душистой нега»   192
«На стоге сена ночью южной»   193
«Как хорош чуть мерцающим утром»   193
Сентябрьская роза (1890)   194

NIKOLÁY NEKRÁSOV (1821–77), the son of a
country squire, was the leading Russian poet of the
second half of the nineteenth century. He was an
admirer of the radical critic Belinsky, and edited the
foremost Russian literary review of his time. Much of
his poetry is excessively sentimental and rhetorical, but
the best of it, describing the misery of the peasants or
reproducing the style of the folk-song, is truly great.
The first of his poems given below has a depth of compassion for human misery and degradation that bears
comparison with Dostoevsky's work. The description,
taken from *Frost the Red-Nosed*, of the death of the
peasant woman who has gone into the frozen forest to
gather firewood after her husband's funeral, has a
timeless enchantment.

«Еду ли ночью по улице тёмной»   196
В деревне (*extract*)   198
Влас   201
Коробейники (*extract*)   206
Мороз, Красный Нос (*extract*)   208

APOLLÓN GRIGÓRIEV (1822–64), a distinguished
literary critic of somewhat Bohemian habits – he spent

a considerable part of his last years in a debtors' prison – wrote poetry of Romantic inspiration in the manner of gipsy songs, anticipating some of Blok's verse.

«О, говори хоть ты со мной»   214

KONSTANTÍN SLUCHÉVSKY (1837–1904), despite a certain technical incompetence, had flashes of genuine poetic originality. The poem presented below is his masterpiece: it is given in the original version of 1880.

После казни в Женеве   216

VLADÍMIR SOLOVIÉV (1853–1900), a notable theologian and philosopher, combined an adherence to the doctrines of the Orthodox Church with efforts to promote the reunion of Christendom under the leadership of the Pope. His mystical intuition of Sophia, the Divine Wisdom (the Eternal Feminine), is a constant theme of his poetry and appears in his lyrics addressed to the Finnish Lake Saimaa. He was a precursor of the Symbolists and strongly influenced the early poetry of Blok.

«У царицы моей есть высокий дворец»   218
«В тумане утреннем неверными шагами»   219
На Сайме зимой   220

INNOKÉNTY ÁNNENSKY (1856–1909) was a poet with a loose yet real connexion with the Symbolist school. A schoolmaster by profession – he became headmaster of the *Gymnasium* at Tsarskoe Selo – he was a distinguished classical scholar, and translated the whole of Euripides into Russian. His lyrical verse influenced several post-Symbolist poets, notably Pasternak. It is subtle, delicate, and precise, and mostly concerned with the anguish of life. Its flawless beauty has not been sufficiently appreciated outside Russia.

Сентябрь (1904)   222
Маки   222
Смычок и струны   223
Старая шарманка   224
Стальная цикада   226
После концерта   227
Decrescendo   228
Тоска миража   229

TABLE OF CONTENTS

FÉDOR SOLOGÚB (1863–1927) – his real name was Teternikov – was one of the Symbolists. His verse, refined and melodious, is concerned with the ugliness of life and with man's search to escape from it into the world of imagination. The contrast between dream and reality he symbolized in two names borrowed from *Don Quixote* – Dulcinea and Aldonsa.

«Что селения наши убогие»	231
«Высока луна Господня»	231
«Забыты вино и веселье»	233
Дон-Кихот (*extract*) (1922)	234

VYACHESLÁV IVÁNOV (1866–1949), a classical scholar who studied under Theodore Mommsen in Berlin, was the unquestioned leader of the St Petersburg Symbolists from 1905 to 1911. His thought was steeped in classical antiquity and influenced by Nietzsche. His poetry of this period, contained in the collection *Cor Ardens* (1911), is majestic and archaic in style. He left Russia in 1924 and settled in Italy. He died in Rome, a convert to Roman Catholicism. His later poetry, simpler and more direct, includes the splendid *Roman Sonnets*.

Голоса	236
Любовь	237
Римские Сонеты I	238
Римские Сонеты IV	239
Римские Сонеты VII	240
«Зачем, о Просперо волшебный» (1944)	241

KONSTANTÍN BÁL'MONT (1867–1943), one of the early Symbolists, enjoyed an extraordinary vogue in the early years of this century largely owing to the mellifluous character of his verse. His phonetic monotony and lack of poetic refinement make him unpopular with the modern reader. He emigrated after the Revolution, and settled in France.

Аккорды	243
Sin miedo (1903)	244

TABLE OF CONTENTS

ZINAÍDA GÍPPIUS (1869–1945), by contrast with Bal'mont, expressed the intellectual aspect of early Russian Symbolism. Wit and a very personal lyricism are combined in her poetry. After the Revolution she and her husband, the writer D. Merezhkovsky, emigrated to France.

Она   245
Нелюбовь (1907)   246

IVÁN BÚNIN (1870–1953) was the only notable Russian poet of the Symbolist period who escaped the influence of Symbolism. His verse is Parnassian in style, and descriptive rather than lyrical. He emigrated to France in 1918. Famous mainly for his prose writings, he was awarded the Nobel Prize for literature in 1933.

«Спокойный взор, подобный взору лани»   247
Вальс   247
Люцифер   248
«И цветы, и шмели, и трава, и колосья» (1918)   248

VALÉRY BRYÚSOV (1873–1924) was the founder of Russian Symbolism, the main theoretician of its early phase, and the acknowledged leader of the Moscow Symbolists, A painstaking craftsman with a liking for classical themes, he cultivated and sometimes achieved a majestic and rather cold brilliance. After the Revolution he accepted and served the new Soviet regime.

Сонет к форме (1895)   250
Ахиллес у алтаря   251
Поэту (1907)   252

MIKHAÍL KUZMÍN (1875–1936) issued in 1910 the poetical manifesto 'Concerning beautiful clarity' which marked the transition from Symbolism to Acmeism. An accomplished craftsman and a thorough-going aesthete, he excelled in pastiches of earlier foreign styles, notably of French rococo. His verse resembles exquisite and mannered chamber music.

«О, быть покинутым – какое счастье» (1907)   254
Фузий в блюдечке (1917)   254

TABLE OF CONTENTS

MAKSIMILIÁN VOLÓSHIN (1877–1932), a Symbolist, is chiefly remarkable for his poems inspired by the Revolution which he hated and feared, but accepted as part of Russia's spiritual destiny. *Holy Russia* (1918) illustrates this theme.

«Над зыбкой рябью вод встаёт из глубины» 256
Святая Русь 257

ANDRÉY BÉLY (1880–1934) was the literary pseudonym of Boris Bugaev. One of the most influential of the Symbolists, he turned to anthroposophy and spent four years (1912–16) in Switzerland with Rudolf Steiner. Like Blok he was influenced by Soloviëv, and accepted the October Revolution of 1917, which he identified with a mystical rebirth of Christianity. Chiefly known for his novels, *The Silver Dove* (1910) and *Petersburg* (1913), he wrote poetry whose dominant mood is one of cynicism and despair.

Объяснение в любви 259
«Довольно: не жди, не надейся» 260

ALEKSÁNDR BLOK (1880–1921), the greatest of the Russian Symbolists, progressed from the ethereal purity of *Verses about the Beautiful Lady* (1904) to the powerful expressiveness of his mature manner, fully developed by 1909. The wild intoxication of a gipsy woman's love, the spiritual destiny of his native land, and the agonizing limitations of the poet's art, are some of the main themes of his greatest body of poetry, to be found in the third volume of his collected verse (1907–16). His last masterpiece is *The Twelve*, a long poem which expresses his short-lived enthusiasm for the Revolution.

Незнакомка (1906) 262
«О доблестях, о подвигах, о славе» 264
За гробом 266
На поле Куликовом 267
Равенна 274
Шаги Командора 276
К Музе 278
«Ночь, улица, фонарь, аптека» 280
Художник 281
«Ты помнишь? В нашей бухте сонной» 283
«Рождённые в года глухие» (September 1914) 284

TABLE OF CONTENTS

VELIMÍR KHLÉBNIKOV (1885–1922), whose real
Christian name was Viktor, was the founder of the
Russian Futurist movement. He experimented with
'metalogical language' (*zaumny yazyk*), creating new
words from existing Russian roots with the aim of
establishing a new, universal idiom. The poetry he
wrote after the Revolution is, on the whole, straight-
forward and classical. Much of his verse resembles
fragments of some vast unfinished epic poem, pagan
and pantheistic.

Три сестры   286
«Ещё раз, ещё раз»   289

NIKOLÁY GUMILЁV (1886–1921) was one of
the founders of the Acmeist movement. Much of his
early verse was inspired by his travels in Africa and is
marked by a liking for the exotic and a cult of heroism
and adventure. Between 1910 and 1918 he was married
to the poetess Anna Akhmatova. He fought with distinction in the First World War, and became openly
anti-Bolshevik after 1917. Accused of conspiracy
against the Soviet Government, he was shot by a firing-
squad. His later poetry is more earnest and tragic, with
flashes of prophetic intuition.

Воин Агамемнона (1910)   291
Врата рая   292
Капитаны (*extract*)   293
Мужик   295
Рабочий   297
Шестое чувство   299
Заблудившийся трамвай (between 1918 and 1921)   [300

VLADISLÁV KHODASÉVICH (1886–1939) was a
classicist with stylistic affinities with Pushkin and a
violent aversion to Futurism. His poetry, witty and
ironic, is concerned with the tragic dualism between
spirit and matter. His best verse appeared during the
ten years following the Revolution. He emigrated in
1922 and settled in Paris.

Баллада (1921)   304
«Весенний лепет не разнежит»   306
«Жив Бог! Умён, а не заумен»   307
Перед зеркалом (1924)   308

TABLE OF CONTENTS

NIKOLÁY KLYÚEV (1887–1937) belonged to an educated peasant family from the Lake Onega country and was a religious dissenter. His poetry is steeped in the language of ritual and in the imagery of folklore. A friend and teacher of the poet Esenin, he wrote his moving *Lament for Esenin* after the latter's suicide in 1925. Arrested in 1933, he was exiled to Siberia, where he died.

«В златотканные дни Сентября»   310
«Любви начало было летом»   311
Плач о Есенине (*extract*)   312

ÁNNA AKHMÁTOVA (1889–1966) is the literary pseudonym of Anna Andreevna Gorenko. Her first husband was Gumilëv, and she too became one of the leading Acmeist poets. Her second book of poems, *Beads* (1914), brought her fame. Her earlier manner, intimate and colloquial, gradually gave way to a more classical severity, apparent in her volumes *The White Flock* (1917) and *Anno Domini MCMXXI* (1922). The growing distaste which the personal and religious elements in her poetry aroused in Soviet officialdom forced her thereafter into long periods of silence; and the poetic masterpieces of her later years, *A Poem without a Hero* and *Requiem*, were published abroad.

Вечером (1913)   315
«О тебе вспоминаю я редко»   316
«Есть в близости людей заветная черта»   317
«Стал мне реже сниться, слава Богу»   317
Июль 1914   318
«Всё расхищено, предано, продано» (1921)   320
Бежецк   321
«Годовщину весёлую празднуй» (1939)   322
Поэма без героя (*extract*)   323
Два стихотворения (1956–7)   324

NIKOLÁY ASÉEV (1889–1963), a Futurist poet, a friend and disciple of Mayakovsky.

Бык   326
Хор вершин   328

TABLE OF CONTENTS

BORÍS PASTERNÁK (1890–1960), the son of a distinguished painter, published his first verse in 1912. His two major collections of lyric poetry, *My Sister Life* (1922) and *Themes and Variations* (1923), caused him to be widely recognized, alongside Mayakovsky, as the outstanding poet of post-Revolutionary Russia. Between 1935 and 1943 he translated works of foreign literature, publishing notable versions of several of Shakespeare's tragedies. His novel *Doctor Zhivago*, banned in the Soviet Union, was published abroad in 1959, after an Italian translation had appeared in 1957. In 1958 he was awarded the Nobel Prize for literature.

Степь	330
В лесу	332
Спасское (1918)	333
Гамлет	335
Зимняя ночь	336
Земля	338
Гефсиманский Сад	340
Ветер	343
В больнице	347

ÓSIP MANDEL'SHTÁM (1891–1938), one of the three great Acmeist poets, wrote verse distinguished by its classical restraint, majestic conciseness, and sonority. Much of his early poetry is embodied in his two collections *Stone* (1913) and *Tristia* (1922). Arrested in 1934, he was exiled first to the Ural region and then to Voronezh. In 1938 he was rearrested, sentenced to forced labour, and died in harrowing circumstances in Vladivostok.

Айя-София	351
«Есть иволги в лесах, и гласных долгота»	352
«Бессонница. Гомер. Тугие паруса»	352
«В разноголосице девического хора»	353
«На страшной высоте блуждающий огонь» (1918)	354
«Прославим, братья, сумерки свободы» (1918)	355
Tristia	356
«Сёстры – тяжесть и нежность – одинаковы ваши приметы»	358
«В Петербурге мы сойдёмся снова» (1920)	359
Век (1923)	361

TABLE OF CONTENTS

MARÍNA TSVETÁEVA (1892–1941) published her first verse in 1911, wrote poems between 1918 and 1920 in praise of the White armies and their fight against Bolshevism, and produced the greater part of her work in Western Europe, where she emigrated in 1922. Her poetry of whirling and staccato rhythms is uneven in quality, but forceful and original. She returned to Russia in 1939 and committed suicide two years later.

«Из строгого, стройного храма» (1917)	363
Стихи о Сонечке (*extract*)	363
«Есть в стане моём – офицерская прямость» (1920)	364
Попытка ревности	365

VLADÍMIR MAYAKÓVSKY (1893–1930) was the poet of Futurism and of the Revolution. He joined the clandestine Bolshevik party at the age of fourteen and spent nearly a year in prison. From 1917 onwards he placed his Muse at the service of the Soviet regime. His political poetry, violent, coarse, and declamatory, alternated with cycles of purely lyric verse, passionate and tender, dramatizing his unhappiness in love. He was a master of metaphor and hyperbole, and of rich and original rhymes. His travels abroad included a journey to the United States in 1925. He committed suicide. The fragment listed last was found scribbled in his notebook.

Лиличка!	369
Наш марш	372
Хорошее отношние к лошадям	373
Атлантический океан	376
Разговор с фининспектором о поэзии	379
[Неоконченное]	385

GEÓRGY IVÁNOV (1894–1958), at first a minor Acmeist poet, developed an original manner after emigrating to Western Europe. In the last ten years of his life, living in France, he wrote witty and nihilistic poetry about the futility of life.

«С бесчеловечною судьбой»	388
«Как вы когда-то разборчивы были»	389
«Четверть века прошло заграницей» (1950)	390

TABLE OF CONTENTS

SERGÉY ESÉNIN (1895–1925), the son of a peasant of
the Ryazan' province, at first hailed the Revolution
which he identified with a new mystical Christianity.
But he gradually became disillusioned by the industrialization of the village, and lamented the disappearance of 'wooden Russia' in melodious and nostalgic
verses. Another of his themes was the Bohemian life of
the Moscow taverns. After a brief and unsuccessful
marriage with the dancer Isadora Duncan (1922–23), he
took increasingly to drink and fell into mental prostra-
tion. Finally, alone in a Leningrad hotel, he opened
a vein in his wrist, wrote with his own blood the farewell poem given below, and hanged himself.

Песнь о собаке	391
«О пашни, пашни, пашни»	392
Сорокоуст (*extract*)	393
Письмо к матери	394
«Мы теперь уходим понемногу»	396
«Отговорила роща золотая»	398
«До свиданья, друг мой, до свиданья»	399

EDUÁRD BAGRÍTSKY (1895–1934) – his real name
was Dzyubin – a native of Odessa, wrote in a Romantic
and heroic vein of the Revolution and the Civil War.
The latter event forms the subject of his best known
work, the long epic poem *The Lay of Opanas* (1926).

«Я сладко изнемог»	401
Арбуз	402

NIKOLÁY TÍKHONOV (1896–   ) fought in the First
World War and, in the Red army, in the Civil War.
His early poetry (1921–2), with its cult of heroism,
owed much to Gumilëv; in the mid-twenties he was
influenced by Khlebnikov and Pasternak; later he
developed a more realistic style. From 1944 to 1946 he
was President of the Union of Soviet Writers.

«Праздничный, весёлый, бесноватый»	406
«Мы разучились нищим подавать»	407
Ветер	407
«Как след весла, от берега ушедший»	408

TABLE OF CONTENTS

PÁVEL ANTOKÓL'SKY (1896–   ) is a poet with a keen historical insight and an appreciation of cultural values. His journeys abroad in 1923 and 1928 resulted in several accomplished poems about Western Europe.

Портрет Инфанты   410
Полёт светляков   412

NIKOLÁY ZABOLÓTSKY (1903–58) achieved his reputation in 1929 with *Scrolls*, his first volume of poetry: it is an ironic and grotesquely drawn panorama of life in Leningrad, satirizing its soulless materialism and the commonplace standardization of human types (such as the 'Ivanov lads'). From 1938 to 1944 he was in prison and in labour camps; by 1946 he was in Moscow, able to publish again. His later verse is largely free from Futuristic technique, and tends to concentrate on the beauty of life as mirrored in the rapture of spring or seen through the eyes of a little girl.

Ивановы   415
Обводный канал   417
«Уступи мне, скворец, уголок»   419
Детство   421

ALEKSÁNDR TVARDÓVSKY (1910–71) is mainly known for his long poems, *The Land of Muravia* (1934–6) and especially *Vasily Terkin* (1941–5) whose vividly drawn hero is a good humoured and courageous soldier who fights the Germans in the war. For most of the period from 1950 to 1970 Tvardóvsky was the editor of *Novy Mir*, the foremost Soviet literary journal.

«Нет, жизнь меня не обделила» (1955)   423

PÁVEL VASÍLIEV (1910–37), a vigorous and original poet with a boisterous love of life, published his first verse in 1927 and was arrested and executed in 1937.

Стихи в честь Натальи   427

TABLE OF CONTENTS

MARGARÍTA ALIGÉR (1915–) has achieved popularity by her war poetry. The extract given below, written in 1942, is from a poem about the siege of Leningrad.

Весна в Ленинграде (*extract*)   431
«Осень только взялась за работу»   432

VLADÍMIR SOLOÚKHIN (1924–) is noted for his sensitive descriptions of nature and for his experiments with blank verse. The piece given here is taken from a collection of his poetry published in Moscow in 1961.

Ветер   434

EVGÉNY VINOKÚROV (1925–), like Soloukhin, fought in the Second World War and graduated from the Moscow Literary Institute in 1951. He is a lyric poet, distinguished by an expressive rhythm, a liking for precise detail, and – at times – by a sense of humour.

Весна   437
Поэма о движении   438

EVGÉNY EVTUSHÉNKO (1933–), born in the town of Zima in southern Siberia, published his first book of poetry in 1952, and acquired fame by his long poem *Zima Railway Station* which appeared in 1956. One of its episodes, later published by its author in a slightly modified version as a separate poem under the title *Berry-picking*, is given here in extract (the actual description of the berry-picking has been omitted). The outspoken sincerity with which he has treated social and political themes has contributed to his reputation, especially abroad. His popularity in his own country is more firmly based on his achievements as a lyric poet.

По ягоды (*extract*)   442
Битница   448
Тайны   450

TABLE OF CONTENTS

ANDRÉY VOZNESÉNSKY (1933–) graduated from the Moscow Institute of Architecture in 1957, and published his first verse in 1958. His brilliant experiments with rhythms, images, and sounds, and the formal qualities of his style, at once complex and concise, have earned him a leading place among the *avant-garde* poets of his country. A prominent theme of his poetry is the right and duty of the artist to follow freely the path of his own inspiration.

Гойя	453
Параболическая баллада	454
Последняя электричка	456
Кроны и корни	458

BÉLLA AKHMADÚLINA (1937–), formerly the wife of Evgeny Evtushenko, is now married to the Soviet writer Yury Nagibin. Classical in form and not unrelated to the Acmeist tradition, her poetry moves among scenes of the concrete world, described with precision and gentle irony.

Новая домна на КМК	460
INDEX OF TITLES AND FIRST LINES	463
INDEX OF POETS	475

INTRODUCTION

THE belief, current in the West, that Russian poetry has its beginnings in the early nineteenth century is, though misguided, understandable. The unexampled blossoming of this poetry between 1810 and 1830, in a newly developed language easily recognizable as modern Russian and in a literary context avowedly European, makes the age of Pushkin seem like a sudden flowering in a wilderness. Eighteenth-century Russian literature, without which Pushkin himself cannot be properly understood, is in the West largely unknown or dismissed as derivative and 'pseudo-classical'; while further back, the Russian Middle Ages extend in an ill-defined penumbra, out of which inexplicably emerge a number of heroic poems transmitted by word of mouth from generation to generation, some of which have been translated into languages of Western Europe.

Unfamiliarity with the culture of medieval Russia cannot be held solely responsible for the prevalence of these views. There exists no comprehensive history of Russian poetry; nor can any single continuous tradition of written verse be detected in Russia before the middle of the eighteenth century. Yet poetry, both written and oral, was composed in medieval Russia, and some of it is of high quality. The examples presented in the opening section of this anthology are taken from the two fields in which it excelled – the heroic and the religious.

The beginnings of Russian literature are recognizable in the first half of the eleventh century, some fifty years after the country's final conversion to Christianity, at a time when the city of Kiev held a political hegemony over the lands inhabited by the Eastern Slavs. Kiev was the cradle of the Russian nation and the mother of Russian letters. Under the guidance of its princes and churchmen Russian literature and art, in fairly close contact with the West, deeply influenced by the civilization of Byzantium, but already displaying a native originality, acquired in the eleventh and twelfth centuries a European importance. The language of this literature was in part Old Church Slavonic, a learned idiom created by the Byzantine missionaries Cyril and Methodius, which in this early period was close enough to the spoken languages of the Slavs to be easily intelligible to them. On Russian soil this ecclesiastical idiom soon blended with the spoken vernacular, and the synthesis of these two kindred tongues gave rise to the Old Russian literary language which remained the basic medium of the country's literature during the whole of the Middle Ages.

The cultural achievements of the Kievan age had as their background the young Russian nation's ceaseless struggle to survive. Constant feuds among the princes of the land and the growth of local separatism after 1054 tended increasingly to disrupt the unity of the Kievan realm. The internal political crisis was greatly aggravated by the ever-present threat of foreign invasion: in the late eleventh and in the twelfth centuries the Russians were forced to wage an almost constant border warfare against the pagan and nomadic Polovtsy (or Cumans), Turkic tribesmen from Asia whose attacks against the Dnieper valley were the chief cause of the disruption of Kievan Russia. Russian writers of the twelfth century were well aware of the urgency of the struggle; and in response to this double challenge – of internal disunity and foreign attack – the most articulate of them propounded in their works the view that only by rallying to the defence of Kiev could their countrymen save their common national inheritance, and the concomitant belief that life is a heroic struggle in which man can gain honour for himself by showing courage and enterprise. These two themes are united in the twelfth-century *Lay of Igor's Campaign*, the greatest work of medieval Russian literature.

In regarding the *Lay* as a poem, and not, as some literary historians have held it to be, a work of prose, I believe myself to be in agreement with a large number, probably the majority, of present-day scholars. However, on this, as on other aspects of the *Lay*, controversy has been long and heated, and it must be admitted that the numerous attempts to reduce it to a metrical pattern have not so far been successful. This is the main reason why the text of the *Lay* is printed here in prose form: to divide it up into lines and stanzas, as many editors have done, would be to introduce an element of arbitrariness and subjectivity.* The highly musical texture of the poem, the use of repetitions and refrains, the numerous fixed epithets so characteristic of heroic poetry, and the visible signs of strophic composition, leave no doubt that the *Lay* was intended for oral recitation; and the author himself describes his work as a 'song'. But it is equally clear that the *Lay* was composed in writing: the terseness of its style, the richness and complexity of the imagery, the subtlety of its euphonic devices, are quite incompatible with the view that it was ever improvised orally. Yet the author seems to have known and sought inspiration in an earlier, oral, tradition: the figure of the eleventh-century bard Boyan, the 'nightingale of olden times', whom he holds in such esteem, prob-

*The division into paragraphs, aimed at helping the reader to grasp the composition of the work, is, however, my own.

ably stems from this pre-literary stage; while Boyan's 'magic' art seems to go back to a pre-heroic age in which the ideal of self-sufficient manhood had not yet fully emerged out of the supernatural world.

The structure of the *Lay* is exceedingly complex. The narrative thread – the story of Igor's campaign against the Polovtsy in 1185, of his defeat, captivity, and escape – is several times interrupted by historical digressions, lyrical invocations, panegyrics, and laments. This material is grouped round two basic themes which serve as the foci of the poem: the first is narrative and heroic; the other didactic and overtly propagandist. The courage of Igor and his companions, their prowess on the field of battle, the tragic dignity of their defeat are held up for admiration in order to move and exalt the audience, in the true tradition of heroic poetry. But from a national standpoint the Russian defeat was a disaster, and Igor himself was gravely at fault: his campaign was a foolhardy adventure, undertaken for personal glory, without the permission of his sovereign, the Prince of Kiev. The latter's rebukes underline this fact and illustrate the author's other basic theme: that the victories of the infidels over the Christians are a direct result of the disunity among the princes of Russia. To them the author addresses, in words charged with deep emotion, his appeals to unite in defence of Kiev, for the sake of the Russian land. These two themes, the heroic and the patriotic, are balanced and at times blended with remarkable artistry. And the *Lay* is a moving record of the last decades of Kievan Russia, on the eve of the Mongol invasion, and of her struggle to survive in an age of chivalry and disaster, of heroism and folly, of civil strife and barbarian invasions. It is one of the great heroic poems of the world.

The *Lay of Igor's Campaign* provides the most direct, though not the only, evidence of the existence of courtly poetry in medieval Russia. Many of the *byliny*, the oral heroic poems which have been recited by peasant bards in remote districts of Russia, and recorded in writing by scholars during the last two centuries, are undoubtedly medieval in origin. But the heroic outlook and courtly ideals which they once embodied have been diluted, and to some extent modified, by the peasant milieu in which these poems have been preserved in recent centuries. Yet the highly conservative oral tradition through which they have come down to us has retained many of their authentic and archaic features. This is particularly true of those *byliny* in which the action is laid in 'glorious and royal Kiev town', the capital of Russia until the Mongol invasion of the thirteenth century; most of them are grouped round the figure of Prince Vladimir, who seems to combine the features of two outstanding Kievan rulers of that name, who died respectively in 1015 and 1125. His court is the focus for the adventures of a group of knightly heroes, the *bogatyri*, who fight in his service against the country's pagan enemies – usually, and anachronistically, termed Tatars – for 'Holy Russia' and the Christian faith. Whatever changes the Kievan *byliny* may have later undergone, there can be no doubt that their basic stratum goes back at least as far as the eleventh and twelfth centuries; and the best of these poems – including the one about Il'ya of Murom, the most popular of these early epic heroes – reflect something of the ethos and the ideals of what the Russian people have always regarded as their country's heroic age. Another group of medieval *byliny* centres on Novgorod, the great trading city of the north-west. Here the open plains of the Kievan poems and the valorous deeds of their military heroes give way to civic and commercial preoccupations. The heroes of Novgorod move in a society that is turbulent, mercantile, and in many respects post-heroic: their activity seems to relate to the time when the city was at the height of its power and prosperity – the fourteenth and the first half of the fifteenth centuries. But in one of the Novgorod poems – the *bylina* of Sadko, the minstrel who became a rich merchant – the theme of far-flung commerce and worldly success is combined with a much older story of the hero's descent into the depths of the sea and of his encounter with the Sea King. Of all the Russian *byliny* that of Sadko is perhaps artistically the finest.

In modern times the *byliny* have been chanted in a kind of monotonous recitative and, at least in North Russia, without the accompaniment of a stringed instrument. In the Middle Ages they were sung to the *gusli*, a kind of harp, played resting on the knees. Little is known of the original creators and reciters of the *byliny*, who were probably court minstrels in close contact with a heroic milieu. In the late Middle Ages these poems were often sung by the *skomorokhi*, a confraternity of wandering minstrels and jesters who performed at public festivals and who, no less than the peasant bards of recent times, are thought to have exerted a strong influence on the content and form of the *byliny*. The *skomorokhi* were distinct from another group of itinerant professional singers, the *kaliki*, whose repertoire included chiefly the *dukhovnye stikhi*, or oral religious poems, of late medieval Russia. These closely resemble the *byliny* in form, but their content is religious, not heroic. Their themes are derived mostly from hagiographic and apocryphal texts, less often from the Bible, the liturgy, and iconography; but the traditional subject-matter is often interpreted with considerable poetic licence. Such religious poems are first clearly attested in the fifteenth century, and they are apparently still sung in Russia. They reflect several typical features of Russian popular religion – its respect for poverty and asceticism, the warmth of its devotion to Christ, His Mother, and the saints, and its deep-rooted pity for all human suffering.

Russian written poetry developed separately from the *byliny* and the *dukhovnye stikhi*, though – as in the case of the *Lay of Igor's Campaign* – it borrowed some of the technique and conventions of the oral tradition. But the history of this learned poetry before the seventeenth century remains very obscure, and its very existence is denied by some scholars. However, it is difficult to doubt that the *Lay* belonged to a literary tradition which has left its traces in several medieval works. Thus the *Zadonshchina*, a work celebrating the Russian victory over the Tatars at Kulikovo in 1380 and written towards the end of the fourteenth century, is closely modelled on the *Lay of Igor's Campaign*, to the point of repeating many of its expressions; and it is hard to avoid the conclusion that, like its more celebrated prototype, it belongs to the genre of heroic poetry.

The beginnings of a clearly recognizable school of Russian poetry are apparent towards the middle of the seventeenth century. Its practitioners owed nothing to the medieval heroic tradition, and employed a syllabic versification imported from Poland.* Their writings exemplified that wave of western influence upon Russian culture which reached its highest point in the eighteenth century and which is already visible in the decades preceding the reforms of Peter the Great. The baroque, didactic poetry of Simeon of Polotsk (d. 1680) and the satires of Kantemir (d. 1744) written in the classical manner of Horace and Boileau, have earned a permanent place in the history of Russian letters. But for the modern reader, who views them through the prism of nineteenth-century poetry, their prosody seems artificial, and much of their language antiquated.

The true founder of modern Russian poetry was Lomonosov (d. 1765), a genius of European stature and a true representative of the Age of Enlightenment. His knowledge ranged from chemistry and mathematics to grammar and rhetoric. To Russian literature, which he stamped with the standards of French classicism, his services were immense. By propounding in his theoretical works a new and more organic relationship between Church Slavonic and the spoken vernacular, and by putting his linguistic reform into practice in his own writings, Lomonosov laid the foundation of modern literary Russian. In the history of Russian prosody his role

*See the note on Russian versification on p. lv.

was equally decisive: with his keen perception of the character and natural resources of the Russian language, he finally established the type of versification known as the syllabic-accentual, based on the regular alternation of stressed and unstressed syllables. This type of verse had been used before, notably by Trediakovsky (d. 1769); but Lomonosov was the first eminent poet to employ it, and he was primarily responsible for introducing the verse-forms which have dominated Russian poetry ever since. His odes, sacred and panegyrical, are his principal achievement as a poet, and some of them are still impressive for the clarity of their diction and the vigour and majesty of their rhetoric.

The taste for solemn odes on religious, philosophical, and political themes in the manner of Lomonosov was openly challenged, in the sixties and seventies of the eighteenth century, by another school of lyric poetry, which demanded greater simplicity and naturalness of language and style. Its practitioners wrote intimate love lyrics, elegiac and anacreontic verse, satires, and fables. Their master was Sumarokov, who may be regarded as the founder of modern Russian love poetry, and whose best pieces, notably his songs, still have the power to move by their unaffected sincerity and melodious rhythm.

It was left to the greatest poet of the eighteenth century to reconcile and combine the solemn with the intimate manner. Derzhavin's poetry remained in the main stream of the classical tradition: his majestic odes on heroic and patriotic subjects are in the rhetorical style of his master Lomonosov, while his *poésie intime* is distinguished by a mixture of sensuality and sentimentality which reflects the influence of Sumarokov's school. But in other respects Derzhavin's work marks a break with the canons of classical aesthetics. Thus he rejected the principle of rigid distinction between the different poetic genres and between the styles corresponding to each – a principle laid down by Lomonosov and earlier canonized by the authority of Boileau. Derzhavin's ode *Felitsa* (1783) marks a landmark in the history of Russian poetry: this panegyric of Catherine II is written in a semi-humorous, at times bantering style, hitherto considered improper for so lofty a genre as the ode. Derzhavin was fully aware of the significance of his revolt against the standards of French classicism; and in his poem *The Monument* he boasts of being 'the first who dared to proclaim Felitsa's virtues in the Russian language of comedy'. His intimate lyrics, and especially the anacreontic poems of his later years, full of sensuous and joyful epicureanism, likewise sound a new note: the inner world and personal experience of the poet are here given an importance that far exceeds the role they play in classical love poetry; and the world of nature, for the first time in eighteenth-century Russian poetry, is described with visual acumen and expressive power. In spite of a tendency to rhetoric and prolixity, and occasional lapses into bathos, Derzhavin is one of the truly great Russian lyric poets. In his power to convey impressions of light and colour, to evoke the rich variety of the visible world, he has few equals. Into the frigid rationalism of so much of eighteenth-century literature his poetry injects a strong current of passion, which is aroused by the sight of social injustice, by a nightingale's song, by a gipsy woman's frenzied dance, or by the realization that the manifold splendour of this world will be borne away by the river of time.

The last decade of the eighteenth century and the first twenty years of the nineteenth were marked by a literary movement associated with the name of Karamzin. Without fully breaking with the traditions of classicism, which lived on in Russia until at least 1825, this movement brought the cult of the new sensibility into Russian poetry and prose. Karamzin also played a leading role in a new reform of the literary language which, through the influence of his writings, was brought closer to the speech of the educated gentry, enriched with Gallicisms, and modelled on the French elegant style. This Europeanized language, later perfected by Pushkin, was to become the standard idiom of nineteenth-century Russian literature.

The Karamzinian movement was extended into the field of poetry by Zhukovsky. His first mature work, written around 1808, may be said to mark the beginning of the Golden Age of Russian poetry. This period, which reached its culmination in the eighteen-twenties and came to an end in the next decade, had four striking and original characteristics: poetry enjoyed a complete monopoly over all other literary genres; the writings of even minor poets reached an exceedingly high level of technical efficiency; the poetry of this age, while retaining in form and style many links with the eighteenth century, revolted against the rules of French classicism and, marching under the banner of Byron and Shakespeare, proclaimed itself romantic; finally, literature and literary opinion were largely monopolized by the educated and Europeanized gentry. The remarkable group of poets which this age produced, and who shared to some extent the same poetic outlook, was dominated by Pushkin.

By the use he made of Karamzin's reforms, Zhukovsky has a strong claim to be considered as the creator of the poetic vocabulary and diction which set the standard for the whole nineteenth century His poetry provides a link between the intimate lyrics of

Derzhavin and the early poetry of Pushkin, on whom he exerted a notable influence. From 1810 to 1820 Zhukovsky was the acknowledged leader of Russian poetry; but the reputation he enjoyed in his lifetime was, on the whole, due to reasons other than those which explain his appeal to the modern reader. His contemporaries admired him above all for his patriotic pieces celebrating the victories over Napoleon and for his numerous poetic translations. For the modern reader his permanent value lies in his short lyrics in which he evokes, with a simplicity, melodiousness, and purity of diction which few Russian poets have equalled, the intimate stirrings of his heart: his quiet and resigned melancholy, the sadness of two lovers' separation, the belief in their reunion after death, the enchantment of memory, and the beauty of the Inexpressible. Zhukovsky is the master of the melodic type of poetry; the 'enchanting sweetness' of his verse, much admired by Pushkin, provides a striking contrast to the rugged virility and rhetoric of Derzhavin, and points the way forward, through the lyrics of Fet, to the musical experiments of the Symbolists.

Another poet of the Karamzinian school was Batyushkov, whose verse, by contrast with Zhukovsky's romantic cult of the 'beyond', is earthy and pagan in inspiration. He sought to reproduce in his poetry the melodious sweetness of Italian; but Batyushkov's melodiousness is restrained and unobtrusive, and he avoids overtly euphonic effects. In this, as in the balance and reticence of his style, he was Pushkin's model. Both poets express that canon of classical harmony which was the prevailing ideal of the age of Alexander I and is typified by the Russian variety of the *style Empire* in architecture.

Pushkin's early poetry displays the influence of Zhukovsky and Batyushkov, also of the French classical poets Voltaire, Parny, and Chénier. The elegiac style of Zhukovsky he soon surmounted and transformed; the others taught him the neatness, clarity, and restraint which remained dominant in his poetry. But Pushkin's fundamental classicism was much more than the product of literary influences: it was rooted in the character of his own genius – in the precision of his language, his artistic concentration, his simple and direct approach to experience, his infallible sense of balance, and the deep humanity of his outlook. He had, moreover, a strongly developed critical taste, constantly controlling his inspiration; and an astonishing ability to assimilate the styles of his literary models, Russian and foreign, only to transform them in accordance with his own poetic design. These last two features are already apparent in the poetry he wrote between 1820 and 1823, when he came under the influence of Byron. From Byron he borrowed the form of the narrative poem, several romantic themes, and a lyrical tonality: this last feature proved important in the development of Pushkin's style by endowing it with a new expressiveness and enabling him to infuse fresh life and vigour into the somewhat conventional and mannered idiom of the followers of Karamzin. But Byron's rhetoric and self-dramatization remained quite alien to Pushkin's poetry.

Pushkin's 'Byronic' poems are chiefly remarkable for the mellifluousness of their language, comparable to the most euphonic effects of Zhukovsky. But after about 1823 Pushkin abandoned this manner and developed a style peculiarly his own, simple and vigorous, depending for its effect on the choice and position of words and on a subtle, and most characteristic, correspondence between rhythm and intonation. Much of his greatest lyric poetry, composed between 1823 and 1830, is in this manner. In this period he also wrote most of his long poems, including *Evgeny Onegin*, perhaps the most influential, and within Russia the most widely popular, work of Russian literature.

Though Pushkin applied himself increasingly to prose after 1830, his poetic output in the last years of his life shows the same mastery. His style, now more austere and bereft of ornament than ever, further gained in vigour and aphoristic concision. At the same time his view of life acquired a new and tragic dimension from his increasing awareness of man's defencelessness before the powers of Fate. It is perhaps this awareness of life's tragedy that explains Pushkin's concern, in the last years of his life, with paradoxical or contrasting human situations. This concern is expressed most powerfully in the *Bronze Horseman*, whose basic theme is the unresolved conflict between the ruthless and inhuman workings of power and the individual's claim to happiness – a problem which, like Pushkin himself, is at once so Russian and so universal.

The term 'the Pushkin Pleiad', often applied to a group of poets who were contemporaries of Pushkin and active in the eighteen-twenties, would be misleading if it were taken to imply that its members had a uniform poetic outlook and programme. Yet, despite the diversity of their individual styles, the group had enough homogeneity to deserve to be called a school. Vyazemsky, Del'vig, Baratynsky, Yazykov, and Venevitinov belonged to this group: of these the greatest poet was unquestionably Baratynsky. He was also the most original. For while his early work largely reflects the literary fashion of the eighteen-twenties – a combination of a classical, eighteenth-century style with a liking for romantic themes, the cult of melancholy, a delight in the pleasures of life, and the influence of Batyushkov – his mature poetry, written after 1829, has that 'singular expression' which Baratynsky himself regarded as the distinctive mark of his Muse. It seems to have developed out of the conflicting tendencies to follow the path laid down by Pushkin and to write differently from him. The result is a refined and intellectual poetry, classical in form, sometimes concise to the point of syntactical obscurity, and deliberately eschewing obvious euphony, in which thought and emotion are blended. Baratynsky is a poet of solitude; and his reflections on the illusory nature of happiness and the loneliness of the poet in modern society bring a dominant mood of pessimism into his later poetry. This, and other features of his work – such as the astringency of his style, his constant search for linguistic precision, and the fusion of sensation and thought – make him perhaps the most 'modern' of all Russian poets of the nineteenth century.

The Golden Age of Russian poetry may be said to have come to an end about 1830. After that date the tastes of the reading public began to change; the poetry of Pushkin and his school was received with increasing indifference; and Pushkin himself, reflecting the growing fashion, turned his attention to prose. The vogue of poetry itself, which had reached unprecedented heights in the previous decade, started to decline. The eighteen-thirties, to be sure, were far from barren in this field: two of the greatest Russian poets, Tyutchev and Lermontov, produced most of their best work during that decade. Yet, by contrast with their predecessors or contemporaries of the Golden Age, they were both lonely figures, lacking the stimulus of a sympathetic literary environment. It was not until 1854 that Tyutchev's poems were published in book form; the selection of his poetry that appeared in 1836 was met with almost total indifference. Lermontov, it is true, had a large and appreciative audience in his lifetime. Yet the greater part of his work was published posthumously.

Tyutchev's lyric verse is a complex amalgam of different poetic traditions, combined with a highly personal view of the universe. Several features of his style and much of his vocabulary go back to the eighteenth-century classics, notably to Derzhavin, whose influence is visible in Tyutchev's predilection for archaic turns of phrase and rhetorical diction. Many of his poems are in effect short speeches, constructed according to the rules of oratory. At the same time the highly musical texture of much of his verse owes something at least to Zhukovsky's melodic experiments. Finally, some of Tyutchev's themes and imagery have a close affinity with German Romantic poetry, and with that of Heine. The typically romantic view that true poetry is rooted in the Inexpressible (*das Unaussprechliche*) is argued, with characteristic lucidity, in Tyutchev's celebrated *Silentium*. Another romantic feature is the theme of night, which is central to his poetry. Night, he believed, reveals the ontological depths of being; Day, its opposite, is but a resplendent and flimsy veil drawn over the basic reality – which is Chaos. And the duality of night and day is but the visible manifestation of the ultimate duality of Chaos and Cosmos. This dualism pervades the world of nature, as it does man's inner life. Between nature and man's soul – the two poles of Tyutchev's lyric poetry – there is a constant interpenetration, which he illustrates by means of metaphor. His dualistic outlook is a tragic one, for man, a plaything of two eternities, recognizes Chaos as the true heritage of his race. Love, a theme to which he devoted some of the most passionate and poignant lyrics in the Russian language, brings no solution to the divided soul: for it is not only a union, but a duel as well. Christianity seems at times to have taught him humility and resignation; but it has never more than a peripheral importance in his poetry. After a period of eclipse, Tyutchev's poetry was rediscovered at the turn of the nineteenth century by the Russian Symbolists who, not without some justification, hailed him as a literary ancestor. His reputation and popularity as Russia's greatest metaphysical poet are firmly established today.

The position of Lermontov in the history of Russian poetry is a curious one. The relationship of his poetry to Pushkin's is a particularly controversial problem which is further complicated by the eclectic character of Lermontov's lyric verse. His debt to Zhukovsky is apparent in the rhythm and the syntax of his poetry, and especially in the astonishing mellifluousness of his diction: this feature, evident in his exquisite early lyric *The Angel* and still more in his narrative poem *The Demon*, was, in the nineteenth century, the most widely admired of Lermontov's qualities as a poet. To the poetic traditions of the Golden Age his attitude appears to have been ambiguous. There is no doubt that, as a craftsman, he learnt from Pushkin; and in the last years of his life he developed a new manner of writing whose simplicity and directness are reminiscent of the latter. Yet on the whole Lermontov's style shows a tendency to depart from Pushkin's canon of classical perfection which was deemed incapable of further development. He brought instead into Russian verse an expressive energy, an emotional tension, and a rhetorical diction peculiarly his own. Yet Lermontov's eloquence is far removed from the precise, classical rhetoric of Tyutchev: it is unrestrained and exuberant, achieving its effect not by single words, but by verbal clusters, dominated by emotionally charged epithets. *The Last House-warming* is a striking example of this kind of rhetorical monologue. This style is the very opposite of Pushkin's terseness, precision, and stress on the autonomy of the individual word. For all the greater realism of his later years, Lermontov remains a romantic poet, with a strong and conscious affinity with Byron. His immediate influence on Russian poetry was not great. The literary historian may be able to detect threads that run from his rhetorical verse to the poetry of Nekrasov, and from his later lyrics to those of A. Grigoriev and Fet; but the full creative impact of his verse was felt only in the present century: its heirs were Blok and Pasternak.

After the death of Lermontov in 1841 it was generally believed in Russia that the age of poetry was over. The prestige of prose, already ensured by Pushkin, Lermontov, and Gogol, was growing, and the next two decades, which saw the appearance of the early works of Dostoevsky and the mature writings of Turgenev and Goncharov, established the hegemony of the realistic novel which lasted in Russia until about 1900. And in the eighteen-sixties the influential radical critics launched a vigorous campaign against poetry as such in the name of the prevailing belief that literature is useless unless it is concerned with social issues. The implied assertion of Pisarev, one of the leaders of this utilitarian school, that Shakespeare's poetry was worth less than a sound pair of boots, is an extreme though characteristic example of how far literary opinion had moved from poetic standards of the eighteen-twenties. It is all the more remarkable that this prosaic age should have produced two outstanding poets, Fet and Nekrasov. Their literary destinies were very different. Fet, after publishing between 1840 and 1863, fell silent for twenty years, discouraged by the critics' disapproval of his uncivic poetry. Nekrasov escaped the pundits' censure owing to the democratic and humanitarian impulse of his verse, and was recognized between 1845 and his death in 1877 as the leading poet of his generation. He is the dominant figure in the history of Russian poetry between the death of Lermontov and the rise of the Symbolist movement in the nineties.

Fet was an uncompromising adherent of the principle of 'art for art's sake', an accomplished craftsman, and a master of the short nature lyric and love poem. His is perhaps the most purely 'musical' of all Russian poets of the nineteenth century. The predominantly melodic structure of his verse was a development of the 'singing' manner of Zhukovsky. Later it was carried still further by the Symbolists: it is significant that a poem such as Fet's 'Storm in the evening sky', with its complex assonances and expressive rhythm, was hailed by Bal'mont as a model of musical verse.

The group of poets who consciously struggled against the prevailing utilitarian current – it included, alongside Fet, Aleksey

Tolstoy, a distinguished lyric poet, dramatist and humorist – was overshadowed by the more popular and powerful genius of Nekrasov. In two respects Nekrasov was much more in tune with the needs of the public: his poetry was mainly concerned with the sufferings of the people, especially of the peasants, and thus appeared to satisfy the demand that literature should be a mouthpiece for indignant denunciation of social and political injustice; and he wrote in a realistic manner about the world in which he lived, thus fulfilling, like the great novelists of the time, the current requirement that literature should take its subject-matter from contemporary life. The misery of the Russian people, in town and country, is evoked by Nekrasov with a mixture of bitterness and compassion: eschewing ornamental trappings, using a vigorous rhythm, rising sometimes to heights of impassioned rhetoric, he combines a tortured pity for the people's sufferings with brutal satire directed against those responsible for it. His 'Muse of vengeance and sorrow', to use his own expression, was something new in Russian poetry. Nekrasov is also unique among Russian poets of the nineteenth century in the virtuosity with which he reproduced the manner and style of the folk song. He had no need to imitate its spirit: he could recreate its authentic ring. His greatest achievements in this field are *The Pedlars,* whose opening verses have in fact become a folk song, and especially *Frost the Red-Nosed,* his masterpiece, with its incomparable description of the enchantment of the frozen forest.

The early eighteen-nineties, when the first signs of the Symbolist movement became visible, were a turning point in the history of Russian poetry. The previous decade had already seen a slow revival of poetry and a timid reaction against utilitarian positivism. Russian Symbolism was part of a wider cultural movement which transformed the country's literature and art between 1900 and 1910. The large number of poets which this movement produced, the high level of their craftsmanship, and the relative coherence of their aesthetic outlook, were unexampled since the eighteen-twenties, and make the heyday of Symbolism a second Golden Age of Russian poetry. The original impulse of this movement came largely from France, and the early Russian Symbolists, such as Bryusov, were powerfully influenced both in their poetic theory and their technique by Baudelaire, Verlaine, and Mallarmé. Yet the movement had native roots as well: in the poetry of Tyutchev, whose poem *Silentium* was quoted in support of the Symbolists' endeavour to penetrate to a reality beyond the world of the senses; in the melodic experiments of Fet, which foreshadowed their attempts to bring the art of poetry closer to music; and in the mystical poetry of Vladimir Soloviev, which found an echo in Blok's early verse. It is in its poetic doctrine that Russian Symbolism, at least in its early phase, has the closest affinity with West European poetry of the period between 1890 and 1910. It laid the same stress upon the value and relevance of the poet's personal vision of reality; it had the same belief that the roots of this reality are in the ideal, supernatural world, and that there exists a true correspondence between the visible and the invisible realms, which the poet can reveal by the use of symbols: thus the early Russian Symbolists wholeheartedly accepted Baudelaire's theory of *correspondances*, and endorsed his celebrated statement that the natural world is filled with 'forests of symbols'. Like their French masters they were deeply conscious of the affinity between poetry and music, and Verlaine's dictum *de la musique avant toute chose* was one of their battle-cries.

Yet Russian Symbolism was a complex and not wholly homogeneous phenomenon; and it gradually became more and more of a national movement. Among its adherents a conflict existed – it became particularly acute in 1910 – between those who held, with Bryusov, that Symbolism was a purely literary school, and those, like Vyacheslav Ivanov, Bely, and Blok, who believed that it was also, and primarily, a form of mystical religion of which the poet is the high priest. There were also considerable differences of style and technique between individual Symbolist poets. Except for their common acceptance of the principle of 'correspondences', and their use of images with multiple meanings to express the link between the visible and invisible worlds, there is, for instance, little in common between the poetry of Vyacheslav Ivanov and that of Annensky: the former – in this period – solemn, hieratic, and ornate; the latter subtle, intimate, ironic, unemphatic and seemingly simple in manner. Both were remarkable and in different ways influential poets.

The greatest Russian poet of that generation was Blok. He was a consistent Symbolist in his use of metaphorical language to convey spiritual or psychic experience, but much of his religious and love poetry and his view of poetic inspiration may broadly be termed romantic. The rhythms and imagery of his early verse owe much to Fet, Polonsky, and Soloviev; and the latter's mystical philosophy of Sophia, the Divine Wisdom, found poetic expression in Blok's *Verses about the Beautiful Lady* (1904). The growing originality of his poetry after that year is reflected both in the range of his themes and the increasing richness of his imagery. The mystical mistress of his early verse, without wholly losing her heavenly features, became to some extent identified with more tangible and compelling realities: with Blok's wife, with the image of a sensual enchantress, with his Muse, with Russia, with the Revolution. The vision of the Beautiful Lady is still evoked in his celebrated poem *The Stranger* (1906), but she is now divested of most of her heavenly attributes and, by a characteristically ironic twist, appears in the sordid and grotesque setting of a suburban drinking-place. In 1905 Blok, together with the majority of the poets of the day, was carried away by a wave of enthusiasm for the Revolution. Its failure, and the political reaction that followed, induced in him a mood of grim and tragic despair. Yet in those 'years of stagnation' he heard the rumble of approaching events that were to transform the face of his country. In one of his greatest poems, *On the Field of Kulikovo* (1908), which contains more than an echo of the medieval heroic tradition, he evoked the Russian victory over the Tatars in 1380, an event which was for him both symbolic and prophetic. The apocalyptic expectation of an approaching catastrophe, and the sense of Russia's mission and destiny – which are the main themes of this poem – seemed to be fulfilled in the Bolshevik Revolution of 1917, which Blok hailed with enthusiasm. He saw in it not the victory of Marxism – to which he was largely indifferent – but the collapse of the old moribund western humanism and a world-wide conflagration which would ensure the triumph of the Spirit of Music. This belief, which he expressed with incomparable power and technical mastery in his long poem *The Twelve* (1918), crumbled before long. He died a broken man, empty of inspiration, conscious that the Spirit of Music had forsaken him, as it was forsaking his country. His influence on modern Russian poetry has been considerable, particularly in the field of technique; and it is mainly due to Blok that accentual verse, based on a set number of stresses in each line, regardless of the total number of its syllables, was established in Russian poetry, alongside the more traditional syllabic-accentual type of versification.

Symbolism as a movement had lost most of its creative force by 1910. The conflict between the protagonists of its aesthetic and its metaphysical aspects was a sign of its approaching disintegration. The growing posthumous influence of Annensky was leading the young generation of poets towards a quieter and more restrained lyricism. In that same year an article by the poet Kuzmin, significantly entitled 'Concerning beautiful clarity', urged young poets to cultivate accuracy, conciseness, and economy of language. This programme, which was in essence a reaction against the mysticism and stylistic vagueness of the Symbolists, was developed and systematized by the Acmeist school, which came into being in 1912 and retained the leadership in Russian poetry until 1917. The

Acmeists rejected the Symbolists' doctrine of 'correspondences' and criticized their concern with musical effects: their own poetic credo demanded the use of words in their exact, logical meaning, precise and concrete imagery, visual vividness, and conciseness of style. By contrast with the mystical romanticism of the Symbolists, their poetry was concerned with the visible world and marked a return to the classical tradition. The struggle between Acmeism and Symbolism, a leading spokesman of the former movement claimed, was 'first and foremost a struggle for *this* world . . . for our planet the Earth'.

As a literary movement, Acmeism was of less lasting significance than either Symbolism, against which it rebelled (while using some of the Symbolists' technical achievements), or Futurism. Its importance lies in the fact that it produced three poets of considerable stature – Gumilev, Anna Akhmatova, and Mandel'shtam. Gumilev, the leader of the Poets' Guild – as the Acmeist movement was called by its votaries – is mostly known in the West as a romantic with stylistic affinities with the French Parnassians, who wrote in virile and colourful fashion of Africa, conquistadors, and war. Some of his poems on these themes have a vividness and precision that are impressive. But more significant still is his later poetry, written between 1918 and 1921, in which he achieved remarkable emotional tenseness and visionary power – as in *The Sixth Sense* or the hauntingly suggestive *Tram that Lost its Way*. Anna Akhmatova's poetry has likewise a dual aspect. Her early verse, mostly love lyrics, reads like an intimate diary in which the author's sorrow and happiness are expressed simply and directly. Its style is colloquial and epigrammatic, it avoids metaphors and the melodic intonations beloved by the Symbolists, and is distinguished by brevity and expressive energy. Gradually, however, a new manner, more severe and majestic, appeared in her poetry: already apparent in the solemn sequence *July 1914*, and fully developed in her poetry published in 1921 and 1922, it was particularly well-suited to the evocation of the ordeals of war and revolution through which her country was passing. Yet she never wholly abandoned her earlier intimate manner, and her most recent poetry contains striking examples of both styles. Mandel'shtam, the third great Acmeist poet, was both in subject matter and style a thoroughgoing classicist. Greece and Rome were among his favourite themes, and his verse, solemn, slow-moving and impersonal, has an architectural quality epitomized by the title *Stone* which he gave to his first published collection of poetry (1913). Russian classicism has always been closely bound up with the cult of St Petersburg, the stately imperial capital on the Neva. Mandel'shtam wrote of St Petersburg in verses of haunting and poignant beauty, filled with nostalgia for its former glory and with distress at the sight of the great city dying destitute and hungry in the 'twilight of freedom'. In his later work he, like Gumilev, deviated from the strict canon of Acmeist clarity: the metaphorical language and the surrealistic imagery of Mandel'shtam's poetry of the nineteen-thirties are closer to Futurism.

Futurism was the third major trend in Russian poetry in the present century. Despite a passing interest shown by its adherents in Marinetti, Russian Futurism had little in common with the Italian movement of that name; its roots were largely autochthonous, some of them even lying in Symbolism, against which the Futurists rebelled so violently. Their first manifesto was issued in 1912, over the signature of four authors, including Khlebnikov and Mayakovsky, and under the characteristic title *A Slap in the Face of Public Taste*. The title was certainly well chosen: one of its more mildly phrased injunctions was: 'Throw Pushkin, Dostoevsky, Tolstoy, etc., overboard from the steamship of modernity'. The aggressively anti-traditionalist programme of the Futurists had three principal aims: to dissociate poetry from the metaphysical abstractions of the Symbolists, making it reflect the industrial and political realities of contemporary life (the poets, as Mayakovsky put it, 'should be requested to climb down from heaven to the earth'); to banish from poetry everything conventionally 'beautiful', especially those 'poetic' images which, in their view, had become nauseatingly outworn and stale; and to create a new language of poetry, whose words, freed of hackneyed associations, would be capable of conveying a genuine poetic thrill. This led several of the Russian Futurists to experiment with a new type of language of their own invention, which they called *zaum'*, or *zaumny yazyk* (usually rendered as 'trans-sense language', though a better translation would be 'metalogical', if this term were divorced from its philosophical connotation). In its extreme forms this language resulted in a gibberish of sounds aimed at suggesting a picture or an emotion. In its more moderate form *zaum'* consisted in creating new words from existing roots and assembling them according to the principle of analogy into a new, but philologically conceivable, semantic system. The latter method was used by Khlebnikov, the founder of Russian Futurism, who wrote 'metalogical' poetry with the aim both of freeing the national idiom of its associative meanings and of creating a new, universal, language. Much of his work resembles the unfinished products of a workshop. But his influence on modern Russian poetry has been considerable; few of the major poets of the Soviet period have

xlvii

escaped it. His later verse, written after 1917, is often free of verbal experimentation and inclines to an almost classical simplicity. Some of his best pieces are epic in character, and reflect his interest in pagan mythology and in *The Lay of Igor's Campaign*.

In the years that immediately preceded and followed the 1917 Revolution Futurism succeeded in expressing the prevailing mood of liberation and revolt: the repudiation of outworn literary conventions, the freedom felt by the poet to unleash the elemental creative forces within him, and his readiness to identify himself with the vast process of social and political change that seemed to be leading humanity into a new and wonderful era. These factors explain the violent assertiveness, the joyful optimism, and the deliberate coarseness of much of the *avant-garde* poetry of the Revolutionary period. Futurism produced a poet of genius in Mayakovsky, whose verse alternated between the two genres in which he excelled: political and patriotic poems, and love lyrics. His political poetry reflects a rapturous joy in the Revolution and a glowing pride in the newly-established Soviet regime. Its emphatic rhythms and declamatory style suggest the manner of a public orator. In such poems as *Our March* Mayakovsky triumphantly vindicated his claim to be 'the drummer of the October Revolution'. He combined passionate rhetoric with biting satire, directed at its enemies abroad and at home. Among the latter he listed the philistines and the bureaucrats of the government apparatus, such as the 'inspector of taxes', before whom he upholds the freedom and dignity of the poet's calling. His love poetry, with its characteristic blend of violence, self-pity, and tenderness, is one of the most effective and moving of its kind in the Russian language. It is mainly concerned with the loneliness and agony of unrequited love. The greater part of Mayakovsky's poetry is rhetorical, and was written to be read aloud: some of his poems sound like slogans or public proclamations. He achieved comic effects by mockery, caricature, and a frequent use of puns. His imagery is highly original, and his metaphors, stripped of everything conventionally poetic, often develop into an elaborate visual picture. Unlike other Futurists, he did not write 'metalogical' poetry: his language, which at first, remarkably enough in so anti-religious a poet, displayed some influence of the Bible and the liturgy, became increasingly colloquial in his later work, absorbing elements of street slang and popular songs. It is coarse, lyrical, and passionate. Mayakovsky's versification marks a further development of the prosodic reforms of the Symbolists. While laying great emphasis on rhyme, he continued Blok's experiments with accentual verse, greatly extending its use; this type of versification, without altogether superseding the syllabic-accentual, became dominant in his poetry.

Though Futurism as a literary school lost much of its coherence soon after 1917, its influence on Soviet poetry remained powerful until about 1930. Its violence, optimism, and modernism fitted well into the *Sturm und Drang* atmosphere of early Soviet literature. Few major poets of this remarkably creative period escaped the influence of either Khlebnikov or Mayakovsky. This is true even of those who belonged to literary movements hostile to Futurism, such as the Imaginists who achieved notoriety between 1919 and 1924 and who – indirectly borrowing some of their ideas from Western poets such as Ezra Pound – stressed the paramount, virtually exclusive, importance of the image as the basis of poetry. The Imaginists would matter little in the history of Russian poetry were it not for the fact that a considerable poet, Esenin, joined forces with them for a time. The best of Esenin's verse, touchingly sincere, wistful, and melodious, describes the Russian countryside, evoking its peaceful simplicity and lamenting the gradual disappearance of traditional village life under the impact of industrialization. A more direct offspring of Futurism was Constructivism, a movement that made itself felt in Soviet literature between 1924 and 1930. In their attempt to create a new poetic style that would reflect the building of the Socialist society, the Constructivists held that a poem's form should be determined by its subject-matter, concentrated on technical and scientific terminology, and attempted to introduce into poetry some of the methods of prose. The leading Constructivist poet was Il'ya Sel'vinsky whose early verse, deliberately non-lyrical and at times exuberantly individualistic, experimented with novel rhythms. Bagritsky, another notable poet of the nineteen-twenties, had a nominal though somewhat tenuous connexion with the Constructivists. His poetry is remarkable for its romantic overtones and zest for life. Although both he and Sel'vinsky identified themselves with the aspirations of the Soviet regime, their basic individualism was by 1930 already at variance with the Party's growing demand for conformity in literature. Bagritsky died in 1934; Sel'vinsky, about that time, abandoned formal experimentation and turned to historical poems and lyric verse.

Futuristic devices are apparent in the early work of Zabolotsky, surely one of the most gifted of the poets who emerged in the Soviet period. His first collection of verse, *Scrolls* (1929), is a work of subtle and sophisticated technique; it is a series of pictures of the coarse and unromantic aspects of Leningrad, of its beerhouses and football stadium, its circuses and brothels, described with irony and a wealth of realistic detail deliberately distorted into the grotesque. Zabolotsky's later verse is very different in style: it shows that his experimental manner has given way to a more classical and traditional kind of poetry. At the same time his early vision of a fantastic, ghostly world was superseded by an affirmation of the beauty of life, mirrored in nature and in man. This late poetry, published after 1948, lacks the pungency and originality of his *Scrolls*; but much of it has real lyric beauty, and several of his recent poems sound a poignant note of human sympathy and pity reminiscent of Nekrasov.

Zabolotsky's abandonment of Futuristic technique for a more direct and classical manner reflects the general trend in Soviet poetry since 1930. That year, in which Mayakovsky committed suicide, marked the beginning of a radical change in Soviet literature which was accomplished during the next four years: the age of revolutionary experiment was over; its place was taken by organization, discipline, and the ideological dictatorship of the Party. Mayakovsky's prestige as the poet laureate of the Revolution remained undiminished; but revolutionary romanticism was now frowned upon, and formal experimentation was condemned. Poets considered guilty of 'idealism' or 'formalism' were either silenced – some of them brutally – or compelled to accept the official doctrine of 'Socialist Realism'. The promulgation of this doctrine in 1934 was a sequel to the compulsory merging, two years earlier, of the different literary groups into the state-controlled Union of Soviet Writers. The enforcement of 'Socialist Realism' led in practice to a partial return to the poetic traditions of the nineteenth century, and to the use of a relatively simple, neo-classical, and somewhat eclectic style. Despite the limitations imposed upon the form and content of their craft, Soviet poets produced some good poetry during the nineteen-thirties and in the more relaxed literary atmosphere of the war. Yet conditions remained unfavourable to any flowering of poetry in Russia, and even the successful attempt of Tvardovsky to revive narrative verse fell far short of the creative originality displayed by poets in the nineteen-twenties. In the years immediately following the war, and more especially after the summer of 1946, Soviet literature was subjected to renewed and powerful pressure aimed at forcing it into the exclusive service of party and state. This bleak and artistically sterile period, associated with the name of Zhdanov, came to a gradual end after Stalin's death in 1953. In terms of published work, it marks the lowest level in quality achieved by Russian poetry in the present century.

The position of Pasternak in Soviet poetry is in several respects

1

a peculiar one. His first volume of verse was published in 1914; his most productive period as a poet lies between 1917 and 1922; though he was in close touch with several of the poetical movements of that time, he identified himself with none; frequently attacked for his alleged indifference to current social and political problems, he was yet, next to Mayakovsky, the most influential poet of the Soviet epoch; in 1946, with Zhdanov's violent onslaught on writers declared to have deviated from official doctrine, he stopped publishing new poetry for eight years; and in the last years of his life, having preserved his artistic integrity to the end, he survived to see several new collections of his verse, containing many masterpieces and including the poems which form part of his great novel *Doctor Zhivago*, published and acclaimed abroad.

Pasternak's early poetry, the best of which is embodied in his two collections, *My Sister Life* and *Themes and Variations*, shows affinities with Symbolism, Imaginism, and Futurism. From the Symbolists, and especially Blok, whom he particularly admired, he seems to have learnt that musical quality which was always a salient feature of his verse; his liking for rare and striking metaphors connects his early poetry with that of the Imaginists; while the Futurists, whose group he joined for a time, taught him to avoid conventionally 'beautiful' imagery and to concentrate on the expressive power of the individual word. Yet Pasternak's poetry is far from being an amalgam of these contemporary movements. From the very first he strove to achieve that originality of diction which is so striking a feature of his mature verse. In one of his autobiographical essays he wrote of his successful efforts to break free from the influence of Mayakovsky's manner to which he felt himself too powerfully attracted. Pasternak's early poetry is distinguished by an intensity of poetic passion and a sharpness of vision. The first of these traits, which connects him with Lermontov, appears in his treatment of love and of poetic creation, the two basic themes of *My Sister Life*, both of which are identified by him with the power latent in the universe, capable of transforming life itself. The second, the acuteness of his vision and the exactness of his imagery, gives his reader the impression of seeing the world with a new, almost child-like, directness. Pasternak has been aptly compared to a man who, armed with a magnifying glass, walks about in a room, making new discoveries. Even more remarkable were the discoveries he made out of doors, in the world of nature which is the principal source of his early poetry and in which he saw the same creative power that is latent in love and art. His lyrical poetry abounds in marvellously evocative and exciting

li

descriptions of the Russian countryside – the primeval splendour of the steppe at midnight, a hot summer day in the wood, the sad decay of autumn, the fall of snow, and the sudden intoxication of spring. For him nature is intimately bound up with man's inner life, and, like man, she is nearly always in a state of movement and flux: his favourite pictures are of showers, thunderstorms, blizzards, and the bursting of the ice in spring.

Despite Pasternak's early connexion with Futurism, the form of his verse remained, on the whole, strictly traditional. Moreover, in the course of time he moved increasingly away from modernism and experimentation towards a poetry which has its roots in the heritage of Pushkin, Tyutchev, Lermontov, and Blok. After about 1930 Pasternak's verse, without losing its sharp-sighted imagery or musical diction, shows a conscious striving for greater simplicity. The twenty-five poems that appear in the final section of *Doctor Zhivago* are a triumph of his new manner. They are mostly about love, nature, and religion. The religious poems are surely the most outstanding of their kind in the Russian language. Deriving much of their subject-matter and some of their phraseology from the Gospels, they combine the simplicity and directness of the language of the New Testament with the dramatic lyricism of the liturgy of the Orthodox Church. They propound the Christian idea of redemption through suffering and the belief that death is overcome by Christ's resurrection. In *Hamlet*, the most strikingly original poem of this cycle, Pasternak expresses his belief in the poet's mission in life; Hamlet, with whom he identifies himself, speaks with the words of Christ in Gethsemane: for Hamlet, like Christ, has been sent by his Father, and all three – Christ, Hamlet, and the Poet – stand alone on their path of sacrifice. The Poet, surrounded by falsehood and pharisaism, must accept with dignity and humility the task for which he has been sent into this world: to live his life obedient to his calling, and to offer it so that others may live by his poetry and his example.

Pasternak's personal and literary influence can be detected in the present revival of poetry in Russia, the first signs of which appeared soon after 1953. This revival is connected with the rise of a new movement in Soviet poetry. Its protagonists, some of whom grew up in the post-war years, display a number of common characteristics: their technique is experimental rather than conformist, modernistic rather than classical, and at least to that extent looks back to the poetic traditions of the nineteen-twenties; they are deeply concerned with the formal aspect of verse; and, in the choice and treatment of their subject-matter, they reveal a dislike of all that is false and insincere, a belief in the value of human relationships, and a faith in the poet's individual vision of reality. The leading poets of this group – both born in 1933 – are Evgeny Evtushenko and Andrey Voznesensky.

For all his preoccupation with social themes and his occasional – and artistically less successful – excursions into political verse, Evtushenko is essentially a lyric poet; yet the social and the intimate, the public and the personal, motifs are so closely interwoven in his work that he appears at once as deeply 'engaged' and defiantly independent. His natural eloquence, controlled exuberance, and free-flowing rhythm are not easy to communicate in translation: yet they are essential qualities of his verse; and, together with the humour, tenderness, and compassion with which he explores human relationships and describes scenes of everyday life, they explain the considerable success enjoyed by his poetry in his own country, especially among the young. Voznesensky resembles Evtushenko in his artistic nonconformity and in his belief that the task of contemporary poetry is to gain insight into man's inner consciousness. In other respects, however, he is a very different poet. Voznesensky's more intellectual approach to his craft, his bold experiments with words, rhythms, and images, his conscious use of metaphors to reveal the interconnexion and interpenetration of phenomena, and his almost surrealistic technique of verbal association, appear to be more deeply rooted than is Evtushenko's poetry in the tradition of Russian Futurism. Yet despite his acknowledged debt to Khlebnikov, Mayakovsky, and Pasternak, he is a distinctly original poet, at once subtle and powerful, achieving in much of his work a high degree of dynamic expressiveness. In different ways Evtushenko and Voznesensky epitomize the most vital and creative elements in Soviet poetry today. Their popularity in Russia, and their youth, augur well for the future of this poetry.

NOTE ON RUSSIAN VERSIFICATION*

I. SYLLABIC VERSE

Modern Russian poetry dates from the middle of the seventeenth century, when the principle of syllabic verse was imported from Poland. This syllabic versification, based on the sole constant principle of a set number of syllables in each line, was of the type used in Romance languages, notably in French poetry. It proved, however, unsuited to Russian, in which word-stress plays a very important role, and was abandoned about 1740. No example of syllabic verse is given in this anthology.

II. SYLLABIC-ACCENTUAL VERSE

Syllabic verse was succeeded by the syllabic-accentual type, in which a given number of stresses is combined within each line with a set number of syllables whose stresses are distributed regularly. This system of versification was introduced into Russia from Germany towards the middle of the eighteenth century, and is, in the main, the type prevalent in German and English poetry. Syllabic-accentual verse, popularized by Trediakovsky and especially by Lomonosov, and based on the regular alternation of stressed and unstressed syllables, has remained dominant in Russian poetry ever since. Borrowing the principles of its metrical scheme from ancient Greek prosody, Russian versification substituted the stressed for the long syllable and the unstressed for the short. Thus there are, in Russian syllabic-accentual verse, five different metres, based on feet of two or three syllables:

1. *Binary Metres*

(a) *The Iambic Metre*. This has been, from the eighteenth century to the present day, the most frequently used metre in Russian poetry. It was the favourite metre of Pushkin (84 per cent of whose poetic output is in iambic verse), of Baratynsky, and of many other poets of the Golden Age. In the iambic line, in principle, every even syllable is stressed, and every odd syllable is unstressed. Lomonosov's *Evening Meditation* is a classic example of the four-foot iambic line:

*This note is based largely on B. O. Unbegaun's excellent survey *Russian Versification* (Oxford, 1956). The examples I have chosen are taken from poems printed in this anthology.

Лицé своé скрывáет дéнь,

— ‿́ | — ‿́ | — ‿́ | — ‿́

Поля́ покры́ла мрáчна нóчь,

‿́ | ‿́ | ‿́ | — ‿́

Взошлá на гóры чóрна тéнь,

— ‿́ | — ‿́ | — ‿́ | — ‿́

Лучи́ от нáс склони́лись прóчь.

— ‿́ | — ‿́ | — ‿́ | — ‿́

The complete regularity with which unstressed and stressed syllables follow each other in these lines would in the long run produce an over-scanned and monotonous effect. In fact, few Russian poems, at least after the eighteenth century, have so regular a cadence. The poet can introduce variety into his metrical scheme by using his own rhythmic pattern and omitting one or several of the stresses from the strong syllables; this has the effect of bringing the rhythm of the line closer to the cadence of spoken Russian. Pushkin's *Prophet*, written in four-foot iambic verse, is a good example of this:

Духóвной жáждою томи́м,

— ‿́ | — ‿́ | — (‿) | — ‿́

В пусты́не мрáчной я́ влачи́лся,

— ‿́ | — ‿́ | — ‿́ | — ‿́ | —

И шестикры́лый серафи́м

— (‿) | — ‿́ | — (‿) | — ‿́

На перепýтье мнé яви́лся.

— (‿) | — ‿́ | — ‿́ | — ‿́ | —

The final unstressed syllables in the second and fourth lines are independent of the metrical pattern. Similar divergences between the rhythmic pattern and the metrical scheme occur in many other of Pushkin's poems written in four-foot iambics, e.g. *Grapes, Evgeny Onegin, To —, The Poet, The Upas-Tree,* and *The Bronze Horseman.* Such variations are also common in five- and six-foot iambic verse; the former is the usual metre of the sonnet:

В Испáнии Амýр не чужестрáнец,

— ‿́ | — — | — ‿́ | — — | — ‿́ | —

Он тáм не гóсть, но рóдственник и свóй,

— ‿́ | — ‿́ | — ‿́ | — — | — ‿́

Под кастаньéт с весёлой красотóй

— — | — ‿́ | — ‿́ | — — | — ‿́

Поёт ромáнс и пля́шет, как испáнец.

— ‿́ | — ‿́ | — ‿́ | — — | — ‿́ | —

(Del'vig)

Other examples of five-foot iambic verse are the sonnets by Vyacheslav Ivanov, and Pushkin's *Boris Godunov* and *I loved you*; the six-foot iambic line is used in the first of the two poems by Voloshin and by Anna Akhmatova ('In human intimacy there is a secret boundary ').

(b) *The Trochaic Metre*. In trochaic lines every odd syllable is strong and in principle stressed, while every even syllable is weak and unstressed; stresses can be omitted in accordance with the rhythmic pattern of the poem, as in iambic verse. The trochaic line has often been used to reproduce the cadence of Russian folk-poetry, as in the two poems by Kol'tsov:

Соловьём залётным
— — | ´ — | ´ —
Юность пролетéла
´ — | — — | ´ —

A four-foot trochaic metre is used by Derzhavin (*A Nightingale in a Dream*), Pushkin (*Winter Evening, The Talisman, Evil Spirits*), Tyutchev ('Those poor villages'), Fet ('I have come to you with greeting'), and Bryusov (*Achilles at the Altar*); examples of five-foot trochaic verse are found in Lermontov ('Alone, I come out on to the road'), Annensky (*The Old Barrel-Organ*), Gumilev (*The Workman*), and in Pasternak's *Hamlet*:

Гул затих. Я вышел на подмóстки.
´ — | ´ — | ´ — | — — | ´ —
Прислонясь к дверному косяку,
— — | ´ — | ´ — | — — | ´
Я ловлю в далёком отголóске,
´ — | ´ — | ´ — | — — | ´ —
Что случится на моём веку.
´ — | ´ — | — — | ´ — | ´

The six-foot trochaic line is rare: it can be found in Sumarokov's poem (where it alternates with a five-foot trochaic line) and in Bal'mont's *Sin miedo*.

2. *Ternary Metres*

Rare in the eighteenth century, and still exceptional in Pushkin's poetry, ternary metres were popularized by the romantic poets, Zhukovsky and Lermontov. They were used frequently and to great effect by Nekrasov, whose lines with dactylic endings (e.g. the odd lines of *Vlas* and the extracts from *In the Village* and *The*

Pedlars) evoke the rhythm of folk poetry. There are three types of ternary metres in Russian:

(a) *The Dactylic Metre* is the commonest of the three. Two examples follow, taken from the opening lines of poems printed in this anthology:

Бу́ря на не́бе вече́рнем,

 ´ — — | ´ — — | ´ —

Мо́ря серди́того шу́м –

 ´ — — | ´ — — | ´

Бу́ря на мо́ре и ду́мы,

 ´ — — | ´ — — | ´ —

Мно́го мучи́тельных ду́м –

 ´ — — | ´ — — | ´

(Fet)

Е́ду ли но́чью по у́лице тёмной,

 ´ — — | ´ — — | ´ — — | ´ —

Бу́ри заслу́шаюсь в па́смурный де́нь, –

 ´ — — | ´ — — | ´ — — | ´

Дру́г беззащи́тный, больно́й и бездо́мный,

 ´ — — | ´ — — | ´ — — | ´ —

Вдру́г предо мно́й промелькнёт твоя те́нь!

 ´ — — | ´ — — | ´ — — | ´

(Nekrasov)

Other examples will be found in Tyutchev ('How beautiful you are, O sea at night'), Blok (*The Artist*), and Gumilev (*Agamemnon's Warrior*).

(b) *The Amphibrachic Metre.* An example is provided by Lermontov's *The Angel*:

По не́бу полу́ночи а́нгел лете́л

 — ´ — | — ´ — | — ´ — | — ´

И ти́хую пе́сню он пе́л;

 — ´ — | — ´ — | — ´

И ме́сяц, и звёзды, и ту́чи толпо́й

 — ´ — | — ´ — | — ´ — | — ´

Внима́ли той пе́сне свято́й.

 — ´ — | — ´ — | — ´

Other instances will be found in Zhukovsky (*The Night*), in the extract from Nekrasov's *Frost the Red-Nosed*, in Annensky (*The Anguish of a Mirage*), and Khodasevich (*Ballad*).

(c) *The Anapaestic Metre.* This is used in Blok's poem *To the Muse*:

Есть в напéвах твоúх сокровéнных

— — ′ | — — ′ | — — ′ | —

Роковáя о гúбели вéсть.

— — ′ | — — ′ | — — ′

Есть прокля́тье завéтов свящéнных,

— — ′ | — — ′ | — — ′ | —

Поругáние счáстия éсть.

— — ′ | — — ′ | — — ′

Other examples will be found in Bal'mont (*Chords*), Gumilev (*The Captains*), Pasternak (*Spasskoe*), and Zabolotsky ('Starling, let me have a little corner').

III. ACCENTUAL VERSE

Alongside syllabic-accentual verse, another type of versification, the purely accentual, gradually gained ground in modern Russian poetry. It is characterized solely by a given number of stresses in each line, irrespective of its total number of syllables, the number of unstressed syllables between the stresses being variable. Accentual verse predominates in Russian folk poetry and in the *byliny,* or heroic poems, which mostly consist of unrhymed lines, each having three irregularly distributed stresses and a dactylic ending. It seems, however, that modern Russian accentual verse owes less to native oral tradition than to the influence of German poetry, in which this type of versification has been prominent since the late eighteenth century. In some respects, moreover, Russian accentual verse may well have developed out of deliberate deviations introduced into syllabic-accentual poetry. Thus in Tyutchev's poem *Silentium,* as published in 1836, the regular four-foot iambic metre is broken in lines 4, 5, and 17 by the insertion of amphibrachic lines. This device, which seems to spring from the poet's desire to vary the monotony of too rigid a rhythm, and marks a step towards accentual verse, was disapproved of by Turgenev who, when editing Tyutchev's works in 1854, felt obliged to 'correct' the poem by altering the offending lines into regular iambics. The original version has been restored in the text printed in this anthology. Accentual verse began to compete with the syllabic-accentual towards the middle of the nineteenth century, in the poetry of Polonsky and Fet. Its real architect, however, was Blok – from whom it passed into the poetry of Akhmatova, Gumilev, Mayakovsky, Esenin, and others. Esenin's *Song about a Bitch* and

the extract from his *Prayers for the Dead*, and the poems by
Mayakovsky printed in this anthology are examples of accentual
verse. Particularly striking is the rhythm of Mayakovsky's *Our
March* which opens with two accentual lines of trochaic cadence,
followed by two anapaestic lines, followed in their turn by four
purely accentual lines. The poem aims at evoking the rhythm of a
beating drum:

> Бéйте в плóщади бýнтов тóпот!
> ´ — ´ — — ´ — ´ —
>
> Вы́ше, гóрдых голóв грядá!
> ´ — ´ — — ´ — ´
>
> Мы разли́вом вторóго потóпа
> — — ´ — — ´ — — ´ —
>
> перемóем мирóв городá.
> — — ´ — — ´ — — ´
>
> Днéй бы́к пéг.
> ´ ´ ´
>
> Мéдленна лéт арбá.
> ´ — — ´ — ´
>
> Нáш бóг бéг.
> ´ ´ ´
>
> Сéрдце нáш барабáн.
> ´ — ´ — — ´

Aseev's poem *The Bull*, and Mayakovsky's *The Atlantic Ocean*
and *Conversation with an Inspector of Taxes about Poetry* were
printed by their authors in broken, echelonned, lines. In this book,
in order to save space, this has not been done, but the caesuras
within each line are indicated by means of raised circles.

To facilitate pronunciation, the letter *ë* is printed in all poems
written after 1800, except when the sound *e* is required by the
rhyme; the diaeresis was not introduced into Russian orthography
until the very end of the eighteenth century.

I wish to record my special gratitude to Mrs Natalie Duddington
and Mr J. S. G. Simmons, and also to Sir Isaiah Berlin, Sir
Maurice Bowra, Mr J. M. Cohen, and Mr Max Hayward for
checking parts of my translations and for many helpful suggestions.
I am further indebted to Professor B. O. Unbegaun, who gave
me invaluable assistance in proof; and to Mr Hayward for his
masterly translation of Mayakovsky's *Conversation with an Inspector
of Taxes*, of which I have made much use. I am also grateful to
Mr B. Filippov, Professor N. Gorodetzky, Mr R. R. Milner-

Gulland, Miss Elizabeth Schouvaloff, and Professor G. Struve, who have helped me with this book in a variety of ways, and to the Librarian and staff of the Taylor Institution, Oxford, for many kindnesses. To my wife for her help at every stage, and for her patience, my debt is great indeed.

Oxford, August 1960   D.O.

ACKNOWLEDGMENTS

Grateful acknowledgment is made to the following:

Mr R. N. Grynberg for an extract from a poem by Anna Akhmatova, published in *Vozdushnye Puti* (New York, 1960);

Mme Odoevzev-Ivanoff for three poems by Georgy Ivanov, published by the *New Review* (New York, 1958);

The Clarendon Press, Oxford, and Mr Dimitri Ivanov, for six poems by Vyacheslav Ivanov;

Giangiacomo Feltrinelli for four poems from *Dr Zhivago* (Milan, 1957),

and Mrs Lydia Slater for five others by Boris Pasternak;

Professor Gleb Struve for two poems by Marina Tsvetaeva, from *Lebediny Stan* (Munich, 1957)

The Heritage of
RUSSIAN VERSE

SLOVO O POLKU IGOREVE

Слово о плъку Игоревъ, Игоря сына Святъславля,
внука Ольгова

Не лѣпо ли ны бяшетъ, братие, начяти старыми
словесы трудныхъ повѣстий о пълку Игоревѣ,
Игоря Святъславлича? Начати же ся тъй пѣсни по
былинамъ сего времени, а не по замышлению
Бояню. Боянъ бо вѣщий, аще кому хотяше пѣснь
творити, то растѣкашется мыслию по древу, сѣрымъ
вълкомъ по земли, шизымъ орломъ подъ облакы.
Помняшеть бо, рече, първыхъ временъ усобицѣ.
Тогда пущашеть 10 соколовь на стадо лебедѣй: кото-
рыи дотечаше, та преди пѣснь пояше старому Ярославу, храброму Мстиславу, иже зарѣза Редедю
предъ пълкы касожьскыми, красному Романови
Святъславличю. Боянъ же, братие, не 10 соколовь
на стадо лебедѣй пущаше, нъ своя вѣщиа пръсты на
живая струны въскладаше; они же сами княземъ
славу рокотаху.

Почнемъ же, братие, повѣсть сию отъ стараго

The Lay of Igor's Campaign – of Igor the Son
of Svyatoslav and the Grandson of Oleg

WOULD it not be fitting, brothers, for us to begin in the manner of
the ancient lays the grievous tale of the campaign of Igor, of Igor
the son of Svyatoslav? But rather let this song begin in accord
with the events of our own time, and not with the design of Boyan.
For Boyan the wizard, if he wished to make a song for someone,
would fly in thought through the tree, like a grey wolf over the
earth, like a blue-grey eagle beneath the clouds. For he recalled, as
he said, the wars of olden times. Then he would let loose ten falcons
upon a flock of swans: whichever swan was overtaken was the first to
sing a song – to Yaroslav of old, to valiant Mstislav who slew Rededya
before the Circassian hosts, to fair Roman, the son of Svyatoslav.
But, brothers, it was not ten falcons that Boyan would let loose
upon a flock of swans – but he would lay his magic fingers upon the
living strings, and of themselves they thundered glory to the princes.

Let us then, brothers, begin this tale from Vladimir of old

Владимера до нынѣшняго Игоря, иже истягну умь крѣпостию своею и поостри сердца своего мужествомъ; наплънився ратнаго духа, наведе своя храбрыя плъкы на землю Половѣцькую за землю Руськую.

Тогда Игорь възрѣ на свѣтлое солнце и видѣ отъ него тьмою вся своя воя прикрыты. И рече Игорь къ дружинѣ своей: «Братие и дружино! Луце жъ бы потяту быти, неже полонену быти; а всядемъ, братие, на свои бръзыя комони, да позримъ синего Дону». Спала князю умь похоти и жалость ему знамение заступи искусити Дону великаго. «Хощу бо, – рече, – копие приломити конець поля Половецкаго, съ вами, русици, хощу главу свою приложити, а любо испити шеломомъ Дону».

О Бояне, соловию стараго времени! Абы ты сиа плъкы ущекоталъ, скача, славию, по мыслену древу, летая умомъ подъ облакы, свивая славы оба полы сего времени, рища въ тропу Трояню чресъ поля на горы, пѣти было пѣснь Игореви, того

to Igor of our time, who girded his mind with firmness and sharpened his heart with valour, and, filled with a warlike spirit, led his brave hosts against the land of the Polovtsy, for the land of Russia.

Then Igor looked at the bright sun and saw that all his warriors were covered by the darkness it cast. And Igor said to his retainers: 'Brothers and retainers! Better it would be to be slain than to be taken prisoner; so let us, brothers, mount our swift horses, that we may look upon the blue Don.' The Prince's mind was ablaze with eagerness and his longing to taste the great Don veiled the omen from him. 'I want', he said, 'to break a lance at the limit of the Polovtsian steppe; with you, O Russians, I want to lay down my life, or else to drink of the Don from my helmet.'

O Boyan, nightingale of olden times! If you had sung these campaigns, flitting, O nightingale, through the tree of thought, flying in your mind beneath the clouds, weaving together the glories of both halves of this time, racing along the path of Troyan over plains and up mountains – thus would you have sung a song for

внуку: «Не буря соколы занесе чрезъ поля широкая, – галици стады бѣжать къ Дону великому». Чи ли въспѣти было, вѣщей Бояне, Велесовь внуче: «Комони ржуть за Сулою, – звенить слава въ Кыевѣ; трубы трубять въ Новѣградѣ, – стоять стязи въ Путивлѣ!»

Игорь ждетъ мила брата Всеволода. И рече ему буй туръ Всеволодъ: «Одинъ братъ, одинъ свѣтъ свѣтлый – ты, Игорю! оба есвѣ Святъславличя! Сѣдлай, брате, свои брѣзыи комони, а мои ти готови, осѣдлани у Курьска напереди. А мои ти куряни свѣдоми къмети: подъ трубами повити, подъ шеломы възлѣлѣяни, конець копия въскръмлени, пути имъ вѣдоми, яругы имъ знаеми, луци у нихъ напряжени, тули отворени, сабли изъострени; сами скачють, акы сѣрыи влъци въ полѣ, ищучи себе чти, а князю славѣ».

Тогда въступи Игорь князь въ златъ стремень, и поѣха по чистому полю. Солнце ему тъмою путь за-

Igor, grandson/ of Troyan: 'It is not a storm that has swept falcons across the wide steppes – flocks of jackdaws are in flight towards the great Don.' Or thus would you have begun your song, O wizard Boyan, grandson of Veles: 'Horses neigh beyond the Sula, glory rings out in Kiev, trumpets sound in Novgorod, standards are raised in Putivl'!'

Igor awaits his dear brother Vsevolod. And Vsevolod the fierce aurochs said to him: 'My one brother, you are my one bright light, Igor; we both are sons of Svyatoslav! Saddle your swift horses, brother; mine indeed are prepared – saddled near Kursk in readiness. And my men of Kursk are renowned warriors – swaddled to the sound of trumpets, nursed beneath helmets, fed at the spear's point; the roads are known to them, the ravines familiar to them, their bows are strung, their quivers open, their sabres whetted; they race across the steppe like grey wolves, seeking honour for themselves and glory for their prince.'

Then Prince Igor stepped into his golden stirrup and rode out into the open plain. The sun barred his path with darkness; . .

3

ступаше; нощь стонущи ему грозою птичь убуди;
свистъ звѣринъ въста; збися дивъ, кличетъ връху
древа: велитъ послушати – земли незнаемѣ, Влъзѣ,
и Поморию, и Посулию, и Сурожу, и Корсуню, и
тебѣ, Тьмутораканьскый блъванъ! А половци него-
товами дорогами побѣгоша къ Дону великому: кры-
чатъ тѣлѣгы полунощы, рци, лебеди роспущени.
Игорь къ Дону вои ведетъ! Уже бо бѣды его пасетъ
птиць по дубию; влъци грозу въсрожатъ по яругамъ;
орли клектомъ на кости звѣри зовутъ; лисици
брешутъ на чрълѣныя щиты. О Руская земле! Уже
за шеломянемъ еси!

Длъго ночь мрькнетъ. Заря свѣтъ запала. Мъгла
поля покрыла. Щекотъ славий успе; говоръ галичь
убуди. Русичи великая поля чрълеными щиты прегородиша, ищучи себѣ чти, а князю славы.

Съ зарания въ пятокъ потопташа поганыя плъкы
половецкыя, и рассушясь стрѣлами по полю, по-
мчаша красныя дѣвкы половецкыя, а съ ними злато,

night, as it groaned to him with the voice of thunder, awakened the
birds; the howling of beasts arose; Div started up and cries from the
top of a tree: bids the unknown land hearken – the Volga, the sea-
coast, the Sula country, Surozh, Chersonesus, and you, O idol of
Tmutorokan'! And the Polovtsy hastened by untrodden roads to
the great Don; their carts screech at midnight like swans let loose:
Igor is leading his warriors towards the Don. Now the birds in the
oak-trees lie in wait for his misfortune; the wolves stir up a storm
in the ravines; the eagles by their screeching call the beasts to [a
feast of] bones; the foxes yelp at the scarlet shields. O land of
Russia, you are already beyond the hill!

The night is slow in falling. The glow of sunset has faded. Mist
has covered the plain. The nightingales' songs are stilled, the jackdaws' chatter is aroused. The Russians have barred the great plain
with their scarlet shields, seeking honour for themselves and glory
for their prince.

From dawn on Friday they trampled the infidel Polovtsian
hosts and, scattering like arrows over the plain, they carried off the
fair Polovtsian maidens, and with them gold . . . . .

и паволокы, и драгыя оксамиты. Орьтъмами, и япончицами, и кожухы начашя мосты мостити по болотомъ и грязивымъ мѣстомъ, и всякыми узорочьи половѣцкыми. Чрьленъ стягъ, бѣла хорюговь, чрьлена чолка, сребрено стружие — храброму Святъславличю!

Дремлетъ въ полѣ Ольгово хороброе гнѣздо. Далече залетѣло! Не было оно обидѣ порождено ни соколу, ни кречету, ни тебѣ, чръный воронъ, поганый половчине! Гзакъ бежитъ сѣрымъ влькомъ, Кончакъ ему слѣдъ править къ Дону великому.

Другаго дни велми рано кровавыя зори свѣтъ повѣдаютъ; чръныя тучя съ моря идутъ, хотятъ прикрыти 4 солнца, а въ нихъ трепещуть синии млъьнии. Быти грому великому! Итти дождю стрѣлами съ Дону великаго! Ту ся копиемъ приламати, ту ся саблямъ потручяти о шеломы половецкыя, на рѣцѣ на Каялѣ, у Дону великаго! О Руская землѣ! Уже за шеломянемъ еси!

Се вѣтри, Стрибожи внуци, вѣютъ съ моря

---

and brocades and precious cloths of samite. With coverlets, mantles, cloaks lined with fur, and with all manner of Polovtsian finery, they began to lay pathways over swamps and marshy places. Scarlet is the standard, white is the banner, scarlet the horse-tail, silver the shaft for the valiant son of Svyatoslav.

The valiant brood of Oleg slumbers in the steppe. Far have they flown! They were not begotten to suffer injury, not from falcon, nor from gerfalcon, nor from you, black raven, infidel Polovtsian! Gzak races like a grey wolf, Konchak shows him the way to the great Don.

On the next day, very early, a blood-red glow heralds the dawn; black clouds come in from the sea, they would veil the four suns, and streaks of blue lightning quiver within them. There will be a mighty thunder! Rain will come, a rain of arrows, from the great Don! Here lances will break, here sabres will strike against the Polovtsian helmets, on the river Kayala, by the great Don. O land of Russia, you are already beyond the hill!

Behold, the winds, grandsons of Stribog, blow arrows from the sea

5

стрѣлами на храбрыя плъкы Игоревы. Земля тут-
нетъ, рѣкы мутно текуть, пороси поля прикрываютъ,
стязи глаголютъ: половци идуть отъ Дона, и отъ
моря, и отъ всѣхъ странъ Рускыя плъкы оступиша.
Дѣти бѣсови кликомъ поля прегородиша, а храбрии
Русици преградиша чрълеными щиты.

Яръ туре Всеволодѣ! стоиши на борони, прыщеши
на вои стрѣлами, гремлеши о шеломы мечи харалужными! Камо, туръ, поскочяше, своимъ златымъ
шеломомъ посвѣчивая, тамо лежатъ поганыя головы
половецкыя. Поскепаны саблями калеными шеломы оварьскыя отъ тебе, яръ туре Всеволоде! Кая
раны дорога, братие, забывъ чти и живота, и града
Чрънигова отня злата стола, и своя милыя хоти,
красныя Глѣбовны, свычая и обычая?

Были вѣчи Трояни, минула лѣта Ярославля; были
плъци Олговы, Ольга Святьславличя. Тъй бо
Олегъ мечемъ крамолу коваше и стрѣлы по земли
сѣяше. Ступаетъ въ златъ стремень въ градѣ

upon the valiant hosts of Igor. The earth rumbles, the rivers
flow with turbid stream, dust covers the plain, the banners
announce: the Polovtsy are coming from the Don and from the sea;
on all sides they have surrounded the Russian hosts. The devil's
children have barred the plain with their war-cry, and the valiant
Russians have barred it with their scarlet shields.

O Vsevolod, you raging aurochs! You stand in battle, you shower
arrows upon the warriors, you thunder against their helmets with
swords of Frankish steel. Wherever you have leapt, O aurochs,
flashing with your golden helmet, there lie infidel Polovtsian heads.
By you the Avar helmets are cloven with tempered sabres, O
Vsevolod, raging aurochs! What do wounds matter, brothers, to
him who has forgotten his honours, his possessions, his father's
golden throne in the city of Chernigov, and the love and caresses
of his dear wife, the fair Glebovna?

There were the ages of Troyan, the years of Yaroslav have
passed; there were the campaigns of Oleg, Oleg the son of Svyatoslav. That Oleg forged strife with his sword, and sowed arrows
over the land. He steps into his golden stirrup in the city . . .

Тьмуторока́нѣ, той же звонъ слыша давный великый Ярославъ, а сынъ Всеволожь Владимиръ по вся
утра уши закладаше въ Черниговѣ. Бориса же
Вячеславлича слава на судъ приведе и на Канину
зслену паполому постла за обиду Олгову, храбра и
млада князя. Съ тоя же Каялы Святоплъкъ повелѣ
яти отца своего междю угорьскими иноходьци ко
святѣй Софии къ Киеву. Тогда, при Олзѣ Гори-
славличи сѣяшется и растяшеть усобицами, погиба-
шеть жизнь Даждьбожа внука; въ княжихъ
крамолахъ вѣци человѣкомь скратишась. Тогда по
Руской земли рѣтко ратаевѣ кикахуть, нъ часто
врани граяхуть, трупіа себѣ дѣляче, а галици свою
рѣчь говоряхуть, хотять полетѣти на уедие.

То было въ ты рати и въ ты плъкы, а сицей рати
не слышано! Съ зараниа до вечера, съ вечера до
свѣта летятъ стрѣлы каленыя, гримлютъ сабли о
шеломы, трещатъ копіа харалужныя въ полѣ незнаемѣ, среди земли Половецкыи. Чръна земля

of Tmutorokan'; that same sound was heard by the great Yaroslav
of old; while Vsevolod's son Vladimir stopped his ears every morning in Chernigov. And vainglory brought Boris the son of Vyacheslav to his doom, and spread out on the Kanina a green shroud for
this valiant young prince, because of the injury done to Oleg.
From the same Kayala Svyatopolk had his father carried between
Hungarian amblers to St Sophia in Kiev. Then, in the days of
Oleg Gorislavich, feuds were sown and sprouted forth, the
substance of Dazhbog's grandson went to ruin, the lives of men
grew short in princely strife. Then over the land of Russia rarely
did the ploughmen call out, but often did the ravens croak as
they shared the corpses; and the jackdaws chattered in their own
tongue, preparing to fly to the feast.

So was it in those battles and in those campaigns, but a like
battle was never heard of: from dawn till evening, from evening till
dawn tempered arrows fly, sabres thunder against helmets, lances
of Frankish steel crash in the unknown steppe amid the Polovtsian
land. The black earth . . . . . . ∘

подъ копыты костьми была посѣяна, а кровию польяна: тугою взыдоша по Руской земли.

Что ми шумить, что ми звенить – далече рано предъ зорями? Игорь плъкы заворочаетъ: жаль бо ему мила брата Всеволода. Бишася день, бишася другый; третьяго дни къ полуднию падоша стязи Игоревы. Ту ся брата разлучиста на брезѣ быстрой Каялы; ту кроваваго вина не доста; ту пиръ докончаша храбрии русичи: сваты попоиша, а сами полегоша за землю Рускую. Ничить трава жалощами, а древо с тугою къ земли преклонилось.

Уже бо, братие, не веселая година въстала, уже пустыни силу прикрыла. Въстала обида въ силахъ Дажьбожа внука, вступила дѣвою на землю Трояню, въсплескала лебедиными крылы на синѣмъ море у Дону плещучи, упуди жирня времена. Усобица княземъ на поганыя погыбе, рекоста бо братъ брату: «Се мое, а то мое же». И начяша князи про малое «се великое» мльвити, а сами на себѣ

beneath the hooves was sown with bones and watered with blood: a harvest of sorrow came up over the land of Russia.

What is this noise, what is this ringing that I hear far away, early before dawn? Igor is wheeling his troops: for he has pity on his dear brother Vsevolod. They fought for a day, they fought for a second day; on the third day, towards noon, Igor's standards fell. Here the two brothers parted on the bank of the swift Kayala; here there was not enough bloody wine, here the brave Russians ended the feast: they plied the wedding guests with wine, and themselves were laid low for the land of Russia. The grass bows low with pity, and the tree in sorrow bends to the ground.

For now, brothers, a sorrowful time is come, now the wild-growing steppe has swallowed up the [Russian] force. Injury has arisen in the forces of the grandson of Dazhbog, and, in the guise of a maiden, has stepped on to the land of Troyan; she flapped her swan-wings on the blue sea by the Don, and by flapping them she has driven away the times of abundance. The war of the princes against the infidels has ceased, for brother said to brother: 'This is mine, and that is mine, too.' And the princes began to say of little things, 'this is a great matter', and to . . . . .

крамолу ковати. А погании съ всѣхъ странъ при-
хождаху съ побѣдами на землю Рускую.

О, далече зайде соколъ, птиць бья, – къ морю! А
Игорева храбраго плѣку не крѣсити! За нимъ
кликну Карна, и Жля поскочи по Руской земли,
смагу мычючи въ пламянѣ розѣ. Жены рускія
въсплакашась, аркучи: «Уже намъ своихъ милыхъ
ладъ ни мыслію смыслити, ни думою сдумати,
ни очима съглядати, а злата и сребра ни мало того
потрепати».

А въстона бо, братие, Киевъ тугою, а Черниговъ
напастьми. Тоска разлияся по Руской земли; печаль
жирна тече средь земли Рускыи. А князи сами на
себе крамолу коваху, а погании сами, побѣдами на-
рищуще на Рускую землю, емляху дань по бѣлѣ отъ
двора.

Тии бо два храбрая Святъславлича, Игорь и
Всеволодъ – уже лжу убудиста, которую ту бяше
успилъ отецъ ихъ – Святъславь грозный великый

---

forge strife each against the other. And from all sides the victorious
infidels invaded the land of Russia.

O far has the falcon flown, killing the birds – towards the sea!
And Igor's valiant host shall not rise again! In its wake Karna [the
Mourner] raised her wail, and Zhlya [Lamentation?] swept over
the land of Russia, scattering fire from her flaming horn. The
women of Russia began to lament, saying: 'No more shall we
conceive our dear loved ones in our minds, nor imagine them in
our thoughts, nor behold them with our eyes, nor so much as touch
gold and silver.'

And Kiev, brothers, groaned with sorrow, and Chernigov with
affliction. Anguish flowed over the land of Russia, sorrow in abundance spread across the Russian land. And the princes forged strife
each against the other, while the infidels, victoriously invading the
land of Russia, took tribute of a squirrel-skin from every home-
stead.

For Igor and Vsevolod, those two valiant sons of Svyatoslav,
now roused the dissensions which their father, the redoubtable
Svyatoslav the Great . . . . . .

киевскый грозою: бяшеть притрепалъ своими сильными плъкы и харалужными мечи; наступи на землю Половецкую, притопта хлъми и яругы, взмути рѣкы и озеры, иссуши потокы и болота. А поганаго Кобяка изъ луку моря отъ желѣзныхъ великыхъ плъковъ половецкыхъ яко вихръ, выторже: и падеся Кобякъ въ градѣ Киевѣ, въ гридницѣ Святъславли. Ту нѣмци и венедици, ту греци и морава поютъ славу Святъславлю, каютъ князя Игоря, иже погрузи жиръ во днѣ Каялы рѣкы половецкыя, рускаго злата насыпаша. Ту Игорь князь высѣдѣ изъ сѣдла злата, а въ сѣдло кощиево. Уныша бо градомъ забралы, а веселие пониче.

А Святъславь мутенъ сонъ видѣ въ Киевѣ на горахъ. «Си ночь съ вечера одѣвахуть мя, – рече, – чрьною папаломою на кроваты тисовѣ; чрьпахуть ми синее вино, съ трудомъ смѣшено, сыпахуть ми тъщими тулы поганыхъ тльковинъ великый женчюгъ на лоно и нѣгуютъ мя. Уже дьскы безъ кнѣса

of Kiev, had curbed by the fear he inspired. He struck terror [into his enemies] with his mighty hosts and his swords of Frankish steel; he invaded the land of the Polovtsy, trampled the hills and ravines, muddied the rivers and lakes, dried up the torrents and swamps. Like a whirlwind, he tore the infidel Kobyak from the arm of the sea out of the great iron Polovtsian hosts; and Kobyak fell in the city of Kiev, in Svyatoslav's great hall. Now Germans and Venetians, Greeks and Moravians sing the glory of Svyatoslav and rebuke Prince Igor who sank his wealth at the bottom of the Kayala, the Polovtsian river, and scattered Russian gold. Now Prince Igor exchanged his golden saddle for the saddle of a slave. The ramparts of the cities are downcast, and joy bowed down.

And Svyatoslav dreamed a troubled dream in Kiev on the hills. 'This night from evening onwards', he said, 'they were clothing me in a black shroud on a bed of cedar; they poured out for me blue wine mixed with sorrow; from the empty quivers of the pagan [Turkic] tribesmen they scattered large pearls on my breast, and caressed me. Now are the beams without a roof-tree in . . .

в моемъ теремѣ златовръсѣмъ. Всю нощь съ
вечера бусови врани възграяху; у Плѣсньска на
болони бѣша дебрьски сани, и несошася къ синему
морю».

И ркоша бояре князю: «Уже, княже, туга умь по-
лонила; се бо два сокола слѣтѣста съ отня стола злата
поискати града Тьмутороканя, а любо испити шело-
момь Дону. Уже соколома крильца припѣшали
поганыхъ саблями, а самаю опуташа въ путины
желѣзны. Темно бо бѣ въ 3 день: два солнца по-
мѣркоста, оба багряная стлъпа погасоста и съ нима
молодая мѣсяца, Олегъ и Святъславъ, тьмою ся по-
волокоста и въ морѣ погрузиста, и великое буйство
подаста хинови. На рѣцѣ на Каялѣ тьма свѣтъ покрыла; по Руской земли простроша половци, акы
пардуже гнѣздо. Уже снесеся хула на хвалу; уже
тресну нужда на волю; уже врьжеся дивь на землю.
Се бо готьскыя красныя дѣвы въспѣша на брезѣ
синему морю: звоня рускымъ златомъ, поютъ время

my gold-roofed palace. All night from evening onwards dark ravens
were croaking; at the approaches to Plesensk there was a wooden
sledge(?), and it was borne towards the blue sea.'

And the boyars said to the prince: 'O Prince, grief has now taken
your mind captive; for two falcons have flown from their father's
golden throne to gain the city of Tmutorokan', or else to drink of
the Don from their helmets. The falcons' wings have now been
clipped by the sabres of the infidels, and they themselves are
fettered in fetters of iron. It was dark on the third day: two suns
ceased to shine, both purple pillars were extinguished, and with
them two young moons, Oleg and Svyatoslav, were veiled in darkness and sank into the sea, and roused great audacity among the
Huns(?). On the river Kayala darkness veiled the light. Over the
Russian land the Polovtsy have scattered like a brood of panthers.
Now shame has descended upon glory; now violence has struck
down freedom; now Div has thrown himself on to the land. For,
behold, the fair Gothic maidens have started to sing on the shores
of the blue sea; jingling Russian gold, they sing of the times . .

Бусово, лелѣютъ месть Шароканю. А мы уже, дружина, жадни веселия!»

Тогда великый Святьславъ изрони злато слово слезами смѣшено и рече: «О моя сыновчя, Игорю и Всеволоде! Рано еста начала Половецкую землю мечи цвѣлити, а себѣ славы искати. Нъ нечестно одолѣсте, нечестно бо кровь поганую пролиясте. Ваю храбрая сердца въ жестоцемъ харалузѣ скована, а въ буести закалена. Се ли створисте моей сребреней сѣдинѣ? А уже не вижду власти сильнаго, и богатаго, и многовоя брата моего Ярослава, съ черниговь-скими былями, съ могуты, и съ татраны, и съ шельбиры, и съ топчакы, и съ ревугы, и съ ольберы. Тии бо бес щитовь съ засапожникы кликомъ плъкы побѣждаютъ, звонячи въ прадѣднюю славу. Нъ рекосте: Мужаимѣся сами: преднюю славу сами по-хитимъ, а заднюю си сами подѣлимъ! А чи диво ся, братие, стару помолодити? Коли соколъ въ мытехъ бываетъ, высоко птицъ възбиваетъ: не дастъ гнѣзда

of Bus, they glorify the vengeance [exacted] for Sharokan's [defeats]. And we, retainers, are thirsting for joy!'

Then the great Svyatoslav let fall a golden word, mingled with tears, and said: 'O my nephews, Igor and Vsevolod! Early have you begun to harry the Polovtsian land with your swords, and to seek glory for yourselves. But you have triumphed without honour, for without honour you have shed the blood of the infidels. Your valiant hearts are forged of hard Frankish steel and tempered in boldness. What have you done to my silver grey hair? No longer do I see the power of my brother Yaroslav, mighty and wealthy and rich in warriors, with his grandees of Chernigov and his magnates, with the Tatrany and Shel'biry and Topchaky and Revugy and Ol'bery. For they, without shields, armed with knives stuck in their boot-legs, vanquish hosts with their war-cry, sounding their fore-fathers' glory. But you said: Let us by ourselves prove our courage: let us seize the glory to come and divide that of the past among ourselves! Is it a marvel, brothers, that an old man should grow young again? If a falcon has moulted, high up does it strike the birds; it will allow .   .   .   .   .   .

своего въ обиду. Нъ се зло – княже ми непособие: наниче ся годины обратиша. Се у Римъ кричатъ подъ саблями половецкыми, а Володимиръ подъ ранами. Туга и тоска сыну Глѣбову!»

Великый княже Всеволоде! Не мыслию ти прелетѣти издалеча отня злата стола поблюсти? Ты бо можеши Волгу веслы раскропити, а Донъ шеломы выльяти! Аже бы ты былъ, то была бы чага по ногатѣ, а кощей по резанѣ. Ты бо можеши посуху живыми шереширы стрѣляти, удалыми сыны Глѣбовы.

Ты буй Рюриче и Давыде! Не ваю ли вои злачеными шеломы по крови плаваша? Не ваю ли храбрая дружина рыкаютъ акы тури, ранены саблями калеными на полѣ незнаемѣ? Вступита, господина, въ злата стремень за обиду сего времени, за землю Рускую, за раны Игоревы, буего Святъславлича!

Галичкы Осмомыслѣ Ярославе! Высоко сѣдиши на своемъ златокованнѣмъ столѣ, подперъ горы

no injury to be done to its nest. But here is the evil: the princes are no help to me. The times have turned inside out. Now in Rimov they cry beneath the Polovtsian sabres, and Vladimir lies wounded: woe and sorrow for the son of Gleb!'

O Great Prince Vsevolod! Will you not even in thought fly here from afar to guard your father's golden throne? For you can drain the Volga of water by splashing it with your oars, and empty the Don by drinking it from your helmets. If only you were here, a slave-girl would cost a farthing, and a male captive a mite. For you can shoot over dry land with live fire-bearing missiles – with the valiant sons of Gleb.

You, bold Ryurik, and David! Did not your warriors with their gilded helmets swim in blood? Do not your valiant retainers roar like aurochses wounded by tempered sabres in the unknown plain? Then step, my lords, into your golden stirrups, for the injury of this age, for the land of Russia, for the wounds of Igor, the bold son of Svyatoslav!

O Prince of Galicia, Yaroslav Osmomysl! High are you seated upon your throne wrought of gold, upbearing the Hungarian

Угорскыи своими желѣзными плъки, заступивъ королеви путь, затворивъ Дунаю ворота, меча бремены чрезъ облакы, суды рядя до Дуная. Грозы твоя по землямъ текутъ, отворяеши Киеву врата, стрѣляеши съ отня злата стола салътани за землями. Стрѣляй, господине, Кончака, поганого кощея, за землю Рускую, за раны Игоревы, буего Святъславлича!

А ты, буй Романе, и Мстиславе! Храбрая мысль носитъ вашъ умъ на дѣло. Высоко плаваеши на дѣло въ буести, яко соколъ на вѣтрехъ ширяяся, хотя птицю въ буйствѣ одолѣти. Суть бо у ваю желѣзныи папорзи подъ шеломы латиньскыми. Тѣми тресну земля, и многы страны – Хинова, Литва, Ятвязи, Деремела, и половци сулищи своя повръгоша, а главы своя подклониша подъ тыи мечи харалужныи.

Нъ уже, княже Игорю, утръпѣ солнцю свѣтъ, а древо не бологомъ листвие срони: по Рси и по Сули гради подѣлиша. А Игорева храбраго плъку не

mountains with your iron hosts, barring the way to the King, closing the gates of the Danube, hurling weights through the clouds, executing justice as far as the Danube. Your thunder hurtles over the lands, you open the gates of Kiev, from your father's golden throne you shoot at sultans beyond your lands. Shoot then, my lord, at Konchak, the infidel slave, for the land of Russia, for the wounds of Igor, the bold son of Svyatoslav!

And you, bold Roman, and Mstislav! Brave thoughts carry your minds to action. High up you bravely glide to action, like a falcon sailing on the wind, eager in its boldness to overpower a bird. For you have iron breast-plates beneath your Latin helmets. They made the earth rumble, and many nations – the Huns(?), the Lithuanians, the Yatvingians, the Deremela and the Polovtsy – have dropped their lances and bowed their heads beneath those swords of Frankish steel.

But now, Prince Igor, the light of the sun has been dimmed, and the tree has shed its leaves as a sign of misfortune: [the Polovtsy] have shared among themselves the cities on the Ros' and on the Sula. And Igor's valiant host shall not .   .   .   .   .   .

крѣсити! Донъ ти, княже, кличетъ и зоветь князи на побѣду. Олговичи, храбрыи князи, доспѣли на брань.

Инъгварь и Всеволодъ и вси три Мстиславичи, не худа гнѣзда шестокрилци! Не побѣдными жребии собѣ власти расхытисте! Кое ваши златыи шеломы и сулицы ляцкыи и щиты? Загородите полю ворота своими острыми стрѣлами за землю Рускую, за раны Игоревы, буего Святъславлича!

Уже бо Сула не течетъ сребреными струями къ граду Переяславлю, и Двина болотомъ течетъ онымъ грознымъ полочаномъ подъ кликомъ поганыхъ. Единъ же Изяславъ, сынъ Васильковъ, позвони своими острыми мечи о шеломы литовьскыя, притрепа славу дѣду своему Всеславу, а самъ подъ чрълеными щиты на кровавѣ травѣ притрепанъ литовскыми мечи, акы съ хотию на кровать. А тъи рекъ: «Дружину твою, княже, птиць крилы приодѣ, а звѣри кровь полизаша». Не бысть ту брата Брячя-

rise again! The Don calls to you, Prince, and summons the princes to victory. The scions of Oleg, valiant princes, went out to the battle.

Ingvar' and Vsevolod, and all three sons of Mstislav – six-winged hawks of no mean nest! Not by the fortune of victory have you seized lands for yourselves. Where then are your golden helmets, your Polish lances, and your shields? Bar the gates of the steppe with your sharp arrows, for the land of Russia, for the wounds of Igor, the bold son of Svyatoslav!

For the Sula no longer flows with silvery stream towards the city of Pereyaslavl', and the Dvina flows like a swamp for those redoubtable men of Polotsk under the infidels' battle-cry. Only Izyaslav, son of Vasil'ko, clanged with his sharp swords against the helmets of the Lithuanians; he struck down the glory of Vseslav, his forefather, and, himself struck down by Lithuanian swords, fell on the blood-stained grass beneath the scarlet shields, as though upon a couch with his beloved. And [?Boyan] had said: 'The birds, O Prince, have covered your retainers with their wings, and the wild beasts have licked their blood.' His brother Bryachislav was not there, ...

слава, ни другаго Всеволода: единъ же изрони жемчюжну душу изъ храбра тѣла чресъ злато ожерелие. Уныли голоси, пониче веселие, трубы трубятъ Городьчьскыѣ.

Ярославе, и вси внуце Всеславли! Уже понизите стязи свои, вонзите свои мечи вережени. Уже бо выскочисте изъ дѣдней славѣ. Вы бо своими крамолами начясте наводити поганыя на землю Рускую, на жизнь Всеславлю. Которою бо бѣше насилие отъ земли Половецкыи!

На седьмомъ вѣцѣ Трояни връже Всеславъ жребий о дѣвицю себѣ любу. Тъй клюками подпръ ся о копии и скочи къ граду Кыеву и дотчеся стружиемъ злата стола киевьскаго. Скочи отаи лютымъ звѣремъ въ плъночи изъ Бѣлаграда, обѣсися синѣ мыглѣ; утръже вазни съ три кусы, – отвори врата Новуграду, разшибе славу Ярославу, скочи влъкомъ до Немиги съ Дудутокъ.

На Немизѣ снопы стелютъ головами, молотятъ

nor his other brother Vsevolod: alone he let fall his pearl-like soul from his valiant body through the neck of his garment edged with gold. Voices have died down, joy is bowed low, the trumpets of Gorodets are sounding.

Yaroslav and all the scions of Vseslav! Lower now your banners, sheathe your damaged swords. For you have forfeited your forebear's glory; with your dissensions you began to invite the infidels to attack the land of Russia, the domains of Vseslav: for through your feuds came oppression from the land of the Polovtsy.

In the seventh age of Troyan Vseslav cast lots for the maiden he loved. Cunningly he leant on his spear, leapt to the city of Kiev and touched with his spear-shaft the golden throne of Kiev. In the guise of a wild beast he secretly leapt out of Belgorod at midnight, and was swathed in a blue mist. Some three times he snatched a streak of good fortune – he opened the gates of Novgorod, shattered the glory of Yaroslav, leapt in the guise of a wolf towards the Nemiga from Dudutki.

On the Nemiga they are laying out sheaves of heads and thresh-

чепи харалужными, на тоцѣ животъ кладутъ, вѣютъ
душу отъ тѣла. Немизѣ кровави брезѣ не бологомъ
бяхуть посѣяни, посѣяни костьми рускихъ сыновъ.

Всеславъ князь людемъ судяше, княземъ грады
рядяше, а самъ въ ночь влькомъ рыскаше: изъ
Кыева дорискаше до куръ Тмутороканя, великому
Хръсови влькомъ путь прерыскаше. Тому въ По-
лотьскѣ позвониша заутренюю рано у святыя Софеи
въ колоколы, а онъ въ Кыевѣ звонъ слыша. Аще и
вѣща душа въ дръзѣ тѣлѣ нъ часто бѣды страдаше.
Тому вѣщей Боянъ и пръвое припѣвку, смысленый,
рече: «Ни хытру, ни горазду, ни птицю горазду суда
Божиа не минути».

О стонати Руской земли, помянувше пръвую
годину и пръвыхъ князей! Того стараго Владимира
нельзѣ бѣ пригвоздити къ горамъ киевьскымъ: сего
бо нынѣ сташа стязи Рюриковы, а друзии –
Давидовы, нъ розно ся имъ хоботы пашутъ. Копиа
поютъ!

ing/ them with flails of Frankish steel; they are laying down their
lives on the threshing-floor, and winnowing soul from body. The
Nemiga's blood-soaked banks were sown with no good seed – they
were sown with the bones of Russia's sons.

Prince Vseslav administered justice to the people, allotted cities
to the princes, but at night he raced in the guise of a wolf: he
would race from Kiev to Tmutorokan' before cock-crow and, in the
shape of a wolf, would cross the path of the great Khors. For him
in Polotsk early in the morning they would ring the bells of St
Sophia for matins, and he heard them still pealing by the time he
got to Kiev. Though he had a wizard's soul in a valiant body, yet
he often suffered misfortune. For him the wizard Boyan, the wise,
long ago made this song: 'Neither the cunning man, nor the skilful,
nor the clever bird shall escape the fate decreed by God.'

Oh, the Russian land shall moan, as it recalls the olden times and
the princes of old! Vladimir of old could not be nailed to the hills
of Kiev. But now some of his standards have become Ryurik's, and
others – those of David, and their pennons flutter apart in strife.
The lances sing!

На Дунаи Ярославнынъ гласъ ся слышитъ, зегзицею незнаема рано кычеть: «Полечю, – рече, – зегзицею по Дунаеви, омочю бебрянъ рукавъ въ Каялѣ рѣцѣ, утру князю кровавыя его раны на жестоцѣмъ его тѣлѣ».

Ярославна рано плачетъ въ Путивлѣ на забралѣ, аркучи: «О вѣтрѣ, вѣтрило! Чему, господине, насильно вѣеши? Чему мычеши хиновьскыя стрѣлкы на своею нетрудною крилцю на моея лады вои? Мало ли ти бяшетъ горѣ подъ облакы вѣяти, лелѣючи корабли на синѣ морѣ? Чему, господине, мое веселие по ковылию развѣя?»

Ярославна рано плачетъ Путивлю городу на забаролѣ, аркучи: «О Днепре Словутицю! Ты пробилъ еси каменныя горы сквозѣ землю Половецкую. Ты лелѣялъ еси на себѣ Святославли насады до плъку Кобякова. Възлелѣй, господине, мою ладу къ мнѣ, а быхъ не слала къ нему слезъ на море рано».

On the Danube Yaroslavna's* voice is heard; like a desolate cuckoo she cries early in the morning. 'I will fly', she says, 'like a cuckoo along the Danube, I will dip my sleeve of beaver-fur in the river Kayala, I will wipe the Prince's bleeding wounds on his strong body.'

Yaroslavna, early in the morning, laments on the rampart of Putivl' saying: 'Wind, O Wind! Why, O Lord, do you blow so hard? Why do you carry the Huns' (?) arrows on your light wings against the warriors of my beloved? Was it not enough for you to blow on high beneath the clouds, rocking the ships upon the blue sea? Why, O Lord, have you scattered my happiness over the feather grass?'

Yaroslavna, early in the morning, laments on the rampart of the city of Putivl' saying: 'O Dnieper Slovutich! You have battered your way through the rocky mountains across the land of the Polovtsy. You have rocked Svyatoslav's boats upon your waters, and carried them to Kobyak's camp. Carry, O Lord, my beloved back to me, that I may no more send him my tears down to the sea, early in the morning.'

* Yaroslavna was Igor's wife.

Ярославна рано плачетъ въ Путивлѣ на забралѣ,
аркучи: «Свѣтлое и тресвѣтлое слъньце! Всѣмъ тепло
и красно еси: чему, господине, простре горячюю
свою лучю на ладѣ вои? Въ полѣ безводнѣ жаждею
имъ лучи съпряже, тугою имъ тули затче?»
Прысну море полунощи; идутъ сморци мыглами.
Игореви князю Богъ путь кажетъ изъ земли По-
ловецкой на землю Рускую, къ отню злату столу. По-
гасоша вечеру зори. Игорь спитъ, Игорь бдитъ,
Игорь мыслию поля мѣритъ отъ великаго Дону до
малаго Донца. Комонь въ полуночи Овлуръ свисну
за рѣкою; велить князю разумѣти: князю Игорю не
быть! Кликну, стукну земля, въшумѣ трава, вежи ся
половецкии подвизашася. А Игорь князь поскочи
горнастаемъ къ тростию и бѣлымъ гоголемъ на воду.
Въвръжеся на бръзъ комонь, и скочи съ него босымъ
влькомъ. И потече къ лугу Донца, и полетѣ соколомъ подъ мыглами, избивая гуси и лебеди зав-
троку, и обѣду, и ужинѣ. Коли Игорь соколомъ

Yaroslavna, early in the morning, laments on the rampart of
Putivl' saying: 'O bright and thrice-bright Sun! You are warm and
beautiful to all. Why, O Lord, did you dart your burning rays
against the warriors of my beloved? In the waterless steppe why did
you shrivel their bows with thirst and stop their quivers with sorrow?'
   The sea broke into foam at midnight; waterspouts advance like
mists. God shows Prince Igor the way out of the land of the
Polovtsy to the land of Russia, to his father's golden throne. The
glow of sunset has faded. Igor sleeps, Igor is awake, Igor
measures in his mind the steppe from the great Don to the little
Donets. Ovlur, [having brought] a horse, whistled from across the
river: he bids the Prince understand: Prince Igor shall not be [? a
captive any longer]! He shouted, the earth rumbled, the grass
rustled, the tents of the Polovtsy stirred. And Prince Igor sped
like an ermine into the rushes and like a white duck on to the
water. He sprang upon his swift horse, and leapt from it like a
white-footed wolf. He sped towards the meadows of the Donets,
and flew like a falcon beneath the mists, slaying geese and swans
for his morning, midday, and evening meals. When Igor flew like
a falcon, ...

полетѣ, тогда Влуръ влькомъ потече, труся собою студеную росу: претръгоста бо своя бръзая комоня.

Донецъ рече: «Княже Игорю! Не мало ти величия, а Кончаку нелюбия, а Руской земли веселиа». Игорь рече: «О Донче! Не мало ти величия, лелѣявшу князя на влънахъ, стлавшу ему зелѣну траву на своихъ сребреныхъ брезѣхъ, одѣвавшу его теплыми мъглами подъ сѣнию зелену древу; стрежаше его гоголемъ на водѣ, чайцами на струяхъ, чрьнядьми на ветрѣхъ». Не тако ти рече рѣка Стугна; худу струю имѣя, пожръши чужи ручьи и стругы ростепа к усту, уношу князю Ростиславу затвори. Днѣпрь темнѣ березѣ плачется мати Ростиславля по уноши князи Ростиславѣ. Уныша цвѣты жалобою, и древо с тугою къ земли прѣклонило.

А не сорокы втроскоташа: на слѣду Игоревѣ ѣздитъ Гзакъ съ Кончакомъ. Тогда врани не граахуть, галици помлъкоша, сорокы не троскоташа, полозие ползоша только. Дятлове тектомъ путь къ

then Vlur ran like a wolf, shaking off the cold dew: for they had overridden their swift horses.

The Donets said: 'O Prince Igor! There is much glory for you, and chagrin for Konchak, and joy for the land of Russia!' Igor said: 'O Donets! There is much glory for you who have rocked the Prince upon your waves, spread out green grass for him upon your silvery banks, draped him in warm mists beneath the shade of green trees, and caused the sea-duck on the water, the gulls on the stream, and the black ducks on the winds to watch over him.' Not so did the Stugna speak: with its meagre stream, having swallowed up other rivulets and tossed the boats to its estuary (?), it closed over the young Prince Rostislav. On the dark bank of the Dnieper Rostislav's mother weeps for the young Prince Rostislav. The flowers droop for pity, and the tree in sorrow bends to the ground.

These are not magpies chattering: it is Gzak and Konchak riding on Igor's trail. Then the ravens did not croak, the jackdaws fell silent, the magpies did not chatter – only the snakes crawled. The woodpeckers by the sound of their pecking . . . . . .

рѣцѣ кажутъ, соловіи веселыми пѣсньми свѣтъ повѣдаютъ.

Млъвитъ Гзакъ Кончакови: «Аже соколъ къ гнѣзду летитъ, – соколича рострѣляевѣ своими злачеными стрѣлами». Речс Кончакъ ко Гзѣ: «Аже соколъ къ гнѣзду летитъ, а вѣ соколца опутаевѣ красною дивицею». И рече Гзакъ къ Кончакови: «Аще его опутаевѣ красною дѣвицею, ни нама будетъ сокольца, ни нама красны дѣвице, то почнутъ наю птици бити въ полѣ Половецкомъ».

Рекъ Боянъ и до сына Святъславля, пѣснотворьць стараго времени – Ярославля, Ольгова, коганя: «Хотя тяжко ти головѣ кромѣ плечю, зло ти тѣлу кромѣ головы», – Руской земли безъ Игоря.

Солнце свѣтится на небесѣ – Игорь князь въ Руской земли. Дѣвици поютъ на Дунаи, – вьются голоси чрезъ море до Киева. Игорь ѣдетъ по Боричеву къ Святѣй Богородици Пирогощей. Страны ради, гради весели.

show the way to the river, the nightingales with their joyous songs announce the dawn.

Says Gzak to Konchak: 'If the falcon flies towards its nest, we will shoot the young falcon with our gilded arrows.' Konchak said to Gzak: 'If the falcon flies towards its nest, we will entangle the young falcon in the toils of a fair maiden.' And Gzak said to Konchak: 'If we entangle him in the toils of a fair maiden, we shall have neither the young falcon nor the fair maiden, and the birds will begin to assail us in the Polovtsian steppe.'

Boyan, the bard of olden times – of the days of Yaroslav, of Prince Oleg – said [foreboding] even the son of Svyatoslav: 'If it is hard for you, O head, parted from the shoulders, it goes ill with you, O body, without the head': and so it is with the land of Russia without Igor.

The sun shines in the heavens: Prince Igor is in the land of Russia. Maidens sing on the Danube, their voices twine across the sea to Kiev. Igor rides up by Borichev to the church of Our Lady of the Tower. The countryside is happy, the cities are joyful.

Пѣвше пѣснь старымъ княземъ, а потомъ моло-
дымъ пѣти: слава Игорю Святъславличю, буй туру
Всеволоду, Владимиру Игоревичу! Здрави князи и
дружина, побарая за христьяны на поганыя плъки!
Княземъ слава а дружинѣ! Аминь.

Having sung a song for the princes of old, now we must sing in
honour of the young: Glory to Igor, son of Svyatoslav; to Vsevolod, the fierce aurochs; to Vladimir, son of Igor! Long live the
princes and the retinue, who fight for the Christians against the
infidel hosts! Glory to the princes and to the retinue! Amen.

BYLINY

Первая Поездка Ильи Муромца.
Илья и Соловей-Разбойник

Не сырой дуб к земле клонится,
Не бумажные листочки расстилаются, –
Расстилается сын перед батюшком,
Он и просит сее благословеньица:
«Ох ты гой еси, родимый милый батюшка!
Дай ты мне свое благословеньице,
Я поеду в славный стольный Киев-град,
Помолиться чудотворцам киевским,
Заложиться за князя Володимира,
Послужить ему верой-правдою,
Постоять за веру христьянскую».
    Отвечает старой крестьянин Иван Тимофеевич:
«Я на добрые дела тее благословенье дам,
А на худые дела благословенья нет.
Поедешь ты путем и дорогою,
Не помысли злом на татарина,
Не убей в чистым поле крестьянина».

Il'ya of Murom's First Journey
Il'ya and Nightingale the Robber

It is not a green oak tree bending low to the earth, nor paper leaves fluttering down to the ground – a son is falling down before his father, and begging his blessing: 'O dear father mine, give me your blessing, that I may go to glorious and royal Kiev town, there to pray to the wonder-workers of Kiev, to do fealty to Prince Vladimir, to serve him in truth and honour, to defend the Christian faith.'

The old peasant Ivan Timofeevich replied: 'I will give you my blessing that you may perform good deeds, but you have not my blessing for evil ones. When you go on your way, do not harbour evil designs against any Tatar, nor kill any Christian man in the open plain.'

Поклонился Илья Муромец отцу дó земли,
Сам он сел на добрá коня,
Поехал он во чистó поле.
Он и бьет коня по крутым бедрам,
Пробиват кожу до чернá мяса:
Ретивóй его конь осержается,
Прочь óт земли отделяется,
Он и скачет выше дерева стоячего,
Чуть пониже оболока ходячего.
Первый скок скочил на пятнадцать верст,
В другой скочил – колодезь стал;
У колодезя срубил сырой дуб,
У колодезя поставил часовенку,
На часовне подписал свое имечко:
«Ехал такой-то сильный могучий богатырь,
Илья Муромец сын Иванович»;
В третий скочил – под Чернигов-град.
Под Черниговом стоит сила – сметы нет;
Под Черниговом стоят три царевича,
С каждым силы сорок тысячей.
Богатырско сердце разгóрчиво и неуемчиво:
Пуще огня-огничка сердце разыграется,
Пуще пляштого мороза разгорается.

Il'ya of Murom bowed to the ground before his father, mounted his good steed and rode out into the open plain. He strikes the horse on its steep flanks, he strikes through the hide to the black flesh; his fiery steed grows angry, frees itself from the ground, and leaps higher than the standing trees and only a little lower than the passing clouds. At its first leap, it leapt fifteen versts; at its second leap, a well sprung up; by the well he felled a green oak and built a chapel; on the chapel he inscribed his name: 'A strong and mighty hero rode by here – Il'ya of Murom, son of Ivan.' The third leap brought him to the neighbourhood of Chernigov town. At the approaches to Chernigov stood a numberless host, at the approaches to Chernigov there stood three princes, each with an army of forty thousand men. The hero's heart is ardent and impetuous: it flared up hotter than fire, hotter than burning frost.

Тут возгово́рит Илья Муромец таково слово:
«Не хотелось было батюшку супротивником бы́ть,
Еще знать-то его заповедь переступить».

Берет он в руки саблю боёвую,
Учал по силушке погуливать:
Где повернется – делал улицы,
Поворотится – часты площади;
Добивается до трех царевичей.

Тут возговорит Илья таково слово:
«Ох вы гой есте, мои три царевича!
Во полон ли мне вас взять,
Аль с вас буйны головы снять?
Как в полон мне вас взять, –
У меня дороги заезжие и хлебы завозные;
А как головы снять, – царски се́мена погубить.
Вы поедьте по свым местам,
Вы чините везде такову славу,
Что святая Русь не пуста стоит,
На святой Руси есть сильны́ могучи бога́тыри».

Увидал его воевода черниговский:
«Что это Господь сослал нам за сослальника!
Очистил наш славный Чернигов-град».

Then Il'ya of Murom spoke these words: 'I did not want to oppose my father nor indeed to break his commandment.'

He seized his battle sabre and began to walk through the host: wherever he wheeled, he hacked out streets, wherever he turned round, [public] squares appeared; he slashed his way through to the three princes.

Then Il'ya of Murom spoke these words: 'O my three princes! Shall I take you prisoners, or shall I cut off your unruly heads? If I take you prisoners I shall have roads for people to ride along and bring me bread. But if I cut off your heads I shall destroy the seed of kings. Go back to your homes and spread the report everywhere that Holy Russia does not stand empty, and that there are strong and mighty heroes in Holy Russia.'

The governor of Chernigov caught sight of him: 'What a messenger the Lord has sent us! He has liberated our glorious Chernigov town.'

Возговорит воевода свым князьям, боярам:
«Подите позовите добра мо́лодца
Ко мне хлеба-соли кушати».

Пошли тут князи, бояра к Муромцу:
«Ох ты гой еси, дородный добрый молодец!
Как тея честным именем зовут,
Как тея величают по отечеству?» –
«Меня именем зовут – Илейкой,
А величают – сын Иванович».

Возговорят ему князи, бояра:
«Ох ты гой еси, Илья Муромец!
Ты пойдешь-ка к воеводе нашему,
Ты изволь у него хлеба-соли кушати» –.
«Нейду я к воеводе вашему,
Не хочу у него хлеба-соли кушати;
Укажите мне прямую дороженьку
На славный стольный Киев-град».

Ответ держат князи, бояра:
«Ох ты гой еси, Илья Муромец!
Пряма дорожка не проста стоит, –
Заросла дорога лесы Брынскими,
Протекла тут река Самородина;
Еще на дороге Соловейко-разбойничек

The governor said to his princes and boyars: 'Go summon the stout young fellow to my board.' The princes and boyars then went to Muromets: 'O you stately, stout young fellow! What is your honourable name, and what is the name of your father?' – 'My name is Il'ya, and they call me the son of Ivan.'

The princes and boyars said to him: 'O Il'ya of Murom! Go to our governor and, pray, eat at his board' – 'I will not go to your governor, I do not want to eat at his board. Show me the straight road to glorious and royal Kiev town.'

The princes and boyars made answer: 'O Il'ya of Murom! The straight road is not open: it is overgrown with the Bryn' forests, the river Smorodina flows there; and, furthermore, above the road Nightingale the Robber . . . . . .

Сидит на тридевяти дубах, сидит тридцать лет;
Ни конному, ни пешему пропуску нет».
    Поклонился им Илья Муромец,
Поехал он лесами Брынскими.
Услыхал Соловейко богатырский топ,
И свистнул он громким голосом.
Конь под Муромцем спотыкается.
Возговорит Илья своему коню доброму:
«Ох ты гой еси, мой богатырский конь!
Аль не езживал ты по темны́м лесам,
Аль не слыхивал пташьего посвисту?»
    Берет Илья калены стрелы:
Перво́ стре́лил – недостре́лил;
А вдруго́рядь – перестрелил;
В третьи стрелил – попал в правый глаз
И сошиб его с тридевяти дубов.
Привязал его к коню во ка́раки;
Поехал Муромец в славный Киев-град.
    Возговорит Соловейко-разбойничек:
«Ох ты гой еси, Илья Муромец!
Мы заедем-ка с тобою ко мне в гости».
    Увидала Соловейкина ма́ла дочь:

---

sits on twenty-seven oak trees, he has sat there for thirty years, and no one can pass, on horseback or on foot.'

Il'ya of Murom saluted them and rode off through the forests of Bryn'. Nightingale heard the thud of the hero's horse, and he whistled loudly. The horse stumbled under Muromets. Il'ya said to his good horse: 'O my horse, you hero's horse! Have you never ridden through dark forests, have you never heard birds whistle?'

Il'ya brought out his tempered arrows: he shot once – the arrow fell short; he shot a second time – he overshot his mark; he shot a third time – he pierced Nightingale's right eye, and shot him down from the twenty-seven oak trees. He strapped him to the back of his horse's saddle; and Muromets rode off to glorious Kiev town.

Nightingale the Robber said: 'O Il'ya of Murom! Let us visit my home.' Nightingale's youngest daughter saw them coming:

«Еще вон едет наш батюшка,
Везет кривого мужика коня в караках».
    Взглянула Соловейкина большая дочь:
«Ах ты, дура неповитая! Это едет добрый молодец
И ведет нашего батюшка коня в караках».
И бросилúсь они на Илью Муромца с дрéкольем.
    Возговорит Соловейко-разбойничек:
«Не тумашúтеся, мои малые детушки,
Не взводите в задор доброго молодца».
    Возговорит Илья Соловейке-разбойнику:
«Что у тея дети во единый лик?»
    Отвечат Соловейко-разбойничек:
«Я сына-то выращу – за него дочь отдам;
Дочь ту выращу – отдам зá сына,
Чтобы Соловейкин род не перевóдился».
    За досаду Илье Муромцу показалося;
Вынимал он саблю свою вострую,
Прирубил у Соловья всех детушек.
Приехал Илья Муромец во Киев-град,
И вскричал он громким голосом:
«Уж ты, батюшка Володимир-князь!

'Here comes our father – he is carrying, strapped to the back of his horse's saddle, a peasant, blind in one eye.' Nightingale's eldest daughter looked out: 'O you unswaddled fool! It is a stout young fellow who is riding hither, and he is carrying our father, strapped to the back of his horse's saddle.' And they fell upon Il'ya of Murom with cudgels.

Nightingale the Robber said: 'Do not bestir yourselves, my little children, do not provoke the stout young fellow.' Il'ya said to Nightingale the Robber: 'Why do your children all look alike?' Nightingale the Robber answered: 'When I have bred a son, I marry my daughter to him; when I have bred a daughter, I marry her to my son, so that Nightingale's brood may never perish.'

This seemed impudent to Il'ya of Murom; he drew his sharp sabre and cut down all Nightingale's children. Il'ya of Murom arrived in Kiev town, and he called out in a loud voice: 'O Prince Vladimir, our father!   .   .   .   .   .   .

Тее надо ль нас, принимаешь ли
Сильных могучих богатырей,
Тее, батюшке, на почéсть-хвалу,
Твому граду стольному на йзберечь,
А татаровьям на посéченье?»
   Отвечат батюшка Володимир-князь:
«Да как мне вас не надо-то?
Я везде вас ищу, везде спрашиваю.
На приезде вас жалую по добру коню,
По добру коню по латынскому, богатырскому»,
   Возговорит Илья Муромец таково слово:
«У меня свой конь латынский, богатырский;
Стоял я с родимым батюшком у заутрени,
Хотелось постоять с тобой у обеденки;
Да на дороге мне было три помешинки:
Перва помеха – очистил я Чернигов-град;
Друга помеха – я мостил мосты на пятнадцать
                                            верст
Через ту реку через Самородину;
Третья помеха – я сошиб Соловья-разбойника».
   Возговорит сам батюшка Володимир-князь:
«Ох ты гой еси, Соловейко-разбойничек!

Do you need us, do you accept strong and mighty heroes, that we may bring honour and glory to you, our father, defend your royal city and slay the Tatars?'
   Father Vladimir the Prince replied: 'How could I not need you? I seek and inquire for you everywhere. On your arrival I bestow on each of you a good horse, a good Latin horse, a hero's one.' Il'ya of Murom spoke these words: 'I have my own Latin horse, a hero's one; I attended Matins with my own father, and I wished to attend Mass with you; but three obstacles delayed me on my way: I was delayed for the first time when I liberated Chernigov town; I was delayed for the second time when I bridged the river Smorodina for fifteen versts; I was delayed for the third time when I shot down Nightingale the Robber.'
   Father Vladimir the Prince said: 'O Nightingale the Robber!

Ты взойди ко мне в палату белу-каменну».
Ответ держит Соловейко-разбойник:
«Не твоя слуга, не тее служу, не тея и слушаю;
Я служу и слушаю Илью Муромца.»
Возговорит Володимир: «Ох ты гой еси,
Муромец,
Илья Муромец сын Иванович!
Прикажи ему взойти в палату белу-каменну».
Приказал ему взойти Илья Муромец.
Тут возговорит Володимир-князь:
«Ох ты гой еси, дородный добрый молодец,
Илья Муромец сын Иванович!
Прикажи ему свистнуть громким голосом».
Возговорит Илья Муромец таково слово:
«Уж ты, батюшка наш Володимир-князь!
Не во гнев бы тее, батюшка, показалося:
Я возьму тея, батюшку, под пазушку,
А княгиню ту закрою под другою».
И говорит Илья Муромец таково слово:
«Свистни, Соловейко, в полсвиста».
Свистнул Соловейка во весь голос:
Сня́ло у палат верх по оконички,
Разломало все связи железные,

Come into my palace of white stone.' Nightingale the Robber made answer: 'I am not your servant, it is not you whom I serve and obey: I serve and obey Il'ya of Murom.' Vladimir said: 'O Muromets, Il'ya of Murom, son of Ivan! Bid him come into my palace of white stone.' Il'ya Muromets bade him enter. Then Prince Vladimir said: 'O you stately, stout young fellow, Il'ya of Murom, son of Ivan! Bid him whistle loudly.' Il'ya Muromets spoke these words: 'O Prince Vladimir, our father! Do not take it in bad part, father, if I take you, father, under one arm, and hide your princess under the other.' And Il'ya of Murom spoke these words: 'Nightingale, whistle at half-strength!'

Nightingale whistled at full strength: the roof of the palace was blown off down to the window-frames, all the iron hinges were broken, ...

Попадали все сильны могучи богатыри,
Упали все знатны князи, бояра,
Один устоял Илья Муромец.
Выпущал он князя со княгиней из-под пазушек.
　　Возговорит сам батюшка Володимир-князь:
«Исполать тее, Соловейко-разбойничек!
Как тея взял это Илья Муромец?»
　　Ответ держит Соловейко-разбойничек:
«Ведь на ту пору больно пьян я был,
У меня большая дочь была именинница».
　　Это слово Илье Муромцу не показалося,
Взял он Соловейку за вершиночку,
Вывел его на княженецкий двор,
Кинул его выше дерева стоячего,
Чуть пониже оболока ходячего;
До сырой земли допускивал – ино подхватывал;
Расшиб Соловейко свои все тут косточки.
Пошли теперь к обеду княженецкому.
　　Возговорит сам батюшка Володимир-князь:
«Ох ты гой еси, Илья Муромец сын Иванович!
Жалую тебя тремя я местами:

and all the strong and mighty heroes, all the noble princes and boyars fell to the ground; Il'ya of Murom alone stood firm. He released the prince and the princess from under his arms.

Father Vladimir the Prince said: 'Well done, Nightingale the Robber! How ever did Il'ya of Murom manage to capture you?' Nightingale the Robber made answer: 'I was roaring drunk at the time – it was my eldest daughter's nameday.' This remark did not please Il'ya of Murom: he seized Nightingale by his head, carried him out into the courtyard of the prince's palace, and hurled him higher than the standing trees and only a little lower than the passing clouds; several times he let him fall to the ground and then seized him and threw him up again. All Nightingale's bones were thus broken. Then they went in to the prince's dinner.

Father Vladimir the Prince said: 'O Il'ya of Murom, son of Ivan! I bestow on you three seats at my table: . . . . . .

Перво место – подле меня ты сядь,
Другó место – супротив меня,
Третье – где ты хочешь, тут и сядь».

Зашел Илья Муромец со кóничка,
Пожал он всех князей и бóярей
И сильных могучих богатырей;
Очутился он супротив князя Володимира.

За досаду Алеше Поповичу показалося;
Взял Алеша булатный нож,
Он и кинул его в Илью Муромца.
Поймал на полетý Илья булатный нож,
Взоткнул его в дубовый стол.

Садко и Морской Царь

На свою бессчетну золоту казну
Построил Садко тридцать кораблей,
Тридцать кораблей, тридцать черленыих;
На ты на корабли на черленые
Свалил товары новгородские,
Поехал Садко по Волхову,
Со Волхово во Ладожско,

the first seat is the one next to me; the second is the one opposite me; the third gives you the right to sit where you want.'

Il'ya of Murom walked round the bench, and made all the princes and boyars and the strong and mighty heroes squeeze closer together; he found himself opposite Prince Vladimir.

Alesha Popovich was annoyed at this; he drew his steel knife and threw it at Il'ya of Murom. Il'ya caught the steel knife in the air and drove it into the oak table.

Sadko and the King of the Sea

WITH his countless treasure of gold Sadko built thirty ships, thirty red ships; he loaded these red ships with the wares of Novgorod; Sadko sailed down the Volkhov, from the Volkhov into Lake Ladoga, ...

А со Ладожска во Неву-реку,
А со Невы-реки во сине море.
Как поехал он по синю морю,
Воротил он в Золоту Орду,
Продавал товары новгородские,
Получал барыши великие,
Насыпал бочки-сороковки красна золота, чиста
серебра,
Поезжал назад во Новгород.
Поезжал он по синю морю,
На синем море сходилась погода сильная,
Застоялись черлены корабли на синём море:
А волной-то бьет, паруса рвет,
Ломает кораблики черленые;
А корабли нейдут с места на синем море.
    Говорит Садко-купец, богатый гость,
Ко своей дружины ко хороброей:
«Ай же ты, дружинушка хоробрая!
Как мы век по морю ездили,
А морскому царю дани не плачивали;
Видно, царь морской от нас дани требует,
Требует дани во сине море.
Ай же братцы, дружина хоробрая!

from Lake Ladoga into the river Neva, and from the river Neva into
the blue sea. Sailing over the blue sea he turned [and made for]
the Golden Horde; he sold the Novgorod wares and got large profits,
he filled hundred-gallon barrels with red gold and pure silver,
and sailed back to Novgorod. While he was sailing over the blue sea,
a great storm gathered on the blue sea, and the red ships stood
still on the blue sea; yet the waves beat, the wind tore the sails and
battered the red ships; but the ships did not move on the blue sea.
    Sadko the trader, the rich merchant, said to his brave retainers:
'O my brave retainers! Long have we sailed the seas, yet we have
never paid tribute to the King of the Sea; it seems that the King of
the Sea demands tribute from us, demands tribute in the blue sea.
O brothers, my brave retainers, ...

Взимайте бочку-сороковку чиста серебра,
Спущайте бочку во сине море».
   Дружина его хоробрая
Взимала бочку чиста серебра,
Спускала бочку во сине море:
А волной-то бьет, паруса рвет,
Ломает кораблики черленые;
А корабли нейдут с места на синем море.
Тут его дружина хоробрая
Брали бочку-сороковку красна золота,
Спускали бочку во сине море:
А волной-то бьет, паруса рвет,
Ломает кораблики черленые;
А корабли все нейдут с места на синем море.
   Говорит Садко-купец, богатый гость:
«Видно, царь морской требует
Живой головы во сине море.
Делайте, братцы, жеребья волжаны,
Я сам сделаю на красноем на золоте;
Всяк свои имена подписывайте,
Спущайте жеребья на сине море:
Чей жеребей ко дну пойдет,
Таковому идти в сине море.»

take a hundred-gallon barrel of pure silver and cast the barrel into
the blue sea.'
   His brave retainers took a barrel of pure silver and cast the barrel
into the blue sea. The waves beat, the wind tore the sails and
battered the red ships; but the ships did not move on the blue sea.
Then his brave retainers took a hundred-gallon barrel of red gold
and cast the barrel into the blue sea. The waves beat, the wind tore
the sails and battered the red ships; but still the ships did not move
on the blue sea.
   Sadko the trader, the rich merchant, said: 'It seems that the King
of the Sea demands that a living man be cast into the blue sea.
Brothers, make yourselves lots out of meadow-sweet, and I shall
make one out of red gold; let every man write his name upon his
own lot; then fling the lots into the blue sea: the man whose lot
sinks shall go into the blue sea.'

Делали жеребья волжаны,
А сам Садко делал на красноем на золоте;
Всяк свое имя подписывал,
Спущали жеребья на сине море:
Как у всей дружины хороброей
Жеребья гоголем по воды плывут,
А у Садка-купца ключом на дно.
    Говорит Садко-купец, богатый гость:
«Ай же братцы, дружина хоробрая!
Этые жеребья неправильны:
Делайте жеребья на красноем на золоте,
А я сделаю жеребей волжаный».
    Делали жеребья на красноем на золоте,
А сам Садко делал жеребей волжаный,
Всяк свое имя подписывал,
Спущали жеребья на сине море:
Как у всей дружины хороброей
Жеребья гоголем по воды плывут,
А у Садка-купца ключом на дно.
    Говорит Садко-купец, богатый гость:
«Ай же братцы, дружина хоробрая!

They made themselves lots out of meadow-sweet, and Sadko
made one out of red gold; every man wrote his name upon his own,
and they flung the lots into the blue sea: the lots of all the brave
retainers floated like ducks on the water, but that of Sadko the
trader went to the bottom like a stone.
Sadko the trader, the rich merchant, said: 'O brothers, my brave
retainers, these lots are all wrong; make yourselves lots out of red
gold, and I will make one out of meadow-sweet.' They made lots
out of red gold, and Sadko made one out of meadow-sweet; every
man wrote his name upon his own, and they flung the lots into the
blue sea: the lots of all the brave retainers floated like ducks on the
water, but that of Sadko the trader went to the bottom like a
stone.
Sadko the trader, the rich merchant, said: 'O brothers, my
brave retainers! , ...

Видно, царь морской требует
Самого Садка богатого в сине море.
Несите мою чернилицу вальяжную,
Перо лебединое, лист бумаги гербовый».

   Несли ему чернилицу вальяжную,
Перо лебединое, лист бумаги гербовый.
Он стал именьице отписывать:
Кое именье отписывал Божьим церквам,
Иное именье нищей братии,
Иное именье молодой жене,
Остатнее именье дружине хороброей.

   Говорил Садко-купец, богатый гость:
«Ай же братцы, дружина хоробрая!
Давайте мне гуселки яровчаты,
Поиграть-то мне в остатнее:
Больше мне в гуселки не игрывати.
Али взять мне гусли с собой во сине море?»

   Взимает он гуселки яровчаты,
Сам говорит таковы слова:
«Свалите дощечку дубовую на воду;
Хоть я свалюсь на доску дубовую,

It seems that the King of the Sea wants the rich Sadko himself
down in the blue sea. Bring me my finely carved inkstand, a swan-
quill pen, and a sheet of stamped paper.'

   They brought him his finely carved inkstand, a swan-quill pen,
and a sheet of stamped paper. He began to sign away his possessions: some he made over to God's churches, some to the poor,
some to his young wife, and the remainder of his possessions to his
brave retainers.

   Sadko the trader, the rich merchant, said: 'O brothers, my brave
retainers! Hand me my *gusli** of sycamore that I may play for the
last time: never again shall I play on the *gusli*. Or shall I take my
gusli with me into the blue sea?' He took his sycamore *gusli* and
spoke these words: 'Cast an oak plank on to the water; at least I
shall be cast on to the oak plank, ...

---

*A kind of harp, played on the knees, used by medieval Russian minstrels.

Не толь мне страшно принять смерть на синем
море».
Свалили дощечку дубовую на воду,
Потом поезжали корабли по синю морю,
Полетели, как черные вороны.
Остался Садко на синем море.
Со тоя со страсти со великия
Заснул на дощечке на дубовой.
Проснулся Садко во синем море,
Во синем море, на самом дне.
Сквозь воду увидел пекучись красное сол-
нышко,
Вечернюю зорю, зорю утреннюю.
Увидел Садко, – во синем море
Стоит палата белокаменная;
Заходил Садко в палату белокаменну:
Сидит в палате царь морской,
Голова у царя как куча сенная.
Говорит царь таковы слова:
«Ай же ты, Садко-купец, богатый гость!
Век ты, Садко, по морю езживал,
Мне, царю, дани не плачивал,
А нонь весь пришел ко мне во подарочках.

and I shall not be so frightened of meeting death on the blue sea.'
They cast the oak plank on to the water. Then the ships sailed
away over the blue sea, like black ravens in flight.

Sadko remained alone on the blue sea. Because of the great fear
that came over him he fell asleep on the oak plank. Sadko awoke
in the blue sea, at the very bottom of the blue sea. He saw the
beautiful sun shining warm through the water, he saw both dawn
and sunset. Sadko saw a palace of white stone standing in the blue
sea; Sadko entered the palace of white stone: in the palace sat the
King of the Sea, and his head was like a heap of hay. The King
spoke these words: 'O Sadko the trader, you rich merchant! Long,
Sadko, have you sailed the seas, yet you paid no tribute to me, their
king; and now you have come to me, loaded with gifts. . . .

Скажут, мастер играть в гуселки яровчаты;
Поиграй же мне в гуселки яровчаты».

Как начал играть Садко в гуселки яровчаты,
Как начал плясать царь морской во синем море,
Как расплясался царь морской.
Играл Садко сутки, играл и другие,
Да играл еще Садко и третии,
А все пляшет царь морской во синем море.
Во синем море вода всколыбалася,
Со желтым песком вода смутилася,
Стало разбивать много кораблей на синем море,
Стало много гинуть именьицев,
Стало много тонуть людей праведныих:
Как стал народ молиться Миколе Можайскому.

Как тронуло Садка в плечо во правое:
«Ай же ты, Садко новгородскиий!
Полно играть в гуселышки яровчаты».

Обернулся, глядит Садко новгородскиий:
Ажно стоит старик седатыий.

Говорил Садко новгородскиий:
«У меня воля не своя во синем море,
Приказано играть в гуселки яровчаты».

They say you are a master-player on your sycamore *gusli*; so play for me on your sycamore *gusli*.'

Sadko began to play on his sycamore *gusli*, and the King of the Sea began to dance in the blue sea; the King of the Sea was carried away by his dancing. Sadko played for a day and a night, he played for a second day and night, and he played for a third day and night, and still the King of the Sea danced in the blue sea. The water in the blue sea became agitated and was churned with yellow sand; many a ship was broken asunder on the blue sea, many possessions were lost, many righteous men were drowned.

The people began to pray to St Nicholas of Mozhaisk. Someone touched Sadko on his right shoulder: 'O Sadko, man of Novgorod! Enough of your playing on your sycamore *gusli*!' Sadko, the man of Novgorod, turned round to look: a grey-haired old man stood there. Sadko, the man of Novgorod, said: 'I am not a free man in the blue sea – I have been ordered to play on my sycamore *gusli*.'

Говорит старик таковы слова:
«А ты струночки повырывай,
А ты шпенечки повыломай.
Скажи: – У меня струночек не случилося,
А шпенечков не пригодилося,
Не во что больше играть,
Приломалися гуселки яровчаты. –
Скажет тебе царь морской: –
Не хочешь ли жениться во синем море
На душечке на красныя девушке? –
Говори ему таковы слова: –
У меня воля не своя во синем море. –
Опять скажет царь морской: –
Ну, Садко, вставай поутру ранешенько,
Выбирай себе девицу-красавицу. –
Как станешь выбирать девицу-красавицу,
Так перво триста девиц пропусти,
И друго триста девиц пропусти,
И третье триста девиц пропусти:
Позади идет девица-красавица,
Красавица девица Чернавушка,
Бери тую Чернаву за себя замуж.
Как ляжешь спать во перву ночь,
Не твори с женой блуда во синем море:

The old man spoke these words: 'What you should do is to snap the strings, break off the pegs and say: "I have no strings, my pegs are missing, I have no longer an instrument on which to play, my sycamore *gusli* are broken." The King of the Sea will ask you: "Would you like to wed some sweet fair maid in the blue sea?" And you say to him: "I am not a free man in the blue sea." Again the King of the Sea will say to you: "Well, Sadko, rise early in the morning and choose yourself a fair maid." When you start choosing a fair maid, pass over the first three hundred maidens, and the second three hundred, and the third three hundred; behind them will come a fair maid – the fair maid Chernava. Take this Chernava to wife. When you go to bed on the first night, do not sin with your wife in the blue sea; . . . . . ·

Останешься навеки во синем море;
А ежели не сотворишь блуда во синем море,
Ляжешь спать о девицу-красавицу,
Будешь, Садко, во Новеграде.
А на свою бессчетну золоту казну
Построй церковь соборную Миколы Можай-
                                    скому».

Садко струночки во гуселках повыдернул,
Шпенечки во яровчатых повыломал.

Говорит ему царь морской:
«Ай же ты, Садко, новгородскиий!
Что же не играешь в гуселки яровчаты?» –
«У меня струночки во гуселках выдернулись,
А шпенечки во яровчатых повыломались,
А струночек запасных не случилося,
А шпенечков не пригодилося».

Говорит царь таковы слова:
«Не хочешь ли жениться во синем море
На душечке на красныя девушке?»

Говорит ему Садко новгородскиий:
«У меня воля не своя во синем море».

Опять говорит царь морской:
«Ну, Садко, вставай поутру ранешенько,
Выбирай себе девицу-красавицу».

if you do, you will stay forever in the blue sea; but if you do not sin with her in the blue sea, you will lie down in your bed beside a fair maid, and then, Sadko, you will be in Novgorod. And with your countless treasure of gold build a cathedral church to St Nicholas of Mozhaisk.'

Sadko snapped the strings of his sycamore *gusli*, and broke off the pegs. The King of the Sea said to him: 'O Sadko, man of Novgorod! Why are you not playing on your sycamore *gusli*?' – 'The strings on my sycamore *gusli* have snapped, the pegs have broken off, and I have no spare strings or pegs.' The King spoke these words: 'Would you like to wed some sweet fair maid in the blue sea?' Sadko, the man of Novgorod, said to him: 'I am not a free man in the blue sea.' Again the King of the Sea said: 'Well, Sadko, rise early in the morning and choose yourself a fair maid.'

Вставал Садко поутру ранешенько,
Поглядит – идет триста девушек красныих;
Он перво триста девиц пропустил,
И друго триста девиц пропустил,
И третье триста девиц пропустил;
Позади шла девица-красавица,
Красавица-девица Чернавушка, –
Брал тую Чернаву за себя замуж.
Как прошел у них столованье, почестен пир,
Как ложится спать Садко во перву ночь, –
Не творил с женой блуда во синем море.
Как проснулся Садко во Новеграде,
О реку Чернаву на крутом кряжу,
Как поглядит, – ажно бежат
Свои черленые корабли по Волхову.
Поминает жена Садка со дружиной во
синем море:
«Не бывать Садку со синя моря!»
А дружина поминает одного Садка:
«Остался Садко во синем море!»
А Садко стоит на крутом кряжу,
Встречает свою дружинушку со Волхова.
Тут его дружина сдивовалася:

Sadko rose early in the morning; he looked – three hundred fair maidens were approaching; he passed over the first three hundred maidens, and the second three hundred, and the third three hundred; behind them came a fair maid – the fair maid Chernava; he took this Chernava to wife. After the marriage feast, the banquet in their honour, Sadko went to bed on the first night; and he did not sin with his wife in the blue sea. Sadko awoke in Novgorod, beside the Chernava river, on its steep bank. And as he looked, he saw his own red ships sailing up the Volkhov.

His wife was praying for the souls of Sadko and of his retainers [drowned] in the blue sea: 'Sadko will not be returning from the blue sea!' And his retainers were praying for Sadko alone: 'Sadko has remained behind in the blue sea!' And Sadko stood on the steep bank and welcomed his retainers as they landed from the Volkhov. His retainers marvelled at this: . . . . . .

«Остался Садко во синем море,
Очутился впереди нас во Новеграде,
Встречает дружину со Волхова!»
    Встретил Садко дружину хоробрую
И повел в палаты белокаменны.
Тут его жена зрадовалася,
Брала Садка за белы руки,
Целовала во уста во сахарные.
Начал Садко выгружать со черленых со
                                   кораблей
Именьице – бессчетну золоту казну.
Как повыгрузил со черленыих кораблей,
Состроил церкву соборную Миколе Можай-
                                        скому,
Не стал больше ездить Садко во сине море,
Стал поживать Садко во Новеграде.

'Sadko remained behind in the blue sea, yet he has reached Novgorod before us, and is welcoming his retainers as we land from the
Volkhov!'
    Sadko welcomed his brave retainers and led them into his palace
of white stone. His wife was full of joy, she seized Sadko by his
white hands and kissed him on his lips as sweet as sugar. Sadko
began to unload his possessions – the countless treasure of gold –
from his red ships. When he had unloaded it from his red ships he
built a cathedral church to St Nicholas of Mozhaisk.
    And Sadko sailed no more upon the blue sea, and lived hence-
forth in Novgorod.

DUKHOVNYE STIKHI

Плач Иосифа

Кому повем печаль мою,
Кого призову к рыданию?
Токмо тебе, Владыко мой:
Известна тебе печаль моя,
Моему творцу, создателю,
Всех благих подателю.
Буду просить я милости
От всея своея крепости.
Кто бы мне дал источник слез?
Я плакал бы и день, и нощь,
Рыдал бы я о гресех своих,
Пролиял бы слезы от очию,
Аки реки Едемские,
Погасил бы я геенский огнь.
Кто бы мне дал голубицу
Вещающу беседами?
Послал бы я ко Иякову,
Отцу моему Израилю:
Отче, отче Иякове,
Святый муж Израилев!
Пролей слезы ко Господу
О своем сыне Иосифе!

Joseph's Lament

To whom shall I tell my sorrow, to whom shall I call that he may weep? Only to Thee, my Lord. To Thee my sorrow is known – to Thee, my Maker and Creator and Giver of all good things. With all my strength I shall ask for mercy. Who will give me a fount of tears? I would weep day and night, I would bewail my sins, I would shed tears that would flow from my eyes like the rivers of Paradise, I would quench the fire of Hell. Who will give me a dove that can speak? I would send it to Jacob, to my father Israel: Father, father Jacob, O holy man of Israel! Shed tears unto the Lord for your son Joseph! . . . . . .

Твои дети, моя братия,
Продаша мене во ину землю.
Исчезнуша мои слезы
О моем с тобою разлучении,
И несть того, кто бы утешил мя.
Земле, земле,
Возопившая ко Господу за Авеля,
Возопи ныне ко Иякову,
Отцу моему Израилю!

Царевич Иосаф, Пустынник

При долине, при долине
Стояла мать прекрасная пустыня,
К которой пустыни
Приходил тут младой царевич,
А младой царевич Асафей:
«Прекрасная мать пустыня,
Любимая моя мати!
Приими меня во пустыню:
Я рад на тебя, мати, работати,
Земные поклоны исправляти».
Отвеща ему мать пустыня
Ко младому царевичу Асафью:

Your children, my brethren, have sold me into an alien land.
Vanished are my tears at my parting from you, and there is no
one who can comfort me. Earth, O earth, you who cried out to the
Lord on behalf of Abel, cry out now to Jacob, to my father Israel!

Prince Josaphat, the Hermit

By a valley, by a valley there stood Fair Mother Desert, and to this
Desert there came a young prince, even the young prince Josaphat:
'Fair Mother Desert, my beloved mother! Accept me into the
desert: I would be happy to serve you, mother, and to make
prostrations.' Mother Desert replied to the young prince Josaphat:

«Ты младой царевич Асафей!
Не жить тебе во пустыни:
Кому владеть волным царством,
Твоею белой каменнуй палатуй,
Твоею казною золотою?»
Отвеща ей млад Асафей:
«Прекрасная мать пустыня,
Любимая моя мати!
Не хощу я на волное царство зрети,
На свою белу каменну полату,
На свою казну золотую.
Хощу пребыть во пустыни:
Я рад на тебя, мати, работати,
Земные поклоны исправляти».
Отвеща ему мать пустыня
Ко младому царевичу Асафью:
«Ты младой царевич Асафей!
Не жить тебе во пустыни:
Как придет весна та мать красная,
И лузи-болоты разольются,
Древа все листами оденутся,
Воспоют птицы все райские, –
А ты из пустыни вон и выйдешь,
Меня, мать прекрасную, покинешь».

'O young prince Josaphat! You will not live in the desert: who would then hold your sovereign realm, your palace of white stone, and your treasury of gold?' Young Josaphat replied to her: 'Fair Mother Desert, my beloved mother! I do not wish to behold my sovereign realm, nor my palace of white stone, nor my treasury of gold. I want to live in the desert: I would be happy to serve you, mother, and to make prostrations.' Mother Desert replied to the young prince Josaphat: 'O young prince Josaphat! You will not live in the desert: when Fair Mother Spring comes, and the pools and ponds overflow, and all the trees clothe themselves in leaves, and all the birds from paradise start singing, then you will come forth out of the desert, and will forsake me, the Fair Mother.' . .

Отвеща младой царевич Асафей:
«О прекрасная мать пустыня,
Любимая моя мати!
Как придет весна та мать красная
И лузи-болоты разольются,
Древа все листами оденутся,
Воспоют птицы все райские:
А я из пустыни вон не выйду,
Тебя, мать прекрасная, не покину».

И все святые праведные
Асафью царевичу вздивовались,
Ево ли младому царскому смыслу.
    Ему поем слава
    И во веки веков аминь.

Дмитровская Суббота

На кануне суботы Дмитровской,
Во соборе святом Успенскиим,
Обедню пел Киприян святой,

The young prince Josaphat replied: 'O Fair Mother Desert, my beloved mother! When Fair Mother Spring comes, and the pools and ponds overflow, and all the trees clothe themselves in leaves, and all the birds from paradise start singing, then I will not come forth out of the desert, nor will I forsake you, Fair Mother.'

And all the righteous saints marvelled at the prince Josaphat, and at his young royal understanding. To him we sing glory for ever and ever. Amen.

The Saturday of St Dimitri

ON the vigil of the Saturday of St Dimitri, in the holy cathedral of the Assumption, Saint Cyprian was celebrating the Liturgy; . .

За обедней был Димитрей князь
С благоверною княгиней Евдокиею,
Со князьями ли со боярами,
Со теми со славными воеводами.

Перед самой то было перед достойной,
Перестал Димитрей князь молиться;
Ко столбу князь прислонился,
Умом князь Димитрей изумился;
Открылись душевные его очи,
Видит он дивное виденье:
Не горят свечи перед иконами,
Не сияют камни на златых окладах,
Не слышит он пения святого,
А видит он чистое поле,
То ли чисто поле Куликово.
Изустлано поле мертвыми телами,
Христиаными да Татарами:
Христиане-то как свечки теплятся,
А Татары-то как смола черна.
По тому ль полю Куликову
Ходит сама Мать Пресвятая Богородица,

at this Liturgy Prince Dimitri was present, with his Orthodox Princess Evdokiya, with his princes and boyars, and his glorious generals.

It was just before the singing of 'It is meet'* that Prince Dimitri ceased to pray; he leant against a pillar: Prince Dimitri was rapt in contemplation, his spiritual eyes were opened, and he beheld a marvellous vision: he sees not the candles burning before the icons nor the gems sparkling on the gold casings of the images, he hears not the sacred chanting: he sees the open plain, the open plain of Kulikovo. The plain is strewn with corpses of Christians and Tatars: the Christians glimmer like candles, and the Tatars are like black pitch. Over the plain of Kulikovo walks the most holy Mother of God, ...

* 'It is meet, in truth, to bless thee . . .', the opening words of a hymn to the Mother of God, which follows the consecration of the Bread and the Wine in the Liturgy of St John Chrysostom.

А за ней апостоли Господни,
Архангели-ангели святьи,
Со светлыми со свещами,
Отпевают они мощи православных,
Кадит на них сама Мать Пресвятая
                                    Богородица
И венцы с небес на них сходят.
Вопросила Мать Пресвятая Богородица.
«А где жь да князь Димитрей?»
Отвечает ей Петр апостол:
«А Димитрей князь в Московском граде,
Во святом Успенскиим соборе,
Да и слушает он обедню,
Со своей княгиней Евдокией,
Со своими князьями-боярами,
Со теми ли со славными воеводами».
И рече Мать Пресвятая Богородица:
«Не в своем Димитрей князь месте:
Предводить ему лики мучеников,
А его княгине в моем стаде».

Тут явление пропало,
Свечи во храме загорелись,

and behind her come the Apostles of the Lord, the holy archangels
and angels, with brightly burning candles. They are chanting the
requiem over the relics of the Orthodox [warriors]; the most holy
Mother of God censes them, and crowns descend from Heaven
upon the dead. The most holy Mother of God inquired: 'And
where is Prince Dimitri?' The Apostle Peter answered her: 'Prince
Dimitri is in the city of Moscow, in the holy cathedral of the
Assumption; he is attending the Liturgy with his Princess
Evdokiya, with his princes and boyars, and his glorious generals.'
The most holy Mother of God said: 'Prince Dimitri is not in his
place: he shall lead the throngs of martyrs, and his princess shall
be in my train.'

Then the vision faded. The candles began to burn in the
church, ...

На окладах камни засияни:
Образумился князь Димитрей,
Да слезно он восплакнул,
Таково слово он промолвил:
«Ах, знать, близок час моей смерти!
Скоро буду в гробе я лежати,
А моей княгине быть в черницах!»

А на память дивного видения
Уставил он Дмитровску суботу.

Сон Пресвятыя Богородицы

«Мати, мати, Мать Божия, Мария Пресвятая!
Где ты, мати, ночи ночевала?» –
«Ночевала я в городе Салиме,
Во Божией во церкви за престолом;
Не много спалось, много виделось:
Будто я Христа Сына породила,
Во пелены Его пеленала,
Во шолковы поясы свивала».

the gems began to sparkle on the casings of the images: Prince
Dimitri came to himself, and he wept tears; he spoke these words:
'Ah, the hour of my death is at hand, it seems; soon shall I be lying
in my tomb, and my princess will become a nun.'

And in memory of the marvellous vision he instituted the
Saturday of St Dimitri.

The Dream of the Most Holy Mother of God

'MOTHER, Mother of God, Mary most holy! Where, mother, did
you spend the night?' – 'I spent the night in the city of Jerusalem
in God's church behind the altar; I slept little, but I saw much in
my dreams: I dreamt that I had given birth to a son who was
Christ, and that I swaddled Him in swaddling-clothes and
swathed Him in silken bands.'

Речет Ей Иисус Христос Небесный:
«Мати Моя, мати!
Не сказывай, мати, этот сон:
Я Сам этот сон знаю,
Я Сам про него рассуждаю». –
«Как на реке на Иордане
Выростало дерево святое,
Святое дерево кипарисово;
Да на том ли на дереве кипарисе
Да чудесный крест проявлялся,
Да чуден крест животворящий:
На том на кресту Тебе быть распяту».
    В пятницу под субботу
Жиды Христа распя́ли,
Понапрасну святу кровь проливали,
Руцы и нози приковали,
Скрость ребер копьем прободали,
Головушку тростью проломали.
Послышала матушка Мария,
Бежит ко Христу, сама плачет:
«Чадо мое милое!
За что Ты такую муку принимаешь?
На кого Ты меня, чадо, покидаешь?» –

Jesus Christ the Heavenly One says to Her: 'O mother, my mother! Do not tell me this dream, mother: I know this dream myself, I myself interpret it.' –

'By the river Jordan there grew a holy tree, a holy cypress tree; and on that cypress tree the wondrous Cross was made manifest – the wondrous life-giving Cross. On that Cross You will be crucified.'

On the Friday before the Sabbath the Jews crucified Christ; wantonly they shed His holy blood, they nailed His hands and feet [to the Cross], they pierced His side with the spear, they broke His head with the reed. Mary, His mother, heard of this and ran weeping to Christ: 'My beloved Son! Why are You enduring such torments? To whom are You abandoning me, my Son?' –   .

«Не плачь, Моя матушка, Мария,
Не одну тебя Я покидаю,
Покидаю Я, тебя, мати, на Иоанна Богослова,
На Своего друга на Христова.
Я Сам, мати, теперь умру,
Я во третий день, матушка, воскресну,
Да Я Сам, мати, со неба сойду,
Я Сам из тебя душу выну,
Погребу твои мощи с ангелами,
С херувимами да со славными серафимы;
И спишу твой лик на иконе,
Поставлю во Божией во церкви за престолом:
Будут души-рабы Богу молиться,
Будут тебя, мати, поминати,
Меня, Христа, прославляти».
   Слава Тебе, Христе Боже!

'Weep not, Mary My mother, I am not leaving you all alone, I am leaving you, mother, in the care of John the Theologian, my friend – Christ's friend. I Myself am now going to die, mother, but on the third day I shall rise again; I shall Myself descend from heaven, mother, and shall take out your soul, and, attended by angels and by the cherubim and the glorious seraphim, I shall bury your relics; and I shall paint your face upon an icon and shall put it in God's church behind the altar: the souls, my servants, will pray to God, will be mindful of you, and will glorify me, who am Christ.'
Glory to Thee, O Christ God!

MIKHAIL LOMONOSOV

Вечернее размышление о Божием величестве
при случае великого северного сияния

Лице свое скрывает день,
Поля покрыла мрачна ночь,
Взошла на горы чорна тень,
Лучи от нас склонились прочь.
Открылась бездна звезд полна;
Звездам числа нет, бездне дна.

Песчинка как в морских волнах,
Как мала искра в вечном льде,
Как в сильном вихре тонкий прах,
В свирепом как перо огне,
Так я в сей бездне углублен
Теряюсь, мысльми утомлен!

Уста премудрых нам гласят:
Там разных множество светов,
Несчетны солнца там горят,
Народы там и круг веков:

An Evening Meditation on the Divine Majesty on the
Occasion of the Great Northern Lights

DAY hides its face, dark night has covered the plains, a black
shadow has climbed up the mountains, and the [sun's] rays have
declined away from us. The abyss is revealed, filled with stars; the
stars are countless, the abyss bottomless.

Like a grain of sand in the waves of the sea, like a tiny spark in
perpetual ice, like a speck of dust in a powerful whirlwind, like a
feather in a raging fire, so am I lost, plunged in this abyss and
exhausted by my thoughts.

The mouths of wise men tell us that there is a multitude of
different worlds there, that countless suns burn, and peoples and a
cycle of ages exist there: . . . . . .

Для общей славы Божества
Там равна сила естества.

Но где ж, натура, твой закон?
С полночных стран встает заря!
Не солнце ль ставит там свой трон?
Не льдисты ль мещут огнь моря?
Се хладный пламень нас покрыл!
Се в ночь на землю день вступил!

О вы, которых быстрый зрак
Пронзает в книгу вечных прав,
Которым малый вещи знак
Являет естества устав,
Вам путь известен всех планет;
Скажите, что нас так мятет?

Что зыблет ясный ночью луч?
Что тонкий пламень в твердь разит?
Как молния без грозных туч
Стремится от земли в зенит?
Как может быть, чтоб мерзлый пар
Среди зимы рождал пожар?

to the general glory of the Divinity the force of nature is the same there.

But, nature, where are your laws? The dawn appears from the northern regions! Is not the sun setting up its throne there? Are not the ice-bound seas emitting fire? Behold, a cold flame has covered us! Behold, day has stepped on to the earth at night!

O you, whose penetrating glance plumbs the book of eternal laws, to whom a slight sign in an object reveals a law of nature – you know the course of all the planets; tell us, what is it that disturbs us so?

What causes bright rays to vibrate in the night? Why does a thin flame strike the heavens? How does lightning without thunderclouds race from the earth to the zenith? How can it be that frozen steam generates a conflagration in the midst of winter?

Там спорит жирна мгла с водой;
Иль солнечны лучи блестят,
Склонясь сквозь воздух к нам густой;
Иль тучных гор верьхи горят;
Иль в море дуть престал зефир,
И гладки волны бьют в ефир.

Сомнений полон ваш ответ
О том, что окрест ближних мест.
Скажите ж, коль пространен свет?
И что малейших дале звезд?
Несведом тварей вам конец?
Скажите ж, коль велик Творец?

There thick gloom contends with water; or the rays of the sun glimmer as they are refracted towards us by the dense atmosphere; or the summits of fertile mountains are on fire; or else the zephyr has ceased to blow on the sea, and smooth waves beat against the ether.

Your answer is full of doubts concerning that which lies around the neighbouring regions. Tell us then – how vast is the universe? What lies beyond the smallest stars? You know not the limits of creation? Tell us then – how great is the Creator?

ALEKSANDR SUMAROKOV

Тщетно я скрываю сердца скорби люты,
  Тщетно я спокойною кажусь.
Не могу спокойна быть я ни минуты,
  Не могу, как много я ни тщусь.
Сердце тяжким стоном, очи током слезным
  Извлекают тайну муки сей;
Ты мое старанье сделал бесполезным,
  Ты, о хищник вольности моей!

Ввергнута тобою я в сию злу долю,
  Ты спокойный дух мой возмутил,
Ты мою свободу пременил в неволю,
  Ты утехи в горесть обратил;
И, к лютейшей муке, ты, того не зная,
  Может быть, вздыхаешь о иной,
Может быть, бесплодным пламенем сгорая,
  Страждешь ею так, как я тобой.

Зреть тебя желаю, а узрев, мятуся
  И боюсь, чтоб взор не изменил;

In vain do I hide the fierce anguish of my heart, in vain do I appear
calm. I cannot be calm for a minute, I cannot, however much I try.
My heart by its sorrowful groans, my eyes by a flood of tears
divulge the secret of these torments; you have made my efforts
useless – you who have robbed me of my freedom!

You have brought this cruel fate upon me, you have disturbed
my tranquil spirit, changed my freedom into captivity, and turned
delight into sorrow; unaware of this, and to my most bitter torment,
perhaps you are sighing for another woman; perhaps, consumed by
a fruitless passion, you suffer on her account as I am suffering on
yours.

I long to see you, but when I do, I am seized with agitation and
am afraid that my eyes will betray me; . . . . . .

ALEKSANDR SUMAROKOV

При тебе смущаюсь, без тебя крушуся,
   Что не знаешь, сколько ты мне мил.
Стыд из сердца выгнать страсть мою стремится,
   А любовь стремится выгнать стыд.
В сей жестокой брани мой рассудок тьмится,
   Сердце рвется, страждет и горит.

Так из муки в муку я себя ввергаю,
   И хочу открыться, и стыжусь,
И не знаю прямо, я чего желаю,
   Только знаю то, что я крушусь;
Знаю, что всеместно пленна мысль тобою
   Вображает мне твой милый зрак;
Знаю, что, вспаленной страстию презлою,
   Мне забыть тебя нельзя никак.

in your presence I am full of confusion, in your absence I grieve at the thought that you do not know how much I love you. Shame strives to drive this passion out of my heart, while love strives to drive out shame; in this fierce contest my reason is clouded, my heart is rent, it suffers and burns.

Thus I throw myself from one torment into another; I long to open my heart, and I am ashamed to do so; I do not know in truth what I want, I only know that I am full of sorrow. I know that, wherever I am, my mind is held captive by you and conjures up your beloved image; I know that, inflamed by a most cruel passion, I am quite unable to forget you.

GAVRIIL DERZHAVIN

Властителям и судиям

Восстал Всевышний Бог, да судит
Земных богов во сонме их;
Доколе, рек, доколь вам будет
Щадить неправедных и злых?

Ваш долг есть: сохранять законы,
На лица сильных не взирать,
Без помощи, без обороны
Сирот и вдов не оставлять.

Ваш долг: спасать от бед невинных,
Несчастливым подать покров;
От сильных защищать бессильных,
Исторгнуть бедных из оков.

Не внемлют! видят – и не знают!
Покрыты мздою очеса:
Злодействы землю потрясают,
Неправда зыблет небеса.

To Rulers and Judges*

THE Most High God has risen to judge the earthly gods in their congregation; how long – He said – how long will you spare the unjust and the wicked?

Your duty is to maintain the laws, to show no favour to the strong, to leave neither orphans nor widows without help and protection.

Your duty is to save the innocent from harm, to give shelter to the unfortunate; to protect the weak from the strong, to release the poor from their fetters.

They hear not! They see – and they know not! Their eyes are veiled by bribes; wicked deeds shake the earth, injustice convulses the heavens.

* An adaptation of Psalm 82.

Цари! Я мнил, вы боги властны,
Никто над вами не судья,
Но вы, как я подобно, страстны,
И так же смертны, как и я.

И вы подобно так падете,
Как с древ увядший лист падет!
И вы подобно так умрете,
Как ваш последний раб умрет!

Воскресни, Боже! Боже правых!
И их молению внемли:
Приди, суди, карай лукавых,
И будь един Царем земли!

Памятник

Я памятник себе воздвиг чудесный, вечный,
Металлов тверже он и выше пирамид;
Ни вихрь его, ни гром не сломит быстротеч-
ный,
И времени полет его не сокрушит.

O kings! I thought that you were powerful gods, and that no one was a judge over you; yet you are subject to passions, as I am, and as mortal as I.

And you shall fall, as the withered leaf will fall from the tree. And you shall die, as the last of your slaves will die!

Arise, O God, God of the just! And hearken to their supplication; come, judge, chastise the wicked, and be Thou alone King of the earth!

The Monument

I HAVE raised up to myself a wonderful, everlasting monument: it is more solid than metal, higher than the pyramids; neither the whirlwind nor the sudden thunderbolt shall shatter it, nor the flight of time overthrow it.

Так! – весь я не умру, но часть меня большая,
От тлена убежав, по смерти станет жить,
И слава возрастет моя, не увядая,
Доколь славянов род вселенна будет чтить.

Слух пройдет обо мне от Белых вод до Черных,
Где Волга, Дон, Нева, с Рифея льет Урал;
Всяк будет помнить то в народах неисчетных,
Как из безвестности я тем известен стал,

Что первый я дерзнул в забавном русском
слоге
О добродетелях Фелицы возгласить,
В сердечной простоте беседовать о Боге
И истину царям с улыбкой говорить.

О муза! возгордись заслугой справедливой,
И презрит кто тебя, сама тех презирай;
Непринужденною рукой неторопливой
Чело твое зарей бессмертия венчай.

Indeed, not all of me shall die: a great part of me, escaping corruption, shall live after death, and my glory, unfading, shall not cease to grow so long as the Slavonic race is held in honour by all the nations of the earth.

My fame shall spread from the White Sea to the Black, where flow the Volga, the Don, the Neva, and the Ural running down from the [Ural] mountains; among numberless peoples all shall remember how, emerging from obscurity, I became renowned

As the first who dared to proclaim Felitsa's* virtues in the Russian language of comedy, to speak of God in all simplicity of heart, and to tell the truth to kings with a smile.

O Muse, glory in your well-deserved merit; if anyone should scorn you, scorn him yourself; with an unconstrained, unhurried hand garland your brow with the day-spring of immortality.

* Felitsa (from the Latin 'felicitas') was a sobriquet applied to the Empress Catherine II.

GAVRIIL DERZHAVIN

Соловей во сне

Я на хо́лме спал высоком,
Слышал глас твой, соловей,
Даже в самом сне глубоком
Внятен был душе моей:
То звучал, то отдавался,
То стенал, то усмехался
В слухе издалече он;
И в объятиях Калисты
Песни, вздохи, клики, свисты
Услаждали сладкий сон.

Если по моей кончине,
В скучном, бесконечном сне,
Ах! не будут так, как ныне,
Эти песни слышны мне;
И веселья, и забавы,
Плясок, ликов, звуков славы
Не услышу больше я, –
Стану ж жизнью наслаждаться,
Чаще с милой целоваться,
Слушать песни соловья.

A Nightingale in a Dream

On a high hill I was sleeping and heard your voice, O nightingale. My soul could hear it even in my deepest sleep – now resounding, now echoing, now moaning, now laughing in my ear from far away; and, while I lay in Callisto's embrace, songs, sighs, cries, and whistling delighted me in my sweet sleep.

If, when I lie after my death in tedious, endless sleep, these songs, alas, will no longer reach my ear as they do now, and if I will no longer hear the sounds of happiness and gaiety, of dancing, of choirs, and of glory – then I may as well enjoy life on earth, kiss my beloved more often, and hearken to the songs of the nightingale.

GAVRIIL DERZHAVIN

Цыганская пляска

Возьми, египтянка, гитару,
Ударь по струнам, восклицай;
Исполнясь сладострастна жару,
Твоей всех пляской восхищай.
    Жги души, огнь бросай в сердца
    От смуглого лица.

Неистово, роскошно чувство,
Нерв трепет, мление любви,
Волшебное зараз искусство
Бакханок древних оживи.
    Жги души, огнь бросай в сердца
    От смуглого лица.

Как ночь – с ланит сверкай зарями,
Как вихорь – прах плащом сметай,
Как птица – подлетай крылами,
И в длани с визгом ударяй.
    Жги души, огнь бросай в сердца
    От смуглого лица.

The Gipsy's Dance

TAKE up your guitar, gipsy woman, strike the strings, cry out; filled with voluptuous fever, entrance everyone with your dance. Burn men's souls, hurl fire into their hearts from your swarthy face.

Call back to life at the same time the frenzied, sensuous feeling, the nervous tremor, the languor of love, and the magic art of the ancient Bacchantes. Burn men's souls, hurl fire into their hearts from your swarthy face.

Like night, flash light from your cheeks; like a whirlwind, sweep away the dust with your cloak; like a bird, rise into the air on your wings; and scream and clap your hands. Burn men's souls, hurl fire into their hearts from your swarthy face.

Под лесом нощию сосновым,
При блеске бледныя луны,
Топоча по доскам гробовым,
Буди сон мёртвой тишины.
    Жги души, огнь бросай в сердца
    От смуглого лица.

Да вопль твой, эвоа! ужасный,
Вдали мешаясь с воем псов,
Лиёт повсюду гулы страшны,
А сластолюбию – любовь.
    Жги души, огнь бросай в сердца
    От смуглого лица.

Нет, стой, прелестница! довольно,
Муз скромных больше не страши;
Но плавно, важно, благородно,
Как русска дева, пропляши.
    Жги души, огнь бросай в сердца
    И в нежного певца.

*

Stamping on the tombstones in the pine forest at night in the pale moonshine, wake the dead silence from its sleep. Burn men's souls, hurl fire into their hearts from your swarthy face.

Let your fearful shriek *euhoe*,* blending in the distance with the baying of hounds, spread a terrifying clamour all around, and mingle love with sensuality. Burn men's souls, hurl fire into their hearts from your swarthy face.

No, stop, temptress! Enough! Frighten the modest Muses no more; and perform your dance with measured step, in a stately and noble fashion, like a Russian maiden. Burn men's souls, hurl fire into their hearts – and at the sensitive poet.

*

* *Euhoe* = the cry of the revellers at the festivals of Bacchus.

GAVRIIL DERZHAVIN

Река времён в своём стремленьи
Уносит все дела людей
И топит в пропасти забвенья
Народы, царства и царей.
А если что и остаётся
Чрез звуки лиры и трубы,
То вечности жерлом пожрётся
И общей не уйдёт судьбы.

THE river of time in its current bears away all the affairs of men, and drowns nations, kingdoms, and kings in the abyss of oblivion. And if, through the sounds of the lyre and the trumpet, anything shall remain, it shall be devoured in the jaws of eternity and shall not escape the common fate.

IVAN KRYLOV

Гуси

Предлинной хворостиной
Мужик Гусей гнал в город продавать;
  И, правду истинну сказать,
Не очень вежливо честил свой гурт гусиной:
На барыши спешил к базарному он дню
  (А где до прибыли коснётся,
Не только там гусям, и людям достаётся).
  Я мужика и не виню;
Но Гуси иначе об этом толковали,
  И, встретяся с прохожим на пути,
  Вот как на мужика пеняли:
«Где можно нас, Гусей, несчастнее найти?
  Мужик так нами помыкает,
И нас, как будто бы простых Гусей, гоняет;
  А этого не смыслит неуч сей,
  Что он обязан нам почтеньем,
Что мы свой знатный род ведём от тех Гусей,
Которым некогда был должен Рим спасеньем:
Там даже праздники им в честь учреждены!»

The Geese

WITH a very long switch a peasant was driving his geese to town, to sell them; and, to tell the simple truth, he treated his flock of geese none too civilly. Driven by the thought of profit, he was hurrying to get there by market day; and when it's a matter of gain, not only geese but men, too, sometimes get it in the neck. I don't blame the peasant; but the geese took a different view and, encountering a passer-by, complained of the peasant thus: 'Where could you find creatures unhappier than we geese? The peasant pushes us around and jostles us along like any common geese. The ignoramus doesn't realize that he owes us respect, and that we trace our high descent from those same geese to which Rome once owed its salvation. Why, there are even feasts instituted there in their honour!' . . . . .

– «А вы хотите быть за что отличены?»
Спросил прохожий их. «Да наши предки . . .»
                              – «Знаю,
    И всё читал; но ведать я желаю,
    Вы сколько пользы принесли?»
    – «Да наши предки Рим спасли!»
    – «Всё так, да вы что сделали такое?»
– «Мы? Ничего!» – «Так что ж и доброго в
                              вас есть?
    Оставьте предков вы в покое:
    Им поделом была и честь;
А вы, друзья, лишь годны на жаркое».

—

Баснь эту можно бы и боле пояснить –
    Да чтоб гусей не раздразнить.

Квартет

Проказница-Мартышка,
    Осёл,
    Козёл,
  Да косолапый Мишка
Затеяли сыграть Квартет.

– 'But what claim have you to be singled out?' the passer-by
asked them. 'But our ancestors . . .' – 'Yes, I know, I've read all
about it; but I would like to know of what use you have been.' –
'But our ancestors saved Rome!' – 'Yes, yes, but what have you
done in this line?' – 'We? Why, nothing.' – 'Then what's the
good of you? Leave your ancestors in peace; they were honoured
in accordance with their deserts; but you, my friends, are fit only
for the roast.'

One could make this fable clearer still: but let's not provoke the
geese.

The Quartet

THE mischievous little monkey, the ass, the goat, and the clumsy
bear decided to play a quartet. . . . . . .

Достали нот, баса́, альта, две скрипки
    И сели на лужок под липки
Пленять своим искусством свет.
Ударили в смычки, дерут, а толку нет.
«Стой, братцы, стой!» кричит Мартышка.
                                    «Погодите!
Как музыке идти? Ведь вы не так сидите.
Ты с басом, Мишенька, садись против альта;
    Я, прима, сяду против вторы;
    Тогда пойдёт уж музыка не та:
        У нас запляшут лес и горы!»
        Расселись, начали Квартет;
        Он всё-таки на лад нейдет.
        «Постойте ж, я сыскал секрет»,
    Кричит Осёл, «мы, верно, уж поладим,
        Коль рядом сядем».
Послушались Осла – уселись чинно в ряд;
    А всё-таки Квартет нейдёт на лад.
Вот пуще прежнего пошли у них разборы
            И споры,
        Кому и как сидеть.
Случилось Соловью на шум их прилететь.

They got the music, the bass, the viola, and the two fiddles, and
sat down under the lime-trees in a meadow to charm the world
with their art. They struck the strings with their bows: they scrape,
but to no purpose. 'Stop, boys, stop,' cries the little monkey.
'Wait a bit! How can the music go right? You're seated all wrong.
You, Bruin, with your bass sit down opposite the viola, and I,
the first fiddle, will face the second fiddle; then, you'll see, it will
be a different sort of music: and the forest and the hills will dance
to our tune.' They take their seats and begin the quartet; but it's
still no good. 'Wait,' cries the ass, 'I've got the answer: I'm sure
we'll make it go if we all sit in a row.' They followed the ass's
advice and seated themselves solemnly in a row; but the quartet is
still no good. Worse than ever, now, they started debating and
wrangling as to who should sit where. Attracted by the noise, a
nightingale came flying. . . . . .

Тут с просьбой все к нему, чтоб их решить сомненье
«Пожалуй, – говорят, – возьми на час терпенье,
Чтобы Квартет в порядок наш привесть:
И ноты есть у нас, и инструменты есть,
Скажи лишь, как нам сесть!»
– «Чтоб музыкантом быть, так надобно уменье
И уши ваших понежней»,
Им отвечает Соловей,
«А вы, друзья, как ни садитесь,
Всё в музыканты не годитесь».

They all appeal to him to solve their doubts. 'Please,' they say, 'have patience for an hour and put our quartet in order; we've got the music and the instruments, too: tell us only how we should sit!' The nightingale replies: 'To be a musician you must know how to play, and have ears somewhat more delicate than yours! But you, my friends, however you seat yourselves, will still be useless as musicians.'

VASILY ZHUKOVSKY

К ней

Имя где для тебя?
Не сильно смертных искусство
Выразить прелесть твою!

Лиры нет для тебя!
Что песни? Отзыв неверный
Поздней молвы об тебе!

Если бы сердце могло быть
Им слышно, каждое чувство
Было бы гимном тебе!

Прелесть жизни твоей,
Сей образ чистый, священный,
В сердце, как тайну, ношу.

Я могу лишь любить,
Сказать же, как ты любима,
Может лишь вечность одна!

To Her

Where is there a name for you? Mortals' art is powerless to express your charm.

There is no lyre for you! What are songs? A false echo of a tardy report about you!

If they could hear what is in my heart, every feeling would be a hymn to you.

The charm of your life, this pure and sacred image, I carry as a secret in my heart.

I can only love; eternity alone can say how much you are loved!

Песня

Минувших дней очарованье,
Зачем опять воскресло ты?
Кто разбудил воспоминанье
И замолчавшие мечты?
Шепнул душе привет бывалой;
Душе блеснул знакомый взор;
И зримо ей минуту стало
Незримое с давнишних пор.

О милый гость, святое *Прежде*,
Зачем в мою теснишься грудь?
Могу ль сказать: *живи* надежде?
Скажу ль тому, что было: *будь*?
Могу ль узреть во блеске новом
Мечты увядшей красоту?
Могу ль опять одеть покровом
Знакомой жизни наготу?

Зачем душа в тот край стремится,
Где были дни, каких уж нет?
Пустынный край не населится,
Не узрит он минувших лет;

Song

ENCHANTMENT of bygone days – why have you come to life again? Who has roused the memories and the dreams that had fallen silent? A greeting which I used to know well has whispered to my soul; familiar eyes have shone upon it; and for an instant it beheld what had long been invisible to it.

O beloved guest – sacred past – why do you invade my breast? Can I say to hope, 'Live'? Shall I say to that which was, 'Be'? Shall I be able to see in a new radiance the beauty of a faded dream? Shall I be able once again to clothe the nakedness of the life that I know so well?

Why does the soul long to fly to the land where days were such as are no longer? The deserted land will not be peopled nor see the bygone years; . . . . . .

Там есть *один* жилец безгласный,
Свидетель милой старины;
Там вместе с ним все дни прекрасны
В единый гроб положены.

19-го марта 1823 г.

Ты предо мною
Стояла тихо.
Твой взор унылый
Был полон чувства.
Он мне напомнил
О милом прошлом ..
Он был последний
На здешнем свете.

Ты удалилась,
Как тихий ангел;
Твоя могила,
Как рай, спокойна!
Там все земные
Воспоминанья,
Там все святые
О небе мысли.

Звёзды небес,
Тихая ночь! . . .

there is *one* silent inhabitant of this land, a witness of the beloved times of old; all the beautiful days have been laid in a single grave with him there.

19 March 1823

YOU stood before me in silence. The sad look in your eyes was full of feeling. It reminded me of the beloved past. . . . It was your last in this world.

You departed like a silent angel; your grave is as peaceful as heaven. All earthly memories, all holy thoughts of heaven are there.

Stars of the heavens, silent night!

VASILY ZHUKOVSKY

Ночь

Уже утомившийся день
Склонился в багряные воды,
Темнеют лазурные своды,
Прохладная стелется тень;
И ночь молчаливая мирно
Пошла по дороге эфирной,
И Геспер летит перед ней
С прекрасной звездою своей.

Сойди, о небесная, к нам
С волшебным твоим покрывалом,
С целебным забвенья фиалом.
Дай мира усталым сердцам.
Своим миротворным явленьем,
Своим усыпительным пеньем
Томимую душу тоской,
Как матерь дитя, успокой.

*

Я Музу юную, бывало,
Встречал в подлунной стороне,

The Night

ALREADY the weary day is sinking into the crimson waters; the
blue sky grows dark; the cool shadow is spreading; and the silent
night has begun to move quietly along the ethereal path; and
Hesperus is flying before it with his beautiful star.

O heavenly one, come down to us with your magic veil, with
your healing phial of oblivion. Give peace to weary hearts. Calm
the anguished soul with your soothing presence and with your
lulling songs, as a mother calms her child.

*

IN former times I used to meet the young Muse on earth, . . .

И Вдохновение летало
С небес, незваное, ко мне;
На всё земное наводило
Животворящий луч оно –
И для меня в то время было
Жизнь и Поэзия одно.

Но дарователь песнопений
Меня давно не посещал;
Бывалых нет в душе видений,
И голос арфы замолчал.
Его желанного возврата
Дождаться ль мне когда опять?
Или навек моя утрата
И вечно арфе не звучать?

Но всё, что от времён прекрасных,
Когда он мне доступен был,
Всё, что от милых, тёмных, ясных
Минувших дней я сохранил –
Цветы мечты уединенной
И жизни лучшие цветы, –
Кладу на твой алтарь священный,
О Гений чистой красоты!

and inspiration would fly down to me, uninvited, from heaven. It directed its life-giving ray at all earthly things; and in those days life and poetry for me were one.

But the giver of songs has not visited me for a long time; the former visions are no longer in my soul, and the voice of the harp has fallen silent. When shall I see once again his longed-for return? Or is my loss for ever, and will my harp never be heard again?

But all that I have kept from the wonderful time when he was accessible to me, from the beloved, dark, bright, bygone days – the flowers of solitary fancy and life's finest flowers – I place on your sacred altar, O spirit of pure beauty!

VASILY ZHUKOVSKY

Не знаю, светлых вдохновений
Когда воротится чреда, –
Но ты знаком мне, чистый Гений!
И светит мне твоя звезда!
Пока ещё её сиянье
Душа умеет различать:
Не умерло очарованье!
Былое сбудется опять.

I know not when the train of bright inspirations will return; but
you are known to me, pure spirit, and your star is shining for me.
My soul can still discern its radiance: enchantment is not dead;
the past will come to life again.

KONSTANTIN BATYUSHKOV

Тень друга

Sunt aliquid manes: letum non omnia finit;
Luridaque evictos effugit umbra rogos.

Propertius

Я берег покидал туманный Альбиона:
Казалось, он в волнах свинцовых утопал.
За кораблём вилася гальциона,
И тихий глас её пловцов увеселял.
Вечерний ветр, валов плесканье,
Однообразный шум и трепет парусов,
И кормчего на палубе взыванье
Ко страже, дремлющей под говором валов, –
Всё сладкую задумчивость питало.
Как очарованный, у мачты я стоял
И сквозь туман и ночи покрывало
Светила севера любезного искал.
Вся мысль моя была в воспоминанье
Под небом сладостным отеческой земли,
Но ветров шум и моря колыханье

The Shade of My Friend

The departed spirits are something
real: death does not end everything;
a pale shadow escapes from the extinguished pyre.   *Propertius*

I WAS leaving Albion's misty shore: it seemed to sink into the
leaden waves. A halcyon hovered in the ship's wake, and its soft
cries delighted the sailors. The evening breeze, the lapping of the
waves, the monotonous rustle and flapping of the sails, and the voice
of the helmsman on deck calling to the watch who slumbered to the
murmur of the waves – all this fostered a sweet reverie. As though
bewitched, I stood by the mast, and through the mist and pall of
night searched for the stars of my beloved northern skies. All my
thoughts were wrapped in memories beneath the gracious skies of
my native land, but the sound of the wind and the rolling of the sea

На вежды томное забвенье навели.
   Мечты сменялися мечтами
И вдруг . . . то был ли сон? . . . предстал
                              товарищ мне,
   Погибший в роковом огне
Завидной смертию, над плейсскими струями.
   Но вид не страшен был; чело
   Глубоких ран не сохраняло,
Как утро майское веселием цвело
И всё небесное душе напоминало.
«Ты ль это, милый друг, товарищ лучших дней!
Ты ль это? – я вскричал, – о воин вечно милой!
Не я ли над твоей безвременной могилой,
При страшном зареве Беллониных огней,
   Не я ли с верными друзьями
Мечом на дереве твой подвиг начертал
И тень в небесную отчизну провождал
   С мольбой, рыданьем и слезами?
Тень незабвенного! Ответствуй, милый брат!
Или протекшее всё было сон, мечтанье;
Всё, всё – и бледный труп, могила и обряд,

brought languor and drowsiness to my eyelids. Fancies followed in each other's wake, when suddenly . . . – was this a dream? – there appeared before me my comrade, who had met an enviable death in a fatal battle by the waters of the Pleisse. But his appearance was not frightening; his brow bore no traces of deep wounds – it shone with gaiety like a May morning and reminded my soul of heavenly things. 'Is that you, dear friend, companion of my fairest days? Is that you' – I cried – 'O warrior whom I shall always cherish? In the dreadful glow of the fires of war did I not, in the company of our faithful friends, inscribe with my sword your exploit on a wooden cross, above your untimely grave, and with prayers, tears, and lamentations bid farewell to your shade on its journey to its heavenly home? O shade of one who will never be forgotten! Answer me, dear brother! Or was all that happened but a dream, a phantom, everything – the pale corpse, the grave, and the rite . . . . . .

Свершённый дружбою в твоё воспоминанье?
О! Молви слово мне! Пускай знакомый звук
    Ещё мой жадный слух ласкает,
Пускай рука моя, о незабвенный друг!
    Твою с любовию сжимает . . .»
И я летел к нему . . . Но горний дух исчез
В бездонной синеве безоблачных небес,
Как дым, как метеор, как призрак полуночи,
    Исчез – и сон покинул очи.

Всё спало вкруг меня под кровом тишины.
Стихии грозные казалися безмолвны.
При свете облаком подёрнутой луны
Чуть веял ветерок, едва сверкали волны.
Но сладостный покой бежал моих очей,
    И всё душа за призраком летела,
Всё гостя горнего остановить хотела:
Тебя, о милый брат! о лучший из друзей!

Мой гений

О память сердца! ты сильней
Рассудка памяти печальной

performed by friendship in memory of you? O speak to me! Let the
familiar sound still caress my eager ears, let my hand clasp yours in
affection, O friend whom I shall never forget!..' And I flew towards
him... But the heavenly spirit vanished in the fathomless blue
of the cloudless sky, like smoke, like a meteor or a midnight phantom: it vanished – and sleep lifted from my eyes.

Everything around me slept under a veil of silence. The dreadful elements seemed mute. By the light of the moon, thinly veiled
by a cloud, a gentle breeze was blowing, the waves were gleaming
faintly. But sweet repose eluded my eyes, and still my soul flew in
pursuit of the phantom, wishing to stay the heavenly guest – you,
dear brother! O best of friends!

My Spirit

O HEART'S memory, you are stronger than the mournful memory

И часто сладостью своей
Меня в стране пленяешь дальной.
Я помню голос милых слов,
Я помню очи голубые,
Я помню локоны златые
Небрежно вьющихся власов.
Моей пастушки несравненной
Я помню весь наряд простой,
И образ милый, незабвенной
Повсюду странствует со мной.
Хранитель гений мой – любовью
В утеху дан разлуке он:
Засну ль? приникнет к изголовью
И усладит печальный сон.

Пробуждение

Зефир последний свеял сон
С ресниц, окованных мечтами,
Но я – не к счастью пробуждён
Зефира тихими крылами.
Ни сладость розовых лучей

of reason;/ and often in a distant land you bewitch me with your sweetness. I remember the sound of the beloved voice, I remember the blue eyes, I remember the golden locks of carelessly curling hair; I remember the whole simple attire of my peerless shepherdess, and the dear, unforgettable image wanders with me everywhere. It is my guardian spirit, given me by love as a solace to separation; let me but fall asleep – it will bend over my pillow and comfort my mournful slumber.

Awakening

ZEPHYR has blown away the last vestige of sleep from my eyelashes fettered by dreams; but not to happiness have I been awakened by Zephyr's gentle wings. Neither the sweetness of the rose-coloured rays . . . . . .

Предтечи утреннего Феба,
Ни кроткий блеск лазури неба,
Ни запах, веющий с полей,
Ни быстрый лёт коня ретива
По скату бархатных лугов
И гончих лай и звон рогов
Вокруг пустынного залива –
Ничто души не веселит,
Души, встревоженной мечтами,
И гордый ум не победит
Любви холодными словами.

of the morning Phœbus's harbinger, nor the soft brilliance of the blue sky, nor the scent wafted from the fields, nor the rapid flight of a fiery steed down the slopes of velvety meadows, nor the baying of hounds and the sound of horns around a deserted bay – nothing gladdens the soul that is troubled by dreams, and proud intellect will not vanquish love by cold words.

PRINCE PETR VYAZEMSKY

Вечер

Прелестный вечер! В сладком обаяньи
Душа притихла, словно в чудном сне.
И небеса в безоблачном сияньи,
И вся земля почила в тишине.

Куда б глаза пытливо ни смотрели,
Таинственной завесой мир одет,
Слух звука ждёт, – но звуки онемели;
Движенья ищет взор – движенья нет.

Не дрогнет лист, не зарябится влага,
Не проскользнёт воздушная струя;
Всё тишь!... Как будто в пресыщеньи блага
Жизнь замерла и не слыхать ея.

Но в видимом бездейственном покое
Не истощенье сил, не мёртвый сон:
Присущны здесь и таинство живое,
И стройного могущества закон.

Evening

DELIGHTFUL evening! My soul, in sweet enchantment, has fallen silent, as though in a wonderful sleep; the heavens in their cloudless radiance and the whole earth are resting in silence.

Wherever my eyes look searchingly the world is draped with a mysterious veil; the ear waits for a sound, but the sounds are stilled; the eye seeks for a movement, but there is no movement.

Not a leaf stirs, no ripple ruffles the water, no current glides through the air – all is stillness...as though from a surfeit of blessings life has stopped still and cannot be heard.

But in this apparent, inert stillness there is no exhaustion of strength, no dead sleep: both living mystery and the law of harmonious power are inherent in it.

И молча жизнь кругом благоухает,
И в неподвижной красоте своей
Прохладный вечер молча расточает
Поэзию без звуков, без речей.

И в этот час, когда, в тени немея,
Всё, притаясь, глубокий мир хранит,
И тихий ангел, крыльями чуть вея,
Землёй любуясь, медленно парит,

Природа вся цветёт, красуясь пышно,
И, нас склоня к мечтам и забытью,
Передаёт незримо и неслышно
Нам всю любовь и душу всю свою.

*

Жизнь наша в старости – изношенный халат:
И совестно носить его, и жаль оставить:
Мы с ним давно сжились, давно, как с братом
                                        брат;
Нельзя нас починить и заново исправить.

And all around life exhales sweet smells in silence, and silently
the cool evening in its motionless beauty diffuses a soundless and
wordless poetry.

And in the hour when all things, growing silent and hiding in the
shade, preserve a profound peace, and a quiet angel, his wings
barely moving, slowly flies over the earth, gazing on it with
admiration,

the whole of nature blossoms in all her beauty and magnificence,
inclines us to reverie and drowsiness, and communicates to us in-
visibly and inaudibly all her love and her entire soul.

*

OUR life when we are old is a threadbare dressing-gown: ashamed
to wear it, we are yet loath to throw it away; we've lived with it so
long and grown used to it, as if it were our brother; we can't be
repaired or restored anew.

Как мы состарились, состарился и он;
В лохмотьях наша жизнь, и он в лохмотьях
тоже,
Чернилами он весь расписан, окроплён,
Но эти пятна нам узоров всех дороже;

В них отпрыски пера, которому во дни
Мы светлой радости иль облачной печали
Свои все помыслы, все таинства свои,
Всю исповедь, всю быль свою передавали.

На жизни также есть минувшего следы:
Записаны на ней и жалобы, и пени,
И на неё легла тень скорби и беды,
Но прелесть грустная таится в этой тени.

В ней есть предания, в ней отзыв наш родной
Сердечной памятью ещё живёт в утрате,
И утро свежее, и полдня блеск и зной
Припоминаем мы и при дневном закате.

As we have grown old, so has it; our life is in rags, and it's in rags too; it's scribbled all over and spattered with ink, but we value these stains more than any design.

They are the marks of a spluttering pen to which, in days of bright happiness or of clouded sorrow, we entrusted all our thoughts, secrets, and confessions, the whole story of our life.

On life, too, there are marks of the past: complaints and laments are recorded upon it, and across it lies the shadow of grief and misfortune; yet a sad charm is hidden in this shadow.

There is in it a legacy of the past, and an echo of something dear and familiar which, thanks to the heart's memory, lives on in the loss we have suffered; and at the decline of day we recall both the fresh morning and the brilliance and heat of noon.

PRINCE PETR VYAZEMSKY

Ещё люблю подчас жизнь старую свою
С её ущербами и грустным поворотом,
И, как боец свой плащ, простреленный в бою,
Я холю свой халат с любовью и почётом.

At times I am still fond of my old life with its bereavements and
its sad deflection, and I cherish my dressing-gown with affection
and respect like a soldier his cloak bullet-riddled in battle.

BARON ANTON DEL'VIG

В Испании Амур не чужестранец,
Он там не гость, но родственник и свой,
Под кастаньет с весёлой красотой
Поёт романс и пляшет, как испанец.

Его огнём в щеках блестит румянец,
Пылает грудь, сверкает взор живой,
Горят уста испанки молодой;
И веет мирт, и дышет померанец.

Но он и к нам, всесильный, не суров,
И к северу мы зрим его вниманье:
Не он ли дал очам твоим блистанье,

Устам коралл, жемчужный ряд зубов,
И в кудри свил сей мягкий шёлк власов
И всю тебя одел в очарованье!

CUPID is no stranger in Spain; he is no guest there, but is at home and among his own kin; to the accompaniment of the castanets he sings a gay and beautiful love-song and dances like a Spaniard.

His fire flushes the cheeks of a young Spanish woman, sets her breast aflame, makes her lively eyes sparkle and her lips burn, while the myrtle and the bitter orange-tree waft their fragrance.

But to us too he, the all-powerful, shows no harshness, and we can see his benevolent interest in the northern climes: is it not he who has given sparkle to your eyes,

coral lips and a row of pearl-like teeth to your mouth, has woven this soft silken hair into curls and clothed the whole of you in enchantment?

ALEKSANDR PUSHKIN

Виноград

Не стану я жалеть о розах,
Увядших с лёгкою весной;
Мне мил и виноград на лозах,
В кистях созревший под горой,
Краса моей долины злачной,
Отрада осени златой,
Продолговатый и прозрачный,
Как персты девы молодой.

[Разговор Татьяны с няней из «Евгения Онегина»]

. . . Тоска любви Татьяну гонит,
И в сад идёт она грустить,
И вдруг недвижны очи клонит,
И лень ей далее ступить.
Приподнялася грудь, ланиты
Мгновенным пламенем покрыты,
Дыханье замерло в устах,

Grapes

I SHALL feel no regret for roses which have faded with the passing of fleeting spring; I also love the grapes on the vine, which have ripened in bunches beneath the hill – the beauty of my fertile valley, the delight of golden autumn – elongated and transparent, like a young girl's fingers.

[Tat'yana's Conversation with her Nurse
from 'Evgeny Onegin']

LOVE'S anguish impels Tat'yana, and she goes into the garden to abandon herself to sadness; suddenly she lowers her gaze, and feels too languorous to walk on . . . Her bosom heaves, her cheeks are suffused with a sudden flame, her breath grows faint, . . .

И в слухе шум, и блеск в очах . .
Настанет ночь; луна обходит
Дозором дальный свод небес,
И соловей во мгле древес
Напевы звучные заводит.
Татьяна в темноте не спит
И тихо с няней говорит:

«Не спится, няня: здесь так душно!
Открой окно, да сядь ко мне».
– «Что, Таня, что с тобой?» – «Мне скучно,
Поговорим о старине».
– «О чём же, Таня! Я, бывало,
Хранила в памяти не мало
Старинных былей, небылиц
Про злых духов и про девиц;
А нынче всё мне тёмно, Таня:
Что знала, то забыла. Да,
Пришла худая череда!
Зашибло . . .» – «Расскажи мне, няня,
Про ваши старые года:
Была ты влюблена тогда?»

there is a noise in her ears, and flashing in her eyes ... It is night; the moon is patrolling the distant vault of heaven, and the nightingale in the darkness of the trees strikes up its sonorous melodies. Tat'yana, sleepless in the dark, talks softly to her nurse:

'I can't sleep, nanny: it's so stifling here! Open the window, and come and sit by me.' – 'What is it, Tanya, what's the matter with you?' – 'I feel depressed; let's talk about the old times.' – 'What about, Tanya? I used to remember not a few old tales and fables about evil spirits and maidens; but now all is dark in my mind, Tanya: I have forgotten what I knew. Yes, bad times have come! My memory's gone...' – 'Tell me, nanny, about your own early years: were you ever in love in those days?'

– «И, полно, Таня! В эти лета
Мы не слыхали про любовь;
А то бы согнала со света
Меня покойница свекровь».
– «Да как же ты венчалась, няня?»
– «Так, видно, Бог велел. Мой Ваня
Моложе был меня, мой свет,
А было мне тринадцать лет.
Недели две ходила сваха
К моей родне, и наконец
Благословил меня отец.
Я горько плакала со страха,
Мне с плачем косу расплели,
Да с пеньем в церковь повели.

И вот ввели в семью чужую . . .
Да ты не слушаешь меня . . .»
– «Ах, няня, няня, я тоскую,
Мне тошно, милая моя:
Я плакать, я рыдать готова! . . .»
– «Дитя моё, ты нездорова;
Господь помилуй и спаси!
Чего ты хочешь, попроси . . .
Дай окроплю святой водою,

– 'Whatever next, Tanya! At that age we hadn't even heard of love; if there had been any talk of it, my late mother-in-law would have been the death of me.' – 'But how did you get married, nanny?' – 'Such, it seems, was God's will. My Vanya, my dear one, was younger than I, and I was thirteen. For about two weeks, the match-maker called on my family, and at last my father gave me his blessing. I wept bitterly for fear; they wept as they un-plaited my hair, and sang as they led me to church.

'And so they brought me into a strange family . . . But you aren't listening . . .' – 'Oh, nanny, nanny dear, my heart aches, I am so miserable, I feel like crying, sobbing! . . .' – 'My child, you're not well: the Lord have mercy and save you! What is it you want, tell me. Let me sprinkle you with holy water .   .   .   .   .   .

Ты вся горишь . . .» – «Я не больна:
Я . . . знаешь, няня . . . влюблена».
– «Дитя моё, Господь с тобою!»
И няня девушку с мольбой
Крестила дряхлою рукой.

«Я влюблена», шептала снова
Старушке с горестью она.
– «Сердечный друг, ты нездорова».
– «Оставь меня: я влюблена».
И между тем луна сияла
И томным светом озаряла
Татьяны бледные красы,
И распущённые власы,
И капли слёз, и на скамейке
Пред героиней молодой,
С платком на голове седой,
Старушку в длинной телогрейке;
И всё дремало в тишине
При вдохновительной луне.

- you're burning hot . . .' – 'I'm not ill: I'm . . . oh, nanny . . . I'm in love.' – 'God preserve you, my child!' And, as she prayed, the nurse made the sign of the cross over the girl with her frail old hand.

'I'm in love,' she whispered again sorrowfully to the old woman. 'My dearest, you are not well.' – 'Leave me alone: I'm in love.' Meanwhile, the moon was shining with a languorous light and lighting up Tat'yana's pale beauty, her hair falling loose, her tears, and the old woman in her long warm jacket, with a kerchief on her grey head, sitting on a bench before our young heroine; and all things slumbered in silence beneath the inspiring moon.

[*Монолог Пимена из «Бориса Годунова»*]

Пимен (*пишет перед лампадой*).

Ещё одно, последнее сказанье –
И летопись окончена моя,
Исполнен долг, завещанный от Бога
Мне, грешному. Недаром многих лет
Свидетелем Господь меня поставил
И книжному искусству вразумил;
Когда-нибудь монах трудолюбивый
Найдёт мой труд усердный, безымянный,
Засветит он, как я, свою лампаду –
И, пыль веков от хартий отряхнув,
Правдивые сказанья перепишет,
Да ведают потомки православных
Земли родной минувшую судьбу,
Своих царей великих поминают
За их труды, за славу, за добро –
А за грехи, за тёмные деянья,
Спасителя смиренно умоляют.

На старости я сызнова живу,
Минувшее проходит предо мною –

[*Pimen's Monologue from 'Boris Godunov'*]

Pimen (*writing by lamplight*)

ONE record more, the last, and my chronicle is finished, the duty laid by God upon me, a sinner, is done. Not in vain did the Lord make me a witness of many years, and instruct me in the lore of books. One day some industrious monk will find my zealous, nameless work; he will light his lamp, as I did, and, shaking the dust of ages from the manuscripts, will transcribe these truthful tales, so that the future generations of the Orthodox may know the bygone fortunes of their native land, remember their great tsars for their labours, their glory, their good actions, and humbly implore the Saviour for their sins, their dark deeds.

In my old age I live anew; the past unrolls before me.

Давно ль оно неслось, событий полно,
Волнуяся, как море-окиян?
Теперь оно безмолвно и спокойно:
Не много лиц мне память сохранила,
Не много слов доходят до меня,
А прочее погибло невозвратно . . .
Но близок день, лампада догорает –
Ещё одно, последнее сказанье (*пишет*).

К * * *

Я помню чудное мгновенье:
Передо мной явилась ты,
Как мимолётное виденье,
Как гений чистой красоты.

В томленьях грусти безнадежной,
В тревогах шумной суеты,
Звучал мне долго голос нежный
И снились милые черты.

Is it long since it swept by, teeming with events and turbulent
like the ocean? Now it is silent and tranquil. Few are the faces which
memory has preserved for me, and few the words which have come
down to me – the rest have perished, never to return! . . . But day
draws near, the lamp is burning low – one record more, the last.
(*Writes*)

To —

I REMEMBER the wonderful moment: you appeared before me like
a fleeting vision, like a spirit of pure beauty.

As I languished in hopeless melancholy, amid the anxieties of
the noisy and restless world, your tender voice long echoed in my
mind, and I dreamt of your beloved features.

Шли годы. Бурь порыв мятежный
Рассеял прежние мечты,
И я забыл твой голос нежный,
Твои небесные черты.

В глуши, во мраке заточенья
Тянулись тихо дни мои
Без божества, без вдохновенья,
Без слёз, без жизни, без любви.

Душе настало пробужденье:
И вот опять явилась ты,
Как мимолётное виденье,
Как гений чистой красоты.

И сердце бьётся в упоенье,
И для него воскресли вновь
И божество, и вдохновенье,
И жизнь, и слёзы, и любовь.

Зимний вечер

Буря мглою небо кроет,
Вихри снежные крутя;

Years passed. The storm's turbulent gusts scattered the dreams of yore, and I forgot your tender voice and your heavenly features.

In a remote corner of the earth, in the darkness of exile, my days dragged slowly on, without divinity, without inspiration, without tears, without life, without love.

Awakening came to my soul: and lo, you appeared again, like a fleeting vision, like a spirit of pure beauty.

And my heart beats in ecstasy, and once more within it divinity, inspiration, life, tears, and love are born.

Winter Evening

THE storm covers the sky in darkness, spinning the snowy whirl-winds; . . . . . .

То, как зверь, она завоет,
То заплачет, как дитя,
То по кровле обветшалой
Вдруг соломой зашумит,
То, как путник запоздалый,
К нам в окошко застучит.

Наша ветхая лачужка
И печальна и темна.
Что же ты, моя старушка,
Приумолкла у окна?
Или бури завываньем
Ты, мой друг, утомлена,
Или дремлешь под жужжаньем
Своего веретена?

Выпьем, добрая подружка
Бедной юности моей,
Выпьем с горя; где же кружка?
Сердцу будет веселей.
Спой мне песню, как синица
Тихо за морем жила;
Спой мне песню, как девица
За водой поутру шла.

now, it howls like a wild beast, now it cries like a child, now
it suddenly rustles the thatch on the ramshackle roof, now, like a
belated traveller, it knocks at our window.

Our tumble-down hut is gloomy and dark. Why, my little old
lady,* have you fallen silent by the window? Are you wearied, my
dear, by the storm's howling, or are you dozing to the hum of your
spindle?

Let's drink, good friend of my luckless youth, let's drink to
drown our sorrows; where's the tankard? It will cheer our hearts.
Sing me a song about the blue-tit which lived quietly beyond the
sea; sing me a song about the maiden who went to fetch water in
the morning.

* The poem is addressed to Pushkin's old nurse.

Буря мглою небо кроет,
Вихри снежные крутя;
То, как зверь, она завоет,
То заплачет, как дитя.
Выпьем, добрая подружка
Бедной юности моей,
Выпьем с горя; где же кружка?
Сердцу будет веселей.

Пророк

Духовной жаждою томим,
В пустыне мрачной я влачился,
И шестикрылый серафим
На перепутье мне явился;
Перстами лёгкими как сон
Моих зениц коснулся он:
Отверзлись вещие зеницы,
Как у испуганной орлицы.
Моих ушей коснулся он,
И их наполнил шум и звон:
И внял я неба содроганье,
И горний ангелов полёт,

The storm covers the sky in darkness, spinning the snowy whirl-winds; now it howls like a wild beast, now it cries like a child. Let's drink, good friend of my luckless youth, let's drink to drown our sorrows; where's the tankard? It will cheer our hearts.

The Prophet

TORMENTED by spiritual thirst I dragged myself through a sombre desert. And a six-winged seraph appeared to me at the crossing of the ways. He touched my eyes with fingers as light as a dream: and my prophetic eyes opened like those of a frightened eagle. He touched my ears and they were filled with noise and ringing: and I heard the shuddering of the heavens, and the flight of the angels in the heights, ...

И гад морских подводный ход,
И дольней лозы прозябанье.
И он к устам моим приник,
И вырвал грешный мой язык,
И празднословный и лукавый,
И жало мудрыя змеи
В уста замершие мои
Вложил десницею кровавой.
И он мне грудь рассек мечом,
И сердце трепетное вынул
И угль, пылающий огнём,
Во грудь отверстую водвинул.
Как труп в пустыне я лежал,
И Бога глас ко мне воззвал:
«Восстань, пророк, и виждь, и внемли,
Исполнись волею Моей,
И, обходя моря и земли,
Глаголом жги сердца людей».

Поэт

Пока не требует поэта
К священной жертве Аполлон,

and the movement of the beasts of the sea under the waters, and the sound of the vine growing in the valley. He bent down to my mouth and tore out my tongue, sinful, deceitful, and given to idle talk; and with his right hand steeped in blood he inserted the forked tongue of a wise serpent into my benumbed mouth. He clove my breast with a sword, and plucked out my quivering heart, and thrust a coal of live fire into my gaping breast. Like a corpse I lay in the desert. And the voice of God called out to me: 'Arise, O prophet, see and hear, be filled with My will, go forth over land and sea, and set the hearts of men on fire with your Word.'

The Poet

UNTIL Apollo summons the poet to the holy sacrifice, . ₀ .

В заботах суетного света
Он малодушно погружён;
Молчит его святая лира;
Душа вкушает хладный сон,
И меж детей ничтожных мира,
Быть может, всех ничтожней он.

Но лишь божественный глагол
До слуха чуткого коснётся,
Душа поэта встрепенётся,
Как пробудившийся орёл.
Тоскует он в забавах мира,
Людской чуждается молвы,
К ногам народного кумира
Не клонит гордой головы;
Бежит он, дикий и суровый,
И звуков и смятенья полн,
На берега пустынных волн,
В широкошумные дубровы . . .

Талисман

Там, где море вечно плещет
На пустынные скалы,
Где луна теплее блещет

faint-hearted, he is immersed in vain and worldly cares; his sacred lyre is silent; his soul lies in wintry sleep, and among the insignificant children of this world he is, perhaps, the most insignificant.

But no sooner does the divine word touch his keen hearing than the poet's soul starts like an eagle that has been roused. He pines among the world's diversions, shuns the rumour of the crowd, and does not bend his proud head at the feet of the people's idol; he flees, wild and austere, full of sounds and confusion, to the shores of deserted seas, into spacious and resonant forests . . .

The Talisman

In the land where the sea is for ever breaking on deserted rocks, where the moon shines with a warmer radiance . . . . . .

В сладкий час вечерней мглы,
Где, в гаремах наслаждаясь,
Дни проводит мусульман,
Там волшебница, ласкаясь,
Мне вручила талисман.

И, ласкаясь, говорила.
«Сохрани мой талисман:
В нём таинственная сила!
Он тебе любовью дан.
От недуга, от могилы,
В бурю, в грозный ураган,
Головы твоей, мой милый,
Не спасёт мой талисман.

И богатствами Востока
Он тебя не одарит,
И поклонников пророка
Он тебе не покорит;
И тебя на лоно друга,
От печальных чуждых стран,
В край родной на север с юга
Не умчит мой талисман . . .

in the delightful hour of evening twilight, where the Mussulman spends his days revelling in the pleasures of the harem, there an enchantress, caressing me, handed me a talisman.

And, as she caressed me, she said: 'Take care of my talisman: in it there is a mysterious power. It is the gift of love. My talisman will not save you, my beloved, from sickness or death, in storm or fearful tempest.

'Nor will it endow you with the riches of the Orient, nor subdue the votaries of the Prophet to your will; nor will my talisman carry you off from the south to the north, from a cheerless alien land to your native home, to a friend's bosom . . .

Но когда коварны очи
Очаруют вдруг тебя,
Иль уста во мраке ночи
Поцелуют не любя –
Милый друг! от преступленья,
От сердечных новых ран,
От измены, от забвенья
Сохранит мой талисман!»

[*Пролог к «Руслану и Людмиле»*]

У лукоморья дуб зелёный;
Златая цепь на дубе том:
И днём и ночью кот учёный
Всё ходит по цепи кругом;
Идёт направо – песнь заводит,
Налево – сказку говорит.

Там чудеса: там леший бродит,
Русалка на ветвях сидит;
Там на неведомых дорожках
Следы невиданных зверей;
Избушка там на курьих ножках
Стоит без окон, без дверей;

'But when perfidious eyes bewitch you suddenly, or lips kiss you without love in the dark of night – my beloved, my talisman will preserve you from crime, from fresh wounds of the heart, from betrayal, from oblivion.'

[*Prologue to 'Ruslan and Lyudmila'*]

BY the shores of a bay there is a green oak-tree; there is a golden chain on that oak; and day and night a learned cat ceaselessly walks round on the chain; as it moves to the right, it strikes up a song, as it moves to the left, it tells a story.

There are marvels there: the wood-sprite roams, a mermaid sits in the branches; there are tracks of strange animals on mysterious paths; a hut on hen's legs stands there, without windows or doors;

Там лес и дол видений полны;
Там о заре прихлынут волны
На брег песчаный и пустой,
И тридцать витязей прекрасных
Чредой из вод выходят ясных,
И с ними дядька их морской;
Там королевич мимоходом
Пленяет грозного царя;
Там в облаках перед народом
Через леса, через моря
Колдун несёт богатыря;
В темнице там царевна тужит,
А бурый волк ей верно служит;
Там ступа с Бабою Ягой
Идёт, бредёт сама собой;
Там царь Кащей над златом чахнет;
Там русский дух . . . там Русью пахнет!
И там я был, и мёд я пил;
У моря видел дуб зелёный;
Под ним сидел, и кот учёный
Свои мне сказки говорил.
Одну я помню: сказку эту
Поведаю теперь я свету . . .

forest and vale are full of visions; there at dawn the waves come washing over the sandy and deserted shore, and thirty fair knights come out one by one from the clear water, attended by their sea-tutor; a king's son, passing on his way, takes a dreaded king prisoner; there, in full view of the people, a sorcerer carries a knight through the clouds, across forests and seas; a princess pines away in prison, and a brown wolf serves her faithfully; a mortar with Baba-Yaga* in it walks along by itself. There King Kashchey† grows sickly beside his gold; there is a Russian odour there . . . it smells of Russia! And I was there, I drank mead, I saw the green oak-tree by the sea and sat under it, while the learned cat told me its stories. I remember one – and this story I will now reveal to the world . . .

* A wicked sorceress of Russian folk-tales.
† A rich and wicked old man of Russian folk-tales.

Воспоминание

Когда для смертного умолкнет шумный день
  И на немые стогны града
Полупрозрачная наляжет ночи тень
  И сон, дневных трудов награда,
В то время для меня влачатся в тишине
  Часы томительного бденья:
В бездействии ночном живей горят во мне
  Змеи сердечной угрызенья;
Мечты кипят; в уме, подавленном тоской,
  Теснится тяжких дум избыток;
Воспоминание безмолвно предо мной
  Свой длинный развивает свиток:
И с отвращением читая жизнь мою,
  Я трепещу и проклинаю,
И горько жалуюсь, и горько слёзы лью,
  Но строк печальных не смываю.

Анчар

В пустыне чахлой и скупой,
  На почве, зноем раскаленной,

Remembrance

When the noisy day is stilled for mortal man, and the translucent shadow of night, and sleep, the reward of the day's toil, descend upon the city's wide and silent streets, then hours of tormenting wakefulness drag on for me in silence: in the blankness of night, remorse, like a serpent's bite, burns more fiercely in my heart; fancies seethe; a throng of oppressive thoughts crowds my mind, weighed down by anguish; memory silently unfolds its long scroll before me; and, reading the chronicle of my life with loathing, I tremble and curse, and complain bitterly, and shed bitter tears, yet I do not wash away the sorrowful lines.

The Upas-tree

In the parched and barren desert, on a soil burning with heat, . .

Анчар, как грозный часовой,
Стоит, один во всей вселенной.

Природа жаждущих степей
Его в день гнева породила,
И зелень мёртвую ветвей
И корни ядом напоила.

Яд каплет сквозь его кору,
К полудню растопясь от зною,
И застывает ввечеру
Густой, прозрачною смолою.

К нему и птица не летит
И тигр нейдёт: лишь вихорь чёрный
На древо смерти набежит –
И мчится прочь, уже тлетворный.

И если туча оросит,
Блуждая, лист его дремучий,
С его ветвей, уж ядовит,
Стекает дождь в песок горючий.

Но человека человек
Послал к анчару властным взглядом;

the upas-tree, like a fearsome sentinel, stands alone in the whole world.

The life of the thirsting desert begot it on a day of wrath, and fed the dead foliage of its boughs and its roots with poison.

The poison oozes through its bark, melting from the heat at midday and hardening in the evening into a thick transparent gum.

No bird flies towards it, no tiger goes near: only the black whirlwind bears down upon the tree of death and speeds away, now pestilent.

And if a roving cloud moistens its dense leaves, a poisoned rain trickles down from its branches into the burning sand.

But man sent man to the upas-tree with a commanding glance;

И тот послушно в путь потек
И к утру возвратился с ядом.

Принёс он смертную смолу
Да ветвь с увядшими листами,
И пот по бледному челу
Струился хладными ручьями;

Принёс — и ослабел и лёг
Под сводом шалаша на лыки,
И умер бедный раб у ног
Непобедимого владыки.

А князь тем ядом напитал
Свои послушливые стрелы
И с ними гибель разослал
К соседам в чуждые пределы.

*

Я вас любил: любовь ещё, быть может,
В душе моей угасла не совсем;
Но пусть она вас больше не тревожит;
Я не хочу печалить вас ничем.

and he set out obediently on his way and came back at dawn with
the poison.

He brought the deadly gum, and with it a branch with withered
leaves, and cold sweat poured down his pale brow.

He brought it, and grew weak and lay down on the matting
beneath the roof of the tent; and the poor slave died at the feet of
the invincible lord.

And the prince soaked his obedient arrows in that poison and
with them he disseminated death to his neighbours in alien lands.

*

I LOVED you: it may be that love has not completely died in my
soul; but let it not trouble you any more; I do not wish to sadden
you in any way. . . . . . .

Я вас любил безмолвно, безнадежно,
То робостью, то ревностью томим;
Я вас любил так искренно, так нежно,
Как дай вам Бог любимой быть другим.

Бесы

Мчатся тучи, вьются тучи;
Невидимкою луна
Освещает снег летучий;
Мутно небо, ночь мутна.
Еду, еду в чистом поле;
Колокольчик дин-дин-дин . . .
Страшно, страшно поневоле
Средь неведомых равнин!

«Эй, пошёл, ямщик! . . .» – «Нет мочи:
Коням, барин, тяжело;
Вьюга мне слипает очи;
Все дороги занесло;
Хоть убей, следа не видно;
Сбились мы. Что делать нам!

I loved you silently, hopelessly, tormented now by diffidence and now by jealousy; I loved you so truly, so tenderly as God may grant you to be loved by another.

Evil Spirits

THE clouds scurry, the clouds whirl; the moon, invisible, lights up the flying snow; the sky is turbid, and so is the night. On and on I drive in the open plain; ding-ding-ding rings the little bell. . . . I can't help feeling frightened amid the unknown expanses.
　'Drive on, coachman! . . .' 'I can't, sir: the horses are hard put to it, the blizzard is blinding me, all the roads are snowed up; strike me dead, but I can't see the track; we've lost our way. What are we to do ? . . .　.　.

В поле бес нас водит, видно,
Да кружит по сторонам.

Посмотри: вон, вон играет,
Дует, плюет на меня;
Вон – теперь в овраг толкает
Одичалого коня;
Там верстою небывалой
Он торчал передо мной;
Там сверкнул он искрой малой
И пропал во тьме пустой».

Мчатся тучи, вьются тучи;
Невидимкою луна
Освещает снег летучий;
Мутно небо, ночь мутна.
Сил нам нет кружиться доле;
Колокольчик вдруг умолк;
Кони стали . . . «Что там в поле?»
– «Кто их знает? пень иль волк?»

Вьюга злится, вьюга плачет;
Кони чуткие храпят;
Вон уж он далече скачет;
Лишь глаза во мгле горят;

It seems that an evil spirit is leading us through the plain and making us go round and round in circles.

Look! There he is, over there, playing, blowing, spitting at me; there he is – now he is pushing into a ravine our horse which is running wild; here he loomed before me like a fantastic milestone; there he flashed like a tiny spark and vanished into the empty night.'

The clouds scurry, the clouds whirl; the moon, invisible, lights up the flying snow; the sky is turbid, and so is the night. We've no strength left to circle any longer; suddenly the bell falls silent; the horses halt. ... 'What's that, out there in the plain?' – 'Who knows? – the stump of a tree, or a wolf?'

The blizzard rages, the blizzard wails; the sensitive horses snort; there he is now, scurrying off into the distance – only his eyes are burning in the dark. . . . . . .

Кони снова понеслися;
Колокольчик дин-дин-дин. . . .
Вижу: духи собралися
Средь белеющих равнин.

Бесконечны, безобразны,
В мутной месяца игре
Закружились бесы разны,
Будто листья в ноябре . . .
Сколько их! куда их гонят?
Что так жалобно поют?
Домового ли хоронят,
Ведьму ль замуж выдают?

Мчатся тучи, вьются тучи;
Невидимкою луна
Освещает снег летучий;
Мутно небо, ночь мутна.
Мчатся бесы рой за роем
В беспредельной вышине,
Визгом жалобным и воем
Надрывая сердце мне . . .

The horses have dashed off again; ding-ding-ding rings the little bell . . . I see the phantoms assembled in the white plain.

Countless, hideous, the manifold spirits are whirling in the dim moonlight, like leaves in November. . . . Legions of them! Where are they being driven? Why are they singing so plaintively? Are they burying a house-sprite? Celebrating a witch's wedding?

The clouds scurry, the clouds whirl; the moon, invisible, lights up the flying snow; the sky is turbid, and so is the night. The spirits, swarms of them, scurry in the boundless height, rending my heart with their plaintive screeching and howling. . .

*

Для берегов отчизны дальной
Ты покидала край чужой;
В час незабвенный, в час печальный
Я долго плакал пред тобой.
Мои хладеющие руки
Тебя старались удержать;
Томленья страшного разлуки
Мой стон молил не прерывать.

Но ты от горького лобзанья
Свои уста оторвала;
Из края мрачного изгнанья
Ты в край иной меня звала.
Ты говорила: «В день свиданья
Под небом вечно голубым,
В тени олив, любви лобзанья
Мы вновь, мой друг, соединим».

Но там, увы, где неба своды
Сияют в блеске голубом,
Где тень олив легла на воды,
Заснула ты последним сном.

Bound for the shores of your distant home you were leaving an alien land. In an hour full of sadness, which I shall never forget, I wept before you for a long time. My hands, growing numb, tried to hold you back. My moans implored you not to end the dreadful agony of parting.

But you tore away your lips from our bitter kiss; from a land of dismal exile you called me to another land. You said: 'When we meet again, in the shade of olive trees beneath a sky that is always blue, we shall once more, my beloved, be joined together in a kiss of love.'

But there – alas! – where the sky's vault shines with blue radiance, where the shadow of olive-trees lies on the waters, you have fallen asleep for ever. . . . . . .

Твоя краса, твои страданья
Исчезли в урне гробовой –
Но сладкий поцелуй свиданья . . .
Его я жду; он за тобой . . .

Осень

(Отрывок)

Чего в мой дремлющий тогда не входит ум?

Державин

I

Октябрь уж наступил – уж роща отряхает
Последние листы с нагих своих ветвей;
Дохнул осенний хлад, дорога промерзает,
Журча ещё бежит за мельницу ручей,
Но пруд уже застыл; сосед мой поспешает
В отъезжие поля с охотою своей,
И страждут озими от бешеной забавы,
И будит лай собак уснувшие дубравы.

Your beauty, your sufferings have vanished in the grave. But the sweet kiss of our meeting – I wait for it; you owe it to me.

Autumn

A Fragment

What does not enter then my drowsy mind? *Derzhavin*

I

OCTOBER has come. The grove is already shaking the last leaves from its naked branches. The autumn cold has breathed, the road is becoming frozen; the stream still runs, babbling, beyond the mill, but ice has already formed on the pond; my neighbour with his pack makes in haste for the hunting-fields, the winter crops suffer from the furious sport, and the hounds' baying rouses the sleeping woods.

2

Теперь моя пора: я не люблю весны;
Скучна мне оттепель; вонь, грязь – весной я
                                        болен
Кровь бродит; чувства, ум тоскою стеснены.
Суровою зимой я более доволен,
Люблю её снега; в присутствии луны
Как лёгкий бег саней с подругой быстр и волен,
Когда под соболем, согрета и свежа,
Она вам руку жмёт, пылая и дрожа!

3

Как весело, обув железом острым ноги,
Скользить по зеркалу стоячих, ровных рек!
А зимних праздников блестящие тревоги?...
Но надо знать и честь; полгода снег да снег,
Ведь это наконец и жителю берлоги,
Медведю надоест. Нельзя же целый век
Кататься нам в санях с Армидами младыми
Иль киснуть у печей за стёклами двойными.

2

This is my season: spring I do not like; thaw I find a nuisance – the smell, the slush – spring makes me ill: my blood is in ferment, my feelings and my mind are hampered by longing. I like stern winter better, I love her snows; how smoothly, rapidly, and freely the sleigh glides in the moonlight when you are with a friend and when, warm and fresh beneath her sable fur, flushed and trembling, she squeezes your hand.

3

What fun it is to glide, shod with sharp steel, over the glassy and even face of still rivers! And what of the glittering stir of winter festivals?... But there is a limit: snow for half the year at a stretch – even the bear, dwelling in its lair, will have had enough of it in the end. You cannot for ever go sleigh-riding with young Armidas,* or sit moping by the stove behind double windows.

* Armida is a beautiful sorceress in Tasso's *Jerusalem Delivered*.

4

Ох, лето красное! любил бы я тебя,
Когда б не зной, да пыль, да комары, да мухи.
Ты, все душевные способности губя,
Нас мучишь; как поля, мы страждем от засухи;
Лишь как бы напоить да освежить себя –
Иной в нас мысли нет, и жаль зимы старухи,
И, проводив её блинами и вином,
Поминки ей творим мороженым и льдом.

5

Дни поздней осени бранят обыкновенно,
Но мне она мила, читатель дорогой,
Красою тихою, блистающей смиренно.
Так нелюбимое дитя в семье родной
К себе меня влечет. Сказать вам откровенно,
Из годовых времён я рад лишь ей одной.
В ней много доброго; любовник не тщеславный,
Я нечто в ней нашёл мечтою своенравной.

4

Oh, fair summer! I would be fond of you, were it not for the heat, the dust, the mosquitoes, and the flies. You torment us by sapping all our mental faculties; like the fields, we suffer from drought; we think of nothing except of drinking and refreshing ourselves – and we regret old Dame Winter. And, after bidding her farewell with pancakes and wine, we now commemorate her with ice-cream and ice.

5

The days of late autumn are abused as a rule, but I, dear reader, love this season for its quiet beauty and its humble glow. She attracts me like a child unloved in its own family. Of all the seasons of the year, to tell you the truth, I welcome her alone. There is much in her that's good, and I, who am not a vainglorious lover, have found in my whimsical fancy something special in her.

6

Как это объяснить? Мне нравится она,
Как, вероятно, вам чахоточная дева
Порою нравится. На смерть осуждена,
Бедняжка клонится без ропота, без гнева.
Улыбка на устах увянувших видна;
Могильной пропасти она не слышит зева;
Играет на лице ещё багровый цвет.
Она жива ещё сегодня, завтра нет.

7

Унылая пора! очей очарованье,
Приятна мне твоя прощальная краса —
Люблю я пышное природы увяданье,
В багрец и в золото одетые леса,
В их сенях ветра шум и свежее дыханье,
И мглой волнистою покрыты небеса,
И редкий солнца луч, и первые морозы,
И отдалённые седой зимы угрозы.

6

How can I explain this? She pleases me as you, perhaps, have sometimes taken a fancy to a consumptive girl. Condemned to death, the poor creature droops, uncomplaining, without resentment; a smile is seen on her faded lips; she does not notice the grave's yawning abyss. A crimson hue still plays on her face. She is alive today – tomorrow she is gone.

7

O mournful season! How enchanting to the eye! Your beauty with its message of farewell delights me: I love nature's sumptuous fading, the woods clothed in purple and gold, the noise of the wind and the fresh breeze in the tree-tops, the skies covered with rolling mist, the infrequent sun-ray, the first frost, and the distant threats of hoary winter.

8

И с каждой осенью я расцветаю вновь;
Здоровью моему полезен русский холод;
К привычкам бытия вновь чувствую любовь:
Чредой слетает сон, чредой находит голод;
Легко и радостно играет в сердце кровь,
Желания кипят – я снова счастлив, молод,
Я снова жизни полн – таков мой организм
(Извольте мне простить ненужный прозаизм).

9

Ведут ко мне коня; в раздолии открытом,
Махая гривою, он всадника несёт,
И звонко под его блистающим копытом
Звенит промёрзлый дол, и трескается лёд.
Но гаснет краткий день, и в камельке забытом
Огонь опять горит – то яркий свет лиёт,
То тлеет медленно – а я пред ним читаю,
Иль думы долгие в душе моей питаю.

8

Every autumn I blossom anew; the Russian cold is good for my health; once more I relish the everyday habits of life. Sleep comes at its proper time, and so does hunger; my heart beats lightly and joyfully, desires seethe, and once again I am happy, young, and full of life – such is my organism (if you will, please, excuse this unnecessarily prosaic term).

9

They bring me a horse; shaking its mane, it carries its rider through the wide open spaces, the frozen valley echoes to the resonant clatter of its sparkling hooves, and the ice cracks. But the short day fades away, and the fire burns again in the forgotten fire-place, now flaring up brightly, now slowly smouldering; in front of it I read, or else cherish lingering thoughts.

10

И забываю мир, – и в сладкой тишине
Я сладко усыплён моим воображеньем,
И пробуждается поэзия во мне:
Душа стесняется лирическим волненьем,
Трепещет и звучит, и ищет, как во сне,
Излиться наконец свободным проявленьем –
И тут ко мне идёт незримый рой гостей,
Знакомцы давние, плоды мечты моей.

11

И мысли в голове волнуются в отваге,
И рифмы лёгкие навстречу им бегут,
И пальцы просятся к перу, перо к бумаге,
Минута – и стихи свободно потекут.
Так дремлет недвижим корабль в недвижной
влаге,
Но чу – матросы вдруг кидаются, ползут
Вверх, вниз – и паруса надулись, ветра полны,
Громада двинулась и рассекает волны.

10

And I forget the world, and in the sweet silence am sweetly lulled
by my imagination; and poetry awakens within me; my soul is
gripped by lyric excitement, it trembles and resounds, and, as in a
dream, seeks release at last in free expression; and now an invisible
throng of guests comes towards me – old acquaintances, creatures
of my fancy.

11

And thoughts seethe fearlessly in my mind, airy rhymes run
forth to meet them, fingers cry out for a pen, the pen – for paper;
one minute more, and verses will freely flow. So a ship slumbers
motionless in still waters, but hark: suddenly all hands leap forward, they crawl up and down the masts, the sails are filled, they
belly in the wind – the monster moves and cleaves the waves.

12

Плывёт. Куда ж нам плыть ? . . .

[*Вступление к «Медному Всаднику»*]

На берегу пустынных волн
Стоял *он*, дум великих полн,
И вдаль глядел. Пред ним широко
Река неслася; бедный чёлн
По ней стремился одиноко.
По мшистым, топким берегам
Чернели избы здесь и там,
Приют убогого чухонца;
И лес, неведомый лучам
В тумане спрятанного солнца,
Кругом шумел.
                И думал он:
«Отсель грозить мы будем шведу.
Здесь будет город заложён
На зло надменному соседу.
Природой здесь нам суждено

12

It sails. Where then shall we sail ? . . .

[*Prologue to 'The Bronze Horseman'*]

ON a deserted, wave-swept shore, *he** stood, filled with lofty thoughts, and gazed into the distance. Before him the river sped on its wide course; a humble, lonely skiff moved fast on its surface. On the mossy and swampy banks black huts were dotted here and there – the homes of miserable Finns; and the forest, impenetrable to the rays of the sun shrouded in mist, murmured all around.

And thus he thought: 'From here we shall threaten the Swede; here a city shall be founded, to spite our arrogant neighbour. Here we are destined by Nature . . . . . .

* Peter the Great.

В Европу прорубить окно,
Ногою твёрдой стать при море.
Сюда по новым им волнам
Все флаги в гости будут к нам,
И запируем на просторе».

Прошло сто лет, и юный град,
Полнощных стран краса и диво,
Из тьмы лесов, из топи блат
Вознёсся пышно, горделиво;
Где прежде финский рыболов,
Печальный пасынок природы,
Один у низких берегов
Бросал в неведомые воды
Свой ветхий невод, ныне там
По оживлённым берегам
Громады стройные теснятся
Дворцов и башен; корабли
Толпой со всех концов земли
К богатым пристаням стремятся;
В гранит оделася Нева;
Мосты повисли над водами;
Темнозелёными садами
Её покрылись острова,

to cut a window into Europe; and to gain a firm foothold by the sea. Here, over waters new to them, ships of every flag will come to visit us, and we shall make merry on the open seas.'

A hundred years passed, and the young city, the ornament and marvel of the northern climes, rose, resplendent and stately, from the dark forests and the swamps. Where once the Finnish fisherman, Nature's wretched stepson, alone on the low-lying banks, cast his ancient net into unknown waters, now along the banks astir with life tall and graceful palaces and towers cluster; ships from all the ends of the earth hasten in throngs to the rich quays; the Neva has clothed herself in granite; bridges hang above the waters; her islands have become covered with dark-green gardens; . . .

И перед младшею столицей
Померкла старая Москва,
Как перед новою царицей
Порфироносная вдова.

Люблю тебя, Петра творенье,
Люблю твой строгий, стройный вид,
Невы державное теченье,
Береговой её гранит,
Твоих оград узор чугунный,
Твоих задумчивых ночей
Прозрачный сумрак, блеск безлунный,
Когда я в комнате моей
Пишу, читаю без лампады,
И ясны спящие громады
Пустынных улиц, и светла
Адмиралтейская игла,
И, не пуская тьму ночную
На золотые небеса,
Одна заря сменить другую
Спешит, дав ночи полчаса.
Люблю зимы твоей жестокой
Недвижный воздух и мороз,
Бег санок вдоль Невы широкой,

and old Moscow has paled before the younger capital, like a
dowager clad in purple before a new empress.
    I love you, Peter's creation, I love your severe, graceful appear-
ance, the Neva's majestic current, the granite of her banks, the
tracery of your cast-iron railings, the transparent twilight, the
moonless gleam of your still nights, when I write and read in my
room without a lamp, and the huge sleeping buildings in the
deserted streets are clearly seen, the Admiralty spire is bright, and
dawn hastens to succeed sunset, not letting the night's darkness
rise to the golden heavens and leaving a bare half-hour for the
night. I love the still air and the frost of your severe winter, the
sleighs racing on the banks of the wide Neva, . . .

Девичьи лица ярче роз,
И блеск, и шум, и говор балов,
А в час пирушки холостой
Шипенье пенистых бокалов
И пунша пламень голубой.
Люблю воинственную живость
Потешных Марсовых полей,
Пехотных ратей и коней
Однообразную красивость,
В их стройно зыблемом строю
Лоскутья сих знамён победных,
Сиянье шапок этих медных,
Насквозь простреленных в бою.
Люблю, военная столица,
Твоей твердыни дым и гром,
Когда полнощная царица
Дарует сына в царский дом,
Или победу над врагом
Россия снова торжествует,
Или, взломав свой синий лёд,
Нева к морям его несёт
И, чуя вешни дни, ликует.

the girls' faces brighter than roses, the sparkle, the noise, and the murmur of voices at the balls, and, at the hour of the bachelors' feasting, the hissing of the foaming wine-glasses and the blue flame of the punch. I love the warlike animation of the playing-fields of Mars, the uniform beauty of the troops of foot and horse, and, in their ranks swaying in ordered rhythm, those tattered flags of victory, the glitter of those bronze helmets, shot through in battle. I love, O warlike capital, the smoke and the booming gun of your fortress, when the northern empress presents a son to the imperial house, or when Russia celebrates another victory over an enemy, or when the Neva, breaking up her blue ice, carries it to the sea and exults, scenting the days of spring.

Красуйся, град Петров, и стой
Неколебимо, как Россия!
Да умирится же с тобой
И побеждённая стихия;
Вражду и плен старинный свой
Пусть волны финские забудут
И тщетной злобою не будут
Тревожить вечный сон Петра!

*

Пора, мой друг, пора! покоя сердце просит –
Летят за днями дни, и каждый час уносит
Частичку бытия, а мы с тобой вдвоём
Предполагаем жить ... И глядь – как раз –
                                умрём.
На свете счастья нет, но есть покой и воля.
Давно завидная мечтается мне доля –
Давно, усталый раб, замыслил я побег
В обитель дальнюю трудов и чистых нег.

City of Peter, stand in all your splendour, stand unshakeable as Russia! May the conquered elements, too, make their peace with you; let the Finnish waves forget their ancient enmity and bondage, and not disturb with their vain rancour Peter's everlasting sleep!

*

Iᴛ's time, my dear, it's time! The heart begs for peace; the days fly past, and every hour carries off a fragment of life: and you and I make plans together to live, yet suddenly we shall die. There is no happiness in the world, but there is peace and freedom. I have long been dreaming of an enviable fate: long have I, a weary slave, planned to flee to a distant home of work and pure delight.

EVGENY BARATYNSKY

Две доли

Дало две доли Провидение
  На выбор мудрости людской:
Или надежду и волнение,
  Иль безнадежность и покой.

Верь тот надежде обольщающей,
  Кто бодр неопытным умом,
Лишь по молве разновещающей
  С судьбой насмешливой знаком

Надейтесь, юноши кипящие!
  Летите, крылья вам даны;
Для вас и замыслы блестящие
  И сердца пламенные сны!

Но вы, судьбину испытавшие,
  Тщету утех, печали власть,
Вы, знанье бытия приявшие
  Себе на тягостную часть!

Two Fates

PROVIDENCE has given human wisdom the choice between two fates: either hope and agitation, or hopelessness and calm.

Let him put his trust in seductive hope who is confident because he is inexperienced in mind and who is acquainted with mocking fate only through many-voiced rumour.

Have hope, ardent young men! Fly – wings are given to you: for you the brilliant projects and the heart's fiery dreams!

But you who have experienced human fate, the vanity of pleasures, and the power of grief, you who have gained knowledge of life at the price of suffering –

Гоните прочь их рой прельстительный;
Так! доживайте жизнь в тиши
И берегите хлад спасительный
Своей бездейственной души.

Своим бесчувствием блаженные,
Как трупы мёртвых из гробов,
Волхва словами пробужденные,
Встают со скрежетом зубов, –

Так вы, согрев в душе желания,
Безумно вдавшись в их обман,
Проснётесь только для страдания,
Для боли новой прежних ран.

Любовь

Мы пьём в любви отраву сладкую;
Но всё отраву пьём мы в ней,
И платим мы за радость краткую
Ей безвесельем долгих дней.
Огонь любви – огонь живительный,
Все говорят; но что мы зрим?
Опустошает, разрушительный,
Он душу, объятую им!

Drive away their tempting swarm. Yes, live the rest of your days in quiet, and guard the salutary coldness of your inert soul.

As the corpses of the dead, blessed in their insensibility, are awakened by the words of a wizard and rise from their graves, gnashing their teeth,

so you, if you kindle desires in your soul and foolishly surrender to their deception, will awake only to suffer, only to endure fresh pain from your old wounds.

Love

WE drink sweet poison in love; but still, it is poison we drink in it, and for a brief joy we pay with the unhappiness of many days. The fire of love is a life-giving fire, so everyone says; but what do we see? Destructive, it lays waste the soul which it embraces!

Кто заглушит воспоминания
О днях блаженства и страдания,
  О чудных днях твоих, любовь?
Тогда я ожил бы для радости,
Для снов златых цветущей младости
  Тебе открыл бы душу вновь.

Подражателям

Когда, печалью вдохновенный,
Певец печаль свою поёт,
Скажите: отзыв умиленный
В каком он сердце не найдёт?
Кто, вековых проклятий жаден,
Дерзнёт осмеивать её?
Но для притворства всякий хладен,
Плач подражательный досаден,
Смешно жеманное вытьё!
Не напряжённого мечтанья
Огнём услужливым согрет —
Постигнул таинства страданья
Душемутительный поэт.

O love, who will stifle the memories of days of bliss and suffering, of your wonderful days? Then I would come to life to taste of joy, and once again I would open my soul to you, that I might dream the golden dreams of youth in bloom.

To Imitators

WHEN, by sorrow inspired, the poet sings of his own sorrow, tell me – whose is the heart that will not be moved by and respond to him? Who would wish to incur perpetual execration by daring to scoff at his sorrow? But pretence leaves everyone cold, imitated tears are irksome, affected wailing is absurd! But the poet who stirs the soul and is not warmed by some complaisant flame kindled by laboured musings, has understood the mystery of suffering. . .

В борьбе с тяжёлою судьбою
Познал он меру вышних сил,
Сердечных судорог ценою
Он выражснье их купил.
И вот нетленными лучами
Лик песнопевца окружён,
И чтим земными племенами,
Подобно мученику, он.
А ваша муза площадная,
Тоской заёмною мечтая
Родить участие в сердцах,
Подобна нищей развращённой,
Молящей лепты незаконной
С чужим ребёнком на руках.

Муза

Не ослеплён я музою моею:
Красавицей её не назовут,
И юноши, узрев её, за нею
Влюблённою толпой не побегут.
Приманивать изысканным убором,
Игрою глаз, блестящим разговором
Ни склонности у ней, ни дара нет;

In his struggle with cruel fate he has taken the measure of the heavenly powers, and learnt to give them expression, at the price of an anguished heart. And now the poet's countenance is encircled by rays of unfading light, and he is honoured as a martyr by the nations of the earth. But your meretricious Muse, which aspires to rouse sympathy in men's hearts by her borrowed melancholy, is like a depraved beggar-woman who craves an illicit penny with someone else's child in her arms.

The Muse

I AM not blinded by my Muse: she will not be called a beauty; and, on seeing her, young men will not run after her in an enamoured throng. She has neither the wish nor the ability to seduce by elegant attire, by the play of her eyes, or by brilliant conversation; . . . . . .

Но поражён бывает мельком свет
Её лица необщим выраженьем,
Её речей спокойной простотой;
И он, скорей чем едким осужденьем,
Её почтит небрежной похвалой.

*

Болящий дух врачует песнопенье.
Гармонии таинственная власть
Тяжёлое искупит заблужденье
И укротит бунтующую страсть.
Душа певца, согласно излитая,
Разрешена от всех своих скорбей;
И чистоту поэзия святая
И мир отдаст причастнице своей.

*

На что вы, дни! Юдольный мир явленья
Свои не изменит!
Все ведомы, и только повторенья
Грядущее сулит.

but at times the world is struck for a moment by the singular expression of her face, by the quiet simplicity of her speech; and, rather than pass biting censure on her, it will honour her with perfunctory praise.

*

POETRY heals an ailing spirit. The mysterious power of harmony will redeem a grievous fault and curb rebellious passion. The poet's soul, poured out in harmony, is delivered from all its sorrows; and holy poetry will give back purity and peace to the soul that communes with it.

*

OF what use are you, days? The earthly world will not change its phenomena: all of them are known, and the future promises only recurrence.

Недаром ты металась и кипела,
　　Развитием спеша,
Свой подвиг ты свершила прежде тела,
　　Безумная душа!

И, тесный круг подлунных впечатлений
　　Сомкнувшая давно,
Под веяньем возвратных сновидений
　　Ты дремлешь; а оно

Бессмысленно глядит, как утро встанет,
　　Без нужды ночь сменя,
Как в мрак ночной бесплодный вечер
　　　　　　　　　　　　　канет,
　　Венец пустого дня!

Скульптор

Глубокий взор вперив на камень,
Художник нимфу в нём прозрел,
И пробежал по жилам пламень,
И к ней он сердцем полетел.

Not in vain did you toss and seethe as you hastened to grow: you have achieved your lofty purpose in advance of the body, O my frenzied soul!

Having long ago closed the narrow circuit of the world's impressions, you drowse under the breath of recurrent dreams; while the body

watches with vacant gaze the dawn of day aimlessly supplanting the night, and the fruitless evening sinking into nocturnal darkness – the crown of an empty day!

The Sculptor

FIXING a penetrating gaze upon the stone, the artist divined a nymph in it, and fire ran through his veins, and in his heart he flew towards her.

Но, бесконечно вожделенный,
Уже он властвует собой:
Неторопливый, постепенный
Резец с богини сокровенной
Кору снимает за корой.

В заботе сладостно-туманной
Не час, не день, не год уйдёт,
А с предугаданной, с желанной
Покров последний не падёт,

Покуда, страсть уразумея
Под лаской вкрадчивой резца,
Ответным взором Галатея
Не увлечёт, желаньем рдея,
К победе неги мудреца.

*

Люблю я вас, богини пенья,
Но ваш чарующий наход,
Сей сладкий трепет вдохновенья, –
Предтечей жизненных невзгод.

But, though full of boundless desire, he is already master of himself: unhurriedly, gradually, the chisel removes layer after layer
from the hidden goddess.

In the sweet and vague preoccupation more than an hour, or a
day, or a year will pass; but the last veil will not fall from her whom
he has divined and desired,

until, perceiving his passion under the chisel's insinuating caress,
Galatea, glowing with desire, carries the sage away by her answer-
ing gaze to a triumphant rapture.

*

I LOVE you, goddesses of song; but your enchanting onslaught,
that exquisite tremor of inspiration, is a harbinger of life's misfortunes.

Любовь камен с враждой Фортуны –
Одно. Молчу! Боюся я,
Чтоб персты, падшие на струны,
Не пробудили вновь перуны,
В которых спит судьба моя.

И отрываюсь, полный муки,
От музы, ласковой ко мне.
И говорю: до завтра, звуки,
Пусть день угаснет в тишине.

The love of the Muses and the enmity of Fortune are one. I hold
my peace, I am afraid that my fingers, plucking the strings, might
awaken again the disasters in which my fate lies asleep.

And, filled with torment, I tear myself away from the Muse who
favours me. And I say: 'Till tomorrow, sounds. Let the day die
away in silence.'

NIKOLAY YAZYKOV

Элегия

Блажен, кто мог на ложе ночи
Тебя руками обогнуть:
Челом в чело, очами в очи,
Уста в уста и грудь на грудь!
Кто соблазнительный твой лепет
Лобзаньем пылким прерывал
И смуглых персей дикий трепет
То усыплял, то пробуждал!..
Но тот блаженней, дева ночи,
Кто в упоении любви
Глядит на огненные очи,
На брови дивные твои,
На свежесть уст твоих пурпурных,
На черноту младых кудрей,
Забыв и жар восторгов бурных
И силы юности своей!

Elegy

BLESSED is he who has been able to clasp you in his arms upon a
bed at night, with brow on brow, eyes on eyes, lips on lips and
breast on breast; who interrupted your seductive murmur with a
passionate kiss, and now lulled, now aroused the wild trembling of
your dark breasts. But more blessed is he, O maiden of night, who
in the ecstasy of love gazes into your fiery eyes, at your marvellous
eyebrows, at the freshness of your scarlet lips, at your black youthful curls, having forgotten the heat of stormy raptures and the
strength of his youth!

NIKOLAY YAZYKOV

К Рейну

Я видел, как бегут твои зелёны волны:
    Они при вешнем свете дня,
Играя и шумя, летучим блеском полны,
    Качали ласково меня;
Я видел яркие, роскошные картины:
    Твои изгибы, твой простор,
Твои весёлые каштаны, и раины,
    И виноград по склонам гор,
И горы, и на них высокие могилы
    Твоих былых богатырей,
Могилы рыцарства и доблести и силы
    Давно, давно минувших дней!
Я волжанин: тебе приветы Волги нашей
    Принёс я. Слышал ты об ней?
Велик, прекрасен ты! Но Волга больше, краше,
    Великолепнее, пышней,
И глубже, быстрая, и шире, голубая!
    Не так, не так она бурлит,
Когда поднимется погодка верховая
    И белый вал заговорит!

To the Rhine

I SAW your green waters flowing; in the light of a spring day,
sparkling and splashing, full of flying brilliance, they rocked me
lovingly; I saw vivid and splendid scenery: your bends, your broad
expanse, your gay chestnut-trees and poplars, the vines on the hill-
sides, the hills, surmounted with the lofty tombs of your past
heroes – sepulchres of knighthood, of valour and power of long,
long ago! I am from the Volga country: I bring you greetings from
our Volga. Have you heard of her? You are great and beautiful; but
the Volga is larger, fairer, grander, and more magnificent; her fast-
flowing waters are deeper, her pale blue stream is wider. Not like
you does she surge when a storm comes blowing from upstream and
the white waves begin to speak! . . . . . .

А какова она, шумящих волн громада,
  Весной, как с выси берегов
Через её разлив не перекинешь взгляда,
  Чрез море вод и островов!
По царству и река! . . Тебе привет заздравный
  Её, властительницы вод,
Обширных русских вод, простершей ход свой
                                     славный,
  Всегда торжественный свой ход,
Между холмов, и гор, и долов многоплодных
  До тёмных Каспия зыбей!
Приветы и её притоков благородных,
  Её подручниц и князей:
Тверцы, которая безбурными струями
  Лелеет тысячи судов,
Идущих пёстрыми, красивыми толпами
  Под звучным пением пловцов;
Тебе привет Оки поёмистой, дубравной,
  В раздолье муромских песков
Текущей царственно, блистательно и плавно,
  В виду почтенных берегов, –
И храмы древние с лучистыми главами

And how splendid is the mass of her noisy waters in spring, when,
as you look from the top of her bank, your eye cannot reach to the
far side of her flooded course, across a sea of water and islands!
As the Empire – so the river! Greetings and good wishes to you
from her, the sovereign of the vast Russian waters, who wends
her glorious and always majestic way between hills and mountains
and fertile valleys to the dark waters of the Caspian! Greetings,
too, from her noble tributaries, her vassals and attendant princes:
from the Tvertsa, who on her stormless waters gently rocks
thousands of boats which sail along in variegated and graceful
throngs to the sailors' resonant singing; greetings to you from the
Oka whose spates are far-flung and whose banks are wooded, and
who flows smoothly, regal and resplendent, amid the wide expanse
of Murom sands, in sight of her honoured banks where ancient
churches with shining cupolas . . . . . .

Глядятся в ясны глубины,
И тихий благовест несётся над водами,
Заветный голос старины!
Суры – красавицы, задумчиво бродящей,
То в густоту своих лесов
Скрывающей себя, то на полях блестящей
Под опахалом парусов;
Свияги пажитной, игривой и бессонной,
Среди хозяйственных забот,
Любящей стук колёс, и плеск неугомонный,
И гул работающих вод;
Тебе привет из стран Биармии далёкой,
Привет царицы хладных рек,
Той Камы сумрачной, широкой и глубокой,
Чей сильный, бурный водобег,
Под кликами орлов свои валы седые
Катя в кремнистых берегах,
Несёт железо, лес и горы соляные
На исполинских ладиях;
Привет Самары, чьё течение живое
Не слышно в говоре гостей,
Ссыпающих в суда богатство полевое,
Пшеницу – золото полей;

watch their reflection in the clear and deep river, and the soft peal
of bells, the cherished voice of olden times, drifts over the waters;
from the Sura, that beauty who wanders pensively, now hiding in
her dense forests, now sparkling in the plains beneath fan-like sails;
from the Sviyaga, flanked with lush grass-lands, playful and sleepless, immersed in the cares of husbandry, delighting in the clank of
wheels, in the ceaseless splashing and hum of waters at work;
greetings to you from the land of distant Biarmiya, greetings from
the queen of cold rivers, that sombre, wide, and deep Kama whose
current, impetuous and violent, rolls its white-flecked waves
between stony banks to the cries of eagles, and carries iron, timber,
and mountains of salt in gigantic boats; greetings from the
Samara, whose lively current cannot be heard for the voices of
merchants who load the ships with the wealth of the plains – with
wheat, the gold of the plains; . . . . . .

Привет проворного, лихого Черемшана,
    И двух Иргизов луговых,
И тихоструйного, привольного Сызрана,
    И всех, и бо́льших и меньши́х,
Несметных данников и данниц величавой,
    Державной северной реки,
Приветы я принёс тебе! . . . Теки со славой,
    Князь многих рек, светло теки!
Блистай, красуйся, Рейн! Да ни грозы военной,
    Ни песен радостных врага
Не слышишь вечно ты; да мир благословен-
                                      ный
    Твои покоит берега!
Да сладостно, на них мечтая и гуляя,
    В тени раскидистых ветвей,
Целуются любовь и юность удалая
    При звоне синих хрусталей!

greetings from the swift and hasty Cheremshan, and from the two
Irgiz flanked with meadows, and from the slow-flowing, free
Syzran'; and from all the countless tributary subjects, great and
small, male and female, of the stately, imperial northern river I
bring you greetings! Flow with glory, prince of many rivers, flow
with limpid waters! Shine in all your beauty, O Rhine! May you
never hear the thunder of war nor the joyful songs of an enemy;
may blessed peace preserve the quiet of your shores — so that love
and daring youth, walking and day-dreaming on your banks, may
exchange sweet kisses in the shade of spreading branches, to the
tinkle of blue crystal glasses!

FEDOR TYUTCHEV

Видение

Есть некий час, в ночи, всемирного молчанья,
И в оный час явлений и чудес
Живая колесница мирозданья
Открыто катится в святилище небес.

Тогда густеет ночь, как хаос на водах;
Беспамятство, как Атлас, давит сушу;
Лишь Музы девственную душу
В пророческих тревожат боги снах!

Весенняя гроза

Люблю грозу в начале мая,
Когда весенний, первый гром,
Как бы резвяся и играя,
Грохочет в небе голубом.

Гремят раскаты молодые,
Вот дождик брызнул, пыль летит,
Повисли перлы дождевые,
И солнце нити золотит.

A Vision

THERE is an hour in the night when the whole world is silent, and in that hour of visions and marvels the living chariot of the universe openly rolls through the sanctuary of heaven.

The night thickens then, like Chaos upon the waters; oblivion, like Atlas, grips the earth; and only the Muse's virgin soul is, in prophetic dreams, troubled by the gods.

A Spring Thunder-storm

I LOVE a thunder-storm at the beginning of May, when spring's first thunder, as though at play, in a frolic, rumbles in the blue sky.

The young peals of thunder rattle. Now it is drizzling, dust is flying, pearls of rain are hanging, and the sun is gilding the threads.

С горы бежит поток проворный,
В лесу не молкнет птичий гам,
И гам лесной и шум нагорный –
Всё вторит весело громам.

Ты скажешь: ветреная Геба,
Кормя Зевесова орла,
Громокипящий кубок с неба,
Смеясь, на землю пролила.

Сон на море

И море и буря качали наш чёлн;
Я, сонный, был предан всей прихоти волн.
Две беспредельности были во мне,
И мной своевольно играли оне.
Вкруг меня, как кимвалы, звучали скалы,
Окликалися ветры и пели валы.
Я в хаосе звуков лежал оглушён,
Но над хаосом звуков носился мой сон.
Болезненно-яркий, волшебно-немой,
Он веял легко над гремящею тьмой.

A swift torrent rushes down the hill, the birds' clamour in the wood does not cease; the clamour in the wood and the noise on the hillside all gaily echo the thunder-claps.

You will say inconstant Hebe, while feeding Zeus's eagle, laughing, emptied a cup seething with thunder from heaven on to the earth.

A Dream at Sea

THE sea and the storm rocked our boat; I was asleep, abandoned to the whim of the waves; within me there were two infinities, of which I was the plaything. Round me the rocks clanged like cymbals, the winds called out to each other and the waves sang. Deafened, I lay in the chaos of sounds, but my dream coursed above it. Painfully vivid, magically mute, it floated lightly over the

В лучах огневицы развил он свой мир –
Земля зеленела, светился эфир,
Сады-лавиринфы, чертоги, столпы,
И сонмы кипели безмолвной толпы.
Я много узнал мне неведомых лиц,
Зрел тварей волшебных, таинственных птиц,
По высям творенья, как бог, я шагал,
И мир подо мною недвижный сиял.
Но все грёзы насквозь, как волшебника вой,
Мне слышался грохот пучины морской,
И в тихую область видений и снов
Врывалася пена ревущих валов.

Цицерон

Оратор римский говорил
Средь бурь гражданских и тревоги:
«Я поздно встал – и на дороге
Застигнут ночью Рима был!»
Так! но, прощаясь с римской славой,
С Капитолийской высоты
Во всём величье видел ты
Закат звезды её кровавой!..

thundering darkness./ In fever-hot rays it unfolded its world, the earth was green, the ether shone, and also gardens, labyrinths, palaces, pillars, and a silent multitude thronged and seethed. I knew many faces unknown to me, I saw magic creatures, mysterious birds; I strode like a god over the summits of creation, and beneath me the world shone, motionless. Through all these visions I heard the thunder of the deep, like some magician's howl, and into the quiet realm of visions and dreams burst the foam of the roaring waves.

Cicero

THE Roman orator spoke in the midst of civic turmoil and alarm: 'I was late in rising and was overtaken on the way by the night of Rome!' Yes, but, as you bade farewell to Rome's glory, you saw from the Capitoline Hill its bloody star set in all its grandeur. . .

Счастлив, кто посетил сей мир
В его минуты роковые –
Его призвали всеблагие,
Как собеседника на пир;
Он их высоких зрелищ зритель,
Он в их совет допущен был,
И заживо, как небожитель,
Из чаши их бессмертье пил!

Silentium

Молчи, скрывайся и таи
И чувства и мечты свои –
Пускай в душевной глубине
Встают и заходят оне
Безмолвно, как звёзды в ночи, –
Любуйся ими – и молчи.

Как сердцу высказать себя?
Другому как понять тебя?
Поймёт ли он, чем ты живёшь?

Blessed is he who has visited this world at its moments of
destiny: the beneficent gods have bidden him to a feast, to hold
converse with them. He is a spectator of their exalted pageants, he
has been admitted to their council, and, while still alive, he has
drunk of immortality from their cup, as though he were a dweller
in heaven.

Silentium

Be silent, hide yourself, and conceal your feelings and your dreams.
Let them rise and set in the depths of your soul, silently, like stars
in the night; contemplate them with admiration, and be silent.
How will the heart express itself? How will another understand
you? Will he understand what it is that you live by? . . . .

FEDOR TYUTCHEV

Мысль изреченная есть ложь;
Взрывая, возмутишь ключи, –
Питайся ими – и молчи.

Лишь жить в самом себе умей –
Есть целый мир в душе твоей
Таинственно-волшебных дум;
Их оглушит наружный шум,
Дневные разгонят лучи, –
Внимай их пенью – и молчи!..

★

О чём ты воешь, ветр ночной?
О чём так сетуешь безумно?..
Что значит странный голос твой,
То глухо жалобный, то шумный?
Понятным сердцу языком
Твердишь о непонятной муке –
И роешь и взрываешь в нём
Порой неистовые звуки!...

О, страшных песен сих не пой
Про древний хаос, про родимый!

A thought that is spoken is a falsehood; by stirring up the springs you will cloud them: drink of them, and be silent.

Know how to live within yourself: there is in your soul a whole world of mysterious and enchanted thoughts; they will be drowned by the noise without; daylight will drive them away: listen to their singing, and be silent.

★

WHAT are you wailing about, night wind, what are you lamenting so frantically? What does your strange voice, now muffled and plaintive, now loud, signify? In a language intelligible to the heart you speak of torment past comprehension, and you dig and at times stir up frenzied sounds in the heart!

Oh, do not sing these fearful songs about ancient, native Chaos!

133

Как жадно мир души ночной
Внимает повести любимой!
Из смертной рвётся он груди,
Он с беспредельным жаждет слиться ...
О, бурь заснувших не буди —
Под ними хаос шевелится! ...

*

Люблю глаза твои, мой друг,
С игрой их пламенно-чудесной,
Когда их приподымешь вдруг
И словно молнией небесной
Окинешь бегло целый круг ...

Но есть сильней очарованья:
Глаза потупленные ниц,
В минуты страстного лобзанья,
И сквозь опущенных ресниц
Угрюмый, тусклый огнь желанья ...

How avidly the world of night within the soul listens to the loved story! It longs to burst out of the mortal breast and to merge with the Unbounded. .. Oh, do not wake the sleeping tempests: beneath them Chaos stirs.

*

My dearest, I love your eyes, with their fiery, wonderful play, when you suddenly raise them a little and, like lightning in the sky, cast a quick glance around you.

But there is a yet more powerful enchantment: your eyes, downcast during a passionate kiss, and, through your lowered eye-lashes, the sullen, smouldering flame of desire. ..

FEDOR TYUTCHEV

День и Ночь

На мир таинственный духов,
Над этой бездной безымянной,
Покров наброшен златотканный
Высокой волею богов.
День – сей блистательный покров –
День, земнородных оживленье,
Души болящей исцеленье,
Друг человеков и богов!

Но меркнет день – настала ночь;
Пришла – и с мира рокового
Ткань благодатную покрова
Сорвав, отбрасывает прочь . . .
И бездна нам обнажена
С своими страхами и мглами,
И нет преград меж ей и нами:
Вот отчего нам ночь страшна!

Предопределение

Любовь, любовь – гласит преданье –
Союз души с душой родной,
Их съединенье, сочетанье,

Day and Night

By the exalted will of the gods a gold-embroidered veil has been
thrown over the mysterious world of spirits, that nameless abyss.
This resplendent veil is Day: Day that quickens mortals and heals
the ailing soul, the friend of men and gods!

But Day fades away and Night falls; she comes and, tearing off
the blessed fabric of the veil from the fatal world, casts it aside . . .
And the abyss is exposed to our gaze, with its horrors and its darkness, and there is no barrier between it and us: that is why we are
frightened of Night!

Predestination

Love, love – tradition tells us – is the joining of a soul with a
kindred soul, their union, their conjunction, ...

135

И роковое их слиянье,
И . . . поединок роковой . . .

И чем одно из них нежнее
В борьбе неравной двух сердец,
Тем неизбежней и вернее,
Любя, страдая, грустно млея,
Оно изноет наконец . . .

★

Я очи знал – о, эти очи!
Как я любил их – знает Бог!
От их волшебной, страстной ночи
Я душу оторвать не мог.

В непостижимом этом взоре,
Жизнь обнажающем до дна,
Такое слышалося горе,
Такая страсти глубина!

Дышал он грустный, углублённый
В тени ресниц её густой,
Как наслажденье, утомлённый
И, как страданье, роковой.

their fateful fusion and . . . their fateful duel . . .

And whichever is the more tender in the unequal contest of two
hearts, will more inescapably and surely – loving, suffering,
languishing sadly – pine away at last . . .

★

I KNEW two eyes – oh, those eyes! How I loved them God knows.
I could not tear my soul away from their bewitching, passionate
night.

In this unfathomable gaze which laid bare the very foundations
of life, such sorrow, such depths of passion were apparent!

Sad and absorbed, it quivered in the dark shadow of her eye-
lashes, exhausted like sensuous enjoyment and, like suffering, fatal.

И в эти чудные мгновенья
Ни разу мне не довелось
С ним повстречаться без волненья
И любоваться им без слёз.

Последняя любовь

О, как на склоне наших лет
Нежней мы любим и суеверней . . .
Сияй, сияй, прощальный свет
Любви последней, зари вечерней!

Полнеба обхватила тень,
Лишь там, на западе, бродит сиянье, -
Помедли, помедли, вечерний день,
Продлись, продлись, очарованье.

Пускай скудеет в жилах кровь,
Но в сердце не скудеет нежность . . .
О ты, последняя любовь!
Ты и блаженство и безнадежность.

And in those marvellous moments never once did I encounter it without emotion, nor admire it without tears.

The Last Love

Oh, how much more fondly and superstitiously we love in our declining years . . . Shine, O shine, farewell light of the last love, light of sunset!

Shadow has covered half the sky; only there, in the west, there is a roving gleam; do not hasten, evening light, linger, linger, enchantment!

Though the blood runs thinner in the veins, yet tenderness does not wane in the heart . . . O last love, you are both bliss and desperation.

137

FEDOR TYUTCHEV

*

Эти бедные селенья,
Эта скудная природа –
Край родной долготерпенья,
Край ты русского народа!

Не поймёт и не заметит
Гордый взор иноплеменный,
Что сквозит и тайно светит
В наготе твоей смиренной.

Удручённый ношей крестной,
Всю тебя, земля родная,
В рабском виде Царь Небесный
Исходил, благословляя.

*

О вещая душа моя!
О сердце, полное тревоги,
О, как ты бьёшься на пороге
Как бы двойного бытия! . .

THESE poor villages, this humble landscape – native land of long-
suffering, land of the Russian people!

The foreigner's haughty glance will not understand or notice
that which shines dimly and mysteriously through your humble
nakedness.

Weighed down by the burden of the cross, the King of Heaven,
in the likeness of a servant, has walked up and down all of you, my
native land, blessing you.

*

O MY prophetic soul, O heart filled with disquiet, how you flutter
on the threshold, as it were, of two realities! . . .

Так, ты жилица двух миров,
Твой день – болезненный и страстный
Твой сон – пророчески-неясный,
Как откровение духов . . .

Пускай страдальческую грудь
Волнуют страсти роковые, –
Душа готова, как Мария,
К ногам Христа навек прильнуть.

*

Как хорошо ты, о море ночное, –
Здесь лучезарно, там сизо-темно . . .
В лунном сиянии, словно живое,
Ходит, и дышит, и блещет оно . . .

На бесконечном, на вольном просторе
Блеск и движение, грохот и гром . . .
Тусклым сияньем облитое море,
Как хорошо ты в безлюдье ночном!

Yes, you are a denizen of two worlds: your day is sorrowful and passionate, your sleep darkly prophetic, like a revelation of the spirit.

Though fatal passions disturb your suffering breast, the soul is ready, like Mary, to cling forever to Christ's feet.

*

How beautiful you are, O sea at night! Radiant here, grey-blue and dark there...It moves, and breathes, and glitters in the moonlight, as though it were a living creature.

On its boundless and free expanse there is brilliance and movement, roaring and thunder...O sea, bathed in dim radiance, how beautiful you are in the solitude of night!

FEDOR TYUTCHEV

Зыбь ты великая, зыбь ты морская,
Чей это праздник так празднуешь ты?
Волны несутся, гремя и сверкая,
Чуткие звёзды глядят с высоты.

В этом волнении, в этом сиянье,
Весь, как во сне, я потерян стою –
О, как охотно бы в их обаянье
Всю потопил бы я душу свою . . .

★

Est in arundineis modulatio musica ripis.
Ausonius

Певучесть есть в морских волнах,
Гармония в стихийных спорах,
И стройный мусикийский шорох
Струится в зыбких камышах.

Невозмутимый строй во всём,
Созвучье полное в природе, –
Лишь в нашей призрачной свободе
Разлад мы с нею сознаём.

O great surge, surge of the sea! Whose feast are you celebrating in this fashion? The waves roll on, thundering and sparkling; the stars look down attentively from on high . . .

I stand as in a dream, lost in this turmoil and radiance; oh, how gladly would I sink my entire soul in their enchantment!

★

There is a musical rhythm in the reeds that grow by the shore.
Ausonius

THERE is melody in the waves of the sea, harmony in the clash of the elements, and a harmonious musical rustle passes through the swaying reeds.

There is an untroubled harmony in everything, a full consonance in nature; only in our illusory freedom do we feel at variance with it.

Откуда, как разлад возник?
И отчего же в общем хоре
Душа не то поёт, что море,
И ропщет мыслящий тростник?

И от земли до крайних звезд
Всё безответен и поныне
Глас вопиющего в пустыне,
Души отчаянный протест?

Накануне годовщины 4-го августа 1864 г.

Вот бреду я вдоль большой дороги
В тихом свете гаснущего дня,
Тяжело мне, замирают ноги . . .
Друг мой милый, видишь ли меня?

Всё темней, темнее над землёю –
Улетел последний отблеск дня . . .
Вот тот мир, где жили мы с тобою,
Ангел мой, ты видишь ли меня?

Whence, and how, did this discord arise? And why, in the general chorus, is the soul out of tune with the sea, and why does the thinking reed complain?

And why, from the earth to the farthest stars, is there no answer even yet to the voice crying in the wilderness – the soul's despairing protest?

On the Eve of the Anniversary of 4 August 1864

I AM walking along the highway in the peaceful light of the fading day; my heart is heavy, my legs grow numb: my dearest, do you see me?

It grows darker and darker over the earth . . . The last gleam of daylight has flown . . . Here is the world where you and I lived together; my angel, do you see me?

FEDOR TYUTCHEV

Завтра день молитвы и печали,
Завтра память рокового дня . . .
Ангел мой, где б души ни витали,
Ангел мой, ты видишь ли меня?

Tomorrow is a day of prayer and sorrow, tomorrow is the anniversary of the fatal day. My angel, wherever souls may dwell – my angel, do you see me?

DMITRI VENEVITINOV

Три розы

В глухую степь земной дороги,
Эмблемой райской красоты,
Три розы бросили нам боги,
Эдема лучшие цветы.

Одна под небом Кашемира
Цветёт близ светлого ручья;
Она любовница Зефира
И вдохновенье соловья.
Ни день, ни ночь она не вянет;
И если кто её сорвёт,
Лишь только утра луч проглянет,
Свежее роза расцветёт.

Ещё прелестнее другая:
Она, румяною зарёй
На раннем небе расцветая,
Пленяет яркой красотой.
Свежей от этой розы веет,
И веселей её встречать.

Three Roses

INTO the desolate waste through which life's road passes the gods
have thrown to us, as an emblem of heavenly beauty, three roses,
the fairest flowers of Eden.

The first blossoms beneath the sky of Kashmir, beside a clear
stream; it is Zephyr's beloved, and the nightingale's inspiration.
Neither by day nor by night does it fade; and if anyone should
pluck it, the rose will blossom with a fresher flower as soon as the
sun's morning rays break through.

The second is more enchanting still: it blossoms in the early
morning sky at the flush of dawn and charms with its dazzling
beauty. A fresher scent breathes from this rose, and he who
encounters it feels greater joy. . . . . . .

На миг один она алеет,
Но с каждым днём цветёт опять.

Ещё свежей от третьей веет,
Хотя она не в небесах;
Её для жарких уст лелеет
Любовь на девственных щеках.
Но эта роза скоро вянет;
Она пуглива и нежна,
И тщетно утра луч проглянет:
Не расцветёт опять она.

*

Я чувствую, во мне горит
Святое пламя вдохновенья,
Но к тёмной цели дух парит . . .
Кто мне укажет путь спасенья?
Я вижу, жизнь передо мной
Кипит, как океан безбрежный . . .
Найду ли я утёс надежный,
Где твёрдой обопрусь ногой?
Иль, вечного сомненья полный,
Я буду горестно глядеть
На переменчивые волны,
Не зная, что любить, что петь?

It keeps its redness but a moment, yet blossoms anew every day.
   A still fresher scent breathes from the third, though it is not in
the sky; love fosters it upon a maiden's cheeks for burning lips.
But this rose soon fades; it is timid and frail; in vain will the rays
of the morning sun break through: it will not blossom again.

*

I FEEL a holy flame of inspiration burning within me, but my
spirit soars towards a dark goal . . . Who will show me the way of
salvation? I see life seething before me like a boundless ocean . . .
Shall I find some safe ridge for a firm foothold? Or, forever filled
with doubts, shall I gaze in sorrow at the inconstant waves, not
knowing what to love and what to sing?

Открой глаза на всю природу, –
Мне тайный голос отвечал, –
Но дай им выбор и свободу.
Твой час ещё не наступал:
Теперь гонись за жизнью дивной
И каждый миг в ней воскрешай,
На каждый звук её призывный
Отзывной песнью отвечай!
Когда ж минуты удивленья,
Как сон туманный, пролетят,
И тайны вечного творенья
Ясней прочтёт спокойный взгляд:
Смирится гордое желанье
Обнять весь мир в единый миг,
И звуки тихих струн твоих
Сольются в стройные созданья.

Не лжив сей голос прорицанья,
И струны верные мои
С тех пор душе не изменяли.
Пою то радость, то печали,
То пыл страстей, то жар любви,
И беглым мыслям простодушно
Вверяюсь в пламени стихов.

'Open your eyes to the whole of nature,' a secret voice answered
me, 'but leave them freedom of choice. Your hour has not yet
struck: now seek the wonders of life, revive every moment, answer
each of its summoning sounds with an echoing song. And when the
minutes of amazement have flown by like a hazy dream, and your
tranquil gaze reads more clearly the secrets of eternal creation, then
your proud desire to grasp the whole world in a single instant will
be humbled, and the sounds of your soft strings will blend into
harmonious creations.'

This prophetic voice did not lie; and ever since my faithful
strings have not beguiled my soul. I sing now joy, now sorrow, now
passion's flame, now love's ardour, and, in the fire of poetry, I
entrust myself with simple confidence to passing thoughts. . . .

Так соловей в тени дубров,
Восторгу краткому послушный,
Когда на долы ляжет тень,
Уныло вечер воспевает,
И утром весело встречает
В румяном небе ясный день.

So the nightingale, obedient to a momentary rapture, mournfully hymns the evening in the shade of the wood, as the shadows fall upon the vales, and in the morning gaily welcomes the bright day in the rose-coloured sky.

KAROLINA PAVLOVA

О былом, о погибшем, о старом
Мысль немая душе тяжела;
Много в жизни я встретила зла,
Много чувств я истратила даром,
Много жертв невпопад принесла.

Шла я вновь после каждой ошибки,
Забывая жестокий урок,
Безоружно в житейские сшибки:
Веры в слёзы, слова и улыбки
Вырвать ум мой из сердца не мог.

И душою, судьбе непокорной,
Средь невзгод, одолевших меня,
Убежденье в успех сохраня,
Как игрок ожидала упорный
День за днём я счастливого дня.

Смело клад я бросала за кладом, –
И стою, проигравшися в пух;
И счастливцы, сидящие рядом,

THE silent thought of what is past and old and perished brings pain to the soul; in my life I have met with much evil, have squandered many feelings in vain and made many an untimely sacrifice.

After each mistake, I went on again into life's conflicts, defenceless and forgetting the cruel lesson I had received: my reason could not drive the belief in tears, words, and smiles out of my heart.

And, among the trials that overcame me, I clung within my soul, unyielding to fate, to my belief in good fortune, and, like a persistent gambler, I waited day after day for my lucky day.

Boldly I threw down one heap of money after another – and now I stand, having lost my last penny; and the lucky ones who are sitting all around . . . . . .

Смотрят жадным, язвительным взглядом –
Изменяет ли твёрдый мне дух?

Рим

Мы едем поляною голой,
Не встретясь с живою душой;
Вдали, из-под тучи тяжёлой,
Виднеется город большой.

И, будто б его называя,
Чрез мёртвой пустыни предел
От неба стемневшего края
Отрывистый гром прогремел.

Кругом всё сурово и дико;
Один он в пространстве немом
Стоит, многогрешный владыка,
Развенчанный Божьим судом.

Стоит беззащитный, недужный,
И смотрит седой исполин
Угрюмо в угрюмый окружный
Простор молчаливых равнин:

watch me with an avid and caustic expression, to see whether my resolution is failing me.

Rome

WE are driving across flat open country, without encountering a living soul; in the distance, beneath a heavy cloud, a large city can be seen.

And, as though calling the city by its name, a sudden peal of thunder from the edge of the darkened sky rattled from the confines of the lifeless wastes.

All around is austere and wild; the city stands alone in the silent expanse, a monarch weighed down with sin and dethroned by the judgement of God.

The grey-haired giant stands defenceless and ailing, and gloomily gazes at the gloomy expanse of the silent plains all around;

Где вести, и казнь, и законы
Гонцы его миру несли,
Где тесные шли легионы,
Где били челом короли.

Он смотрит, как ветер поляны
Песок по пустыни метёт,
И серые всходят туманы
Из топи тлетворных болот.

over which his messengers carried to the world tidings, sentences of death, and laws, where the legions marched in serried ranks, where kings did homage.

He watches the wind of the plain sweep the sand over the wilderness, and the grey mists rise from the pestilent swamps.

ALEKSEY KOL'TSOV

Горькая доля

Соловьём залётным
Юность пролетела,
Волной в непогоду
Радость прошумела.

Пора золотая
Была, да сокрылась;
Сила молодая
С телом износилась.

От кручины-думы
В сердце кровь застыла;
Что любил, как душу, –
И то изменило.

Как былинку, ветер
Молодца шатает;
Зима лицо знобит,
Солнце сожигает.

До поры, до время
Всем я весь изжился;

Bitter Lot

LIKE a passing nightingale my youth has flown by, happiness has
echoed past like a wave in bad weather.

The golden days were here, but they have vanished; the strength
of youth is exhausted together with my body.

Sorrowful thoughts have made the blood congeal in my heart;
that which I loved even as my own soul – that too has played me
false.

The wind sways the young fellow like a blade of grass; the
winter chills his face, the sun burns it.

I've worn out myself and all I have too soon; .   .   .   .   .   .

И кафтан мой синий
С плеч долой свалился!

Без любви, без счастья
По миру скитаюсь:
Разойдусь с бедою –
С горем повстречаюсь!

На крутой горе
Рос зелёный дуб,
Под горой теперь
Он лежит гниёт . . .

Песня

Ах, зачем меня
Силой выдали
За немилова –
Мужа старова?

Небось весело
Теперь матушке
Утирать мои
Слёзы горькие;

and **my blue** coat has fallen off my shoulders.

I wander through the world without love or happiness; if I part company with ill-fortune, I encounter sorrow.

A green oak used to grow on a steep hill; it now lies rotting beneath the hill . . .

Song

Ah, **why did** they marry me against my will to an old **man** I did not love?

It **must make** my mother glad now to wipe away **my bitter tears!**

Небось весело
Глядеть батюшке
На житьё-бытьё
Горемышное!

Небось сердце в них
Разрывается, –
Как приду одна
На великой день;

От дружка дары
Принесу с собой:
На лице – печаль,
На душе – тоску.

Поздно, родные,
Обвинять судьбу,
Ворожить, гадать,
Сулить радости!

Пусть из-за моря
Корабли плывут:
Пущай золото
На пол сыпится;

It must make my father glad to see my wretched life!

It must make their hearts break when I come to see them alone
on Easter day,

and bring gifts from my beloved – sadness on my face, anguish
in my heart.

It's too late, my dear ones, to blame fate, to tell fortunes, to try
to guess the future, to promise joy!

Let the ships come sailing in from beyond the sea; let gold be
scattered on the floor;

Не расти траве
После осени;
Не цвести цветам
Зимой по снегу!

grass will not grow after the autumn, flowers will not flower in winter on the snow!

MIKHAIL LERMONTOV

Ангел

По небу полуночи ангел летел
И тихую песню он пел;
И месяц, и звёзды, и тучи толпой
Внимали той песне святой.
Он пел о блаженстве безгрешных духов
Под кущами райских садов;
О Боге великом он пел, и хвала
Его непритворна была.
Он душу младую в объятиях нёс
Для мира печали и слёз;
И звук его песни в душе молодой
Остался – без слов, но живой.
И долго на свете томилась она,
Желанием чудным полна;
И звуков небес заменить не могли
Ей скучные песни земли.

The Angel

An angel was flying through the midnight sky, and softly he sang;
and the moon, and the stars, and the clouds in a throng hearkened
to that holy song. He sang of the bliss of innocent spirits in the
shade of the gardens of paradise; he sang of the great God, and his
praise was unfeigned. In his arms he carried a young soul, destined for the world of sorrow and tears; and the sound of his song
stayed, wordless but alive, in the young soul. And for a long time it
languished in the world, filled with a wonderful longing, and earth's
tedious songs could not replace for it the sounds of heaven.

*

Когда волнуется желтеющая нива,
И свежий лес шумит при звуке ветерка,
И прячется в саду малиновая слива
Под тенью сладостной зелёного листка;

Когда, росой обрызганный душистой,
Румяным вечером иль утра в час златой,
Из-под куста мне ландыш серебристый
Приветливо качает головой;

Когда студёный ключ играет по оврагу
И, погружая мысль в какой-то смутный сон,
Лепечет мне таинственную сагу
Про мирный край, откуда мчится он:

Тогда смиряется души моей тревога,
Тогда расходятся морщины на челе,
И счастье я могу постигнуть на земле,
И в небесах я вижу Бога.

WHEN the yellowing cornfield sways, and the cool forest rustles to the sound of the breeze, and in the garden the crimson plum hides beneath the green leaf's luscious shade;

when on a rose-coloured evening or in the golden hour of morning the silvery lily of the valley, sprinkled with fragrant dew, nods its head to me in friendly greeting from underneath a bush;

when the cold spring dances down the glen, and lulling thought into an uncertain dream, murmurs to me a mysterious saga of the peaceful land from which it speeds;

then my soul's anxiety is stilled, the furrows on my brow are smoothed, I am able to comprehend happiness on earth, and in heaven I see God.

MIKHAIL LERMONTOV

[Обращение Демона к Тамаре из «Демона»]

Клянусь я первым днём творенья,
Клянусь его последним днём,
Клянусь позором преступленья
И вечной правды торжеством;
Клянусь паденья горькой мукой,
Победы краткою мечтой;
Клянусь свиданием с тобой
И вновь грозящею разлукой;
Клянуся сонмищем духов,
Судьбою братий мне подвластных,
Мечами ангелов бесстрастных,
Моих недремлющих врагов;
Клянуся небом я и адом,
Земной святыней и тобой;
Клянусь твоим последним взглядом,
Твоею первою слезой,
Незлобных уст твоих дыханьем,
Волною шёлковых кудрей;
Клянусь блаженством и страданьем,
Клянусь любовию моей:
Отрёкся я от старой мести,
Отрёкся я от гордых дум;

[The Demon's speech to Tamara from 'The Demon']

I SWEAR by the first day of Creation, I swear by its last day, I
swear by the infamy of crime and by the triumph of eternal truth;
I swear by the bitter torments of the Fall, by the short-lived dream
of victory; I swear by my meeting with you and by our impending
separation; I swear by the assembly of the spirits, brethren whom
fate has subjected to me, by the swords of the passionless angels,
my ever-watchful enemies; I swear by Heaven and by Hell, by all
that is sacred on earth, and by you; I swear by your last glance,
by your first tear, by the breath of your gentle lips, by the silken
wave of your curly hair; I swear by bliss and by suffering, I swear
by my love: I have renounced my old revenge, I have renounced
my proud thoughts; . . . . . .

Отныне яд коварной лести
Ничей уж не встревожит ум.
Хочу я с небом примириться,
Хочу любить, хочу молиться,
Хочу я веровать добру;
Слезой раскаянья сотру
Я на челе, тебя достойном,
Следы небесного огня,
И мир в неведеньи спокойном
Пусть доцветает без меня!
О, верь мне: я один поныне
Тебя постиг и оценил:
Избрав тебя моей святыней,
Я власть у ног твоих сложил.
Твоей любви я жду, как дара,
И вечность дам тебе за миг, –
В любви, как в злобе, верь, Тамара,
Я неизменен и велик.
Тебя я, вольный сын эфира,
Возьму в надзвездные края,
И будешь ты царицей мира,
Подруга первая моя;
Без сожаленья, без участья
Смотреть на землю станешь ты,
Где нет ни истинного счастья,

henceforth the poison of insidious temptation will trouble no more the minds of men. I want to make my peace with Heaven, I want to love and to pray, I want to believe in good; with tears of repentance I will efface the marks of celestial fire from my brow, now worthy of you, and let the world in peaceful ignorance end its life without me! O believe me – I alone so far have understood and appreciated you; having chosen you for my hallowed shrine, I have laid down my power at your feet; I await your love as a gift, and in exchange for a single moment I will give you eternity: in love as in enmity, believe me, Tamara, I am faithful and great. I, the free son of Ether, will take you to spheres that lie beyond the stars, and you shall be the queen of the world, my first companion; you will look without regret or concern at the earth, where there is no true

Ни долговечной красоты . . .

. . . Оставь же прежние желанья
И жалкий свет его судьбе:
Пучину гордого познанья
Взамен открою я тебе.
Толпу духов моих служебных
Я приведу к твоим стопам;
Прислужниц лёгких и волшебных
Тебе, красавица, я дам;
И для тебя с звезды восточной
Сорву венец я золотой,
Возьму с цветов росы полночной,
Его усыплю той росой;
Лучом румяного заката
Твой стан, как лентой, обовью,
Дыханьем чистым аромата
Окрестный воздух напою;
Всечасно дивною игрою
Твой слух лелеять буду я;
Чертоги пышные построю
Из бирюзы и янтаря;
Я опущусь на дно морское,
Я полечу за облака,
Я дам тебе всё, всё земное –
Люби меня! . . .

happiness,/ no lasting beauty . . . . . . O leave your former desires, and the pitiful world to its fate! In exchange I will reveal to you the abyss of proud knowledge. I will bring the host of my attendant spirits to your feet; I will give you, O beautiful one, airy and magic handmaidens; I will pluck for you the golden crown of the Eastern Star and will sprinkle it with the dew which I will take from the flowers at midnight; I will wind a ray of rosy sunset like a ribbon round your waist; I will imbue the air around you with a breath of pure fragrance; I will ceaselessly charm your ear with marvellous music; I will build splendid palaces of turquoise and amber; I will plunge to the bottom of the sea, I will fly above the clouds, I will give you everything the earth has to offer – love me! . . .

MIKHAIL LERMONTOV

Первое января

Как часто, пёстрою толпою окружён,
Когда передо мной, как будто бы сквозь сон,
  При шуме музыки и пляски,
При диком шопоте затверженных речей,
Мелькают образы бездушные людей,
  Приличьем стянутые маски;
Когда касаются холодных рук моих
С небрежной смелостью красавиц городских
  Давно бестрепетные руки, –
Наружно погружась в их блеск и суету,
Ласкаю я в душе старинную мечту,
  Погибших лет святые звуки.
И если как-нибудь на миг удастся мне
Забыться, – памятью к недавней старине
  Лечу я вольной, вольной птицей;
И вижу я себя ребёнком; и кругом
Родные всё места: высокий барский дом
  И сад с разрушенной теплицей;
Зелёной сетью трав подёрнут спящий пруд,
А за прудом село дымится, и встают

The First of January

WHEN I am surrounded by a motley crowd, and figures of soul-less people – genteelly grimacing masques – flit before my eyes, as in a dream, to the sound of music and dancing, and to the absurd whispering of speeches learnt by heart; when the hands of town beauties, which have long ceased to tremble, touch my cold hands with careless audacity – how often then, outwardly absorbed in their glitter and vanity, do I cherish in my soul an old dream and the sacred sounds of bygone years. And if in some way I succeed for a moment in losing myself in a reverie, I fly in my memory like a free, free bird back to the recent past. I see myself a child again; all around me are familiar places: the tall manor-house and the garden with the broken-down conservatory; the sleeping pond is filmed with a green network of grass, beyond the pond smoke is rising from the village, and in the distance . . . . . . ·

Вдали туманы над полями.
В аллею тёмную вхожу я; сквозь кусты
Глядит вечерний луч, и жёлтые листы
    Шумят под робкими шагами.
И странная тоска теснит уж грудь мою:
Я думаю о ней, я плачу и люблю,
    Люблю мечты моей созданье
С глазами, полными лазурного огня,
С удыбкой розовой, как молодого дня
    За рощей первое сиянье.
Так, царства дивного всесильный господин,
Я долгие часы просиживал один,
    И память их жива поныне
Под бурей тягостных сомнений и страстей,
Как свежий островок безвредно средь морей
    Цветёт на влажной их пустыне.
Когда ж, опомнившись, обман я узнаю,
И шум толпы людской спугнёт мечту мою,
    На праздник незванную гостью,
О, как мне хочется смутить весёлость их,
И дерзко бросить им в глаза железный стих,
    Облитый горечью и злостью! . . .

the mist is lifting from the fields. I am entering a dark alley; a ray of
the evening sun is peering through the bushes, and the yellow leaves
are rustling beneath my diffident steps. And a strange melancholy
lies heavy on my breast: I am thinking of her, weeping, and loving
her – loving this creature of my dreams, with eyes full of azure
light, with a rosy smile like the first brilliance of the young dawn
behind the grove. Thus did I sit for long hours alone, like an all-
powerful sovereign of some marvellous kingdom; and the memory
of those hours still lives beneath the storm of grievous doubts and
passions, like some fresh little island flowering innocently in the
midst of the seas' watery desert. But when, on coming to my senses,
I recognize the delusion, and when the noise of the human crowd
frightens away my dream – the guest that has come uninvited to
the feast – oh, how I long to disturb their gaiety and to cast in-
solently in their faces iron verses, steeped in bitterness and fury! ...

MIKHAIL LERMONTOV

Казачья колыбельная песня

Спи, младенец мой прекрасный,
 Баюшки-баю.
Тихо смотрит месяц ясный
 В колыбель твою.
Стану сказывать я сказки,
 Песенку спою;
Ты ж дремли, закрывши глазки,
 Баюшки-баю.

По камням струится Терек,
 Плещет мутный вал;
Злой чечен ползёт на берег,
 Точит свой кинжал;
Но отец твой – старый воин,
 Закалён в бою:
Спи, малютка, будь спокоен,
 Баюшки-баю.

Сам узнаешь, будет время,
 Бранное житьё;
Смело вденешь ногу в стремя
 И возмёшь ружьё.

Cossack Lullaby

SLEEP, my lovely baby, lullaby. Quietly the bright moon looks into your cradle. I shall tell you stories, and sing you a song; so shut your little eyes and doze, lullaby.

The Terek is flowing over the stones, its turbid waves lapping; the wicked Chechen creeps up the river bank, and sharpens his dagger; but your father is a veteran warrior, tried in battle; sleep, my baby, have no fear, lullaby.

The time will come – you will get to know for yourself the soldier's way of life; boldly you will put your foot into the stirrup and take up your gun. . . . . . .

Я седельце боевое
  Шёлком разошью . . .
Спи, дитя моё родное,
  Баюшки-баю.

Богатырь ты будешь с виду
  И казак душой.
Провожать тебя я выйду –
  Ты махнёшь рукой . . .
Сколько горьких слёз украдкой
  Я в ту ночь пролью! . . .
Спи, мой ангел, тихо, сладко,
  Баюшки-баю.

Стану я тоской томиться,
  Безутешно ждать;
Стану целый день молиться,
  По ночам гадать;
Стану думать, что скучаешь
  Ты в чужом краю . . .
Спи ж, пока забот не знаешь,
  Баюшки-баю.

Дам тебе я на дорогу
  Образок святой:

I shall embroider your war-saddle with silk . . . Sleep, my darling child, lullaby.

You will be a fine fellow to look at and a Cossack at heart. I shall come out to see you off, and you will wave goodbye. How many bitter tears I shall shed that night in secret! Sleep, my angel, quietly, sweetly, lullaby.

I shall pine and wait for you disconsolately; I shall pray the whole day long, and try to foretell the future at night; I shall think that you are fretting in a foreign land . . . So sleep, while you know no care, lullaby.

I shall give you a little holy icon for your journey;

Ты его, моляся Богу,
   Ставь перед собой;
Да готовясь в бой опасный,
   Помни мать свою . . .
Спи, младенец мой прекрасный,
   Баюшки-баю.

*

И скучно, и грустно, и некому руку подать
  В минуту душевной невзгоды . . .
Желанья! . . что пользы напрасно и вечно
                         желать? . . .
  А годы проходят – все лучшие годы!
Любить . . . но кого же? . . . На время – не стоит
                         труда,
  А вечно любить невозможно.
В себя ли заглянешь, там прошлого нет и следа;
  И радость, и муки, и всё там ничтожно . . .
Что страсти? – ведь рано иль поздно их сладкий
                        недуг
  Исчезнет при слове рассудка;

put it before you when you pray to God; and, when you prepare for a dangerous battle, remember your mother . . . Sleep, my lovely baby, lullaby.

*

I AM weary and sad, and there is no one to whom I can stretch out my hand in the hour of my soul's distress . . . Desires! What is the use of desiring vainly and for ever? And the years slip by – all the best years. To love? But whom? For a time it is not worth the trouble, and to love for ever is impossible. If you look within yourself, there is not a trace of the past there; the joys and the torments – everything there is worthless . . . What of passions? Sooner or later their sweet sickness will vanish at the word of reason; . . .

И жизнь, как посмотришь с холодным вниманьем
вокруг, –
Такая пустая и глупая шутка . . .

Последнее новоселье

Меж тем, как Франция, среди рукоплесканий
И кликов радостных, встречает хладный прах
Погибшего давно среди немых страданий
    В изгнаньи мрачном и цепях;

Меж тем, как мир услужливой хвалою
Венчает позднего раскаянья порыв,
И вздорная толпа, довольная собою,
    Гордится, прошлое забыв, –

Негодованию и чувству дав свободу,
Поняв тщеславие сих праздничных забот,
Мне хочется сказать великому народу:
    Ты жалкий и пустой народ!

And life, if you look round with cold attention, is such a hollow and stupid farce . . .

The Last House-warming

WHILE France, amid applause and shouts of joy, bids welcome to the cold ashes of him who perished long ago in silent agony, in grim exile and in chains;

while the world crowns this burst of belated remorse with complaisant plaudits, and the inane, self-satisfied mob, oblivious of the past, is filled with pride –

giving vent to my feelings and my indignation, and aware of the vanity of these festive preoccupations, I want to say to that gteat nation: You are a contemptible and frivolous nation!

Ты жалок потому, что вера, слава, гений,
Всё, всё великое, священное земли,
С насмешкой глупою ребяческих сомнений
    Тобой растоптано в пыли.

Из славы сделал ты игрушку лицемерья,
Из вольности – орудье палача,
И все заветные отцовские поверья
    Ты им рубил, рубил с плеча.

Ты погибал! И он явился, с строгим взором,
Отмеченный божественным перстом,
И признан за вождя всеобщим приговором,
    И ваша жизнь слилася в нём.

И вы окрепли вновь в тени его державы,
И мир трепещущий в безмолвии взирал
На ризу чудную могущества и славы,
    Которой вас он одевал.

Один – он был везде, холодный, неизменный,
Отец седых дружин, любимый сын молвы,
В степях египетских, у стен покорной Вены,
    В снегах пылающей Москвы.

You are contemptible, because all that is noble and sacred on
earth – faith, glory, genius – you have trampled in the dust with a
fatuous sneer of childish disbelief.

You have made of glory a plaything of hypocrisy, of liberty – a
tool of the executioner, with which you lopped off indiscriminately
every cherished tradition of your fathers.

You were perishing – and he appeared, stern of countenance,
singled out by the finger of God; he was acknowledged as your
leader by common decision, and your life merged into him.

And you grew strong again in the shadow of his power, and the
trembling world contemplated in silence the marvellous raiment of
power and glory with which he was clothing you.

Everywhere he was alone, cool and steadfast, the father of his
veteran squadrons, the darling son of fame – in the plains of Egypt,
by the walls of submissive Vienna, in the snows of burning Moscow.

А вы что делали, скажите, в это время,
Когда в полях чужих он гордо погибал?
Вы потрясали власть избранную, как бремя,
    Точили в темноте кинжал!

Среди последних битв, отчаянных усилий,
В испуге не поняв позора своего,
Как женщина, ему вы изменили
    И, как рабы, вы предали его!

Лишённый прав и места гражданина,
Разбитый свой венец он снял и бросил сам,
И вам оставил он в залог родного сына –
    Вы сына выдали врагам!

Тогда, отяготив позорными цепями,
Героя увезли от плачущих дружин,
И на чужой скале, за синими морями,
    Забытый, он угас один –

Один, замучен мщением бесплодным,
Безмолвною и гордою тоской,
И, как простой солдат, в плаще своём походном
    Зарыт наёмною рукой . . .

And what were you doing, tell me, while he was proudly facing
death on alien battlefields? You were sapping the authority which
you had chosen as though it were a yoke, you whetted your dagger
in secret!

During his last battles, his desperate efforts, too frightened to see
your infamy, like a woman you were unfaithful to him, and like
slaves you betrayed him.

Deprived of the rights and the status of a citizen, he himself took
off and cast away his shattered crown, and he left you his own son
as a pledge – you surrendered his son to his enemies!

Then, weighed down by shameful chains, the hero was taken
away from his weeping troops, and on an alien rock beyond blue
seas he died alone and forgotten;

alone, tortured to death by a vain longing for revenge, and by
silent and proud anguish; and, like a simple soldier, he was buried
by the hand of a hireling in his army cloak . . .

Но годы протекли, – и ветреное племя
Кричит: «Подайте нам священный этот прах!
Он наш! Его теперь, великой жатвы семя,
    Зароем мы в спасённых им стенах!»

И возвратился он на родину. Безумно,
Как прежде, вкруг него теснятся и бегут,
И в пышный гроб, среди столицы шумной,
    Останки тленные кладут.

Желанье позднее увенчано успехом!
И, краткий свой восторг сменив уже другим,
Гуляя, топчет их с самодовольным смехом
    Толпа, дрожавшая пред ним!

И грустно мне, когда подумаю, что ныне
Нарушена святая тишина
Вокруг того, кто ждал в своей пустыне
    Так жадно, столько лет – спокойствия и сна!

И если дух вождя примчится на свиданье
С гробницей новою, где прах его лежит,
Какое в нём негодованье
    При этом виде закипит!

But years passed – and the fickle nation cries: 'Give us these sacred ashes! He is ours! We shall now bury him – the seed that has yielded a great harvest – within the walls which he saved!'

And he returned to his native land. Madly, as in the old days, they crowd and bustle round him, and his mortal remains are placed in a sumptuous tomb, in the middle of the noisy capital.

The belated wish is crowned with success, and the strolling crowd which had trembled before him, its short-lived enthusiasm now spent and superseded by another, tramples on his ashes with complacent laughter!

And I feel sad at the thought that the holy silence has now been disturbed round him who, so eagerly and for so many years, waited in his solitude for peace and sleep.

And if the leader's spirit should come flying to visit this new mausoleum where his ashes repose, what indignation would seethe within him at the sight!

Как будет он жалеть, печалию томимый,
О знойном острове под небом дальних стран,
Где сторожил его, как он непобедимый,
Как он великий, океан!

Отчизна

Люблю отчизну я, но странною любовью,
Не победит её рассудок мой!
Ни слава, купленная кровью,
Ни полный гордого доверия покой,
Ни тёмной старины заветные преданья
Не шевелят во мне отрадного мечтанья.

Но я люблю – за что, не знаю сам –
Её степей холодное молчанье,
Её лесов безбрежных колыханье,
Разливы рек её, подобные морям;
Просёлочным путём люблю скакать в телеге
И, взором медленным пронзая ночи тень,
Встречать по сторонам, вздыхая о ночлеге,
Дрожащие огни печальных деревень.

Stricken with grief, how he would regret the sweltering island beneath the distant skies, where the ocean, invincible and great as he was, stood guard over him!

My country

I LOVE my country, but with a strange love. my reason cannot fathom it. Neither glory, purchased with blood, nor peace, steeped in proud confidence, nor the cherished traditions of the dim past will stir pleasant fancies within me. But I love – I know not why – the cold silence of her plains, the swaying of her boundless forests, her flooded rivers, wide as the seas; I love to gallop along a country track in a cart and, peering slowly through the darkness of night and longing for a shelter, to come upon the scattered lights of sad villages, flickering in the distance. . . . . . .

Люблю дымок спалённой жнивы,
В степи ночующий обоз,
И на холме средь жёлтой нивы
Чету белеющих берёз.
С отрадой, многим незнакомой,
Я вижу полное гумно,
Избу, покрытую соломой,
С резными ставнями окно;
И в праздник, вечером росистым,
Смотреть до полночи готов
На пляску с топаньем и свистом,
Под говор пьяных мужичков.

Сон

В полдневный жар, в долине Дагестана,
С свинцом в груди лежал недвижим я;
Глубокая ещё дымилась рана,
По капле кровь точилася моя.

Лежал один я на песке долины;
Уступы скал теснилися кругом,
И солнце жгло их жёлтые вершины,
И жгло меня, – но спал я мёртвым сном.

I love the wispy smoke of the burnt stubble-field, the string of carts standing in the steppe at night, and a couple of birches, gleaming white in the yellow cornfield on the hill. With a pleasure unknown to many I see a well-stocked barn, a cottage covered with thatch, a window with carved shutters. And on a holiday, one dewy evening, I am ready to watch until midnight the dance, with its stamping and whistling, to the hum of drunken peasants' voices.

The Dream

In the heat of noon, in a gorge in Daghestan, I lay motionless, with a bullet in my breast. My deep wound was still steaming, and my blood oozed out, drop by drop.

I lay alone on the sand of the gorge; the ledges of the cliffs clustered around, the sun was scorching their yellow summits, and scorching me; but I slept the sleep of the dead.

И снился мне сияющий огнями
Вечерний пир в родимой стороне;
Меж юных жён, увенчанных цветами,
Шёл разговор весёлый обо мне.

Но, в разговор весёлый не вступая,
Сидела там задумчиво одна,
И в грустный сон душа её младая,
Бог знает чем, была погружена.

И снилась ей долина Дагестана . . .
Знакомый труп лежал в долине той,
В его груди дымясь чернела рана,
И кровь лилась хладеющей струёй . . .

★

Выхожу один я на дорогу.
Сквозь туман кремнистый путь блестит;
Ночь тиха, пустыня внемлет Богу,
И звезда с звездою говорит.

And I dreamed of an evening feast, glittering with lights, in my homeland; young women, garlanded with flowers, were gaily talking about me.

But one of them sat there, sunk in thought, not joining in the gay conversation, and her young soul, God knows why, was plunged into a sad dream.

And in her dream she saw a gorge in Daghestan . . . A familiar figure lay dead in that gorge, a black wound was steaming in his breast, and blood flowed in a stream that was growing cold . . .

★

ALONE, I come out on to the road. The stony way glistens through the mist; the night is still, the wilderness is listening to God, and star is talking to star.

В небесах торжественно и чудно!
Спит земля в сияньи голубом . . .
Что же мне так больно и так трудно?
Жду ль чего? Жалею ли о чём?

Уж не жду от жизни ничего я,
И не жаль мне прошлого ничуть.
Я ищу свободы и покоя;
Я б хотел забыться и заснуть . . .

Но не тем холодным сном могилы:
Я б желал навеки так заснуть,
Чтоб в груди дремали жизни силы,
Чтоб дыша вздымалась тихо грудь;

Чтоб всю ночь, весь день мой слух лелея,
Про любовь мне сладкий голос пел;
Надо мной чтоб, вечно зеленея,
Тёмный дуб склонялся и шумел.

All is solemn and wonderful in the sky; the earth is sleeping in a pale blue radiance . . . Why then do I feel so much pain and heaviness of heart? Am I waiting for something, regretting anything?

I expect nothing more from life, and do not regret the past at all. I seek for freedom and peace, I would like to find oblivion and to fall asleep . . .

But not with the cold sleep of the grave: I would like to fall asleep forever so that the forces of life would slumber in my breast, and that it would heave in gentle breathing;

so that an enchanting voice, delighting my ear, would sing to me of love day and night, and a dark evergreen oak would bend and rustle over me.

COUNT ALEKSEY TOLSTOY

Князь Михайло Репнин

Без отдыха пирует с дружиной удалой
Иван Васильич Грозный под матушкой Москвой.

Ковшами золотыми столов блистает ряд,
Разгульные за ними опричники сидят.

С вечерни льются вина на царские ковры,
Поют ему с полночи лихие гусляры;

Поют потехи брани, дела былых времен,
И взятие Казани, и Астрахани плен.

Но голос прежней славы царя не веселит,
Подать себе личину он кравчему велит.

«Да здравствуют тиуны, опричники мои!
Вы ж громче бейте в струны, баяны-соловьи!

Prince Michael Repnin

IVAN Vasil'evich the Terrible with his valiant retinue is feasting tirelessly near Mother Moscow.

A row of tables glitters with golden jugs; the dissolute *oprichniki** are sitting at the tables.

From Vespers onwards wines flow on to the tsar's carpets, from midnight spirited minstrels sing to him;

they sing of the joys of war, of the battles of olden times, of the capture of Kazan' and the conquest of Astrakhan'.

But the voice of former glory does not gladden the tsar; he bids his cup-bearer hand him a mask.

'Long live my officers, my *oprichniki*! And you bards, you nightingales, pluck the strings more loudly!

* *Oprichniki* were members of the *oprichnina*, a special royal domain created by Ivan IV to break the power of the old landed aristocracy. For several years they established a reign of terror in Russia.

Себе личину, други, пусть каждый изберёт –
Я первый открываю весёлый хоровод!

За мной, мои тиуны, опричники мои!
Вы ж громче бейте в струны, баяны-соловьи!»

И все подъяли кубки. Не поднял лишь один,
Один не поднял кубка, Михайло князь Репнин.

«О, царь, забыл ты Бога! Свой сан ты, царь,
                                        забыл!
Опричниной на горе престол свой окружил!

Рассыпь державным словом детей бесовских
                                        рать!
Тебе ли, властелину, здесь в машкере плясать!»

Но царь, нахмуря брови: «В уме ты, знать, ослаб,
Или хмелён не в меру? Молчи, строптивый раб!

Не возражай ни слова и машкеру надень –
Или клянусь, что прожил ты свой последний
                                        день!»

'Let each of you, my friends, choose himself a mask; I will lead off the gay round dance myself!

'Follow me, my officers, my *oprichniki*! And you bards, you nightingales, pluck the strings more loudly!'

And all of them raised their cups, all save one; one did not raise his cup – Michael, Prince Repnin.

'O tsar, you have forgotten God! You have forgotten your rank, o tsar! To our misfortune you have surrounded your throne with the *oprichnina*.

'Scatter the host of the devil's children by your royal command! Is it fitting for you, our sovereign, to be dancing here in a mask?'

But the tsar frowned: 'You must have gone weak in the head, or have you drunk too much? Be silent, recalcitrant slave!

'Not another word: put on a mask – or else I swear that you have lived your last day!'

Тут встал и поднял кубок Репнин, правдивый
князь.

«Опричнина да сгинет!» он рек, перекрестясь,

«Да здравствует во веки наш православный
царь!
Да правит человеки, как правил ими встарь!

Да презрит, как измену, бесстыдной лести глас!
Личины ж не надену я в мой последний час!»

Он молвил и ногами личину растоптал,
Из рук его на землю звенящий кубок пал . . .

«Умри же, дерзновенный!» царь вскрикнул,
разъярясь –
И пал, жезлом пронзенный, Репнин, правдивый
князь.

И вновь подъяты кубки, ковши опять звучат,
За длинными столами опричники шумят,

И смех их раздаётся, и пир опять кипит –
Но звон ковшей и кубков царя не веселит:

Then Repnin, the truthful prince, rose and raised his cup:
'Perish the *oprichnina*!' he said, making the sign of the cross;
'May he live for ever, our Orthodox tsar! May he rule over men
as he ruled them of old!
'May he spurn, as treason, the voice of shameless flattery! But I
will not don a mask in my last hour.'
He spoke, and trampled the mask under foot; the cup fell clang-
ing from his hands to the ground . . .
'Then die, you insolent one,' shouted the enraged tsar; and
Repnin, the truthful prince, fell, pierced by the [tsar's] staff.
And once again the cups are raised and the jugs ring, the
oprichniki are sitting at the long tables in noisy revelry;
their laughter resounds, and once again the feast is in full swing;
but the clinking of the jugs and cups does not gladden the tsar:

«Убил, убил напрасно я верного слугу!
Вкушать веселье ныне я боле не могу!»

Напрасно льются вина на царские ковры,
Поют царю напрасно лихие гусляры;

Поют потехи брани, дела былых времен,
И взятие Казани, и Астрахани плен.

*

По гребле неровной и тряской,
Вдоль мокрых рыбачьих сетей,
Дорожная едет коляска,
Сижу я задумчиво в ней;

Сижу и смотрю я дорогой
На серый и пасмурный день,
На озера берег отлогий,
На дальний дымок деревень.

'I have killed, I have wrongfully killed a loyal servant! I can no longer taste of joy!'

In vain do wines flow on to the tsar's carpets, in vain do spirited minstrels sing to the tsar;

they sing of the joys of war, of the battles of olden times, of the capture of Kazan' and the conquest of Astrakhan'.

*

ALONG the rough and bumpy causeway, past some wet fishing-nets, the carriage rolls on; I am sitting in it, sunk in reverie.

I sit and, as the road unfolds, I look at the dull and gloomy weather, at the lake's sloping bank, at the far-off smoke of the villages.

По гребле, со взглядом угрюмым,
Проходит оборванный жид;
Из озера с пеной и шумом
Вода через греблю бежит;

Там мальчик играет на дудке,
Забравшись в зелёный тростник.
В испуге взлетевшие утки
Над озером подняли крик;

Близ мельницы старой и шаткой
Сидят на траве мужики;
Телега с разбитой лошадкой
Лениво подвозит мешки . . .

Мне кажется всё так знакомо,
Хоть не был я здесь никогда,
И крыша далёкого дома,
И мальчик, и лес, и вода,

И мельницы говор унылый,
И ветхое в поле гумно,
Всё это когда-то уж было,
Но мною забыто давно.

A ragged Jew with a glum look on his face is walking along the causeway; the water from the lake runs foaming and swashing over the causeway;

over there a boy, ensconced in the green rushes, is playing on a pipe; the startled ducks take wing and cry above the lake;

by an old tumble-down mill peasants are sitting on the grass; a tired old horse is lazily dragging a cart with some sacks . . .

It all seems so familiar, though I have never been here before; the roof of the distant house, and the boy, and the wood, and the water,

and the mournful voice of the mill, and the ramshackle barn in the field – it has all happened before, but I have forgotten it long ago.

Так точно ступала лошадка,
Такие ж тащила мешки;
Такие ж у мельницы шаткой
Сидели в траве мужики;

И так же шёл жид бородатый,
И так же шумела вода –
Всё это уж было когда-то,
Но только не помню когда . . .

[*Тропарь из «Иоанна Дамаскина»*]

Какая сладость в жизни сей
Земной печали непричастна?
Чьё ожиданье не напрасно,
И где счастливый меж людей?
Всё то превратно, всё ничтожно,
Что мы с трудом приобрели –
Какая слава на земли
Стоит тверда и непреложна?
Всё пепел, призрак, тень и дым,
Исчезнет всё, как вихорь пыльный,
И перед смертью мы стоим
И безоружны и бессильны.

The horse plodded on in just the same way, dragging the same
sacks, the same peasants sat in the grass by the tumble-down mill;
and the bearded Jew walked by in the same way, and the water
made the same noise. It has all happened before – only I cannot
remember when . . .

[*The Troparion from 'John Damascene'*]

WHAT joy in this life has no part in earthly sorrow? Whose hope
is not vain, and where among men is there one who is happy? All
that we have acquired with effort is inconstant and worthless; what
earthly glory stands firm and unchangeable? All is but ashes,
phantom, shadow, and smoke, everything will vanish like the dust
of a whirlwind, and we stand before death unarmed and helpless.

Рука могучего слаба,
Ничтожны царские веленья –
Прийми усопшего раба,
Господь, в блаженные селенья!

Как ярый витязь смерть нашла,
Меня как хищник низложила,
Свой зев разинула могила
И всё житейское взяла.
Спасайтесь, сродники и чада,
Из гроба к вам взываю я,
Спасайтесь, братья и друзья,
Да не узрите пламень ада!
Вся жизнь есть царство суеты,
И, дуновенье смерти чуя,
Мы увядаем как цветы –
Почто же мы мятемся всуе?
Престолы наши суть гроба,
Чертоги наши разрушенье –
Прийми усопшего раба,
Господь, в блаженные селенья!

Средь груды тлеющих костей
Кто царь, кто раб, судья иль воин?

The hand of the mighty is feeble, the commands of kings are as nothing. Receive, O Lord, Thy departed servant into Thy blessed habitations!

Death fell upon me like a furious warrior, and like a beast of prey it struck me down; the grave opened wide its jaws and took away all the things of this life. Save yourselves, kinsfolk and children, I call to you from the grave, save yourselves, brothers and friends, so that you see not the flames of hell! The whole of life is a realm of vanity, and as we sense the breath of death we wither like flowers: why then do we toss about in vain? Our thrones are but graves, our palaces but ruins. Receive, O Lord, Thy departed servant into Thy blessed habitations!

Amidst the heap of rotting bones, who is king or slave or judge or warrior? . . . . . .

Кто царства Божия достоин,
И кто отверженный злодей?
О, братья, где сребро и злато,
Где сонмы многие рабов?
Среди неведомых гробов
Кто есть убогий, кто богатый?
Всё пепел, дым, и пыль и прах,
Всё призрак, тень и привиденье –
Лишь у Тебя, на небесах,
Господь, и пристань и спасенье!
Исчезнет всё, что было плоть,
Величье наше будет тленье –
Прийми усопшего, Господь,
В Твои блаженные селенья!

И Ты, предстательница всем,
И Ты, заступница скорбящим,
К Тебе о брате, здесь лежащем,
К Тебе, Святая, вопием!
Моли божественного Сына,
Его, Пречистая, моли,
Дабы отживший на земли
Оставил здесь свои кручины!
Всё пепел, прах, и дым и тень,

Who has deserved the Kingdom of God and who is a rejected evil-doer? O brothers, where is the silver and the gold, where are the hosts of slaves? Among the nameless graves who is the poor man, and who the rich? All is but ashes, smoke, dust, and decay, phantom, shadow, and spectre; only with Thee in heaven, O Lord, is there refuge and salvation. All that was flesh will vanish, our pomp will turn into decay. Receive, O Lord, the departed one into Thy blessed habitations!

And Thou, who dost intercede for us all, Thou, Advocate of those who mourn, to Thee we cry, O most blessed, on behalf of our brother who lies here. Pray to Thy Divine Son, pray to Him, O most pure, that he who has lived out his life on earth may leave his sorrows here. All is but ashes, decay, smoke, and shadow; . . .

О, други, призраку не верьте!
Когда дохнёт в нежданный день
Дыханье тлительное смерти,
Мы все поляжем как хлеба,
Серпом подрезанные в нивах –
Прийми усопшего раба,
Господь, в селениях счастливых!

Иду в незнаемый я путь,
Иду меж страха и надежды;
Мой взор угас, остыла грудь,
Не внемлет слух, сомкнуты вежды;
Лежу безгласен, недвижим,
Не слышу братского рыданья,
И от кадила синий дым
Не мне струит благоуханье;
Но, вечным сном пока я сплю,
Моя любовь не умирает,
И ею, братья, вас молю,
Да каждый к Господу взывает:
Господь! В тот день, когда труба
Вострубит мира преставленье –
Прийми усопшего раба
В Твои блаженные селенья!

O friends, put not your faith in a phantom! When, on an unexpected day, the corruption of death will breathe upon us, we shall all be laid low like corn, mown down by the sickle in the cornfields. Receive, O Lord, Thy departed servant into Thy happy habitations!

I tread an unknown path, my journey lies between fear and hope; my sight is extinguished, my breast has grown cold, my ears do not hear, my eyelids are closed; I am lying voiceless, without movement, I cannot hear the brethren sobbing, and the fragrance of the censer's blue smoke is not for me; but, though I sleep the eternal sleep, my love is not dead, and by that love I implore you, my brethren, each one of you, to call thus unto the Lord: O Lord, on the day when the trumpet shall sound the end of the world, receive Thy departed servant into Thy blessed habitations!

*

То было раннею весной,
Трава едва всходила,
Ручьи текли, не парил зной,
И зелень рощ сквозила;

Труба пастушья поутру
Ещё не пела звонко,
И в завитках ещё в бору
Был папоротник тонкий;

То было раннею весной,
В тени берёз то было,
Когда с улыбкой предо мной
Ты очи опустила . . .

То на любовь мою в ответ
Ты опустила вежды —
О, жизнь! о, лес! о, солнца свет!
О, юность! о, надежды!

И плакал я перед тобой,
На лик твой глядя милый, —
То было раннею весной,
В тени берёз то было!

I т was in the early spring – the grass was barely sprouting, the brooks were flowing, the heat was not oppressive, and light shone through the green groves.

The shepherd's horn was not yet sounding its clear note early in the morning, and the slender fern in the forest was still in curls.

It was in the early spring, it was in the shade of the birches that you lowered your eyes before me with a smile . . .

It was in reply to my love that you lowered your glance – O life! O wood! O sunlight! O youth! O hopes!

And I wept before you, gazing at your sweet face – it was in the early spring, it was in the shade of the birches.

То было в утро наших лет —
О, счастие! о, слёзы!
О, лес! о, жизнь! о, солнца свет!
О, свежий дух берёзы!

Баллада о камергере Деларю

Вонзил кинжал убийца нечестивый
    В грудь Деларю.
Тот шляпу сняв, сказал ему учтиво:
    «Благодарю».
Тут в левый бок ему кинжал ужасный
    Злодей вогнал,
А Деларю сказал: «Какой прекрасный
    У вас кинжал!»
Тогда злодей, к нему зашедши справа,
    Его пронзил,
А Деларю с улыбкою лукавой
    Лишь погрозил.
Истыкал тут злодей ему, пронзая,
    Все телеса,
А Деларю: «Прошу на чашку чая
    К нам в три часа».

It was in the morning of our lives – O happiness! O tears! O wood! O life! O sunlight! O the fresh fragrance of the birches!

Ballad of the Chamberlain Delarue

THE ungodly murderer plunged his dagger into Delarue's breast. Taking off his hat, the latter said to him politely: 'Thank you.' At this the villain drove his horrible dagger into his left side; but Delarue said: 'What a fine dagger you have!' Then the villain approached him from the right and pierced him; but Delarue only wagged his finger with an arch smile. At this the villain riddled all his body with dagger wounds, but Delarue said: 'Come and have a cup of tea with us at three o'clock.'

Злодей пал ниц и, слёз проливши много,
    Дрожал как лист,
А Деларю: «Ах, встаньте ради Бога!
    Здесь пол нечист».
Но всё у ног его в сердечной муке
    Злодей рыдал,
А Деларю сказал, расставя руки:
    «Не ожидал!
Возможно-ль? Как?! Рыдать с такою силой? –
    По пустякам?
Я вам аренду выхлопочу, милый,
    Аренду вам!
Через плечо дадут вам Станислава
    Другим в пример.
Я дать совет властям имею право:
    Я – камергер.
Хотите дочь мою просватать, Дуню?
    А я за то
Кредитными билетами отслюню
    Вам тысяч сто;
А вот пока вам мой портрет на память,
    Приязни в знак.
Я не успел его ещё обрамить, –
    Примите так!»

The villain fell prostrate and, shedding many tears, trembled like a leaf; but Delarue said: 'Oh, for heaven's sake, do get up, the floor here is not clean.' But still the villain sobbed with anguish at his feet; but Delarue, his arms outstretched, said: 'I did not expect this! What? Is it possible? To cry so violently for a mere trifle? I'll arrange for you to have a rise, my dear man – a rise in salary! They'll give you the Order of St Stanislas, and hang it across your shoulder as an example to others. I'm in a position to advise the authorities: I am a chamberlain. Would you like to marry my daughter Dunya? If so, I'll fork out a hundred thousand in banknotes for you; meanwhile, here's my portrait for you to keep, in token of friendship. I've not had time to have it framed: accept it as it is.' . .   · ·

Тут едок стал и даже горче перца
      Злодея вид.
Добра за зло испорченное сердце –
      Ах! – не простит.
Высокий дух посредственность тревожит,
      Тьме страшен свет.
Портрет ещё простить убийца может,
      Аренду-ж – нет.
Зажглась в злодее зависти отрава
      Так горячо,
Что, лишь надел мерзавец Станислава
      Через плечо, –
Он окунул со злобою безбожной
      Кинжал свой в яд
И, к Деларю подкравшись осторожно, –
      Хвать друга в зад!
Тот на пол лёг, не в силах в страшных болях
      На кресло сесть.
Меж тем злодей, отняв на антресолях
      У Дуни честь, –
Бежал в Тамбов, где был, как губернатор,
      Весьма любим.
Потом в Москве, как ревностный сенатор,
      Был всеми чтим.

At this the villain's countenance became sour and more acrid than pepper. Alas, a depraved heart will not forgive the one who renders good for evil! A lofty spirit troubles the small-minded; darkness fears the light. The murderer can, at a pinch, forgive the portrait, but not the rise. The poison of envy began to burn so hot in the villain's heart that, as soon as he had hung the Order of St Stanislas across his shoulder, the scoundrel with devilish malice dipped his dagger in poison, crept up stealthily to Delarue, and stabbed his friend in the backside! The latter lay down on the floor, unable in his dreadful agony to sit in an armchair. The villain, meanwhile, having violated Dunya's honour on the entresol, fled to Tambov, where he became governor and was greatly loved; later, in Moscow, as a zealous senator, he was esteemed by all. . . . . .

Потом он членом сделался совета
В короткий срок . . .
Какой пример для нас являет это,
Какой урок!

Then in a short time he became a member of the State Council
. . . What an example this is for us, what a lesson!

YAKOV POLONSKY

Колокольчик

Улеглася метелица . . . путь озарён . . .
Ночь глядит миллионами тусклых очей . .
Погружай меня в сон, колокольчика звон!
Выноси меня, тройка усталых коней!
Мутный дым облаков и холодная даль
Начинают яснеть; белый призрак луны
Смотрит в душу мою и былую печаль
　　Наряжает в забытые сны.
То вдруг слышится мне, – страстный голос поёт,
　　С колокольчиком дружно звеня:
«Ах, когда-то, когда-то мой милый придёт
　　Отдохнуть на груди у меня!
У меня ли не жизнь! Чуть заря на стекле
Начинает лучами с морозом играть,
Самовар мой кипит на дубовом столе,
И трещит моя печь, озаряя в угле
　　За цветной занавеской кровать . . .
У меня ли не жизнь! Ночью ль ставень открыт, –
По стене бродит месяца луч золотой;

The Bell

THE snow-storm has subsided . . . The road is lit up . . . The night looks at me with millions of dim eyes . . . Send me to sleep, jingle of the bell! Drive me on, tired horses of the troika! The murky clouds and the cold distance are beginning to clear; the moon's white spectre looks into my soul and clothes my past sadness in forgotten dreams. At times, I hear a passionate voice singing in harmony with the jingling bell: 'Ah, when, when, will my sweetheart come to seek rest on my breast! What a life I can offer! Hardly have the dawn's rays started to play with the frost on the window, when my samovar is boiling on the oaken table and my stove is crackling and lighting up the bed behind the coloured curtain in the corner . . . What a life I can offer! When my shutter is open at night the golden moonbeam roams on the wall; . . . . . .

Забушует ли вьюга, – лампада горит,
И, когда я дремлю, моё сердце не спит,
   Всё по нём изнывая тоской!»

То вдруг слышится мне, – тот же голос поёт,
   С колокольчиком грустно звеня:
«Где-то старый мой друг? я боюсь, – он войдёт
   И, ласкаясь, обнимет меня!
Что за жизнь у меня! – И тесна, и темна,
И скучна моя горница; дует в окно . . .
За окошком растёт только вишня одна,
Да и та за промёрзлым окном не видна
   И, быть может, погибла давно . . .
Что за жизнь! Полинял пёстрый полога цвет,
Я больная брожу и не еду к родным;
Побранить меня некому, – милого нет . . .
Лишь старуха ворчит, как приходит сосед,
   Оттого, что мне весело с ним . . .»

when the snow-storm starts to rage my lamp is burning, and when I drowse my heart is awake, still longing with anguish for him!'

And then I hear the same voice singing sadly to the tune of the jingling bell: 'Where is my old friend? I am afraid that he might enter and embrace me tenderly. What a life is mine! My room is narrow and dark and dull; there is a draught blowing from the window . . . Nothing grows outside the window except a single cherry-tree, and even that cannot be seen through the frozen pane – perhaps it has long been dead . . . What a life! The bright colours of the bed-curtain have faded; I wander about, feeling ill, and do not go to visit my people; there's no one to scold me – my sweetheart is not here . . . Only the old woman grumbles when my neighbour comes to see me - because I enjoy his company!'

Лебедь

Пел смычок, – в садах горели
  Огоньки, – сновал народ, –
Только ветер спал да тёмен
  Был ночной небесный свод.

Тёмен был и пруд зелёный,
  И густые камыши,
Где томился бедный лебедь,
  Притаясь в ночной тиши.

Умирая, не видал он, –
  Приручённый, нелюдим, –
Как над ним взвилась ракета
  И рассыпалась над ним;

Не слыхал, как струйка билась,
  Как журчал прибрежный ключ, –
Он глаза смыкал и грезил
  О полёте выше туч:

Как в простор небес высоко
  Унесёт его полёт, –

The Swan

THE fiddlestick was quavering, lights shone in the gardens, people were strolling about; only the wind slept and the night sky was dark.

Dark were also the green pond and the thick rushes where a poor swan was languishing, hiding in the quiet of the night.

Tame and solitary, he did not see in his death-throes that a rocket soared into the air and scattered its fire above him.

He did not hear the jet of water playing, nor the murmur of the stream by the bank; his eyes closed, he was dreaming of a flight above the clouds:

of a flight that would carry him high into the wide expanse of the sky, – . . . . . .

И какую там он песню
   Вдохновенную споёт!

Как на всё, на всё святое,
   Что таил он от людей,
Там откликнутся родные
   Стаи белых лебедей.

И уж грезит он: минута, –
   Вздох – и крылья зашумят,
И его свободной песни
   Звуки утро возвестят.

Но крыло не шевелилось,
   Песня путалась в уме:
Без полёта и без пенья
   Умирал он в полутьме.

Сквозь камыш, шурша по листьям,
   Пробирался ветерок . . .
А кругом в садах горели
   Огоньки и пел смычок.

and what an inspired song he would sing there!

All that he held sacred and concealed from men would find response up there in the echoing song of flocks of white swans, his own kin;

And he dreamed that in a moment he would sigh, his wings would start beating, and the sounds of his unfettered song would proclaim the morning.

But his wings did not stir; the song faltered in his mind; unable to take flight and with his song unsung, he was dying in the half-light.

The leaves rustled, as a breeze passed through the rushes; and in the gardens around, the lights shone and the fiddlestick quavered.

AFANASY FET

Я пришёл к тебе с приветом,
Рассказать, что солнце встало,
Что оно горячим светом
По листам затрепетало;

Рассказать, что лес проснулся,
Весь проснулся, веткой каждой,
Каждой птицей встрепенулся
И весенней полон жаждой;

Рассказать, что с той же страстью,
Как вчера, пришёл я снова,
Что душа всё так же счастью
И тебе служить готова;

Рассказать, что отовсюду
На меня весельем веет,
Что не знаю сам, что буду
Петь – но только песня зреет.

*

I HAVE come to you with greeting, to tell you that the sun has
risen, and that its hot light has started to quiver in the leaves;
    to tell you that the whole forest is awake in its every branch and
full of the thirst of spring, and that every bird within it has stirred;
    to tell you that I have come again with the same passion which
filled me yesterday, and that my soul is as ready as before to serve
happiness and you;
    to tell you that a breath of joy comes to me from everywhere, and
that I do not know what I shall sing; I only know that a song is
ripening.

Ивы и берёзы

Берёзы севера мне милы, –
Их грустный, опущённый вид,
Как речь безмолвная могилы,
Горячку сердца холодит.

Но ива, длинными листами
Упав на лоно ясных вод,
Дружней с мучительными снами
И дольше в памяти живёт.

Лия таинственные слёзы
По рощам и лугам родным,
Про горе шепчутся берёзы
Лишь с ветром севера одним.

Всю землю, грустно-сиротлива,
Считая родиной скорбей,
Плакучая склоняет ива
Везде концы своих ветвей.

*

Буря на небе вечернем,
Моря сердитого шум –

Willows and Birches

THE birches of the North are dear to me: their sad, downcast appearance cools the heart's fever like the grave's soundless speech.

But the willow, its long leaves falling into the clear waters, is more in tune with tormenting dreams and lives longer in memory.

Shedding secret tears over their native groves and meadows, the birches whisper about sorrow to the north wind alone.

Sad and orphaned, believing the whole earth to be the home of sorrow, the weeping willow inclines the tips of its branches all around.

*

STORM in the evening sky, noise of the angry sea; . . . .

Буря на мо́ре и ду́мы,
Мно́го мучи́тельных дум –
Бу́ря на мо́ре и ду́мы,
Хор возраста́ющих дум –
Чёрная ту́ча за ту́чей,
Мо́ря серди́того шум.

*

Ещё весны́ души́стой не́га
К нам не успе́ла низойти́,
Ещё овра́ги полны́ сне́га,
Ещё заре́й греми́т теле́га
На заморо́женном пути́.

Едва́ лишь в по́лдень со́лнце гре́ет,
Красне́ет ли́па в высоте́,
Сквозя́, бере́зник чуть желте́ет,
И солове́й ещё не сме́ет
Запе́ть в сморо́динном кусте́.

Но возрожде́нья весть жива́я
Уж есть в пролётных журавля́х,
И, их глаза́ми провожа́я,
Стои́т краса́вица степна́я
С румя́нцем си́зым на щека́х.

storm on the sea, and thoughts – many tormenting thoughts. Storm
on the sea and thoughts – rising chorus of thoughts – black cloud
after cloud, noise of the angry sea.

*

THE rapture of fragrant spring has not yet had time to come down
to us; the ravines are still full of snow and the cart still clatters at
dawn over the frozen road.

The sun barely becomes warm by midday, high up the lime-
tree has a reddish hue, the translucent birch grove is faintly tinged
with yellow, and the nightingale in the blackcurrant bush has not
yet plucked up courage to break into song.

But already the cranes in their flight bring living tidings of rebirth, and a young beauty of the steppes, a bluish flush on her
cheeks, stands, following them with her eyes.

*

На стоге сена ночью южной
Лицом ко тверди я лежал,
И хор светил, живой и дружный,
Кругом раскинувшись, дрожал.

Земля, как смутный сон немая,
Безвестно уносилась прочь,
И я, как первый житель рая,
Один в лицо увидел ночь.

Я ль нёсся к бездне полуночной,
Иль сонмы звёзд ко мне неслись?
Казалось, будто в длани мощной
Над этой бездной я повис.

И с замираньем и смятеньем
Я взором мерил глубину,
В которой с каждым я мгновеньем
Всё невозвратнее тону.

*

Как хорош чуть мерцающим утром,
Амфитрита, твой влажный венок!

*

On a southern night I lay on a hayrick facing the sky, and the choir
of stars was spread out in a circle, live and trembling in harmony.

The earth, mute as a vague dream, was fast receding into the
unknown, and I, like the first denizen of paradise, alone beheld the
night face to face.

Was I racing towards the midnight abyss, or were the hosts of
stars racing towards me? It seemed as if I were held in a mighty
hand suspended above this abyss.

And with a sinking and bewildered heart, I spanned with my
gaze the depth into which I was sinking more irrevocably every
moment.

*

How beautiful, in the faintly glimmering morning, is your wet
garland, Amphitrite! . . . . . .

Как огнём и сквозным перламутром
Убирает Аврора восток!

Далеко на песок отодвинут
Трав морских бесконечный извив,
Свод небесный, в воде опрокинут,
Испещряет румянцем залив.

Остров вырос над тенью зелёной;
Ни движенья, ни звука в тиши,
И, погнувшись над влагой солёной,
В крупных каплях стоят камыши.

Сентябрьская роза

За вздохом утренним мороза,
Румянец уст приотворя,
Как странно улыбнулась роза
В день быстролётный сентября!

Перед порхающей синицей
В давно безлиственных кустах
Как дерзко выступать царицей
С приветом вешним на устах.

How Aurora decks the East with fire and translucent mother-of-pearl!

The endless coils of seaweed have been washed up far over the sand; the vault of heaven, overturned in the water, speckles the bay with a rosy glow.

An island has emerged above the green shade; there is not a movement, not a sound in the stillness; and, bending over the salty water, the rushes stand, covered with large drops.

The September Rose

HALF-opening her red lips to the frost's morning sigh, how strangely the rose has smiled on a swift-fleeting day of September!

How audacious it is to advance in stately manner before the blue-tit fluttering in the shrubs that have long lost their leaves, like a queen with the spring's greeting on her lips;

Расцвесть в надежде неуклонной –
С холодной разлучась грядой,
Прильнуть последней, опьянённой,
К груди хозяйки молодой!

to bloom with steadfast hope that, parted from the cold
flower-bed, she may be the last to cling, intoxicated, to a young
hostess's breast!

NIKOLAY NEKRASOV

Еду ли ночью по улице тёмной,
Бури заслушаюсь в пасмурный день, –
Друг беззащитный, больной и бездомный,
Вдруг предо мной промелькнёт твоя тень!
Сердце сожмётся мучительной думой.
С детства судьба не взлюбила тебя:
Беден и зол был отец твой угрюмый,
Замуж пошла ты – другого любя.
Муж тебе выпал недобрый на долю:
С бешеным нравом, с тяжёлой рукой;
Не покорилась – ушла ты на волю,
Да не на радость сошлась и со мной . . .

Помнишь ли день, как больной и голодный
Я унывал, выбивался из сил?
В комнате нашей, пустой и холодной,
Пар от дыханья волнами ходил.
Помнишь ли труб заунывные звуки,
Брызги дождя, полусвет, полутьму?
Плакал твой сын, и холодные руки

WHETHER I am driving down a dark street at night, or listening attentively to a storm on a dull day, your shadow suddenly flits before me, my defenceless, sick, and homeless friend. Agonizing thoughts wring my heart. From your childhood fate took a dislike to you: your gloomy father was poor and ill-tempered, you married, loving another. A bad husband fell to your lot, a man of ungovernable temper and with a heavy hand; you did not resign yourself – you went away to be free, and to your sorrow took up with me . . .

Do you remember the day when, ill and hungry, I was exhausted and in despair? In our empty and cold room the steam from our breath floated about in waves. Do you remember the mournful sounds in the chimney, the rain drops, the semi-darkness? Your son was crying, and you were warming his cold hands . . .

Ты согревала дыханьем ему.
Он не смолкал – и пронзительно звонок
Был его крик . . . Становилось темней;
Вдоволь поплакал и умер ребёнок . . .
Бедная! слёз безрассудных не лей!
С горя да с голоду завтра мы оба
Так же глубоко и сладко заснём;
Купит хозяин, с проклятьем, три гроба –
Вместе свезут и положат рядком . . .

В разных углах мы сидели угрюмо.
Помню, была ты бледна и слаба,
Зрела в тебе сокровенная дума,
В сердце твоём совершалась борьба.
Я задремал. Ты ушла молчаливо,
Принарядившись, как будто к венцу,
И через час принесла торопливо
Гробик ребёнку и ужин отцу.
Голод мучительный мы утолили,
В комнате тёмной зажгли огонёк,
Сына одели и в гроб положили . . .
Случай нас выручил? Бог ли помог?
Ты не спешила печальным признаньем,

with your breath. He cried without ceasing, and his screams were piercing . . . It was growing dark. The child wept many tears and died . . . Poor thing! Do not shed useless tears. Tomorrow both of us will fall asleep just as soundly and sweetly from grief and hunger; the landlord, cursing us, will buy three coffins; they'll take us away all together and lay us side by side . . .

Gloomily we sat in separate corners. I remember, you looked pale and faint: a secret thought was ripening within you, a struggle was taking place in your heart. I dozed off. You went out in silence, after dressing yourself up as though for your wedding; and an hour later you hurriedly brought back a little coffin for your child and some supper for its father. We satisfied our cruel hunger, lit a light in the dark room, we dressed our son and laid him in the coffin . . . Had chance come to our rescue? Had God helped us? You were in no hurry to make your sad confession, ...

Я ничего не спросил,
Только мы оба глядели с рыданьем,
Только угрюм и озлоблен я был . . .

Где ты теперь? С нищетой горемычной
Злая тебя сокрушила борьба?
Или пошла ты дорогой обычной,
И роковая свершится судьба?
Кто ж защитит тебя? Все без изъятья
Именем страшным тебя назовут,
Только во мне шевельнутся проклятья –
И бесполезно замрут! . . .

[*Плач старой крестьянки из «В деревне»*]

«Здравствуй, родная.» – «Как можется,
                                  кумушка?
    Всё ещё плачешь никак?
Ходит, знать, пò сердцу горькая думушка,
    Словно хозяин-большак?»
–«Как же не плакать? Пропала я, грешная!
    Душенька ноет, болит . . .

I asked no questions; we only looked and sobbed, and I was morose and embittered . . .

Where are you now? Has the cruel struggle against wretched poverty broken you? Or have you taken the usual road, and will your fatal destiny run its course? Who will protect you? All without exception will call you by a terrible name. Only within me will curses stir and die away to no purpose.

[*The old peasant woman's lament from 'In the Village'**]

'Good day to you, my dear.' – 'How are you, neighbour? Still weeping, it seems? A bitter thought, I see, is pacing your heart as though it were the master of the house.' – 'How could I not weep? I am done for, sinful woman that I am! My heart aches, it hurts . . .

* Two old peasant women are talking.

Умер, Касьяновна, умер, сердешная,
    Умер и в землю зарыт!

Ведь наскочил же на экую гадину!
    Сын ли мой не был удал?
Сорок медведей поддел на рогатину –
    На сорок первом сплошал!
Росту большого, рука, что железная,
    Плечи – косая сажень;
Умер, Касьяновна, умер, болезная –
    Вот уж тринадцатый день!

Шкуру с медведя-то содрали, продали;
    Деньги – семнадцать рублей –
За душу бедного Савушки подали,
    Царство небесное ей!
Добрая барыня Марья Романовна
    На панихиду дала . . .
Умер, голубушка, умер, Касьяновна –
    Чуть я домой добрела.

Ветер шатает избёнку убогую,
    Весь развалился овин . . .

He is dead, Kas'yanovna, he is dead, my dear, dead and buried in the ground!

'He ran up against such a loathsome creature! My son was a fearless fellow, if ever there was one! Forty bears he hooked on to his hunting spear – he slipped up on the forty-first! He was tall and broad-shouldered, his arm was as strong as iron; he is dead, Kas'yanovna, he has been dead, my dear, for twelve days!

'The bear's skin was stripped off and sold; the money – seventeen roubles – was given for the repose of poor Savushka's soul – may God give it eternal rest in His Kingdom! The kind lady Mar'ya Romanovna paid for a requiem . . . He is dead, my dear, he is dead, Kas'yanovna – I just managed to drag myself home.

'The wind shakes my poor little house, the barn is falling to pieces . . .

Словно шальная пошла я дорогою:
Не попадётся ли сын?
Взял бы топорик – беда поправимая –
Мать бы утешил свою . . .
Умер, Касьяновна, умер, родимая –
Надо ль? топор продаю.

Кто приголубит старуху безродную?
Вся обнищала вконец!
В осень ненастную, в зиму холодную
Кто запасёт мне дровец?
Кто, как доносится тёплая шубушка,
Зайчиков новых набьёт?
Умер, Касьяновна, умер, голубушка –
Даром ружьё пропадёт!

Веришь, родная: с тоской да с заботами
Так опостылел мне свет!
Лягу в коморку, покроюсь тенётами,
Словно как саваном . . . Нет!
Смерть не приходит . . . Брожу нелюдимая,
Попусту жалоблю всех . . .

I walked down the road, as though I were out of my mind, thinking that I might meet my son. If only he had taken his axe, all would have been well, and he would have made his mother happy . . . He is dead, Kas'yanovna, he is dead, my dear – Do you need it? I'm selling the axe.

'Who will comfort a lonely old woman? I have fallen into complete poverty! Who will lay in firewood for me for rainy autumn and cold winter? When my warm fur-coat is worn out, who will go out and shoot some more hares? He is dead, Kas'yanovna, he is dead, my dear – the gun will be useless now.

'Believe me, my dear, what with my grief and my worries, I feel life has become so hateful! I lie down in my little room and cover myself with nets as though with a shroud . . . No! Death does not come . . . I wander about, shunning everyone, uselessly making everyone pity me . . .

Умер, Касьяновна, умер, родимая –
   Эх! кабы только не грех . . .

Ну, да и так . . . дай Бог зиму промаяться,
   Свежей травы мне не мять!
Скоро избёнка совсем расшатается,
   Некому поле вспахать.
В город сбирается Марья Романовна,
   По̀ миру сил нет ходить . . .
Умер, голубушка, умер, Касьяновна,
   И не велел долго жить!»

Влас

В армяке с открытым воротом,
С обнажённой головой,
Медленно проходит городом
Дядя Влас – старик седой.

На груди икона медная:
Просит он на Божий храм,
Весь в веригах, обувь бедная,
На щеке глубокий шрам;

He is dead, Kas'yanovna, he is dead, my dear – oh, if it were not for the sin . . .

'Oh well, it will come anyway . . . At the most I'll last out the winter, I'll not tread on fresh grass. Soon my little house will fall into decay, and there is no one to plough the field. Mar'ya Romanovna is moving to the town, I've no strength left to go begging. He is dead, my dear, he is dead, Kas'yanovna – and I've not long to live!'

Vlas

UNCLE Vlas, a grey-haired old man in a peasant's coat, with an open collar and with his head uncovered, slowly passes through the town.

A copper icon hangs at his breast; he is collecting alms to build a godly church; he is hung with chains, poorly shod, with a deep scar on his cheek.

Да с железным наконешником
Палка длинная в руке . . .
Говорят, великим грешником
Был он прежде. В мужике

Бога не было; побоями
В гроб жену свою вогнал;
Промышляющих разбоями,
Конокрадов укрывал;

У всего соседства бедного
Скупит хлеб, а в чёрный год
Не поверит гроша медного,
Втрое с нищего сдерёт!

Брал с родного, брал с убогого,
Слыл кащеем-мужиком;
Нрава был крутого, строгого . . .
Наконец, и грянул гром!

Власу худо; кличет знахаря —
Да поможешь ли тому,
Кто снимал рубашку с пахаря,
Крал у нищего суму?

In his hand he carries a long staff with an iron point . . . They
say that in bygone days he had been a grievous sinner . . . The
fellow
knew no God; his blows drove his wife into her grave; he
sheltered horse-thieves and those who lived by robbery;
He bought up grain from all his needy neighbours, and when
hard times came would not give credit for a brass farthing, but
would sell it back to the poor at three times the price.
He fleeced his kinsfolk, he fleeced the poor, he was renowned as
an old skinflint, he was of a severe and churlish disposition . . .
Then at last the storm broke!
Vlas fell sick; he called in the wise man: but would you help a
man who had stripped the ploughman of his shirt and stolen the
beggar's scrip?

Только пуще всё неможется.
Год прошёл – а Влас лежит,
И построить церковь божится,
Если смерти избежит.

Говорят, ему видение
Всё мерещилось в бреду:
Видел света преставление,
Видел грешников в аду:

Мучат бесы их проворные,
Жалит ведьма-егоза.
Ефиопы – видом чёрные
И, как углие глаза,

Крокодилы, змии, скорпии
Припекают, режут, жгут . . .
Воют грешники в прискорбии,
Цепи ржавые грызут.

Гром глушит их вечным грохотом,
Удушает лютый смрад,
И кружит над ними с хохотом
Чёрный тигр-шестокрылат.

He felt worse and worse. A year passed – Vlas still lay helpless;
and he swore to build a church if he escaped death.

They say that a vision kept on appearing to him in his delirium:
he saw the Day of Doom and the sinners in hell.

Nimble fiends were tormenting them, the frisky witch was
stinging them. Ethiopians – black of aspect, their eyes like burning
coals –

crocodiles and snakes and scorpions were scorching, stabbing,
burning them . . . The sinners howled in anguish and gnawed their
rusty chains.

Thunder deafened them with never-ending peals, a fearful
stench suffocated them, and above them a black six-winged tiger
circled, laughing loudly.

Те на длинный шест нанизаны,
Те горячий лижут пол . . .
Там, на хартиях написаны,
Влас грехи свои прочёл . . .

Влас увидел тьму кромешную
И последний дал обет . . .
Внял Господь – и душу грешную
Воротил на вольный свет.

Роздал Влас свое имение,
Сам остался бос и гол,
И сбирать на построение
Храма Божьего пошёл.

С той поры мужик скитается
Вот уж скоро тридцать лет,
Подаянием питается –
Строго держит свой обет.

Сила вся души великая
В дело Божие ушла:
Словно сроду жадность дикая
Непричастна ей была . . .

Some were strung on to a long pole, others were licking the
burning ground . . . There, inscribed on parchments, Vlas read his
sins . . .

Vlas beheld the outer darkness and made his final vow . . . The
Lord heard him, and led his sinful soul back into the world of
freedom.

Vlas gave away his possessions, remaining himself barefoot and
destitute, and went off to collect money for the building of a godly
church.

Since then the fellow has been wandering for nearly thirty years,
living by alms, strictly keeping his vow.

All the great force of his soul has gone into doing God's work, as
though savage greed had never touched it.

Полон скорбью неутешною,
Смуглолиц, высок и прям,
Ходит он стопой неспешною
По селеньям, городам.

Нет ему пути далёкого:
Был у матушки Москвы,
И у Каспия широкого,
И у царственной Невы.

Ходит с образом и с книгою,
Сам с собой всё говорит,
И железною веригою
Тихо на ходу звенит.

Ходит в зимушку студёную,
Ходит в летние жары,
Вызывая Русь крещёную
На посильные дары, –

И дают, дают прохожие . . .
Так из лепты трудовой
Вырастают храмы Божии
По лицу земли родной . . .

Full of inconsolable grief, swarthy of face, tall and erect, he walks with unhurried gait through villages and towns.

No distance is too great for him; he has been to Mother Moscow, and to the wide Caspian, and to the imperial Neva.

He walks with his icon and his book, all the time talking to himself and softly jingling his iron chains as he goes.

He walks through icy winters, he walks through the summer heat, entreating Christian Russia to give what she can.

And give they do, the passers-by . . . So from hard-earned mites God's churches spring up over the face of our native land.

[*Из «Коробейников»*]

> Кумачу я не хочу,
> Китайки не надо. *Песня*

«Ой, полна, полна коробушка,
Есть и ситцы и парча.
Пожалей, моя зазнобушка,
Молодецкого плеча!
Выди, выди в рожь высокую!
Там до ночки погожу,
А завижу черноокую –
Все товары разложу.
Цены сам платил не малые,
Не торгуйся, не скупись:
Подставляй-ка губы алые,
Ближе к милому садись!»
Вот и пала ночь туманная,
Ждёт удалый молодец.
Чу, идёт! – пришла желанная,
Продаёт товар купец.
Катя бережно торгуется,
Всё боится передать.
Парень с девицей целуется,
Просит цену набавлять.

[*From 'The Pedlars'*]

> Red calico I want not,
> Nankeen I need not – *Song*

'HEY! Full, full is my box – I've got cottons and brocades, too! Have pity, my sweetheart, on a stout fellow's shoulder. Come, come out into the field of high-growing rye. I shall wait there until nightfall, and when I see my black-eyed beauty, I'll spread out all my wares. I paid good prices for them; don't bargain, don't be stingy: come, hold out your bright red lips, nestle closer to your sweetheart.' The misty night has fallen, the bold young fellow is waiting. Hark, here she comes! She has come, the beloved, and the pedlar sells his wares. Katya bargains with discretion, afraid of paying too much. The lad kisses the girl, and begs her to raise the price. . . . . . .

Знает только ночь глубокая,
Как поладили они.
Распрямись ты, рожь высокая,
Тайну свято сохрани!

«Ой, легка, легка коробушка,
Плеч не режет ремешок!
А всего взяла зазнобушка
Бирюзовый перстенёк.
Дал ей ситцу штуку целую,
Ленту алую для кос,
Поясок – рубаху белую
Подпоясать в сенокос –
Всё поклала ненаглядная
В короб, кроме перстенька:
Не хочу ходить нарядная
Без сердечного дружка! –
То-то дуры вы, молодочки!
Не сама ли принесла
Полуштофик сладкой водочки?
А подарков не взяла!
Так постой же! Нерушимое
Обещаньице даю:
У отца дитя любимое!
Ты попомни речь мою:

The dead of night alone knows how they came to terms. Straighten yourself up, you high-growing rye, keep the secret faithfully!

'Hey! Light, light is my box – the strap does not cut into my shoulders! Yet all that my sweetheart took was a turquoise ring. I gave her a whole piece of cotton, a bright red ribbon for her tresses, a girdle to fasten round her shift at hay-making time; my beloved put all of them back into the box, except the ring: I don't want to go about finely dressed when my true love isn't here! Aren't you foolish, you young girls! – Did you not bring yourself a half-bottle of sweet vodka? Yet you did not take the gifts! Just you wait! I give you my firm promise: cherished child of your father, remember these words of mine : . . . . . .

Опорожнится коробушка,
На Покров домой приду
И тебя, душа-зазнобушка,
В Божью церковь поведу!»

[*Из «Мороза, Красного Носа»*]

. . . Не ветер бушует над бором,
Не с гор побежали ручьи,
Мороз-воевода дозором
Обходит владенья свои.

Глядит – хорошо ли метели
Лесные тропы занесли,
И нет ли где трещины, щели
И нет ли где голой земли?

Пушисты ли сосен вершины,
Красив ли узор на дубах?
И крепко ли скованы льдины
В великих и малых водах?

when my box is empty, I'll come home for the feast of Our Lady's Protection and I'll lead you, my heart's beloved, to God's holy church!'

[*From 'Frost the Red-Nosed'*]

IT is not the wind storming above the forest, nor the streams running down from the mountains: General Frost on a patrol is going the round of his domains.

He looks – have the snow-storms covered up the forest paths thoroughly? And is there no crack, no fissure, no bare patch of earth anywhere?

Are the pine-tops feathery? Is the tracery on the oak-trees beautiful? And is the ice solidly clamped on the waters great and small?

Идёт – по деревьям шагает,
Трещит по замёрзлой воде,
И яркое солнце играет
В косматой его бороде.

Дорога везде чародею,
Чу! ближе подходит, седой.
И вдруг очутился над нею,
Над самой её головой!

Забравшись на сосну большую,
По веточкам палицей бьёт
И сам про себя удалую,
Хвастливую песню поёт:

«Вглядись, молодица, смелее,
Каков воевода Мороз!
Навряд тебе парня сильнее
И краше видать привелось?

Метели, снега и туманы
Покорны морозу всегда,
Пойду на моря-окияны –
Построю дворцы изо льда.

He comes. He strides over the trees, his steps crackle on the frozen waters, and the bright sunshine sparkles in his shaggy beard.

All roads are open to the white-haired wizard. Hark! He comes nearer – and all of a sudden he is right above her, straight over her head.

Perched on a tall pine-tree, he smites the branches with his mace and sings a dashing and boastful song about himself:

'Look without fear, fair lady, note well what a fine fellow is General Frost. I'll bet you have never seen a stouter or handsomer fellow!

'The blizzards, the snow, and the mists are always obedient to frost; I'll go to the seas and the oceans and build palaces of ice.

Задумаю – реки большие
Надолго упрячу под гнёт,
Построю мосты ледяные,
Каких не построит народ.

Где быстрые, шумные воды
Недавно свободно текли, –
Сегодня прошли пешеходы,
Обозы с товаром прошли.

Люблю я в глубоких могилах
Покойников в иней рядить,
И кровь вымораживать в жилах,
И мозг в голове леденить.

На горе недоброму вору,
На страх седоку и коню,
Люблю я в вечернюю пору
Затеять в лесу трескотню.

Бабёнки, пеняя на леших,
Домой удирают скорей.
А пьяных, и конных, и пеших
Дурачить ещё веселей.

'I've only to plan it, and I'll hide mighty rivers for long under a load of ice, and build bridges of ice such as men cannot build.

'Where lately fast-flowing and noisy waters sped freely, today pedestrians and cart-trains of merchandise have passed.

'I love to dress up the dead in hoar-frost in their deep graves, to congeal the blood in their veins, and to freeze the brains in their skulls.

'To harass the wicked thief, to startle the rider and horse, I love to start up a salvo of crackling in the forest at nightfall.

'The women, blaming it on the wood-sprites, take to their heels and run home. But to fool the drunks on horseback and on foot is funnier still.

Без мелу всю выбелю рожу,
А нос запылает огнём,
И бороду так приморожу
К вожжам – хоть руби топором!

Богат я, казны не считаю,
А всё не скудеет добро;
Я царство моё убираю
В алмазы, жемчуг, серебро.

Войди в моё царство со мною
И будь ты царицею в нём!
Поцарствуем славно зимою,
А летом глубоко уснём.

Войди! приголублю, согрею,
Дворец отведу голубой . . .»
И стал воевода над нею
Махать ледяной булавой.

«Тепло ли тебе, молодица?»
С высокой сосны ей кричит.
«Тепло!» отвечает вдовица,
Сама холодеет, дрожит.

'Without chalk I'll plaster their faces with white, their noses will start burning like fire, and I'll freeze their beards to the reins so hard that only an axe can sever them!

'I'm rich, I count not my treasure, yet my fortune never shrinks; I adorn my kingdom with diamonds, pearls, and silver.

'Come, enter my kingdom with me, and be its queen. We'll reign gloriously throughout the winter, and in summer we'll fall sound asleep.

'Come, enter! I'll cherish and warm you, I'll assign you a sky-blue palace . . .' And General Frost began to wave his icy mace over her.

'Are you warm, fair lady?', he calls to her from a tall pine-tree. 'I'm warm,' the widow replies, and she grows numb and shivers with cold.

Морозко спустился пониже,
Опять помахал булавой
И шепчет ей ласковей, тише:
«Тепло ли?...» – «Тепло, золотой!»

Тепло – а сама коченеет.
Морозко коснулся её:
В лицо ей дыханием веет
И иглы колючие сеет
С седой бороды на неё.

И вот перед ней опустился!
«Тепло ли?» промолвив опять,
И в Проклушку вдруг обратился
И стал он её целовать.

В уста её, в очи и в плечи
Седой чародей целовал
И те же ей сладкие речи,
Что милый о свадьбе, шептал.

И так-то ли любо ей было
Внимать его сладким речам,

Frost came down a little lower, waved his mace again, and whispered to her more tenderly, more softly: 'Are you warm?' – 'I'm warm, my dearest.'

Warm – yet she is growing numb. Frost has touched her; he breathes into her face and scatters over her sharp needles from his white beard.

And now he has come down and stands in front of her. 'Are you warm?' he murmured once more, and suddenly turned into Proklushka,* and started to kiss her.

The white-haired wizard kissed her on the lips, the eyes, and the shoulders, and whispered to her the same sweet words which her lover whispered at wedding-time.

And so happy was Dar'ya to listen to his sweet words . . .

* The name of her dead husband.

Что Дарьюшка очи закрыла,
Топор уронила к ногам.

Улыбка у горькой вдовицы
Играет на бледных губах,
Пушисты и белы ресницы,
Морозные иглы в бровях . . .

. . . Ни звука! Душа умирает
Для скорби, для страсти. Стоишь
И чувствуешь, как покоряет
Её эта мёртвая тишь.

Ни звука! И видишь ты синий
Свод неба, да солнце, да лес,
В серебряно-матовый иней
Наряженный, полный чудес,

Влекущий неведомой тайной,
Глубоко-бесстрастный . . . Но вот
Послышался шорох случайный –
Вершинами белка идёт.

Ком снегу она уронила
На Дарью, прыгнув по сосне.
А Дарья стояла и стыла
В своём заколдованном сне . . .

that she closed her eyes and dropped the axe to the ground.

A smile is playing on the pale lips of the unhappy widow, her eye-lashes are fluffy and white, ice needles cling to her eyebrows . . .

. . . Not a sound! The soul is dying to sorrow and passion. You stand and feel this dead silence enthralling it.

Not a sound! And you see the blue vault of heaven, the sun, and the forest full of marvels arrayed in lustreless silvery hoar-frost;

alluring in its inscrutable mystery, deep and passionless . . . But suddenly there is a rustling sound: a squirrel is passing over the tree-tops.

Leaping in the pine-tree, it let fall a lump of snow on Dar'ya. And Dar'ya stood and froze in her enchanted sleep . . .

APOLLON GRIGORIEV

О, говори хоть ты со мной,
　　Подруга семиструнная!
Душа полна такой тоской,
　　А ночь такая лунная!

Вон там звезда одна горит
　　Так ярко и мучительно,
Лучами сердце шевелит,
　　Дразня его язвительно.

Чего от сердца нужно ей?
　　Ведь знает без того она,
Что к ней тоскою долгих дней
　　Вся жизнь моя прикована ...

И сердце ведает моё,
　　Отравою облитое,
Что я впивал в себя её
　　Дыханье ядовитое ...

Я от зари и до зари
　　Тоскую, мучусь, сетую ...
Допой же мне – договори
　　Ты песню недопетую.

O YOU at least – speak to me, my seven-stringed friend! My soul is
full of such anguish, and the night is bathed in such [radiant]
moonlight!

Over there a star burns so brightly and tormentingly; its rays
stir the heart, teasing and stinging it.

What does it want of my heart? It knows anyhow that my whole
life is riveted to it by the yearning of many days ...

And my heart, steeped in poison, knows that I have imbibed its
venomous breath ...

And from sunset till dawn I yearn, suffer, and complain: so sing
me the unfinished song to the end.

APOLLON GRIGORIEV

Договори сестры твоей
   Все недомолвки странные . . .
Смотри: звезда горит ярчей . . .
   О, пой, моя желанная!

И до зари готов с тобой
   Вести беседу эту я . . .
Договори лишь мне, допой
   Ты песню недопетую!

Say to the end all those strange things which in your sister's mouth have remained half-said . . . Look: the star burns brighter . . . O sing, my beloved!

I am ready to hold this converse with you till dawn . . . Only sing me the unfinished song to the end!

KONSTANTIN SLUCHEVSKY

После казни в Женеве

Тяжёлый день . . . ты уходил так вяло . . .
Я видел казнь: багровый эшафот
Давил своею тяжестью народ,
И солнце на топор сияло.

Казнили. Голова отпрянула как мяч!
Стёр полотенцем кровь с руки палач,
И эшафот поспешно разобрали;
Пришли пожарные и площадь поливали.

Тяжёлый день . . . ты уходил так вяло . . .
Мне снилось: я лежал на страшном колесе,
Меня коробило, меня на части рвало,
И мышцы лопались, ломались кости все . . .

Я всё вытягивался в пытке небывалой
И став звенящею, чувствительной струной,
К монахине какой-то исхудалой
На балалайку вдруг попал живой!

After an Execution in Geneva

OPPRESSIVE day . . . you passed so sluggishly . . . I saw an execution: the crimson scaffold pressed down with its weight upon the people, and the sun glittered upon the axe.

They executed him. His head bounced off like a ball. The executioner wiped off the blood from his hand with a towel, and the scaffold was hurriedly dismantled; the firemen came and soused the public square.

Oppressive day . . . you passed so sluggishly . . . I dreamed that I lay on a fearful wheel: I writhed, I was being torn to pieces, my muscles were bursting asunder, all my bones were being broken.

I was being more and more distended in unprecedented tortures; and I became a ringing, sensitive string, and suddenly found myself, alive, on the balalaika of some emaciated nun.

Старуха чёрная гнусила и хрипела,
Костлявым пальцем дёргала меня,
«В крови горит огонь желанья» – пела,
И я вторил ей, жалобно звеня! . . .

The black hag was crooning in hoarse and nasal tones and plucking me with a bony finger; she was singing 'the flame of desire burns in the heart', and I was accompanying her, twanging plaintively.

VLADIMIR SOLOVIEV

У царицы моей есть высокий дворец,
О семи он столбах золотых,
У царицы моей семигранный венец,
В нём без счёту камней дорогих.

И в зелёном саду у царицы моей
Роз и лилий краса расцвела,
И в прозрачной волне серебристый ручей
Ловит отблеск кудрей и чела.

Но не слышит царица, что шепчет ручей,
На цветы и не взглянет она:
Ей туманит печаль свет лазурных очей,
И мечта её скорби полна.

Она видит: далёко, в полночном краю,
Средь морозных туманов и вьюг,
С злою силою тьмы в одиночном бою
Гибнет ею покинутый друг.

И бросает она свой алмазный венец,
Оставляет чертог золотой

My queen has a lofty palace with seven golden pillars. My queen has a seven-sided crown inlaid with countless jewels.

In my queen's green garden roses and lilies bloom fair, and a silvery stream catches the reflection of her curls and her brow in its transparent waters.

But my queen does not hear the murmur of the stream, she does not so much as glance at the flowers: sorrow clouds the brightness of her sky-blue eyes, and her thoughts are full of grief.

She sees her beloved, whom she has forsaken, perishing far away in a northern land, amid freezing mists and snow-storms, in solitary battle with the evil powers of darkness.

And she lays down her crown of diamonds, leaves her golden palace, ...

И к неверному другу, – нежданный пришлец, –
Благодатной стучится рукой.

И над мрачной зимой молодая весна –
Вся сияя склонилась над ним
И покрыла его, тихой ласки полна,
Лучезарным покровом своим.

И низринуты тёмные силы во прах,
Чистым пламенем весь он горит
И с любовию вечной в лазурных очах
Тихо другу она говорит:

«Знаю, воля твоя волн морских не верней,
Ты мне верность клялся сохранить, –
Клятве ты изменил, но изменой своей
Мог ли сердце моё изменить?»

*

В тумане утреннем неверными шагами
Я шёл к таинственным и чудным берегам.
Боролася заря с последними звездами,

and – an unexpected visitor – knocks with her hand full of grace at the door of her unfaithful lover.

And, bathed in light, she bends over him like youthful spring over sombre winter and, full of gentle tenderness, covers him with her radiant veil.

And the powers of darkness are stricken to the ground; his whole being burns with a pure flame, and with eternal love in her sky-blue eyes she softly speaks to her beloved:

'I know that your resolve is not more constant than the waves of the sea: you swore to keep faith with me; you broke your oath, but could you by your betrayal alter the constancy of my heart?'

*

IN the morning mist I walked with wavering steps towards a mysterious and wonderful shore. Dawn was contending against the last stars, . . .

Ещё летали сны – и схваченная снами
Душа молилася неведомым богам.

В холодный белый день дорогой одинокой,
Как прежде, я иду в неведомой стране.
Рассеялся туман, и ясно видит око,
Как труден горный путь, и как ещё далёко,
Далёко всё, что грезилося мне.

И до полуночи неробкими шагами
Всё буду я идти к желанным берегам,
Туда, где на горе, под новыми звездами
Весь пламенеющий победными огнями
Меня дождётся мой заветный храм.

На Сайме зимой

Вся ты закуталась шубой пушистой,
В сне безмятежном затихнув лежишь.
Веет не смертью здесь воздух лучистый,
Эта прозрачная, белая тишь.

dreams were still hovering, and my soul, in the grip of dreams, prayed to unknown gods.

In the cold white day I tread, as before, a lonely road in an unknown land. The mist has lifted, and the eye sees clearly how difficult is the mountain track, and how far, far away is still all that I saw in my dreams.

And until midnight I shall still be walking with fearless steps towards the shore of my desires, to where, on a mountain beneath new stars, my promised temple, all ablaze with triumphal lights, awaits me.

Winter on Lake Saimaa

YOU have muffled yourself from head to foot in a thick fur-coat; you lie hushed, in tranquil sleep. There is no breath of death here in the luminous air, in this transparent, white silence.

VLADIMIR SOLOVIEV

В невозмутимом покое глубоком
Нет, не напрасно тебя я искал.
Образ твой тот же пред внутренним оком,
Фся – владычица сосен и скал!

Ты непорочна, как снег за горами,
Ты многодумна, как зимняя ночь,
Вся ты в лучах, как полярное пламя,
Тёмного хаоса светлая дочь!

No, I have not sought you in vain in the unruffled, profound stillness. The inner eye still sees the same image of you, Fairy Queen –
mistress of the pines and the rocks!
   You are immaculate, as the snow beyond the mountains, you are
filled with many thoughts, like the winter night, you are radiant,
like the Northern Lights – O bright daughter of dark Chaos!

INNOKENTY ANNENSKY

Сентябрь

Раззолочённые, но чахлые сады
С соблазном пурпура на медленных недугах,
И солнца поздний пыл в его коротких дугах,
Невластный вылиться в душистые плоды.

И жёлтый шёлк ковров, и грубые следы,
И понятая ложь последнего свиданья,
И парков чёрные, бездонные пруды,
Давно готовые для спелого страданья ...

Но сердцу чудится лишь красота утрат,
Лишь упоение в заворожённой силе;
И тех, которые уж лотоса вкусили,
Волнует вкрадчивый осенний аромат.

Маки

Весёлый   день   горит ... Среди   сомлевших
                                                  трав
Всё маки пятнами – как жадное бессилье,

September

GILDED but decaying gardens, with the lure of purple on the slow-growing ailments, and the sun's tardy heat in its short curved rays, powerless to distil itself into fragrant fruit.

And the yellow silk of the carpets, and the coarse traces, and the avowed falsehood of the last meeting; and the black, bottomless ponds of the parks, long ready for ripe suffering.

But the heart senses only the beauty of bereavement, feels only the lure of spell-bound strength; and those who have already tasted of the lotus, are excited by the insinuating aroma of autumn.

Poppies

THE gay day is ablaze ... In the languid grass patches of poppies are everywhere, like avid impotence, ...

Как губы, полные соблазна и отрав,
Как алых бабочек развёрнутые крылья.

Весёлый день горит . . . Но сад и пуст и глух.
Давно покончил он с соблазнами и пиром, –
И маки сохлые, как головы старух,
Осенены с небес сияющим потиром.

Смычок и струны

Какой тяжёлый, тёмный бред!
Как эти выси мутно-лунны!
Касаться скрипки столько лет
И не узнать при свете струны!

Кому ж нас надо? Кто зажёг
Два жёлтых лика, два унылых . . .
И вдруг почувствовал смычок,
Что кто-то взял и кто-то слил их.

«О, как давно! Сквозь эту тьму
Скажи одно: ты та ли, та ли?»

like lips full of temptation and poison, like the spread-out wings of
scarlet butterflies.

The gay day is ablaze . . . But the garden is empty and overgrown. It has long since done with temptations and feasting, and
the withered poppies, like heads of old women, are overspread by
the radiant chalice of heaven.

The Bow and the Strings

How oppressive, how dark the delirium! How turbid those moon-
lit heights! To have touched the violin for so many years and not to
recognize the strings in the light!

Who needs us? Who has lit up two yellow and melancholy
faces? . . And suddenly the bow felt someone take them up and
merge them.

'Oh, how long it has been! Tell me one thing through this darkness: are you the same one, the same one?' . . . . . .

И струны ластились к нему,
Звеня, но, ластясь, трепетали.

«Не правда ль, больше никогда
Мы не расстанемся ? довольно ? . . .
И скрипка отвечала *да*,
Но сердцу скрипки было больно.

Смычок всё понял, он затих,
А в скрипке эхо всё держалось . . .
И было мукою для них,
Что людям музыкой казалось.

Но человек не погасил
До утра свеч . . . И струны пели . . .
Лишь солнце их нашло без сил
На чёрном бархате постели.

Старая шарманка

Небо нас совсем свело с ума:
То огнём, то снегом нас слепило,
И, ощерясь, зверем отступила
За апрель упрямая зима.

And the strings pressed close to him caressingly, ringing but quivering in this fond caress.

'It's true, is it not, that we shall never part again, that it is enough ?' And the violin replied *yes*, though its heart was gripped with pain.

The bow understood everything, and fell silent; but in the violin the resonance still persisted, and what seemed music to men was torment to them.

But the man did not blow out the candles till morning . . . And the strings sang . . . Only the sun found them, drained of strength, on the black velvet of the bed.

The Old Barrel Organ

THE sky has driven us out of our minds: it has blinded us now with fire, now with snow; and stubborn winter, baring its teeth like a wild beast, has retreated behind April.

Чуть на миг сомлеет в забытьи –
Уж опять на брови шлем надвинут,
И под наст ушедшие ручьи,
Не допев, умолкнут и застынут.

Но забыто прошлое давно,
Шумен сад, а камень бел и гулок,
И глядит раскрытое окно,
Как трава одела закоулок.

Лишь шарманку старую знобит,
И она в закатном мленьи мая
Всё никак не смелет злых обид,
Цепкий вал кружа и нажимая.

И никак, цепляясь, не поймёт
Этот вал, что не к чему работа,
Что обида старости растёт
На шипах от муки поворота.

Но когда б и понял старый вал,
Что такая им с шарманкой участь,
Разве б петь, кружась, он перестал
Оттого, что петь нельзя, не мучась? . .

No sooner has it fallen into lethargy for a moment, than its helmet is once again pulled down over its eyebrows, and the streams which have burrowed beneath the frozen snow-crust fall silent and grow stiff, their songs unfinished.

But the past has long since been forgotten, the garden is full of sound, the stone is white and resonant, and the open window gazes at the grass that has clothed the back street.

Only the old barrel-organ shivers with cold, and, in the languor of a May sunset, still can't grind away its bitter injuries, as it turns and presses on the tenacious barrel.

And, as it strikes the keys, this barrel will never understand that its work is of no avail, and that with each agonized turn the injury of old age grows on the pins.

But even if the old barrel were to understand that this is its fate and the street organ's, would it cease singing as it turns, because there is no singing without torment? . . .

Стальная цикада

Я знал, что она вернётся
И будет со мной – Тоска.
Звякнет и запахнётся
С дверью часовщика . . .

Сердца стального трепет
Со стрекотаньем крыл
Сцепит и вновь расцепит
Тот, кто ей дверь открыл . .

Жадным крылом цикады
Нетерпеливо бьют:
Счастью ль, что близко, рады,
Муки ль конец зовут ? . .

Столько сказать им надо,
Так далеко уйти . . .
Розно, увы! цикада,
Наши лежат пути.

Здесь мы с тобой лишь чудо,
Жить нам с тобою теперь
Только минуту – покуда
Не распахнулась дверь . . .

The Steel Cicada

I KNEW that Anguish would return and remain with me: she will tinkle and slam, with the watchmaker's lid . . .

He who snapped open the lid for her will fasten the steel heart's quivering to the wings' chirping, and again unfasten them.

Impatiently the cicadas beat their avid wings: are they glad of the happiness that is near? Are they calling for an end to their torment?

They have so much to say, so far to go . . . Alas, our paths diverge, O cicada.

Here our companionship is but a miracle; we shall only live together, you and I, for a minute more – until the lid flies open . . .

Звякнет и запахнётся,
И будешь ты так далека . . .
Молча сейчас вернётся
И будет со мной – Тоска.

После концерта

В аллею чёрные спустились небеса,
Но сердцу в эту ночь не превозмочь уста-
                          лость . . .
Погасшие огни, немые голоса, –
Неужто это всё, что от мечты осталось?

О, как печален был одежд её атлас,
И вырез жутко бел среди наплечий чёрных!
Как жалко было мне её недвижных глаз
И снежной лайки рук, молитвенно-
                          покорных!

А сколько было там развеяно души
Среди рассеянных, мятежных и бесслёзных!
Что звуков пролито, взлелеянных в тиши,
Сиреневых, и ласковых, и звёздных!

It will tinkle and slam – and you will be far, far away . . . In a
moment she will silently return, and remain with me – Anguish.

After the Concert

THE black skies have come down on to the garden walk; yet tonight the heart cannot overcome its weariness . . . Lights that have
gone out, silent voices – can this be all that remains of a dream?

Oh, how mournful was the satin of her clothes, and how frighten-
ingly white her décolletage showed against the black shoulder-
straps! How I pitied her motionless eyes and her hands in snow-white
kid gloves, suppliant and submissive!

But oh, how much soul was scattered there, among the inatten-
tive, the restless, and the tearless! How many sounds were spilled,
sounds nurtured in silence, lilac, tender, and star-like!

Так с нити порванной в волненьи иногда,
Средь месячных лучей, и нежны и огнисты
В росистую траву катятся аметисты
И гибнут без следа.

Decrescendo

Из тучи с тучей в безумном споре
  Родится шквал, –
Под ним зыбучий в пустынном море
  Вскипает вал.

Он полон страсти, он мчится гневный,
  Грозя брегам.
А вслед из пастей за ним стозевный
  И рёв и гам . . .

То, как железный, он канет в бездны
  И роет муть,
То, бык могучий, нацелит тучи
  Хвостом хлестнуть . . .

Но ближе . . . ближе, и вал уж ниже,
  Не стало сил,

So at times, from a string broken in a moment of emotion,
amethysts, tender and sparkling, roll into the dewy grass in the
moonlight and are lost without trace.

Decrescendo

FROM a wild dispute between cloud and cloud a squall is born,
beneath it a surging billow is churned up on the empty sea.

Full of passion and anger, it hurtles on, threatening the shores,
and from the troughs it leaves in its wake come a roar and a din as
though from a hundred gaping jaws . . .

Now, as though made of iron, it sinks into abysses and churns
the seething water, now, a mighty bull, it takes aim to lash the
clouds with its tail . . .

But nearer . . . nearer, and the billow is lower, its strength has
ebbed; . . . . . .

К ладье воздушной хребет послушный
    Он наклонил . . .

И вот чуть плещет, кружа осадок,
    Λ гнев иссяк . . .
Песок так мягок, припёк так гладок:
    Плесни – и ляг!

Тоска миража

Погасла последняя краска,
Как шёпот в полночной мольбе . . .
Что надо, безумная сказка,
От этого сердца тебе?

Мои ли без счёта и меры
По снегу не тяжки концы?
Мне ль дали пустые не серы?
Не тускло звенят бубенцы?

Но ты-то зачем так глубоко
Двоишься, о сердце моё?
Я знаю – она далёко,
И чувствую близость её.

---

it has bowed its obedient crest down to a buoyant boat . . .

And now it's barely lapping and whirling the silt; its anger has dissolved . . . The sand is so soft, the sunny beach so smooth: one lap, and then lie down!

The Anguish of a Mirage

THE last colour has faded like a whisper in a midnight prayer . . . O tale of madness, what do you want of this heart of mine?

Are not my journeys over the snow oppressive beyond count or measure? Are the empty distances that lie before me not grey? Is the jingle of the bells not dreary?

But you, my heart, why are you so deeply divided? I know that she is far away, yet I feel her nearness.

Уж вот они, снежные дымы,
С них глаз я свести не могу:
Сейчас разминуться должны мы
На белом, но мёртвом снегу.

Сейчас кто-то сани нам сцепит
И снова расцепит без слов.
На миг, но томительный лепет
Сольётся для нас бубенцов . . .

Он слился . . . Но больше друг друга
Мы в тусклую ночь не найдём . . .
В тоске безысходного круга
Влачусь я постылым путём . . .

Погасла последняя краска,
Как шёпот в полночной мольбе . . .
Что надо, безумная сказка,
От этого сердца тебе?

Here they are now, the snowy mists; I cannot take my eyes off
them: in a moment we shall pass each other on the white but dead
snow.

In a moment someone will silently couple, and then uncouple,
our sleighs. For a single but tormenting instant the bells' murmurs
will merge into one for us . . .

They have merged. But we shall not find each other again in the
dim night . . . In the anguish of a closed circle I wander on my
wearisome way . . .

The last colour has faded like a whisper in a midnight prayer . . .
O tale of madness, what do you want of this heart of mine?

FEDOR SOLOGUB

Что селения наши убогие,
Все пространства и все времена!
У Отца есть обители многие, –
Нам неведомы их имена.

Но, предчувствуя райские радости,
Пред которыми жизнь – только сон.
Отрекаюсь от призрачной сладости,
Отвергаю томленье времён.

Увяданье, страданье и тление, –
Мне суровый венец вы сплели.
Не свершится завет воскресения
Никогда и нигде для земли.

*

Высока луна Господня.
    Тяжко мне.
Истомилась я сегодня
    В тишине.

WHAT are our poor villages, what is the whole of space and time ? The Father has many mansions, but their names are unknown to us.

But I have a presentiment of the joys of paradise, beside which life is only a dream; and I renounce illusory sweetness and repudiate the torment of time.

Decline, suffering, and decay – you have woven me a cruel garland. Never and nowhere will the promise of resurrection be fulfilled for the earth.

*

GOD'S moon is high in the sky. I feel wretched. I've had a miserable day in silence.

Ни одна вокруг не лает
    Из подруг.
Скучно, страшно замирает
    Всё вокруг.

В ясных улицах так пусто,
    Так мертво.
Не слыхать шагов, ни хруста,
    Ничего.

Землю нюхая в тревоге,
    Жду я бед.
Слабо пахнет по дороге
    Чей-то след.

Никого нигде не будит
    Быстрый шаг.
Жданный путник, кто ж он будет, –
    Друг иль враг?

Под холодною луною
    Я одна.
Нет, не в мочь мне, – я завою
    У окна.

Высока луна Господня,
    Высока.

Around me not one of my companions is barking. Everything around is sinking into a tedious and frightening hush.

The brightly lit streets are so empty and dead. You can't hear any tread or crunching of feet – nothing.

I sniff the ground apprehensively, expecting trouble. Someone's track smells faintly along the road.

There are no hurried footsteps anywhere to wake people up. The long-awaited wayfarer, who will he be – friend or foe?

I am alone beneath the cold moon. No, I can't stand it – I'll start howling by the window.

God's moon is high in the sky. . . . . . .

Грусть томит меня сегодня
И тоска.

Просыпайтесь, нарушайте
Тишину.
Сёстры, сёстры! войте, лайте.
На луну!

*

Забыты вино и веселье,
Оставлены латы и меч, –
Один он идёт в подземелье,
Лампады не хочет зажечь.

И дверь заскрипела протяжно,
В неё не входили давно.
За дверью и тёмно и влажно,
Высоко и узко окно.

Глаза привыкают во мраке, –
И вот выступают сквозь мглу
Какие-то странные знаки
На сводах, стенах и полу.

Sadness and anguish are tormenting me today.
   Wake up, break the silence! Sisters, my sisters, howl, bark at the moon!
*

WINE and merry-making are forgotten, armour and sword are left behind; alone he descends into the dungeon, unwilling to light a lamp.
   The door opens with a prolonged creak: no one has entered through it for a long time. It is dark and damp beyond the door, and the window is high and narrow.
   His eyes grow accustomed to the dark; and through the gloom strange marks emerge on the vaults, the walls, and the floor.

Он долго глядит на сплетенье
Непонятых знаков и ждёт,
Что взорам его просветленье
Всезрящая смерть принесёт.

[*Из «Дон-Кихота»*]

Дон-Кихот путей не выбирает,
Россинант дорогу сам найдёт.
Доблестного враг везде встречает,
С ним всегда сразится Дон-Кихот.

Славный круг насмешек, заблуждений,
Злых обманов, скорбных неудач,
Превращений, битв и поражений
Пробежит славнейшая из кляч.

Сквозь скрежещущий и ржавый грохот
Колесницы пламенного дня,
Сквозь проклятья, свист, глумленья, хохот,
Меч утратив, щит, копьё, коня,

Добредёт к ограде Дульцинеи
Дон-Кихот. Открыты ворота,

For a long time he gazes at the interlacement of these incomprehensible marks, and waits for all-seeing death to bring enlightenment to his eyes.

[*From 'Don Quixote'*]

DON Quixote does not choose his paths, Rosinante will find the way by herself. The enemy encounters the valiant one everywhere, Don Quixote will always do battle with him.

Through the glorious round of gibes, delusions, wicked deceptions, grievous failures, transformations, battles, and defeats, the most renowned of hacks will trot her way.

Through the grinding and rusty clangour of the fiery day's chariot, through the curses, whistles, jeers, and laughter – having lost sword, shield, lance, and horse –

Don Quixote will drag himself to the fence of Dulcinea's home. The gates are open, ...

Розами усеяны аллеи,
Срезанными с каждого куста.

Подавив непрошенные слёзы,
Спросит Дон-Кихот пажа: «Скажи,
Для чего загублены все розы?»
– «Весть пришла в чертоги госпожи,

Что стрелой отравленной злодея
Насмерть ранен верный Дон-Кихот.
Госпожа сказала: – Дульцинея
Дон-Кихота не переживёт. –

И, оплаканная горько нами,
Госпожа вкусила вечный сон,
И сейчас над этими цветами
Будет гроб её перенесён.»

И пойдёт за гробом бедный рыцарь,
Что ему глумленье и хула?
Дульцинея, светлая царица
Радостного рая, умерла!

the alleys are strewn with roses, cut from every bush.

Forcing back unbidden tears, Don Quixote will ask a page: 'Tell me, why have all the roses been laid waste?' – 'Tidings came to my lady's palace

that the faithful Don Quixote was wounded to death by the poisoned arrow of a villain. My lady said: "Dulcinea shall not survive Don Quixote."

And, bitterly mourned by us, my lady has fallen into eternal sleep; and presently her coffin will be carried over these flowers.'

And the poor knight will walk behind the coffin. What cares he for jeers and abuse? Dulcinea, the bright queen of joyful paradise, is dead!

VYACHESLAV IVANOV

Голоса

Муз моих вещунья и подруга,
Вдохновенных спутница Мэнад!
Отчего неведомого Юга
    Снится нам священный сад?

И о чём под кущей огнетканой
Чутколистный ропщет Дионис,
И, колебля мрак благоуханный,
    Шепчут лавр и кипарис?

И куда лазурной Нереиды
Нас зовёт певучая печаль?
Где она, волшебной Геспериды
    Золотящаяся даль?

Тихо спят кумиров наших храмы,
Древних грёз в пурпуровых морях;
Мы вотще сжигаем фимиамы
    На забытых алтарях.

Отчего же в дымных нимбах тени
Зыблются, подобные богам,

Voices

ORACLE and friend of my Muses, companion of the inspired Maenads! Why do we dream of the sacred garden of the mysterious South?

And what does tender-leafed Dionysus murmur beneath the fire-woven bower, and what do the laurel and the cypress, swaying in the fragrant darkness, whisper?

And whither does the tuneful sorrow of the azure Nereid call us? Where are they, the gold-gleaming confines of the far-away enchanted Hesperides?

In silence sleep the temples of our idols – those ancient fancies in purple seas; in vain do we burn incense on forgotten altars.

Why then do shades with misty haloes sway, looking like gods,

Будят лир зефирострунных пени –
   И зовут к родным брегам?

И зовут к родному новоселью
Неотступных ликов голоса,
И полны таинственной свирелью
   Молчаливые леса?...

Вдаль влекомы волей сокровенной,
Пришлецы неведомой земли,
Мы тоскуем по дали́ забвенной,
   По несбывшейся дали́.

Душу память смутная тревожит,
В смутном сне надеется она;
И забыть богов своих не может, –
   И воззвать их не сильна!

Любовь

Мы – два грозой зажжённые ствола,
Два пламени полуночного бора;

why do they awaken the plaints of the Zephyr-stringed lyres, and summon [us] to native shores?

And why do insistent voices of choirs summon [us] to a new and familiar home, and why are the silent woods filled with the sound of a mysterious pipe?

Driven on into the distance by a secret will, strangers who have come from an unknown country, we long for the forgotten distant land which never came to be.

Obscure memories trouble the soul: plunged in a confused dream, she cherishes hope; she cannot forget her gods, nor has she the power to call them forth.

Love

WE are two tree-trunks kindled by a thunderstorm, two flames in a midnight forest; . . . . .

Мы – два в ночи летящих метеора,
Одной судьбы двужалая стрела.

Мы – два коня, чьи держит удила
Одна рука, – одна язвит их шпора;
Два ока мы единственного взора,
Мечты одной два трепетных крыла.

Мы – двух теней скорбящая чета
Над мрамором божественного гроба,
Где древняя почиет Красота.

Единых тайн двугласные уста,
Себе самим мы Сфинкс единый оба.
Мы – две руки единого креста.

Римские Сонеты I

Вновь арок древних верный пилигрим,
В мой поздний час вечерним «Ave Roma»
Приветствую как свод родного дома,
Тебя, скитаний пристань, вечный Рим.

we are two meteors, flying through the night, a two-pointed arrow of one destiny.

We are two horses, whose reins are held by one hand, and which are pricked by the same spur; we are two eyes of a single vision, two quivering wings of one dream.

We are a sorrowful pair of shades above the marble of a sacred tomb, where ancient Beauty sleeps.

A two-voiced mouthpiece of the same mysteries, we are one and the same Sphinx for each other. We are the two arms of a single cross.

Roman Sonnets I

ONCE again, a faithful pilgrim of the ancient arches, in my late hour I greet you as the roof of my native home, with an evening 'Ave Roma', you, the wanderer's haven, eternal Rome.

Мы Трою предков пламени дарим;
Дробятся оси колесниц меж грома
И фурий мирового ипподрома:
Ты, царь путей, глядишь, как мы горим.

И ты пылал и восставал из пепла,
И памятливая голубизна
Твоих небес глубоких не ослепла.

И помнит в ласке золотого сна
Твой вратарь кипарис, как Троя крепла,
Когда лежала Троя сожжена.

Римские Сонеты IV

Окаменев под чарами журчанья
Бегущих струй за полные края,
Лежит полу-затоплена ладья;
К ней девушек с цветами шлёт Кампанья.

We abandon the Troy of our ancestors to the flames; the chariots' axles are splintered amid the thunder and the Furies of the world's hippodrome. You, king of all the roads, are watching as we burn.

You, too, burned and rose again from your ashes; and the retentive azure of your deep skies has not grown blind.

And in the caress of a golden dream your gate-keeper, the cypress, remembers how Troy grew strong, when Troy lay consumed by fire.

Roman Sonnets IV

TURNED to stone under the spell of the murmuring waters that flow over the brim, a boat lies, half-submerged.* The Campagna sends to it girls bearing flowers.

* This is the Fountain of the Barcaccia, in the Piazza di Spagna.

И лестница, переступая зданья,
Широкий путь узорами двоя,
Несёт в лазурь двух башен острия
И обелиск над Площадью ди-Спанья.

Люблю домов оранжевый загар
И людные меж старых стен теснины
И шорох пальм на ней в полдневный жар;

А ночью тёмной вздохи каватины
И под аккорды бархатных гитар
Бродячей стрекотанье мандолины.

Римские Сонеты VII

Спит водоём осенний, окроплён
Багрянцем нищим царственных отрепий.
Средь мхов и скал, муж со змеёй, Асклепий,
Под аркою глядит на красный клён.

И синий свод, как бронзой, окаймлён
Убранством сумрачных великолепий

And the staircase, stepping over the buildings, sweeping up-
wards in a double row of wide, ornamented steps, carries into the
blue sky the pinnacles of two towers and the obelisk above the
Piazza di Spagna.

I love the orange sun-tan of the houses, and the crowded narrow
passages between old walls, and the rustle of palm-trees on the
Piazza in the midday heat;

and, in the dark night, the sighs of the *cavatina* and the trill of a
roving mandoline to the accompaniment of velvety guitars.

Roman Sonnets VII

THE autumn fountain sleeps, sprinkled with the beggarly purple
of Imperial rags. Among moss and rocks, Aesculapius, the man
with the serpent, looks from under the arch at the red maple-tree.

And the blue sky is framed, as though with bronze, by the
sombre and splendid apparel . . . . . .

Листвы, на коей не коснели цепи
Мертвящих стуж, ни снежных блеск пелён.

Взирают так, с улыбкою печальной,
Блаженные на нас, как на платан
Увядший солнце. Плещет звон хрустальный:

Струя к лучу стремит зыбучий стан.
И в глади опрокинуты зеркальной
Асклепий, клён, и небо, и фонтан.

★

Зачем, о Просперо волшебный,
    Тебе престол,
Коль Ариель, твой дух служебный,
    Прочь отошёл?

Спешит к закату день Шекспира
    С тех пор, как хмель
Его мечты не строит лира –
    Смолк Ариель.

of the leaves which have not been stiffened by a succession of destructive frosts or by glittering palls of snow.

The blessed ones gaze upon us with a sad smile, like the sun upon a withered plane-tree. The splashing waters ring like crystal.

The jet flings its shifting silhouette towards the sun-ray. And on the mirror-like surface are reflected upside down Aesculapius, the maple-tree, the sky, and the fountain.

★

WHAT need have you of a throne, O Prospero skilled in magic, if Ariel, your attendant spirit, has departed from you?

Shakespeare's day is hastening to its decline now that the lyre has ceased to tune the rapture of his dream; Ariel has fallen silent.

VYACHESLAV IVANOV

Ужели гений – волхв могучий,
    Ты ж, Ариель,
Лишь посланец его певучий, –
    Лишь эльф ужель ?

Иль в гордую вошед обитель
    Из шалаша,
Ты сам владыки повелитель,
    Его душа ?

    Can it be that the genius is a mighty wizard, and that you, Ariel, are but his tuneful messenger ? Can it be that you are but an elf ?
    Or, having passed from a hovel into a stately mansion, are you yourself your lord's sovereign – his soul ?

KONSTANTIN BAL'MONT

Аккорды

В красоте музыкальности,
    Как в недвижной зеркальности,
Я нашёл очертания снов,
    До меня не рассказанных,
    Тосковавших и связанных,
Как растенья под глыбою льдов.

    Я им дал наслаждение,
    Красоту их рождения,
Я разрушил звенящие льды.
    И, как гимны неслышные,
    Дышут лотосы пышные
Над пространством зеркальной воды.

    И в немой музыкальности,
    В этой новой зеркальности,
Создаёт их живой хоровод
    Новый мир, недосказанный,
    Но с рассказанным связанный
В глубине отражающих вод.

Chords

In the beauty of melody, as on a still, mirror-like surface, I discovered the outlines of dreams untold by anyone before me, pining and confined like plants under blocks of ice.

I gave them the power to delight, I gave beauty to their birth, I shattered the ringing blocks of ice; and, like soundless hymns, luxuriant lotuses breathe above the expanse of the mirror-like water.

And in the soundless melody, on this new mirror-like surface, their live round dance generates a new world, not yet fully revealed but linked to the known world in the depth of reflecting waters.

Sin miedo

Если ты поэт, и хочешь быть могучим,
Хочешь быть бессмертным в памяти людей,
Порази их в сердце вымыслом певучим,
Думу закали на пламени страстей.

Ты видал кинжалы древнего Толедо?
Лучших не увидишь, где бы ни искал.
На клинке узорном надпись: «Sin miedo»:
Будь всегда бесстрашным, – властен их закал.

Раскалённой стали форму придавая,
В сталь кладут по черни золотой узор,
И века сверкает красота живая
Двух металлов слитых, разных с давних пор.

Чтоб твои мечты вовек не отблистали,
Чтоб твоя душа всегда была жива,
Разбросай в напевах золото по стали,
Влей огонь застывший в звонкие слова.

Sin miedo*

IF you are a poet and wish to be powerful and to live for ever in the memory of men, strike them to the heart with the melodious creations of your imagination, temper your thought upon the flame of passion.

Have you seen daggers of old Toledo? You won't find better ones, wherever you may search. On their figured blades there is an inscription: 'Sin miedo' – be always fearless: they are powerfully tempered.

When shaping the red-hot steel they inlay with niello the golden design on the steel, and the living beauty of the two alloyed metals, separate of old, glitters for centuries.

In order that your dreams may never cease to shine and your soul may always live, inlay in your melodies the steel with patterns of gold, pour molten fire into resonant words.

* Without fear.

ZINAIDA GIPPIUS

Она

В своей бессовестной и жалкой низости,
Она как пыль сера, как прах земной.
И умираю я от этой близости,
От неразрывности её со мной.

Она шершавая, она колючая,
Она холодная, она змея.
Меня изранила противно-жгучая
Её коленчатая чешуя.

О, если б острое почуял жало я!
Неповоротлива, тупа, тиха.
Такая тяжкая, такая вялая,
И нет к ней доступа – она глуха.

Своими кольцами она, упорная,
Ко мне ласкается, меня душа.
И эта мёртвая, и эта чёрная,
И эта страшная – моя душа!

She

IN her shameless and despicable vileness she is grey as dust, as earthly ashes. And I am perishing from her nearness, from the indissoluble bond between her and me.

She is scabrous, prickly, cold – she is a serpent. Her repulsive, searing, and jagged scales have covered me with wounds.

If only I could feel a sharp sting! She is flaccid, dull, and still, so lumpish and sluggish; there is no access to her – she is deaf.

Coiling round me, she stubbornly and insinuatingly caresses and strangles me. And this dead, black, and fearsome thing is my soul!

ZINAIDA GIPPIUS

Нелюбовь

Как ветер мокрый, ты бьёшься в ставни,
Как ветер чёрный, поёшь: ты мой!
Я древний хаос, я друг твой давний,
Твой друг единый, – открой, открой!

Держу за ставни, открыть не смею,
Держусь за ставни и страх таю.
Храню, лелею, храню, жалею
Мой луч последний – любовь мою.

Смеётся хаос, зовёт безокий:
Умрёшь в оковах, – порви, порви!
Ты знаешь счастье, ты одинокий,
В свободе счастье, – и в Нелюбви.

Охладевая, творю молитву,
Любви молитву едва творю . . .
Слабеют руки, кончаю битву,
Слабеют руки . . . Я отворю!

Non-Love

Like a damp wind you beat at the shutters, like a black wind you sing: 'You are mine! I am primeval Chaos, I am your old friend, your only friend – open, open!'

I hold on to the shutters, I dare not open, I hold on to the shutters and hide my fear. I keep and cherish, I keep and treasure my last ray – my love.

Sightless Chaos laughs and calls: 'You will die in fetters – tear, tear yourself away! You know happiness, you are alone, happiness lies in freedom – and in Non-Love.'

I grow cold and say a prayer, I am barely able to say a prayer of love . . . My hands are weakening, I am giving up the fight, my hands are weakening . . . I will open!

IVAN BUNIN

Спокойный взор, подобный взору лани,
И всё, что в нём так нежно я любил,
Я до сих пор в печали не забыл,
Но образ твой теперь уже в тумане.

А будут дни – угаснет и печаль,
И засинеет сон воспоминанья,
Где нет уже ни счастья, ни страданья,
А только всепрощающая даль.

Вальс

Похолодели лепестки
Раскрытых губ, по-детски влажных –
И зал плывёт, плывёт в протяжных
Напевах счастья и тоски.

Сиянье люстр и зыбь зеркал
Слились в один мираж хрустальный –
И веет, веет ветер бальный
Теплом душистых опахал.

THE tranquil look in your eyes, like that of a doe and all that I loved so tenderly in it, I have not to this day forgotten in my sadness, but now your image is already swathed in mist.

And the time will come when even sadness will die away, and the dream of remembrance will recede into the blue, where there is neither happiness nor suffering, but only an all-forgiving distance.

Waltz

THE petals of parted lips, childlike and moist, have grown cool; and the ballroom is drifting, drifting in slow melodies of happiness and yearning.

The glitter of chandeliers and the swaying movements in the mirrors have merged into a single mirage of crystal; and the wind of the ball is wafting, wafting the warm breath of the scented fans.

Люцифер

В святой Софии голуби летали,
Гнусил мулла. Эректеон был нем.
И боги гомерических поэм
В пустых музеях стыли и скучали.

Великий Сфинкс, исполненный печали,
Лежал в песках. Израиль, чуждый всем,
Сбирал, рыдая, ржавые скрижали.
Христос покинул жадный Вифлеем.

Вот Рай, Ливан. Рассвет горит багряно.
Снег гор – как шёлк. По скатам из пещер
Текут стада. В лугах – моря тумана . . .

Мир Авеля! Дни чистых детских вер!
Из-за нагих хребтов Антиливана
Блистает, угасая, Люцифер.

*

И цветы, и шмели, и трава, и колосья,
И лазурь, и полуденный зной . . .

Lucifer

In St Sophia pigeons were flying. The nasal tones of the imam were heard. The Erechtheum was mute. And in deserted museums the gods of the Homeric poems were growing cold and bored.

The great Sphinx, full of sorrow, lay in the sands. Israel, estranged from all, gathered its time-worn tables with lamentations. Christ had abandoned greedy Bethlehem.

The Lebanon, this is Paradise. The dawn is ablaze with crimson. The snow on the mountains is like silk. From the caves the flocks come wandering down the slopes. The meadows are covered with a sea of mist.

O world of Abel! Days of pure, childlike faith! From behind the bare ridges of the Anti-Lebanon Lucifer shimmers as it dies away.

*

Flowers, and bumble-bees, and grass, and ears [of corn], and the blue sky, and the midday heat . . .

Срок настанет – Господь сына блудного
спросит:
«Был ли счастлив ты в жизни земной?»

И забуду я всё – вспомню только вот эти
Полевые пути меж колосьев и трав –
И от сладостных слёз не успею ответить,
К милосердным коленям припав.

The time will come – the Lord will ask the prodigal son: 'Were you happy in your life on earth?'

And I shall forget everything, and remember only these paths across the fields between the ears of corn and the grass – and, pressed against [His] merciful knees, I shall be unable to reply for the tears of joy in my eyes.

VALERY BRYUSOV

Сонет к форме

Есть тонкие властительные связи
Меж контуром и запахом цветка.
Так бриллиант невидим нам, пока
Под гранями не оживёт в алмазе.

Так образы изменчивых фантазий,
Бегущие, как в небе облака,
Окаменев, живут потом века
В отточенной и завершённой фразе.

И я хочу, чтоб все мои мечты,
Дошедшие до слова и до света,
Нашли себе желанные черты.

Пускай мой друг, открывши том поэта,
Упьётся в нём и прелестью сонета
И буквами спокойной красоты!

A Sonnet to Form

There are subtle but potent affinities between the outline and the scent of a flower; so the diamond is invisible until it comes to life in the cut and polished stone.

So do images of fleeting fancy, drifting like the clouds in the sky, become hard as stone and thereafter live for centuries in a chiselled and finished phrase.

And it is my wish that all my fancies which have reached the realm of words and light may find for themselves the desired outlines.

May my friend, on opening a volume of the poet's verses, take delight both in the loveliness of a sonnet and in the letter of its tranquil beauty.

VALERY BRYUSOV

Ахиллес у алтаря

Знаю я, во вражьем стане
Изогнулся меткий лук,
Слышу в утреннем тумане
Тетивы певучий звук.

Встал над жертвой облак дыма,
Песня хора весела,
Но разит неотвратимо
Аполлонова стрела.

Я спешу склонить колена,
Но не с трепетной мольбой.
Обручён я, Поликсена,
На единый миг с тобой!

Всем равно в глухом Эребе
Годы долгие скорбеть.
Но прекрасен ясный жребий –
Просиять и умереть!

Мать звала к спокойной доле . . .
Нет! не выбрал счастье я!

Achilles at the Altar

I KNOW that a sharp-shooting bow has been bent within the enemy's camp; in the morning mist I hear the bow-string's melodious twang.

A cloud of smoke has risen above the victim, gay is the choir's song, but Apollo's arrow strikes down unerringly.

I hasten to bend my knee, though not in trembling supplication. I am betrothed to you for a single instant, O Polyxene!

All men equally will grieve for long years in dim Erebus. But to shine forth and to die is a fate fair and bright!

My mother called me to a peaceful fate . . . No! I did not choose happiness. . . . . . .

Прошумела в ратном поле
Жизнь мятежная моя.

И, вступив сегодня в Трою
В блеске царского венца, –
Пред стрелою не укрою
Я спокойного лица!

Дай, к устам твоим приникнув,
Посмотреть в лицо твоё,
Чтоб не дрогнув, чтоб не крикнув
Встретить смерти остриё.

И, не кончив поцелуя,
Клятвы тихие творя,
Улыбаясь, упаду я
На помосте алтаря.

Поэту

Ты должен быть гордым, как знамя;
Ты должен быть острым, как меч;
Как Данту, подземное пламя
Должно тебе щёки обжечь.

My restless life has passed resoundingly on the field of battle.

And, on entering Troy today in the radiance of a royal crown, I will not shield my calm face from an arrow.

Let me press my lips to yours and look into your face, that I may meet death's sharp point without a tremor or a cry.

And, softly murmuring vows and smiling, I shall fall, my kiss unfinished, on the scaffold of the altar.

To the Poet

You must be proud as a banner; you must be sharp as a sword; your cheeks, like Dante's, must be scorched by a subterranean flame.

VALERY BRYUSOV

Всего будь холодный свидетель,
На всё устремляя свой взор.
Да будет твоя добродетель –
Готовность взойти на костёр.

Быть может, всё в жизни лишь средство
Для ярко-певучих стихов,
И ты с беспечального детства
Ищи сочетания слов.

В минуты любовных объятий
К бесстрастью себя приневоль,
И в час беспощадных распятий
Прославь исступлённую боль.

В снах утра и в бездне вечерней
Лови, что шепнёт тебе Рок,
И помни: от века из терний
Поэта заветный венок.

Be a coldly dispassionate witness of all things, and turn your gaze
to everything. Let your virtue be a readiness to mount the pyre.

It may be that everything in life is but a means for the creation
of vivid and melodious verses; so from your carefree childhood,
search for combinations of words.

Force yourself to be passionless in moments of loving embrace,
and when you are crucified by merciless agony glorify your frenzied
pain.

In the dreams of morning and in evening's abyss try to grasp
Fate's whispered message, and remember: from time immemorial
the poet's cherished crown has been one of thorns.

MIKHAIL KUZMIN

О, быть покинутым – какое счастье!
Какой безмерный в прошлом виден свет –
Так после лета – зимнее ненастье:
Всё помнишь солнце, хоть его уж нет.

Сухой цветок, любовных писем связка,
Улыбка глаз, счастливых встречи две, –
Пускай теперь в пути темно и вязко,
Но ты весной бродил по мураве.

Ах, есть другой урок для сладострастья,
Иной есть путь – пустынен и широк.
О, быть покинутым – такое счастье!
Быть нелюбимым – вот горчайший рок.

Фузий в блюдечке

Сквозь чайный пар я вижу гору Фузий,
На жёлтом небе золотой вулкан.
Как блюдечко природу странно узит!

Oн, what happiness it is to be forsaken – what boundless light is seen in the past! So summer is followed by the bad weather of winter: you still remember the sun, though it is no longer here.

A dried-up flower, a bundle of love-letters, smiling eyes, a couple of happy meetings – though now your road be dark and marshy, yet you have trodden the fresh grass in spring.

Ah, there is another lesson for sensuality, there is another path – it is deserted and wide. Oh, it's such happiness to be forsaken! To be unloved – that is the bitterest lot.

Fujiyama in a Saucer

Through the steam rising from the tea I see Mount Fujiyama, a golden volcano against a yellow sky. How strangely does a saucer contract a landscape! . . . . . .

Но новый трепет мелкой рябью дан.
Как облаков продольных паутинки
Пронзает солнце с муравьиный глаз,
А птицы-рыбы, чёрные чаинки,
Чертят лазури зыблемый топаз!
Весенний мир вместится в малом мире:
Запахнут миндали, затрубит рог,
И весь залив, хоть будь он вдвое шире,
Фарфоровый обнимет ободок.
Но ветка неожиданной мимозы,
Рассекши небеса, легла на них, –
Так на страницах философской прозы
Порою заблестит влюблённый стих.

But the gently rippling surface imparts a new vibration to it. Look how the gossamer-like clouds, sketched lengthwise, are pierced by a sun the size of an ant's head, and how the black tea-leaves, resembling birds or fish, form lines on the quivering topaz of the blue sky! The world of spring will be contained in a small world: the almond-trees will become fragrant, the horn will sound, and the porcelain rim will encompass the whole bay, though the latter be twice as wide. But an unexpected branch of mimosa, cleaving the sky, lies across it: so on the pages of philosophical prose a line of love poetry will sometimes shine.

MAKSIMILIAN VOLOSHIN

Над зыбкой рябью вод встаёт из глубины
Пустынный кряж земли: хребты скалистых
гребней,
Обрывы чёрные, потоки красных щебней –
Пределы скорбные незнаемой страны.

Я вижу грустные торжественные сны –
Заливы гулкие земли глухой и древней,
Где в поздних сумерках грустнее и напевней
Звучат пустынные гекзаметры волны.

И парус в темноте, скользя по бездорожью,
Трепещет древнею таинственною дрожью
Ветров тоскующих и дышащих зыбей.

Путём назначенным дерзанья и возмездья
Стремит мою ладью глухая дрожь морей,
И в небе теплятся лампады Семизвездья.

ABOVE the gently swelling and rippling water a deserted spur of land rises out of the sea: rocky ridges, black precipices, torrents of red shingle – the sorrowful confines of an unknown land.

I dream sad and solemn dreams: resonant bays of a remote and ancient land, where the waves' lonely hexameters sound sadder and more melodious in the late twilight.

And a sail in the darkness, gliding over the trackless expanse, quivers with the ancient and mysterious tremor of yearning winds and of the heaving swell.

Along the appointed path of daring and retribution my boat is driven by the obscure tremor of the seas, and the lamps of the Great Bear glimmer in the sky.

Святая Русь

Суздаль да Москва не для тебя ли
По уделам землю собирали,
Да тугую золотом суму?
В рундуках приданое копили,
И тебя невестою растили
В расписном да тесном терему?

Не тебе ли на речных истоках
Плотник-Царь построил дом широко –
Окнами на пять земных морей?
Из невест красой да силой бранной
Не была ль ты самою желанной
Для заморских княжих сыновей?

Но тебе сыздетства были любы –
По лесам глубоким скитов срубы,
По степям кочевья без дорог,
Вольные раздолья да вериги,
Самозванцы, воры да расстриги,
Соловьиный посвист да острог.

Holy Russia

WAS it not for you that Suzdal' and Moscow gathered the land apanage by apanage, collected gold in a tightly packed bag, stored up a dowry in their coffers, and reared you as a bride in a narrow, frescoed tower-room?

Was it not for you that the Carpenter-Tsar built by the sources of rivers a spacious house, with windows looking out on to the five seas of the earth? With your beauty and warlike strength were you not the most desirable of brides for the sons of foreign princes?

But from childhood you had a liking for wooden hermitages deep in the forests, for trackless lands of nomads in the steppes, for free open spaces, for ascetics' chains, for pretenders, felons, and unfrocked monks, for the whistling of Nightingale the Robber,* and for prisons.

* A fantastic creature of Russian heroic poetry, half bird, half man. (See p. xi).

Быть Царевой ты не захотела —
Уж такое подвернулось дело:
Враг шептал: развей да расточи,
Ты отдай казну свою богатым,
Власть – холопам, силу – супостатам,
Смердам – честь, изменникам – ключи.

Поддалась лихому подговору,
Отдалась разбойнику и вору,
Подожгла посады и хлеба,
Разорила древнее жилище,
И пошла поруганной и нищей,
И рабой последнего раба.

Я ль в тебя посмею бросить камень?
Осужу ль страстной и буйный пламень?
В грязь лицом тебе ль не поклонюсь,
След босой ноги благословляя, –
Ты – бездомная, гулящая, хмельная,
Во Христе юродивая Русь!

You did not want to belong to the Tsar, and this is the way things turned out: the enemy whispered: 'Scatter and squander, give away your treasure to the rich, your power to slaves, your strength to your enemies, to villeins your honour, to traitors your keys.'

You lent you ear to the evil counsel, you gave yourself to the robber and to the felon, you set fire to your suburbs and crops, you laid waste your ancient dwelling-place, and you went out humiliated and a beggar, and the slave of the meanest slave.

Shall I dare cast a stone at you? Shall I condemn your wild and passionate flame? Shall I not bow down before you with my face in the mud, blessing the trace of your bare foot, you homeless, wanton, drunken Russia – fool in Christ!

ANDREY BELY

Объяснение в любви

Сияет роса на листочках,
И солнце над прудом горит.
Красавица с мушкой на щёчках,
Как пышная роза сидит.

Любезная сердцу картина!
Вся в белых, сквозных кружевах
Мечтает под звук клавесина . . .
Горит в золотистых лучах –

Под вешнею лаской фортуны
И хмелью обвитый карниз,
И стены. Прекрасный и юный
Пред нею склонился маркиз –

В привычно заученной роли,
В волнисто-седом парике,
В лазурно-атласном камзоле,
С малиновой розой в руке.

«Я вас обожаю, кузина,
Извольте цветок сей принять . . .»

Declaration of Love

THE dew sparkles on the leaves, and the sun shines above the pond.
A fair lady with a beauty-spot on her cheek sits like a gorgeous rose.

Picture pleasing to the heart! Dressed all in white semi-transparent lace, she dreams to the sound of the harpsichord . . . She glows in the golden rays of the sun.

Both the cornice entwined with hop and the walls are under Fortune's spring caress. A handsome young marquis bows before her –

in his accustomed and studied role, in a curled grey wig, in a skyblue satin camisole, with a crimson rose in his hand.

'I adore you, cousin – deign to accept this flower . . .'

Смеётся под звук клавесина
И хочет кузину обнять.

Уже вдоль газонов росистых
Туман бледно-белый ползёт.
В волнах фиолетово-мглистых
Луна золотая плывёт.

*

Довольно: не жди, не надейся –
Рассейся, мой бедный народ!
В пространстве пади и разбейся
За годом мучительный год!

Века нищеты и безволья.
Позволь же, о родина мать,
В сырое, в пустое раздолье,
В раздолье твоё прорыдать: –

Туда, на равнине горбатой, –
Где стая зелёных дубов
Волнуется купой подъятой,
В косматый свинец облаков,

He laughs to the sound of the harpsichord and wants to embrace his cousin.

And now a pale white mist is already creeping over the dewy lawns; and a golden moon is floating on the waves of a violet haze.

*

Enough! Don't wait or hope, be scattered, my unhappy people! Agonizing succession of years – be shattered and vanish into space!

Ages of poverty and bondage . . . O my motherland, let me sob my heart out in your damp, empty expanse.

Out there on the humped plain, where a clump of green oaks sways and rises towards the shaggy lead of the clouds;

ANDREY BELY

Где по полю Оторопь рыщет,
Восстав сухоруким кустом,
И в ветер пронзительно свищет
Ветвистым своим лоскутом.

Где в душу мне смотрят из ночи,
Поднявшись над сетью бугров,
Жестокие, жёлтые очи
Безумных твоих кабаков, –

Туда, – где смертей и болезней
Лихая прошла колея, –
Исчезни в пространство, исчезни,
Россия, Россия моя!

where Terror ranges over the open plain, rising like a bush with withered arms, its ragged branches whistling piercingly in the wind;

where the pitiless, yellow eyes of your crazy taverns, hovering over a range of hillocks, peer into my soul out of the night;

where the baleful track of death and disease has passed – vanish, vanish into space, O Russia, my Russia!

ALEKSANDR BLOK

Незнакомка

По вечерам над ресторанами
Горячий воздух дик и глух,
И правит окриками пьяными
Весенний и тлетворный дух.

Вдали, над пылью переулочной,
Над скукой загородных дач,
Чуть золотится крендель булочной,
И раздаётся детский плач.

И каждый вечер, за шлагбаумами,
Заламывая котелки,
Среди канав гуляют с дамами
Испытанные остряки.

Над озером скрипят уключины,
И раздаётся женский визг,
А в небе, ко всему приученный,
Бессмысленно кривится диск.

The Stranger

In the evenings the sultry air above the restaurants is savage and heavy, and the breath of spring and corruption carries the sound of drunken shouts.

In the distance, above the dust of the lanes and the boredom of suburban villas, the gilded sign over the bakery can just be seen, and a child can be heard crying.

And every evening, beyond the toll-gates, their bowler hats tipped at rakish angle, the practised wits stroll about between the ditches with the ladies.

On the lake the rowlocks creak and a woman shrieks, while in the sky the moon's disk, inured to everything, leers senselessly.

И каждый вечер друг единственный
В моём стакане отражён
И влагой терпкой и таинственной,
Как я, смирён и оглушён.

А рядом у соседних столиков
Лакеи сонные торчат,
И пьяницы с глазами кроликов
«In vino veritas!» кричат.

И каждый вечер, в час назначенный
(Иль это только снится мне?),
Девичий стан, шелками схваченный,
В туманном движется окне.

И медленно, пройдя меж пьяными,
Всегда без спутников, одна,
Дыша духами и туманами,
Она садится у окна.

И веют древними поверьями
Её упругие шелка,
И шляпа с траурными перьями,
И в кольцах узкая рука.

And every evening my only friend is mirrored in my wine-glass
and, like myself, is subdued and dazed by the tart and mysterious
liquor.

And near by, sleepy waiters hang about beside the adjoining
tables, while drunkards, with rabbit-like eyes, shout: 'In vino
veritas!'

And every evening at the appointed hour – or am I only dreaming it? – the figure of a girl, swathed in silk, moves across the
misted window.

And, slowly passing among the drunkards, always unescorted,
breathing perfume and mists, she sits down alone by the window.

Her resilient silks, her hat with its black plumes, and her narrow
hand adorned with rings breathe an air of ancient legends.

И странной близостью закованный,
Смотрю за тёмную вуаль,
И вижу берег очарованный
И очарованную даль.

Глухие тайны мне поручены,
Мне чьё-то солнце вручено,
И все души моей излучины
Пронзило терпкое вино.

И перья страуса склонённые
В моём качаются мозгу,
И очи синие бездонные
Цветут на дальнем берегу.

В моей душе лежит сокровище,
И ключ поручен только мне!
Ты право, пьяное чудовище!
Я знаю: истина в вине.

*

О доблестях, о подвигах, о славе
Я забывал на горестной земле,

Entranced by this strange nearness, I look through a dark veil, and see an enchanted shore and an enchanted distance.

Hidden mysteries are entrusted to me, someone's sun has been committed to my care; and the tart wine has pierced all the convolutions of my soul.

And the drooping ostrich plumes wave in my brain, and blue fathomless eyes flower on a distant shore.

A treasure lies buried in my soul, and the key to it is entrusted to me alone. You are right, you drunken monster; I know: truth lies in wine.

*

On the sorrowful earth I forgot about valour, heroic deeds, and glory, ...

Когда твоё лицо в простой оправе
Передо мной сияло на столе.

Но час настал, и ты ушла из дому.
Я бросил в ночь заветное кольцо.
Ты отдала свою судьбу другому,
И я забыл прекрасное лицо.

Летели дни, крутясь проклятым роем . . .
Вино и страсть терзали жизнь мою . . .
И вспомнил я тебя пред аналоем,
И звал тебя, как молодость свою . . .

Я звал тебя, но ты не оглянулась,
Я слёзы лил, но ты не снизошла.
Ты в синий плащ печально завернулась,
В сырую ночь ты из дому ушла.

Не знаю, где приют своей гордыне
Ты, милая, ты, нежная, нашла . . .
Я крепко сплю, мне снится плащ твой синий,
В котором ты в сырую ночь ушла . . .

---

when your face in a simple frame shone before me on the table.

But the hour struck, and you walked out of the house. I flung the cherished ring into the night. You placed your fate in another's hands, and I forgot your beautiful face.

Days flew by, circling in a cursed swarm . . . Wine and passion tormented my life . . . And I remembered you as you stood before the altar, and I called you, as I would my youth . . .

I called you, but you did not look back; I shed tears, but you did not relent. Sadly you wrapped yourself in a blue cloak and walked out of the house into the damp night.

I do not know, O dear and tender one, where you found a shelter for your pride . . . I sleep soundly, I dream of your blue cloak in which you walked out into the damp night . . .

Уж не мечтать о нежности, о славе,
Всё миновалось, молодость прошла!
Твоё лицо в его простой оправе
Своей рукой убрал я со стола.

За гробом

Божья Матерь *Утоли мои печали*
Перед гробом шла, светла, тиха.
А за гробом – в траурной вуали
Шла невеста, провожая жениха . . .

Был он только литератор модный,
Только слов кощунственных творец . . .
Но мертвец – родной душе народной:
Всякий свято чтит она конец.

И навстречу кланялись, крестили
Многодумный, многотрудный лоб.
А друзья и близкие пылили
На икону, на неё, на гроб . . .

No longer can I dream of tenderness, of glory; it is all over, my
youth is past. With my own hand I removed your face in its simple
frame from the table.

Behind the Coffin

An icon of the Mother of God 'Soothe my sorrows', bright and
serene, went before the coffin; and behind the coffin, in a black veil,
walked a bride who was bidding farewell to her betrothed.

He was only a fashionable man of letters, a maker of blas-
phemous words . . . But a dead man is dear to the people's heart:
they hold every death in holy reverence.

And the passers-by who met the procession bowed their heads,
heavy with thought and work, and crossed themselves; while the
friends and relatives raised clouds of dust that settled on the icon,
on her, and on the coffin . . .

И с какою бесконечной грустью
(Не о нём – Бог весть о ком?)
Приняла она слова сочувствий
И венок случайный за венком . . .

Этих фраз избитых повторенья,
Никому не нужные слова –
Возвела она в венец творенья,
В тайную улыбку Божества . . .

Словно здесь, где пели и кадили,
Где и грусть не может быть тиха,
Убралась она фатой от пыли
И ждала Иного Жениха . . .

На поле Куликовом

I

Река раскинулась. Течёт, грустит лениво
И моет берега.
Над скудной глиной жёлтого обрыва
В степи грустят стога.

And she accepted the words of condolence and the succession of casual wreaths with such infinite sadness, grieving not for him – God knows for whom . . .

These repeated, hackneyed phrases – words which no one needs – she raised up into a crown of creation, into a secret smile of God . . .

As though, amid the singing and the incense, in a place where even grief cannot be silent, she arrayed herself in a bridal veil against the dust and awaited another Bridegroom.

On the Field of Kulikovo

I

THE river is spread out wide. It flows, sad and sluggish, and washes its banks. Above the barren clay of the yellow cliff ricks stand sadly in the steppe.

О, Русь моя! Жена моя! До боли
    Нам ясен долгий путь!
Наш путь – стрелой татарской древней воли
    Пронзил нам грудь.

Наш путь – степной, наш путь – в тоске
                    безбрежной,
    В твоей тоске, о, Русь!
И даже мглы – ночной и зарубежной –
    Я не боюсь.

Пусть ночь. Домчимся. Озарим кострами
    Степную даль.
В степном дыму блеснёт святое знамя
    И ханской сабли сталь . . .

И вечный бой! Покой нам только снится
    Сквозь кровь и пыль . . .
Летит, летит степная кобылица
    И мнёт ковыль . . .

И нет конца! Мелькают вёрсты, кручи . . .
    Останови!

O Russia! My wife! Our long road lies painfully clear ahead. Our road has pierced our breast with an arrow of the ancient Tatar power.

Our road lies through the steppe, it lies through boundless anguish – your anguish, O Russia! And even the darkness of night that lies beyond the border I do not fear.

Let night come. We will gallop on to our goal. We will light up with camp-fires the steppe stretching into the distance. In the smoke of the steppe the holy banner and the steel blade of the Khan's sabre will flash . . .

And the battle has no end! We only dream of peace through the blood and dust . . . The mare of the steppe flies on and on, and tramples the feather-grass.

And there is no end . . . The miles and cliffs flash past . . . Stop!

Идут, идут испуганные тучи,
        Закат в крови!

Закат в крови! Из сердца кровь струится!
        Плачь, сердце, плачь . . .
Покоя нет! Степная кобылица
        Несётся вскачь!

2

Мы, сам-друг, над степью в полночь стали:
Не вернуться, не взглянуть назад.
За Непрядвой лебеди кричали,
И опять, опять они кричат . . .

На пути – горючий белый камень.
За рекой – поганая орда.
Светлый стяг над нашими полками
Не взыграет больше никогда.

И, к земле склонившись головою,
Говорит мне друг: «Остри свой меч,

The frightened clouds are drawing nearer and nearer, and the sunset is bathed in blood.

The sunset is bathed in blood. Blood streams from the heart. Weep, heart, weep. There is no peace – the mare of the steppe flies on at a full gallop!

2

At midnight you and I came to a halt in the steppe. There is no turning or looking back. Beyond the Nepryadva the swans were crying, and again, again they cry . . .

On our way is the burning white stone,* beyond the river is the pagan Horde. The shining banner will never again flutter gaily over our host.

And, bending her head to the ground, my friend says to me: 'Sharpen your sword, ...

* An allusion to the sacred and magical 'white burning stone Alatyr' ' of Russian folklore.

Чтоб не даром биться с татарвою,
За святое дело мёртвым лечь!»

Я – не первый воин, не последний,
Долго будет родина больна.
Помяни ж за раннею обедней
Мила друга, светлая жена!

3

В ночь, когда Мамай залёг с ордою
     Степи и мосты,
В тёмном поле были мы с Тобою, –
     Разве знала Ты?

Перед Доном, тёмным и зловещим,
     Средь ночных полей,
Слышал я Твой голос сердцем вещим
     В криках лебедей.

С полунóчи тучей возносилась
     Княжеская рать,
И вдали, вдали о стремя билась,
     Голосила мать.

that you may not fight the Tatars and lay down your life for the
holy cause in vain!'
  I am not the first warrior, nor the last; the motherland will long
be ailing. So pray for your beloved at the early morning Liturgy, O
wife, fair and bright!

3

On the night when Mamai and the Horde went to ground on the
steppe and the bridges, you and I were in the dark plain together –
did you know this?
  In front of the Don, dark and ominous, I heard with my prophetic heart in the plain at night your voice in the cries of the
swans.
  From midnight onwards the prince's host rose up like a cloud,
while in the distance the mother beat against the stirrup and
wailed.

И, чертя круги, ночные птицы
    Реяли вдали.
А над Русью тихие зарницы
    Князя стерегли.

Орлий клёкот над татарским станом
    Угрожал бедой,
А Непрядва убралась туманом,
    Что княжна фатой.

И с туманом над Непрядвой спящей
    Прямо на меня
Ты сошла, в одежде свет струящей,
    Не спугнув коня.

Серебром волны блеснула другу
    На стальном мече,
Освежила пыльную кольчугу
    На моём плече.

И когда, наутро, тучей чёрной
    Двинулась орда,
Был в щите Твой лик нерукотворный
    Светел навсегда.

And night birds were circling and hovering in the distance, while above Russia silent summer lightning watched over the prince.

Above the Tatar camp the eagles' cries portended disaster, while the Nepryadva arrayed herself in mist, like a princess in a veil.

And, together with the mist that lay over the sleeping Nepryadva, you came down straight at me, in a radiant garment, without startling my horse.

Like a silver wave you flashed on your friend's steel sword, you refreshed the dusty armour on my shoulders.

And when next morning the Horde moved forward like a black cloud, your image, not made by human hands, was for ever bright upon my shield.

4

Опять с вековою тоскою
Пригнулись к земле ковыли.
Опять за туманной рекою
Ты кличешь меня издали.

Умчались, пропали без вести
Степных кобылиц табуны,
Развязаны дикие страсти
Под игом ущербной луны.

И я с вековою тоскою,
Как волк под ущербной луной,
Не знаю, что делать с собою,
Куда мне лететь за тобой!

Я слушаю рокоты сечи
И трубные крики татар,
Я вижу над Русью далече
Широкий и тихий пожар.

Объятый тоскою могучей,
Я рыщу на белом коне . . .

4

Once again the feather-grass bends down to the earth with age-old anguish, once again beyond the misty river you call me from afar.

The droves of the steppe mares have sped away and vanished without a trace, wild passions are unleashed under the yoke of the waning moon.

And I, with my age-old anguish, like a wolf under the waning moon, do not know what to do with myself, where to fly in your wake.

I listen to the rumble of battle, and to the trumpet-calls and shouts of the Tatars, I see a vast and silent conflagration raging far over Russia.

Gripped by an immense anguish, I range on my white horse ..

Встречаются вольные тучи
Во мглистой ночной вышине.

Вздымаются светлые мысли
В растерзанном сердце моём,
И падают светлые мысли,
Сожжённые тёмным огнём . . .

«Явись, моё дивное диво!
Быть светлым меня научи!»
Вздымается конская грива . . .
За ветром взывают мечи . . .

5

И мглою бед неотразимых
Грядущий день заволокло,
Вл. Соловьёв

Опять над полем Куликовым
Взошла и расточилась мгла,
И, словно облаком суровым,
Грядущий день заволокла.

За тишиною непробудной,
За разливающейся мглой

I encounter the freely moving clouds high up in the misty night.

Radiant thoughts rise in my lacerated heart, and radiant thoughts fall, consumed by a dark fire . . .

'Reveal yourself, my marvellous marvel, teach me to be radiant!' The horse's mane rises . . . The swords call out in the wake of the wind . . .

5

And the dawning day was clouded with the darkness of inescapable misfortunes.
Vl. Soloviev

Once again the mist rose and spread over the field of Kulikovo, and veiled the dawning day like a lowering cloud.

Behind the total silence and the spreading mist . . . . . .

Не слышно грома битвы чудной,
Не видно молньи боевой.

Но узнаю тебя, начало
Высоких и мятежных дней!
Над вражьим станом, как бывало,
И плеск, и трубы лебедей.

Не может сердце жить покоем,
Недаром тучи собрались.
Доспех тяжёл, как перед боем.
Теперь твой час настал. – Молись!

Равенна

Всё, что минутно, всё, что бренно,
Похоронила ты в веках.
Ты, как младенец, спишь, Равенна,
У сонной вечности в руках.

Рабы сквозь римские ворота
Уже не ввозят мозаик.
И догорает позолота
В стенах прохладных базилик.

---

you cannot hear the thunder of the prodigious battle, nor see the lightning of the struggle.

But I recognize you, dawn of exalted and turbulent days! Above the enemy camp, as before, there are the trumpet-like cries of the swans, and the flapping of their wings.

The heart cannot abide in peace, not in vain have the clouds gathered. The armour is heavy, as before battle. Now your hour has struck. – Pray!

Ravenna

You have buried in the centuries all that is transient and frail. You sleep like a child, Ravenna, in the arms of drowsy eternity.

No longer do slaves bring in mosaic through the Roman gates, and the gilt on the walls of the cool basilicas is burning out.

От медленных лобзаний влаги
Нежнее грубый свод гробниц,
Где зеленеют саркофаги
Святых монахов и цариц.

Безмолвны гробовые залы,
Тенист и хладен их порог,
Чтоб чёрный взор блаженной Галлы,
Проснувшись, камня не прожёг.

Военной брани и обиды
Забыт и стёрт кровавый след,
Чтобы воскресший глас Плакиды
Не пел страстей протекших лет.

Далёко отступило море,
И розы оцепили вал,
Чтоб спящий в гробе Теодорих
О буре жизни не мечтал.

А виноградные пустыни,
Дома и люди – всё гроба.
Лишь медь торжественной латыни
Поёт на плитах, как труба.

The rough vaults of the sepulchres have grown softer under the moisture's lingering kisses, where the sarcophagi of holy monks and empresses are filmed with green.

The burial halls are silent, their thresholds shady and cold, lest the gaze of blessed Galla's black eyes should awake and burn through the stone.

The bloody trail of war and injury is effaced and forgotten, lest Placidia's voice should come to life and sing the passions of bygone years.

Far has the sea receded, and the roses cluster round the rampart, lest Theoderic, sleeping in his tomb, should dream of life's tempests.

And the vine-hung wastes, the houses and the people – all are graves. Only the stately Latin, inscribed in bronze, rings on the tombstones like a trumpet.

ALEKSANDR BLOK

Лишь в пристальном и тихом взоре
Равеннских девушек, порой,
Печаль о невозвратном море
Проходит робкой чередой.

Лишь по ночам, склонясь к долинам,
Ведя векам грядущим счёт,
Тень Данта с профилем орлиным
О Новой Жизни мне поёт.

Шаги Командора

Тяжкий, плотный занавес у входа,
    За ночным окном – туман.
Что теперь твоя постылая свобода,
    Страх познавший Дон Жуан?

Холодно и пусто в пышной спальне,
    Слуги спят, и ночь глуха.
Из страны блаженной, незнакомой, даль-
                                    ней
    Слышно пенье петуха.

Only in the intent and tranquil gaze of the girls of Ravenna does regret for the sea that will never return flicker shyly now and then.

Only at night the shade of Dante with his aquiline profile, bending over the valleys and taking stock of the centuries to come, sings to me of the New Life.

The Commendatore's Footsteps

A THICK and heavy curtain at the entrance, behind the window lies the mist of night. What price now your tedious freedom, Don Juan, now that you know fear?

The sumptuous bedroom is cold and empty, the servants are asleep, and it is the dead of night. From some blessed, unknown, far-away land comes the sound of the cock crowing.

Что изменнику блаженства звуки?
Миги жизни сочтены.
Донна Анна спит, скрестив на сердце руки,
Донна Анна видит сны . . .

Чьи черты жестокие застыли,
В зеркалах отражены?
Анна, Анна, сладко ль спать в могиле?
Сладко ль видеть неземные сны?

Жизнь пуста, безумна и бездонна!
Выходи на битву, старый рок!
И в ответ – победно и влюблённо –
В снежной мгле поёт рожок . . .

Пролетает, брызнув в ночь огнями,
Чёрный, тихий, как сова, мотор.
Тихими, тяжёлыми шагами
В дом вступает Командор . . .

Настежь дверь. Из непомерной стужи,
Словно хриплый бой ночных часов –

What can sounds of bliss mean to a traitor? Life's moments are numbered. Donna Anna sleeps, hands crossed on her bosom, Donna Anna dreams . . .

Whose cruel features are reflected, motionless and rigid, in the mirrors? Anna, Anna, is it sweet to sleep in the grave? Is it sweet to dream unearthly dreams?

Life is empty, senseless, and unfathomable! Go out to battle, ancient Fate! And in reply, triumphant and enamoured, a horn sounds in the snowy darkness . . .

A black, silent motor car flies past like an owl, its lights splashing in the night. With muffled, heavy steps, the Commendatore enters the house . . .

The door flies open. From the immense cold comes a sound like a clock striking hoarsely in the night – . . . . . .

Бой часов: «Ты звал меня на ужин.
   Я пришёл. А ты готов? . . .»

На вопрос жестокий нет ответа,
   Нет ответа – тишина.
В пышной спальне страшно в час рассвета,
   Слуги спят, и ночь бледна.

В час рассвета холодно и странно,
   В час рассвета – ночь мутна.
Дева Света! Где ты, донна Анна?
   Анна! Анна! – Тишина.

Только в грозном утреннем тумане
   Бьют часы в последний раз:
Донна Анна в смертный час твой встанет.
   Анна встанет в смертный час.

К Музе

Есть в напевах твоих сокровенных
Роковая о гибели весть.

---

a clock striking: 'You asked me to supper. I have come. Are you ready? . . .'

To the cruel question there is no answer, no answer – only silence. There is fear in the sumptuous bedroom at the hour of dawn; the servants are asleep, and the night is pale.

At the hour of dawn it is cold and strange, at the hour of dawn the night is dim. Maiden of Light! Where are you, Donna Anna? Anna! Anna! – Silence [reigns].

Only in the fearsome mist of morning the clock strikes for the last time: Donna Anna will rise in the hour of your death, Anna will rise in the hour of death.

To the Muse

In your hidden melodies there are fatal tidings of doom, ...

Есть проклятье заветов священных,
Поругание счастия есть.

И такая влекущая сила,
Что готов я твердить за молвой,
Будто ангелов ты низводила,
Соблазняя своей красотой . . .

И когда ты смеёшься над верой,
Над тобой загорается вдруг
Тот неяркий, пурпурово-серый
И когда-то мной виденный круг.

Зла, добра ли? – Ты вся – не отсюда.
Мудрено про тебя говорят:
Для иных ты – и Муза, и чудо.
Для меня ты – мученье и ад.

Я не знаю, зачем на рассвете,
В час, когда уже не было сил,
Не погиб я, но лик твой заметил
И твоих утешений просил?

---

a curse on sacred traditions, a desecration of happiness;

and a power so alluring that I am ready to repeat the rumour that you have brought angels down from heaven, enticing them with your beauty . . .

And when you mock at faith, that pale, greyish-purple halo which I once saw before suddenly begins to shine above you.

Are you evil, or good? You are altogether from another world. They say strange things about you. For some you are the Muse and a miracle. For me you are torment and hell.

I do not know why in the hour of dawn, when no strength was left to me, I did not perish, but caught sight of your face and begged you to comfort me.

Я хотел, чтоб мы были врагами,
Так за что ж подарила мне ты
Луг с цветами и твердь со звездами –
Всё проклятье своей красоты?

И коварнее северной ночи,
И хмельней золотого аи,
И любови цыганской короче
Были страшные ласки твои . . .

И была роковая отрада
В попираньи заветных святынь,
И безумная сердцу услада –
Эта горькая страсть, как полынь!

*

Ночь, улица, фонарь, аптека,
Бессмысленный и тусклый свет
Живи ещё хоть четверть века –
Всё будет так. Исхода нет.

I wanted us to be enemies; why then did you make me a present of a flowery meadow and of the starry firmament – the whole curse of your beauty?

Your fearful caresses were more treacherous than the northern night, more intoxicating than the golden champagne of Aï, briefer than a gipsy woman's love . . .

And there was a fatal pleasure in trampling on cherished and holy things; and this passion, bitter as wormwood, was a frenzied delight for the heart!

*

NIGHT, a street, a lamp, a chemist's shop, a meaningless and dim light. Even if you live for another quarter of a century, everything will be like this. There is no way out.

Умрёшь – начнёшь опять сначала,
И повторится всё, как встарь:
Ночь, ледяная рябь канала,
Аптека, улица, фонарь.

Художник

В жаркое лето и в зиму метельную,
В дни ваших свадеб, торжеств, похорон,
Жду, чтоб спугнул мою скуку смертельную
Лёгкий, доселе не слышанный звон.

Вот он – возник. И с холодным вниманием
Жду, чтоб понять, закрепить и убить.
И перед зорким моим ожиданием
Тянет он еле приметную нить.

С моря ли вихрь? Или сирины райские
В листьях поют? Или время стоит?
Или осыпали яблони майские
Снежный свой цвет? Или ангел летит?

You will die – and start all over again, and everything will be repeated, as of old: the night, the icy ripples on the canal, the chemist's shop, the street, the lamp.

The Artist

I N hot summer and snow-swept winter, on the days of your weddings, festivals, and funerals, I wait for a faint, hitherto unheard ringing sound to dispel my deadly boredom.

Here it is – it has arisen. And with cold attention I wait – to understand it, to pin it down, and to kill it. And as I wait intently, it stretches a barely perceptible thread before me.

Is a whirlwind blowing from the sea? Or are fabulous birds from Paradise singing among the leaves? Is Time standing still? Have the May-time apple-trees scattered their snowy blossom? Or is it an angel flying past?

Длятся часы, мировое несущие.
Ширятся звуки, движенье и свет.
Прошлое страстно глядится в грядущее.
Нет настоящего. Жалкого – нет.

И, наконец, у предела зачатия
Новой души, неизведанных сил, –
Душу сражает, как громом, проклятие:
Творческий разум осилил – убил.

И замыкаю я в клетку холодную
Лёгкую, добрую птицу свободную,
Птицу, хотевшую смерть унести,
Птицу, летевшую душу спасти.

Вот моя клетка – стальная, тяжёлая,
Как золотая, в вечернем огне.
Вот моя птица, когда-то весёлая,
Обруч качает, поёт на окне.

Крылья подрезаны, песни заучены.
Любите вы под окном постоять?
Песни вам нравятся. Я же, измученный
Нового жду – и скучаю опять.

Hours pass, bearing the weight of the world. Sounds, movement, and light expand. The past gazes passionately at its reflection in the future. There is no present. There is nothing pitiful any more.

And, at last, on the threshold of the birth of a new soul, of unknown forces, a curse strikes down the soul, like thunder: creative reason has mastered – and killed it.

And I shut up in a cold cage the airy, kind, unfettered bird, the bird that wanted to take death away, the bird that was flying to save the soul.

Here is my cage – heavy, made of steel; it gleams golden in the sun's evening fire. Here is my bird – once joyful, and now swinging on a hoop and singing in the window.

Its wings are clipped, its songs are learnt by heart. Do you like to stand under the window? The songs please you. But I, worn out by suffering, wait for something new, and feel boredom again.

*

Ты помнишь? В нашей бухте сонной
Спала́ зелёная вода,
Когда кильватерной колонной
Вошли военные суда.

Четыре – серых. И вопросы
Нас волновали битый час,
И загорелые матросы
Ходили важно мимо нас.

Мир стал заманчивей и шире,
И вдруг – суда уплыли прочь.
Нам было видно: все четыре
Зарылись в океан и в ночь.

И вновь обычным стало море,
Маяк уныло замигал,
Когда на низком семафоре
Последний отдали сигнал . . .

Как мало в этой жизни надо
Нам, детям, – и тебе и мне.
Ведь сердце радоваться радо
И самой малой новизне.

Do you remember? In our sleepy bay the green water was slumbering when some warships sailed in, in line ahead.

Four of them, grey ones. And for a whole hour we were excited by questions, and sunburnt sailors strutted past us.

The world became wider and more alluring; and suddenly the ships sailed away. We could see how all four of them vanished into the ocean and the night.

And once again the sea became ordinary, and the lighthouse began to wink mournfully when the last signal was given from the low semaphore . . .

How little we children – you and I – need in this life! The heart gladly finds joy in the slightest novelty.

Случайно на ноже карманном
Найди пылинку дальних стран –
И мир опять предстанет странным,
Закутанным в цветной туман!

*

Рождённые в года глухие
Пути не помнят своего.
Мы – дети страшных лет России –
Забыть не в силах ничего.

Испепеляющие годы!
Безумья ль в вас, надежды ль весть ?
От дней войны, от дней свободы –
Кровавый отсвет в лицах есть.

Есть немота – то гул набата
Заставил заградить уста.
В сердцах, восторженных когда-то,
Есть роковая пустота.

You have only to find by chance a speck of dust from a distant land on your penknife, and once again the world will appear strange and wrapped in a coloured haze.

*

THOSE who were born in years of stagnation do not remember their way. We, children of Russia's fearful years, can forget nothing.

Years that burnt everything to ashes! Do you bode madness, or bring tidings of hope ? The days of war, the days of freedom have marked our faces with a blood-red glow.

We are struck dumb: the tocsin's clang has made us close our lips. In our hearts, once full of fervour, there is a fateful emptiness.

И пусть над нашим смертным ложем
Взовьётся с криком воронье, –
Те, кто достойней, Боже, Боже,
Да узрят Царствие Твоё!

Let the croaking ravens soar above our death-bed – may those
who are more worthy, O God, O God, behold Thy Kingdom!

VELIMIR KHLEBNIKOV

Три сестры

Как воды далёких озёр
За тёмными ветками ивы,
Молчали глаза у сестёр,
А все они были красивы.
Одна, зачарована Богом
Старинных людских образов,
Стояла под звёздным чертогом
И слушала полночи зов.
А та замолчала навеки,
Душой простодушнее дурочки,
Боролися чёрные веки
С зрачками усталой снегурочки.
Лукавый язык из окошка на птичнике
Прохожего дразнит цыгана,
То, полная песен язычника,
Молчит на вершине кургана.
Она серебристые глины
Любила дикарского тела,
На сене, на стоге овина,
Лежать ей знакомое дело.

Three Sisters

LIKE the waters of distant lakes behind a willow's dark branches, the eyes of the sisters were silent, and they were all beautiful. The first, bewitched by the God of men's ancient icons, stood beneath the starry palace and listened to the call of midnight. The second one, whose soul was more artless than that of a simpleton, had fallen silent for ever; her dark eyelids were competing with the pupils of a tired snow-maiden. Sometimes her mischievous tongue, stuck out through a window of the hen-house, would tease a passing gipsy; at other times, her ears full of pagan songs, she stood silent at the top of an ancient burial-mound. She liked the silvery clay of a savage body, and was no novice in the business of lying on a hay-stack in a barn. . . . .

И полная неба и лени,
Жуёт голубые цветы,
И в мёртвом засохнувшем сене
Плыла в голубые черты.
Порой, быть одстой устав,
Оденет речную волну,
Учить своей груди устав
Дозволит ветров шалуну.
Она одуванчиком тела
Летит к одуванчику мира,
И сказка ручейная пела,
Глаза человека – секира.
И в пропасть вечернего неб
Смотрели девичьи глаза,
И волосы чёрного хлеба
От ветра упали назад.
Была точно смуглый зверок,
Где синие блещут глазёнки;
Небес синева, как намёк,
Блеснёт на ресницах телёнка.
И волосы – золота тёмного мёд,
Похожи на чёрного солнца восток,
Как чёрная бабочка небо сосёт
И хоботом узким пьёт неба цветок.

Filled with the sky and with indolence, she chewed pale blue flowers
and, in the lifeless, dried-up hay, faded into pale blue outlines.
Sometimes, tired of her clothes, she would clothe herself with
wave of the river and allow the playful wind to learn the laws of
her breasts. With her dandelion body she would fly toward the
dandelion world, and the stream murmured a story which said that
man's eyes are an axe. The girl's eyes gazed into the abyss of the
evening sky, and her hair, the colour of rye bread, was swept back
by the wind. She was like a little dark animal with gleaming blue
eyes; so the blue of the sky gleams, as a faint hint, on a calf's eye-
lashes. Her hair, the colour of dark golden honey, was like a black
sun rising in the east. She was like a black butterfly sucking the
sky and drinking from a heavenly flower with its thin proboscis.

И неба священный подсолнух,
То золотом чёрным, то синим отливом
Блеснёт по размётанным волнам,
Проходит, как ветер по нивам.
Идёт, как священник, и тёмной рукой
Даёт тёмным волнам и сон и покой,
То, может быть, Пушкин иль Ленский
По ниве идут деревенской.
И слабая кашка запутает ноги
Случайному гостю сельской дороги.
Другая – окутана сказкой
Умерших событий.
К ней тянутся часто за лаской
Другого дыхания нити.
Она величаво, как мать,
Проходит сквозь призраки вишни
И любит глаза подымать,
Где звёзды раскинул Всевышний.
Дрожали лучи поговоркою,
И время столетьями цедится,
И смотрит, задумчиво зоркая,
Как слабо шагает Медведица.

And, like a sacred sunflower from heaven, she would flash on the scattered waves now like black gold, now with a blue gleam; she would pass like the wind through the cornfields; she walked like a priest, bestowing with her dark hand sleep and peace to the dark waves – so Pushkin, perhaps, or Lensky* walked through the village cornfields; and the tender clover would coil round the feet of the casual passer-by on the village road. The third sister is shrouded in legendary stories of the past. The threads of another's existence often reach out to her in search of affection. Stately as a mother, she passes through the cherry-tree's phantoms and likes to raise her eyes to [the firmament] where the Almighty has scattered the stars. Their light twinkles like a proverb, and time filters in centuries; sharp-sighted and thoughtful, she watches the slow pacing of the Bear, ...

* A character in Pushkin's *Evgeny Onegin*.

И дышит старинная вольница,
Ушкуйницы гордая стать.
О, строгая ликом раскольница,
Поморов отшельница-мать.
Стонавших радостно черёмух
Зовёт бушующий костёр.
Там в стороне от глаз знакомых
Находишь, дикая, шатёр.
И, точно хохот обезьяны,
Взлетели косы выше плеч,
И ветров синие цыганы
Ведут взволнованную речь.
Чтоб мертвецы забыли сны,
Она несёт костёр весны,
Его накинула на плечи,
Забывши облик человечий.

★

Ещё раз, ещё раз,
Я для вас
Звезда.

and stirs up memories of ancient freebooters, of the proud figures of river-pirates. She is like an Old Believer* with an austere countenance, like an abbess of the hermits of the White Sea coast. The raging bonfire calls to itself the bird-cherry trees which were creaking joyfully. There, O wild one, away from eyes that know you, you find yourself a tent. Like a monkey's laughter, your tresses are blown higher than your shoulders, and the winds like blue gipsies speak in excited tones. To make dead men forget their dreams she bears the bonfire of spring, and, forgetful of her human aspect, she has laid it on her shoulders.

★

ONCE again, once again I am a star for you. . . . . .

* A Russian religious dissenter.

Горе моряку, взявшему
Неверный угол своей ладьи
И звезды:
Он разобьётся о камни,
О подводные мели.
Горе и вам, взявшим
Неверный угол сердца ко мне:
Вы разобьётесь о камни
И камни будут надсмехаться
Над вами,
Как вы надсмехались
Надо мной.

Woe to the sailor who has taken the wrong angle of his ship on a star: he will be shattered on the rocks, on the underwater sandbanks. Woe to you also who have taken the heart's wrong angle on me. You will be shattered on the rocks, and the rocks will laugh at you, as you laughed at me.

NIKOLAY GUMILEV

Воин Агамемнона

Смутную душу мою тяготит
Странный и страшный вопрос:
Можно ли жить, если умер Атрид,
Умер на ложе из роз?

Всё, что нам снилось всегда и везде,
Наше желанье и страх,
Всё отражалось, как в чистой воде,
В этих спокойных очах.

В мышцах жила несказанная мощь,
Сказка – в изгибе колен,
Был он прекрасен, как облако, – вождь
Золотоносных Микен.

Что я? Обломок старинных обид,
Дротик, упавший в траву,
Умер водитель народов, Атрид, –
Я же, ничтожный, живу.

Agamemnon's Warrior

A STRANGE and fearful question oppresses my troubled soul: can one live when the son of Atreus has died – has died on a bed of roses?

All that we dreamed of always and everywhere, our longing and fear – all was reflected in those calm eyes, as in pure water.

Ineffable power dwelt in his muscles, a saga – in the curve of his knees; beautiful he was as a cloud – the lord of Mycenae rich in gold.

What am I? A fragment of ancient wrongs, a javelin, fallen in the grass, – the son of Atreus, the leader of nations, is dead – and I, a man of no account, am alive.

Манит прозрачность глубоких озёр,
Смотрит с укором заря,
Тягостен, тягостен этот позор,
Жить, потерявши царя!

Врата рая

Не семью печатями алмазными
В Божий рай замкнулся вечный вход,
Он не манит блеском и соблазнами,
И его не ведает народ.

Это дверь в стене давно заброшенной,
Камни, мох, и больше ничего,
Возле – нищий, словно гость непрошенный,
И ключи у пояса его.

Мимо едут рыцари и латники,
Трубный вой, бряцанье серебра,
И никто не взглянет на привратника,
Светлого апостола Петра.

The clear waters of deep lakes beckon me, the dawn looks on reproachfully: hard, hard to bear is the shame of living when one has lost one's king!

The Gates of Paradise

THE eternal entrance into God's paradise is not closed with seven diamond seals; it has no brilliance nor enticing charms, and the people do not know it.

It's a doorway in a wall abandoned long ago – stones, moss, and nothing more; near by there is a beggar, like an unbidden guest, with keys hanging at his waist.

Knights and men-at-arms ride by to the blare of trumpets and the clatter of silver; and no one spares a glance for the gate-keeper, the glorious Apostle Peter.

Все мечтают: «Там, у Гроба Божия,
Двери рая вскроются для нас,
На горе Фаворе, у подножия,
Прозвенит обетованный час».

Так проходит медленное чудище,
Завывая, трубит звонкий рог,
И апостол Пётр в дырявом рубище,
Словно нищий, бледен и убог.

[*Из «Капитанов»*]

На полярных морях и на южных,
По изгибам зелёных зыбей,
Меж базальтовых скал и жемчужных
Шелестят паруса кораблей.

Быстрокрылых ведут капитаны,
Открыватели новых земель,
Для кого не страшны ураганы,
Кто изведал мальстремы и мель;

They are all dreaming: 'There, beside God's Sepulchre, the doors of paradise will open for us; on Mount Thabor, at its foot, the promised hour will strike.'

So the slow-moving monster goes by; the wailing sound of the horn rings out clearly; and the Apostle Peter in his tattered rags, pale and poor, looks like a beggar.

[*From 'The Captains'*]

IN arctic and southern seas, on the ridges of green waves, among reefs of basalt and pearl, the sails of ships rustle.

Swift-winged [ships] are commanded by captains who discover new lands, for whom hurricanes hold no terrors, who have experienced maelstroms and shoals;

Чья не пылью затерянных хартий, –
Солью моря пропитана грудь,
Кто иглой на разорванной карте
Отмечает свой дерзостный путь,

И, взойдя на трепещущий мостик,
Вспоминает покинутый порт,
Отряхая ударами трости
Клочья пены с высоких ботфорт,

Или, бунт на борту обнаружив,
Из-за пояса рвёт пистолет,
Так что сыплется золото с кружев,
С розоватых брабантских манжет.

Пусть безумствует море и хлещет,
Гребни волн поднялись в небеса, –
Ни один пред грозой не трепещет,
Ни один не свернёт паруса.

Разве трусам даны эти руки,
Этот острый, уверенный взгляд,
Что умеет на вражьи фелуки
Неожиданно бросить фрегат,

whose breasts are saturated not with the dust of mislaid charts, but with the salt of the sea; such a captain plots his daring course with a needle on a tattered map,

and, after climbing on to the shuddering bridge, thinks of the harbour he has left behind, as he slashes flakes of foam off his high jack-boots with his cane;

or, on discovering mutiny on board, whips out a pistol from his belt, so that gold is scattered from his cuffs of pinkish Brabant lace.

The sea may rage and surge, and the crests of the waves rise to the heavens, yet not one of these captains trembles before the storm, not one will reef in his sails.

They are surely no cowards, the men who are endowed with such hands and with the keen, confident eye that can suddenly hurl a frigate against enemy feluccas,

Меткой пулей, острогой железной
Настигать исполинских китов
И приметить в ночи многозвездной
Охранительный свет маяков?

Мужик

В чащах, в болотах огромных,
У оловянной реки,
В срубах мохнатых и тёмных
Странные есть мужики.

Выйдет такой в бездорожье,
Где разбежался ковыль,
Слушает крики Стрибожьи,
Чуя старинную быль.

С остановившимся взглядом
Здесь проходил печенег . . .
Сыростью пахнет и гадом
Возле мелеющих рек.

---

strike giant whales with a well-aimed bullet or an iron harpoon, and pick out the protective beams of lighthouses in the star-spangled night.

The Peasant

IN the thickets, in the vast swamps, by the river the colour of tin, in shaggy and dark huts, there live strange peasants.

One of them goes out into the trackless wastes where the feather-grass has run riot, and, sensing an ancient legend, listens to the cries of Stribog.*

The Pecheneg, with a fixed gaze, used to pass through here . . . It smells of dampness and of reptiles by rivers that are growing shallow.

* A Slavonic pagan god, associated with the wind.

Вот уже он и с котомкой,
Путь оглашая лесной
Песней протяжной, негромкой,
Но озорной, озорной.

Путь этот – светы и мраки,
Посвист разбойный в полях,
Ссоры, кровавые драки
В страшных, как сны, кабаках.

В гордую нашу столицу
Входит он – Боже, спаси! –
Обворожает царицу
Необозримой Руси

Взглядом, улыбкою детской,
Речью такой озорной, –
И на груди молодецкой
Крест просиял золотой.

Как не погнулись, – о, горе! –
Как не покинули мест
Крест на Казанском соборе
И на Исакии крест?

Here he* is now with a scrip, filling the forest path with a song,
slow and soft, but mischievous, so mischievous.

His path is light and darkness, the whistle of robbers in the fields,
quarrels, bloody brawls in taverns horrible as nightmares:

He enters our proud capital – God save us! – and bewitches the
Empress of boundless Russia

by his gaze, his child-like smile, his speech that is so mischievous
– and on his mighty chest there glitters a golden cross.

Alas, why did not the cross on the Kazan' Cathedral and the one
on St Isaac's bend and leave their places?

* The subject of this poem is Rasputin.

Над потрясённой столицей
Выстрелы, крики, набат;
Город ощерился львицей,
Обороняющей львят.

«Что ж, православные, жгите
Труп мой на тёмном мосту,
Пепел по ветру пустите . . .
Кто защитит сироту?

В диком краю и убогом
Много таких мужиков,
Слышен по вашим дорогам
Радостный гул их шагов».

Рабочий

Он стоит пред раскалённым горном,
Невысокий старый человек.
Взгляд спокойный кажется покорным
От миганья красноватых век.

Все товарищи его заснули,
Только он один ещё не спит:

Shots, shouting, and the tocsin are heard over the stunned capital; the city has bared its teeth like a lioness protecting her young.

'Well, Orthodox folk, burn my corpse on a dark bridge, throw the ashes to the wind . . . Who will protect the orphan?

'In the wild and poor country there are many such peasants; the joyful tramp of their footsteps is heard along your roads.'

The Workman

He stands before the red-hot furnace – a small old man. The blinking of his reddish eyelids gives a submissive air to his calm eyes.

All his comrades have gone to sleep; he alone is not sleeping: . .

Всё он занят отливаньем пули,
Что меня с землёю разлучит.

Кончил, и глаза повеселели.
Возвращается. Блестит луна.
Дома ждёт его в большой постели
Сонная и тёплая жена.

Пуля, им отлитая, просвищет
Над седою, вспененной Двиной,
Пуля, им отлитая, отыщет
Грудь мою, она пришла за мной.

Упаду, смертельно затоскую,
Прошлое увижу наяву,
Кровь ключом захлещет на сухую,
Пыльную и мятую траву.

И Господь воздаст мне полной мерой
За недолгий мой и горький век.
Это сделал, в блузе светло-серой,
Невысокий старый человек.

he is still busy casting the bullet which will part me from the earth.

He has finished, and his eyes have grown gayer. He is going home. The moon is shining. At home his sleepy and warm wife is waiting for him in a large bed.

The bullet he has cast will whistle above the white-foamed Dvina; the bullet he has cast will seek out my breast – it has come for me.

I shall fall in mortal anguish, I shall see the past as it really was, and my blood will gush like a fountain on to the dry, dusty, and trampled grass.

And the Lord will requite me in full measure for my brief and bitter life. This is what the small old man in the light grey blouse has done.

Шестое чувство

Прекрасно в нас влюблённое вино
И добрый хлеб, что в печь для нас садится,
И женщина, которою дано,
Сперва измучившись, нам насладиться.

Но что нам делать с розовой зарёй
Над холодеющими небесами,
Где тишина и неземной покой,
Что делать нам с бессмертными стихами?

Ни съесть, ни выпить, ни поцеловать.
Мгновение бежит неудержимо,
И мы ломаем руки, но опять
Осуждены идти всё мимо, мимо.

Как мальчик, игры позабыв свои,
Следит порой за девичьим купаньем
И, ничего не зная о любви,
Всё ж мучится таинственным желаньем;

The Sixth Sense

FINE is the wine that is in love with us, and the goodly bread that goes into the oven for our sake, and the woman whom we enjoy, after she has tormented us to the full.

But what are we to do with the rose-coloured sunset above a sky that is growing cold, where there is silence and unearthly calm, what are we to do with immortal verses?

You can't eat, or drink, or kiss them ... The moment flies unchecked, and we wring our hands, but still we are condemned to pass wide, wide of the mark.

Just as a boy, forgetting his games, sometimes watches the girls bathing and, knowing nothing of love, is yet tormented by a mysterious desire;

Как некогда в разросшихся хвощах
Ревела от сознания бессилья
Тварь скользкая, почуя на плечах
Ещё не появившиеся крылья, –

Так век за веком – скоро ли, Господь ? –
Под скальпелем природы и искусства
Кричит наш дух, изнемогает плоть,
Рождая орган для шестого чувства.

Заблудившийся трамвай

Шёл я по улице незнакомой
И вдруг услышал вороний грай,
И звоны лютни, и дальние громы –
Передо мною летел трамвай.

Как я вскочил на его подножку,
Было загадкою для меня,
В воздухе огненную дорожку
Он оставлял и при свете дня.

just as once upon a time the slippery creature, feeling on its back the still unformed wings, howled from a sense of impotence in the overgrown thickets –

so century after century – how soon, O Lord ? – under the knife of nature and art our spirit cries out, the flesh grows faint, as they bring to birth an organ of the sixth sense.

The Tram that Lost its Way

I WAS walking down an unfamiliar street, when I suddenly heard crows croaking, the sound of a lute, and distant peals of thunder – a tram was flying past me.

How I managed to jump on to its step was a mystery to me even in broad daylight it left behind a trail of fire in the air.

Мчался он бурей тёмной, крылатой,
Он заблудился в бездне времён . . .
«Остановите, вагоновожатый,
Остановите сейчас вагон!»

Поздно. Уж мы обогнули стену,
Мы проскочили сквозь рощу пальм,
Через Неву, через Нил и Сену
Мы прогремели по трём мостам.

И, промелькнув у оконной рамы,
Бросил нам вслед пытливый взгляд
Нищий старик, – конечно тот самый,
Что умер в Бейруте год назад.

Где я ? Так томно и так тревожно
Сердце моё стучит в ответ:
«Видишь вокзал, на котором можно
В Индию Духа купить билет ?»

Вывеска . . . кровью налитые буквы
Гласят – зеленная, – знаю, тут
Вместо капусты и вместо брюквы
Мёртвые головы продают.

It rushed on like a dark, winged storm, it lost its way in time's abyss . . . 'Driver, stop! Stop the tram-car at once!'

Too late! We had already skirted the wall, dashed through a palm-grove, and clattered over three bridges across the Neva, the Nile, and the Seine.

And, flashing past the window, an old beggar threw a searching glance after us – it was, of course, the same one who died in Beirut a year ago.

Where am I ? In reply my heart beats so languidly and apprehensively: 'Do you see the station where you can buy a ticket for the India of the Spirit ?'

A sign-board . . . The letters, suffused with blood, spell 'greengrocer': here, I know, instead of cabbages and swedes they sell dead heads.

В красной рубашке, с лицом как вымя,
Голову срезал палач и мне,
Она лежала вместе с другими
Здесь в ящике скользком, на самом дне.

А в переулке забор дощатый,
Дом в три окна и серый газон . . .
«Остановите, вагоновожатый,
Остановите сейчас вагон!»

Машенька, ты здесь жила и пела,
Мне, жениху, ковёр ткала,
Где же теперь твой голос и тело,
Может ли быть, что ты умерла!

Как ты стонала в своей светлице,
Я же с напудренною косой
Шёл представляться Императрице,
И не увиделся вновь с тобой.

Понял теперь я: наша свобода
Только оттуда бьющий свет,
Люди и тени стоят у входа
В зоологический сад планет.

The executioner, in a red shirt and with a face like an udder, chopped off my head, too; it lay together with the others here in this slippery box, right at the bottom.

In the side-street there is a wooden fence, a house with three windows and a grey lawn . . . 'Driver, stop! Stop the tram-car at once!'

Mashen'ka, it was here that you lived and sang, and wove a carpet for me, your betrothed. But where are now your voice and your body? Can it be that you are dead?

How you moaned in your room, while I, my hair powdered, went to present myself to the Empress, and never saw you again.

Now I understand – our freedom is but a light that breaks through from another world; people and shadows stand by the entrance to the planets' zoo.

NIKOLAY GUMILEV

И сразу ветер знакомый и сладкий,
И за мостом летит на меня
Всадника длань в железной перчатке
И два копыта его коня.

Верной твердынею православья
Врезан Исакий в вышине,
Там отслужу молебен о здравье
Машеньки и панихиду по мне.

И всё ж навеки сердце угрюмо,
И трудно дышать, и больно жить . . .
Машенька, я никогда не думал,
Что можно так любить и грустить.

And all at once a sweet and familiar wind begins to blow, and beyond the bridge a rider's hand in an iron glove and two hooves of his horse are flying towards me.

Like a true stronghold of Orthodoxy, St Isaac's dome is etched on high; there I shall have a service of intercession celebrated for Mashen′ka's good health, and a requiem for myself.

But still my heart is for ever filled with gloom, it is difficult to breathe, and painful to live . . . Mashen′ka, I never knew that it was possible to love and grieve so much.

VLADISLAV KHODASEVICH

Баллада

Сижу, освещаемый сверху,
Я в комнате круглой моей.
Смотрю в штукатурное небо
На солнце в шестнадцать свечей.

Кругом – освещённые тоже,
И стулья, и стол, и кровать.
Сижу – и в смущеньи не знаю,
Куда бы мне руки девать.

Морозные белые пальмы
На стёклах беззвучно цветут.
Часы с металлическим шумом
В жилетном кармане идут.

О, косная, нищая скудость
Безвыходной жизни моей!
Кому мне поведать, как жалко
Себя и всех этих вещей?

И я начинаю качаться,
Колени обнявши свои,

Ballad

BRIGHTLY lit from above, I am sitting in my circular room and looking up at a sky of stucco and at a sixteen candle-power sun.

All around me, also lit up, are chairs, a table, and a bed. I sit, and in my confusion do not know what to do with my hands.

White palm-leaves of frost silently bloom on the window-panes. The watch in my waistcoat pocket is ticking with a metallic sound.

Oh, the stagnant, barren wretchedness of my hopeless life! Whom can I tell how sorry I feel for myself and for all these objects?

And then, clasping my knees, I begin to sway to and fro, . . .

И вдруг начинаю стихами
С собой говорить в забытьи.

Бессвязные, страстные речи!
Нельзя в них понять ничего,
Но звуки правдивее смысла,
И слово сильнее всего.

И музыка, музыка, музыка
Вплетается в пенье моё,
И узкое, узкое, узкое
Пронзает меня лезвиё.

Я сам над собой вырастаю,
Над мёртвым встаю бытиём,
Стопами в подземное пламя,
В текучие звёзды челом.

И вижу большими глазами –
Глазами, быть может, змеи –
Как пению дикому внемлют
Несчастные вещи мои.

И в плавный, вращательный танец
Вся комната мерно идёт,

and, falling into a trance, suddenly start speaking to myself in verse.

Incoherent, passionate words! They make no sense at all. But sounds are more truthful than meaning, and the word is more powerful than anything.

And music, music, music weaves itself into my singing, and a narrow, narrow, narrow blade pierces me.

I rise above myself, above lifeless reality, my feet in subterranean fire, my brow in the moving stars.

And with wide-open eyes, perhaps with the eyes of a serpent, I watch my pitiful objects listening to the wild singing.

And the whole room begins to move rhythmically in a smooth, circular dance, ...

И кто-то тяжёлую лиру
Мне в руки сквозь ветер даёт.

И нет штукатурного неба
И солнца в шестнадцать свечей:
На гладкие чёрные скалы
Стопы опирает – Орфей.

★

Весенний лепет не разнежит
Сурово стиснутых стихов.
Я полюбил железный скрежет
Какофонических миров.

В зиянии разверстых гласных
Дышу легко и вольно я.
Мне чудится в толпе согласных -
Льдин взгромождённых толчея.

Мне мил – из оловянной тучи
Удар изломанной стрелы,
Люблю певучий и визгучий
Лязг электрической пилы.

and someone hands me a heavy lyre through the wind.
   And the sky of stucco and the sixteen candle-power sun have vanished: Orpheus is standing on the smooth black rocks.

★

THE murmur of spring will not loosen severely clenched verses. I have grown to love the iron grating of cacophonous worlds.
   In the gaping of wide-open vowels I breathe easily and freely. In the throng of consonants I seem to hear the crush of piled-up blocks of ice.
   The thrust of a forked arrow coming out of a cloud the colour of tin is dear to me; I love the warbling and shrill whine of an electric saw.

И в этой жизни мне дороже
Всех гармонических красот –
Дрожь, побежавшая по коже,
Иль ужаса холодный пот,

Иль сон, где, некогда единый –
Взрываясь, разлетаюсь я,
Как грязь разбрызганная шиной
По чуждым сферам бытия.

*

Жив Бог! Умён, а не заумен,
Хожу среди своих стихов,
Как непоблажливый игумен
Среди смиренных чернецов.
Пасу послушливое стадо
Я процветающим жезлом.
Ключи таинственного сада
Звенят на поясе моём.
Я – чающий и говорящий.
Заумно, может быть, поёт
Лишь ангел, Богу предстоящий, –
Да Бога не узревший скот

And in this life more precious to me than all the beauties of harmony are the tremor that passes over the skin, or the cold sweat of terror,

or the dream in which, intact at first, I explode and fly asunder like mud spattered by a tyre, into alien spheres of existence.

*

GOD be praised! A logical, but not a metalogical, being* – I stroll among my verses, like a severe abbot among his humble monks. I tend my obedient flock with a flowering staff. The keys of a mysterious garden jingle at my belt. I am one who hopes and speaks. It is, perhaps, only the angel standing before God who sings metalogically; and cattle, which have not seen God, ...

* The poem is an attack on the *zaumny yazyk*, the 'metalogical' language invented and used by several Futurist poets (see Introduction p. xlvii).

Мычит заумно и ревёт.
А я – не ангел осиянный,
Не лютый змий, не глупый бык.
Люблю из рода в род мне данный
Мой человеческий язык:
Его суровую свободу,
Его извилистый закон . . .
О, если б мой предсмертный стон
Облечь в отчётливую оду!

Перед зеркалом

> Nel mezzo del cammin di
> nostra vita.

Я, я, я. Что за дикое слово!
Неужели вон тот – это я?
Разве мама любила такого,
Желтосерого, полуседого
И всезнающего, как змея?

Разве мальчик, в Останкине летом
Танцовавший на дачных балах, –
Это я, тот, кто каждым ответом
Желторотым внушает поэтам
Отвращение, злобу и страх?

---

moo and bellow metalogically. But I am no radiant angel, no fierce serpent, no stupid ox. I love my human language, transmitted to me from generation to generation: I love its stern freedom, its sinuous laws . . . If only my dying groans could be shaped into a lucid ode!

Before the Mirror

> Midway on our journey through life.

I, I, I. What a weird word! Is that man there really I? Can it be that mother loved such a person, greyish-yellow, with hair turning grey, and omniscient as a serpent?

Can it be that the boy who used to dance at country-balls at Ostankino in the summer – is I, who by each of my answers inspire loathing, anger, and fear in newly hatched poets?

Разве тот, кто в полночные споры
Всю мальчишечью вкладывал прыть, –
Это я, тот же самый, который
На трагические разговоры
Научился молчать и шутить?

Впрочем – так и всегда на средине
Рокового земного пути:
От ничтожной причины – к причине,
А глядишь – заплутался в пустыне,
И своих же следов не найти.

Да, меня не пантера прыжками
На парижский чердак загнала.
И Виргилия нет за плечами, –
Только есть одиночество – в раме
Говорящего правду стекла.

Can it be that the same person who used to throw all his boyish
vivacity into midnight arguments – is I, who have learnt to be
silent and to jest when faced with tragic conversations?

Yet it is always like this midway on the fatal journey through life;
[you go] from one trivial cause to another, and behold, you have
lost your way in the desert and cannot find your own tracks.

No panther leaping in pursuit has driven me up into my
Parisian garret, and there is no Virgil standing at my shoulder.
There is only loneliness – framed in the mirror that speaks the truth.

NIKOLAY KLYUEV

В златотканные дни Сентября
Мнится папертью бора опушка.
Сосны молятся, ладан куря,
Над твоей опустелой избушкой.

Ветер-сторож следы старины
Заметает листвой шелестящей.
Распахни узорочье сосны,
Промелькни за берёзовой чащей!

Я узнаю косынки кайму,
Голосок с легковейной походкой . . .
Сосны шепчут про мрак и тюрьму,
Про мерцание звёзд за решёткой,

Про бубенчик в жестоком пути,
Про седые бурятские дали . . .
Мир вам, сосны, вы думы мои,
Как родимая мать, разгадали!

On gold-woven days of September the edge of the pine-forest seems to be the porch of a church. The pine-trees are praying and burning incense above your deserted cottage.

The wind, the forest warden, covers up the tracks of olden times with rustling leaves. Spread out the patterned web of the pines, let me catch a glimpse of you behind the thick birch wood!

I shall recognize the kerchief border, the small voice, and the slightly swaying gait. . . . The pine-trees whisper about darkness and prison, about the twinkling of stars through the bars,

about the bell jingling on a cruel journey, about the grey Buryat horizons . . . Peace be unto you, pine-trees, you have divined my thoughts like my own mother!

В поминальные дни Сентября
Вы сыновнюю тайну узнайте,
И о той, что погибла, любя,
Небесам и земле передайте.

*

Любви начало было летом,
Конец – осенним Сентябрём.
Ты подошла ко мне с приветом
В наряде девичьи-простом.

Вручила красное яичко,
Как символ крови и любви:
Не торопись на Север, птичка,
Весну на Юге обожди!

Синеют дымно перелески,
Насторожённы и немы,
За узорочьем занавески
Не видно тающей зимы.

Но сердце чует: есть туманы,
Движенье смутное лесов,

On memorial days of September discover your son's secret, and tell heaven and earth about her who – loving – perished.

*

Love's beginning was in the summer, its end – in autumnal September. In a girl's simple attire you came up to me with a greeting.

You handed me a red-coloured egg as a symbol of blood and love: don't be in a hurry to fly north, little bird, wait for the spring in the south!

Blue and smoky, the coppices are watchful and silent; one cannot see the melting winter through the patterned curtain.

But the heart senses that there are mists, obscure movements of the forests, ...

Неотвратимые обманы
Лилово-сизых вечеров.

О, не лети в туманы пташкой!
Года уйдут в седую мглу –
Ты будешь нищею монашкой
Стоять на паперти в углу.

И может быть, пройду я мимо,
Такой же нищий и худой . . .
О, дай мне крылья херувима
Лететь незримо за тобой!

Не обойти тебя приветом,
И не раскаяться потом . . .
Любви начало было летом,
Конец – осенним Сентябрём.

[*Успокоение из «Плача о Есенине»*]

Падает снег на дорогу –
Белый ромашковый цвет.
Может, дойду понемногу
К окнам, где ласковый свет?

fated illusions of violet-grey evenings.

Oh, do not fly off into the mists like a little bird! The years will recede into a grey haze: you will be standing as a mendicant nun in a corner of the church's porch;

and perhaps I shall pass by, just as beggarly and thin . . . Oh, give me a cherub's wings, that I may fly invisible in your wake;

and not pass you by without a greeting, nor feel remorse afterwards . . . Love's beginning was in the summer, its end – in autumnal September.

[*'The Coming of Peace' from 'Lament for Esenin'*]

SNOW is falling on the road – the white camomile flowers. Perhaps, little by little, I shall reach the windows where shines a welcoming light? . . . . . .

Топчут усталые ноги
Белый ромашковый цвет.

Вижу за окнами прялку,
Песенку мама поёт,
С нитью весёлой вповалку
Пухлый мурлыкает кот.
Мышку-вдову за мочалку
Замуж сверчок выдаёт.

Сладко уснуть на лежанке . . .
Кот – непробудный сосед.
Пусть забубнит в позаранки
Ульем на странника дед,
Сед он, как пень на полянке –
Белый ромашковый цвет.

Только б коснуться покоя,
В сумке огниво и трут,
Яблоней в розовом зное
Щёки мои расцветут,
Там, где вплетает левкои
В мамины косы уют.

My tired feet tread on the white camomile flowers.

Through the windows I see a spinning-wheel; mother is singing a song, and a plump tom-cat, stretched out happily with a thread, is purring. The cricket is giving away the widowed mouse in marriage to a wisp of woven bast.

How sweet it is to fall asleep on the bench beside the stove . . . The cat lies beside me, fast asleep. Let grandfather at daybreak murmur at the wayfarer like a hive of bees; he is grey-haired, like a stump in a forest clearing – the white camomile flowers.

Could I but touch peace! In my bag there are steel and tinder. My cheeks will bloom like apple-trees in the rose-coloured heat, where cosiness entwines mother's tresses with gillyflowers.

NIKOLAY KLYUEV

Жизнь – океан многозвонный –
Путнику плещет вослед.
Волгу ли, берег ли Роны –
Всё принимает поэт . . .
Тихо ложится на склоны
Белый ромашковый цвет.

Life – a many-voiced ocean – surges in the traveller's wake. The poet accepts everything – whether it's the Volga or the banks of the Rhône. The white camomile flowers fall softly on to the slopes.

ANNA AKHMATOVA

Вечером

Звенела музыка в саду
Таким невыразимым горем.
Свежо и остро пахли морем
На блюде устрицы во льду.

Он мне сказал: «Я верный друг!»
И моего коснулся платья.
Как непохожи на объятья
Прикосновенья этих рук.

Так гладят кошек или птиц,
Так на наездниц смотрят стройных.
Лишь смех в глазах его спокойных
Под лёгким золотом ресниц.

А скорбных скрипок голоса
Поют за стелющимся дымом:
«Благослови же небеса:
Ты первый раз одна с любимым».

In the Evening

THE strains of music in the garden were full of such inexpressible sorrow. A fresh and pungent smell of the sea came from oysters on a dish of ice.

He said to me: 'I am a faithful friend', and touched my dress. How unlike an embrace is the touch of those hands!

That's how one strokes cats or birds; that's how one looks at shapely circus-riders. There is only laughter in his calm eyes beneath his light, golden lashes.

And the voices of mournful violins sing behind the drifting smoke: 'Give thanks to Heaven: for the first time you are alone with the man you love.'

315

★

О тебе вспоминаю я редко
И твоей не пленяюсь судьбой,
Но с души не стирается метка
Незначительной встречи с тобой.

Красный дом твой нарочно минyю,
Красный дом твой над мутной рекой,
Но я знаю, что горько волную
Твой пронизанный солнцем покой.

Пусть не ты над моими устами
Наклонялся, моля о любви,
Пусть не ты золотыми стихами
Обессмертил томленья мои –

Я над будущим тайно колдую,
Если вечер совсем голубой,
И предчувствую встречу вторую,
Неизбежную встречу с тобой.

I THINK of you seldom, and am not captivated by your fate; but the mark left by our insignificant meeting has not been effaced from my soul.

I pass your red house by on purpose – your red house above the muddy river; but I know that I bitterly disturb your sun-pervaded peace.

Though it was not you who bent down over my lips, craving my love, though it was not you who immortalized my yearning in golden verses –

yet I secretly cast spells over the future, whenever the evenings are quite blue, and I have a foreboding of a second meeting, an inevitable meeting, with you.

*

Есть в близости людей заветная черта,
Её не перейти влюблённости и страсти, –
Пусть в жуткой тишине сливаются уста,
И сердце рвётся от любви на части.

И дружба здесь бессильна, и года
Высокого и огненного счастья,
Когда душа свободна и чужда
Медлительной истоме сладострастья.

Стремящиеся к ней безумны, а её
Достигшие – поражены тоскою . . .
Теперь ты понял, отчего моё
Не бьётся сердце под твоей рукою.

*

Стал мне реже сниться, слава Богу,
Больше не мерещится везде,
Лёг туман на белую дорогу,
Тени побежали по воде.

In human intimacy there is a secret boundary; neither the experience of being in love nor passion can cross it, though lips be joined together in awful silence, and the heart break asunder with love.

Friendship, too, is powerless here, and so are years of sublime and fiery happiness, when the soul is free and knows not the slow languor of sensuality.

Those who strive towards this boundary are demented, while those who have reached it are stricken with anguish . . . Now you know why my heart does not beat beneath your hand.

*

I dream of him more rarely now, thank God, no longer do I fancy that I see him everywhere. The mist has settled on the white road, shadows flit across the water.

И весь день не замолкали звоны
Над простором вспаханной земли,
Здесь всего сильнее от Ионы
Колокольни Лаврские вдали.

Подстригаю на кустах сирени
Ветки те, что нынче отцвели;
По валам старинных укреплений
Два монаха медленно прошли.

Мир родной понятный и телесный
Для меня незрячей оживи.
Исцелил мне душу Царь Небесный
Ледяным покоем нелюбви.

Июль 1914

I

Пахнет гарью. Четыре недели
Торф сухой по болотам горит.
Даже птицы сегодня не пели,
И осина уже не дрожит.

And all day long the chime of bells did not cease over the wide
expanse of ploughed-up earth. Here the bells of St Jonas's are
heard best, and the monastery belfries are seen in the distance.

I am pruning the lilac bushes of the branches which have now
shed their blossom; along the top of ancient ramparts two monks
have slowly passed.

Bring to life the familiar, intelligible, material world for me
whose eyes cannot see. The King of Heaven has healed my soul
with the icy calm of love's absence.

July 1914

I

THERE is a smell of burning. For four weeks the dry peat has been
on fire in the bogs. Even the birds have not sung today, and the asp
no longer trembles.

Стало солнце немилостью Божьей,
Дождик с Пасхи полей не кропил.
Приходил одноногий прохожий
И один на дворе говорил:

«Сроки страшные близятся. Скоро
Станет тесно от свежих могил.
Ждите глада, и труса, и мора,
И затменья небесных светил.

Только нашей земли не разделит
На потеху себе супостат:
Богородица белый расстелет
Над скорбями великими плат».

2

Можжевельника запах сладкий
От горящих лесов летит.
Над ребятами стонут солдатки,
Вдовий плач по деревне звенит.

The sun has become a sign of God's disfavour; since Easter no
rain has sprinkled the fields. A one-legged passer-by came and,
alone in the courtyard, said:

'Terrible times are drawing near. Soon the earth will be packed
with fresh graves. You must expect famine, earthquakes, pestilence,
and the eclipse of the heavenly bodies.

'But the enemy shall not dismember our land for his own amuse-
ment: the Mother of God will spread a white veil over our great
sorrows.'

2

A SWEET smell of juniper comes floating from the burning woods.
The soldiers' wives bend over their children and moan, the weeping
of widows echoes through the village.

Не напрасно молебны служились,
О дожде тосковала земля:
Красной влагой тепло окропились
Затоптанные поля.

Низко, низко небо пустое,
И голос молящего тих:
«Ранят тело Твоё пресвятое,
Мечут жребий о ризах Твоих».

*

Всё расхищено, предано, продано,
Чёрной смерти мелькало крыло,
Всё голодной тоскою изглодано,
Отчего же нам стало светло?

Днём дыханьями веет вишнёвыми
Небывалый под городом лес,
Ночью блещет созвездьями новыми
Глубь прозрачных июльских небес.

Not in vain were prayers offered; the earth yearned for rain. The trampled fields were sprinkled with warm and red moisture.

The empty sky is low, so low, and the voice of the one who prays sounds soft: 'They are wounding Your most holy body, and casting lots for Your garments.'

*

ALL has been looted, betrayed, sold; black death's wing flashed [ahead]; all is gnawed by hungry anguish – why then does a light shine for us?

By day a mysterious wood in the vicinity of the town breathes a scent of cherries, by night the depths of the transparent July sky glitter with new constellations.

И так близко подходит чудесное
К развалившимся грязным домам,
Никому, никому неизвестное,
Но от века желанное нам.

Бежецк

Там белые церкви и звонкий, светящийся лёд,
Там милого сына цветут васильковые очи.
Над городом древним алмазные русские ночи
И серп поднебесный желтее чем липовый мёд.
Там вьюги сухие взлетают с заречных полей,
И люди, как ангелы, Божьему Празднику рады,
Прибрали светлицу, зажгли у киота лампады,
И Книга Благая лежит на дубовом столе.
Там строгая память, такая скупая теперь,
Свои терема мне открыла с глубоким поклоном;
Но я не вошла, я захлопнула страшную дверь;
И город был полон весёлым рождественским
звоном.

And the miraculous is coming so near to the ruined and filthy houses, something nobody, nobody has known, though we have longed for it from time immemorial.

Bezhetsk

THERE are white churches there, and resonant, sparkling ice; there blossom my beloved son's eyes, the colour of cornflowers. The Russian nights, speckled with diamonds, are suspended above the ancient town, and the crescent in the sky is yellower than honey. There dry snow-storms blow in from the plains beyond the river, and men rejoice as angels do on God's Holy Day. They have tidied up the best room, lit the lamps by the icons, and the Good Book is lying on the oak table. There stern memory, so parsimonious now, opened her tower-rooms to me with a low bow. But I did not enter, and I slammed the fearful door. And the town was filled with the merry ringing of Christmas bells.

*

Годовщину весёлую празднуй –
Ты пойми, что сегодня точь в точь
Нашей первой зимы – той, алмазной,
Повторяется снежная ночь.

Пар валит из-под жёлтых конюшен,
Погружается Мойка во тьму,
Свет луны как нарочно притушен,
И куда мы идём – не пойму.

В грозных айсбергах Марсово поле,
И Лебяжья лежит в хрусталях . . .
Чья с моею сравняется доля,
Если в сердце веселье и страх, –

И трепещет, как дивная птица,
Голос твой у меня за плечом.
И, внезапным согретый лучом,
Снежный прах так тепло серебрится.

CELEBRATE a joyful anniversary: can't you see? – Today the snowy night of our first winter – that diamond-like winter – is repeated in every detail.

Steam is pouring out from under the yellow stables, the Moika* is sinking into darkness, the moonlight is dimmed as though on purpose, and I cannot make out where we are going.

The Marsovo Pole lies covered with huge icebergs, and the Lebyazh'ya with crystals . . . Whose lot can compare with mine, if gaiety and fear are in my heart?

And if your voice, like some marvellous bird, quivers over my shoulder, and the powdery snow, warmed by a sudden ray, glitters so warm and silvery?

* The Moika is a small river, the Marsovo Pole (Champ de Mars) an open square, and the Lebyazh'ya [Kanavka] a canal, in Leningrad.

[*Петербург в 1913 году из «Поэмы без героя»*]

Были святки кострами согреты,
И валились с мостов кареты,
 И весь траурный город плыл
По невсдомому назначенью,
По Неве иль против теченья, –
 Только прочь от своих могил.
На Галерной чернела арка,
В Летнем тонко пела флюгарка,
И серебряный месяц ярко
 Над серебряным веком стыл.
Оттого, что по всем дорогам,
Оттого, что ко всем порогам
 Приближалась медленно тень, –
Ветер рвал со стены афиши,
Дым плясал вприсядку на крыше,
 И кладбищем пахла сирень.
И, царицей Авдотьей заклятый,
Достоевский и бесноватый
 Город в свой уходил туман,

[*St Petersburg in 1913 from 'A Poem without a Hero'*]

CHRISTMAS-TIDE was aglow with bonfires, the carriages tumbled off the bridges, and the whole funereal city was floating to an unknown destination, either down the Neva or upstream, but in any case away from its graves. In the Galernaya [Street] the arch stood out in black outline, in the Summer Garden a weather-vane sang in shrill tones, and a bright silver moon was growing cold over [Russia's] Silver Age. Along every road a shadow was slowly drawing near to every threshold; and because of this the wind tore posters off the walls, the smoke danced a jig on the roof, and the lilac smelt of the graveyard. And, laid under a spell by the Tsaritsa Avdot'ya,* Dostoevskian and ghostly, the city retreated into its own mist . . . . . .

* A popular form of Evdokiya (Eudoxia), the name of Peter the Great's first wife, whom he compelled to take the veil. A member of an old Muscovite family, she represented those elements in Russian society who were hostile to Peter's new capital of St Petersburg.

И выглядывал вновь из мрака . . .
Старый питерщик и гуляка!
  Как пред казнью бил барабан.
И всегда в духоте морозной,
Предвоенной, блудной и грозной,
  Непонятный таился гул . . .
Но тогда он был слышен глухо,
Он почти не касался слуха
  И в сугробах невских тонул.
Словно в зеркале страшной ночи
И беснуется и не хочет
  Узнавать себя человек,
А по набережной легендарной
Приближался не календарный –
  Настоящий Двадцатый Век.

Два стихотворения

I

Таинственной невстречи
Пустынны торжества,
Несказанные речи,
Безмолвные слова.

and emerged again out of the darkness . . . that old reveller, Petersburg. The drum was beating as before an execution. And all the time in the stifling, frosty, lascivious, and menacing air of the pre-war days an incomprehensible rumble was latent . . . But it sounded hollow then, scarcely reached the ear, and was lost in the snow-drifts of the Neva. It was as though man were possessed, and unwilling to recognize himself in the mirror of some dreadful night, while along the legendary embankment the twentieth century – the real, not the calendar one – was approaching.

Two Poems

I

THE triumphs of a mysterious non-meeting are desolate ones; unspoken phrases, silent words. . . . . .

Нескрещенные взгляды
Не знают, где им лечь,
И только слёзы рады,
Что можно долго течь.
Шиповник Подмосковья
Увы! при чём-то тут . . .
И это всё любовью
Бессмертной назовут.

2

Ты опять со мной, подруга осень!
Ин. Анненский

Пусть кто-то ещё отдыхает на юге
И нежится в райском саду.
Здесь северно очень, и осень в подруги
Я выбрала в этом году.
Сюда принесла я блаженную память
Последней невстречи с тобой —
Холодное, чистое, лёгкое пламя
Победы моей над судьбой.

Glances that do not meet and do not know where to rest; and only tears are glad that they can flow for long. Alas! for some reason, a wild rose-bush near Moscow plays a part in all this . . . And all that will be called immortal love.

2

You are with me once again, autumn, my friend!
I. Annensky

Other people may still be on holiday in the south and basking in the garden of paradise; here it is very northerly, and this year I have chosen autumn to be my friend. I have brought here the blessed memory of my last non-meeting with you – the cold, pure, light flame of my victory over fate.

NIKOLAY ASEEV

Бык

Ворочая°тяжёлыми белками
кровавых глаз,
свирепствуя,°ревя,°не умолкая,
идёт рассказ.
Он землю рвёт,°он бьёт песок, которым
затушит жар,
бросаясь°за вертлявым пикадором
на блеск ножа.
Все ждут, все ждут:°когда ж начнёт он падать,
скользя в грязи?
И первая°Испании эспада
его сразит.
Она блеснёт°язвительным укусом
сквозь трепет лет,
и ноги,°ослабев, уволокутся
в тугой петле!

Откуда ты?°Зачем тебя мне надо,
разбитый хрящ?
Иди сюда,°багряная Гренада,
взвивай°свой плащ!

The Bull

Rolling the heavy whites of its bloodshot eyes, raging and bellowing without a pause, the story proceeds. He tears the ground and beats the sand with which he will quench the fire, as he rushes after the nimble *picador*, at the glittering blade. They are all waiting, waiting: when will he start falling and sliding in the mud, and the first sword of Spain strike him down? It will flash like a biting sting through the shudder of the years, and his legs drained of strength will be dragged away in a tight noose.

    Where are you from? Why do I need you, O shattered cartilage? Come here, crimson Granada, whirl your cape through the air! . .

Вот так и мне°блеснут, зрачки заполнив,
и песнь и страсть,
вот так и мне –°в рукоплесканьях молний
вздохнув –°упасть.
Ведь жить°и значит:°петь, любить и злиться,
и рвать в клочки,
пока°глядят оливковые лица,
горят зрачки!
Амфитеатру –°вечная услада
твоя беда . . .
Иди ко мне, багровая Гренада,
иди сюда!
Ведь так и жил,°и шёл, и падал Пушкин,
и пел, пока
взвивалися горящие хлопушки,
язвя бока.

Все ждут, все ждут:°когда ж начнёшь ты
                                    падать,
ещё горящ,
и первая Испании эспада
проколет хрящ!
Ведь радостнее°всех людских профессий,

Thus will song and passion flash before my eyes, filling their pupils; thus will I fall down, sighing in the applause of lightning. For to live means to sing, to love, to rage, and to tear things to shreds, while olive-coloured faces look on and pupils burn. Your catastrophe is a never-ending delight for the arena . . . Come to me, crimson Granada, come here! After all, this is how Pushkin lived and walked and fell and sang, while blazing crackers rose in the air and wounded his flanks.

They are all waiting, waiting: when will you start falling, while still ablaze, and the first sword of Spain pierce your cartilage? For the most joyous of human occupations . . . . . .

сменясь в лице,
судьбу чужую° взвесив на эфесе,
ударить в цель!

Хор вершин

Широкие плечи гор –
Вершин онемелый хор,
Крутые отроги
У самой дороги –
Времён замолчавший хор.

Высокие тени гор . . .
С беспамятно давних пор
Стоят недотроги
У самой дороги –
Затихший внезапно спор.

Когтистые рёбра круч,
Катящие шумный ключ.
Туманные кряжи
Завеяны в пряже
Вот здесь же
Рождённых туч.

s to balance another's fate upon a sword-hilt and, with a changed
expression, to hit the mark!

The Chorus of Summits

THE broad shoulders of mountains – the silenced chorus of summits, precipitous spurs by the very roadside – the chorus of ages
that has fallen silent.

Tall shadows of mountains . . . From time immemorial the
touch-me-nots stand by the very roadside – [their] argument
suddenly stilled.

The sharp-clawed ribs of cliffs pouring forth a noisy spring.
The misty ridges are enveloped in the yarn of clouds that are born
on this very spot.

Что каменных гряд полоса,
Должна быть и песен краса,
Чтоб в небо вздымались,
Как каменный палец,
Один за другим голоса.

The beauty of songs should be like a range of rocky mountains; voices, one after the other, must soar like stone fingers towards the sky.

BORIS PASTERNAK

Степь

Как были те выходы в тишь хороши!
Безбрежная степь, как марина.
Вздыхает ковыль, шуршат мураши,
И плавает плач комариный.

Стога с облаками построились в цепь
И гаснут, вулкан на вулкане.
Примолкла и взмокла безбрежная степь,
Колеблет, относит, толкает.

Туман отовсюду нас морем обстиг,
В волчцах волочась за чулками,
И чудно нам степью, как взморьем, брести –
Колеблет, относит, толкает.

Не стог ли в тумане? Кто поймёт?
Не наш ли омёт? Доходим. – Он.
– Нашли! Он самый и есть. – Омёт,
Туман и степь с четырёх сторон.

The Steppe

How wonderful were those sallies into the stillness! The boundless steppe is like a sea-scape. The feather-grass sighs, the ants
rustle, and the mosquitoes' whine drifts through the air.

The ricks have fallen into line with the clouds and fade into
darkness, like one volcano on another. The boundless steppe
has grown silent and damp; you sway, you drift, you are buffeted.

The mist has overtaken us and surrounds us like the sea, the
burrs are trailing after the stockings, and it is wonderful to tramp
the steppe like the sea-shore – you sway, you drift, you are buffeted.

Isn't that a rick in the mist? Who can tell? Isn't that our straw-
rick? We are coming up to it. – Yes, it is. We've found it. That's
it all right. The rick and the mist and the steppe all around us.

И млечный путь стороной ведёт
На Керчь, как шлях, скотом пропылён.
Зайти за хаты, и дух займёт:
Открыт, открыт с четырёх сторон.

Туман снотворен, ковыль, как мёд.
Ковыль всем млечным путём рассорён.
Туман разойдётся, и ночь обоймёт
Омёт и степь с четырёх сторон.

Тенистая полночь стоит у пути,
На шлях навалилась звездами,
И через дорогу за тын перейти
Нельзя, не топча мирозданья.

Когда ещё звёзды так низко росли,
И полночь в бурьян окунало,
Пылал и пугался намокший муслин,
Льнул, жался и жаждал финала?

Пусть степь нас рассудит и ночь разрешит.
Когда, когда не: – В Начале

And the Milky Way slants off towards Kerch', like a road made dusty by cattle. If you go behind the houses it will take your breath away: wide open spaces on all sides.

The mist is soporific, the feather-grass is like honey. The feather-grass is strewn over the whole Milky Way. The mist will disperse, and the night will cover the rick and the steppe on all sides.

Shadowy midnight stands by the wayside, it has come right down on to the road and strewn it with stars, and you cannot cross the road to go beyond the fence without treading on the universe.

When did the stars grow so low, midnight sink so deep into the tall wild grass, and the drenched muslin, glowing and frightened, press closer, cling, and long for a dénouement?

Let the steppe arbitrate and night judge between us. When, if not in the Beginning, ...

Плыл Плач Комариный, Ползли Мураши,
Волчцы по Чулкам Торчали?

Закрой их, любимая! Запорошит!
Вся степь, как до грехопаденья:
Вся – миром объята, вся – как парашют,
Вся – дыбящееся виденье!

В лесу

Луга мутило жаром лиловатым,
В лесу клубился кафедральный мрак.
Что оставалось в мире целовать им?
Он весь был их, как воск на пальцах мяк.

Есть сон такой, – не спишь, а только снится,
Что жаждешь сна; что дремлет человек,
Которому сквозь сон палит ресницы
Два чёрных солнца, бьющих из-под век.

Текли лучи. Текли жуки с отливом,
Стекло стрекоз сновало по щекам.

did the mosquitoes whine, the ants crawl, and the burrs cling to the stockings?

Close them, my darling, or you'll be blinded. The whole steppe is as before the Fall: bathed in peace, like a parachute, like a heaving vision!

In the Wood

THE meadows were blurred by a faintly mauve heat; in the wood the darkness of cathedrals swirled. What in the world remained for them to kiss? It was all theirs, like wax growing soft on their fingers.

There is a dream: you are not asleep, but merely dreaming that you long for sleep; that a person is dozing, and two black suns beating from beneath his eyelids are burning his lashes in his sleep.

The sun-rays flowed by, and iridescent beetles; the glass of dragon-flies skimmed over his cheeks. . . . . . .

Был полон лес мерцаньем кропотливым,
Как под щипцами у часовщика.

Казалось, он уснул под стук цифири,
Меж тем как выше, в терпком янтаре,
Испытаннейшие часы в эфире
Переставляют, сверив по жаре.

Их переводят, сотрясают иглы
И сеют тень, и мают, и сверлят
Мачтовый мрак, который ввысь воздвигло,
В истому дня, на синий циферблат.

Казалось, древность счастья облетает.
Казалось, лес закатом снов объят.
Счастливые часов не наблюдают,
Но те, вдвоём, казалось, только спят.

Спасское

Незабвенный сентябрь осыпается в Спас-
                                                                ском.
Не сегодня ли с дачи съезжать вам пора?

The wood was full of minute scintillations, as beneath the clock-maker's tweezers.

It seemed he had fallen asleep to the tick of figures, while high above his head, in harsh amber, the hands of a strictly tested clock are shifted in the ether and set in accordance with the change of heat.

They adjust the clock, shake the pine-needles, scatter shadow, wear out, and pierce the darkness of the trunks which is raised up into the day's fatigue, on to the clock's blue dial.

It seemed that ancient happiness was sinking, that the wood was wrapped in the sunset of dreams. Happy people do not watch the clock, but this couple, it seemed, merely slept.

Spasskoe

AN unforgettable September sheds its leaves in Spasskoe. Is today not the time for you to move out of the summer cottage?

За плетнём перекликнулось эхо с подпаском
И в лесу различило удар топора.

Этой ночью за парком знобило трясину.
Только солнце взошло, и опять – наутёк.
Колокольчик не пьёт костоломных росинок.
На берёзах несмытый лиловый отёк.

Лес хандрит. И ему захотелось на отдых,
Под снега, в непробудную спячку берлог.
Да и то, меж стволов, в почерневших обводах
Парк зияет в столбцах, как сплошной не-
                                    кролог.

Березняк перестал ли линять и пятнаться,
Водянистую сень потуплять и редеть?
Этот – ропщет ещё, и опять вам – пятнадцать,
И опять, – о дитя, о, куда нам их деть?

Их так много уже, что не всё ж – куралесить.
Их – что птиц по кустам, что грибов за межой.

Beyond the fence Echo has exchanged a shout with the herd-boy
and caught the sound of the axe's stroke in the wood.

Last night beyond the park the quagmire shivered. The sun no
sooner rose than it made off again. The bluebell does not drink the
rheumatic dew-drops, and there are dirty mauve stains on the
birches.

The wood is despondent. It, too, wants a rest beneath the snow,
in the deep sleep of the bear-dens. As it is, the park, framed by the
tree trunks, stands gaping in columns with blackened borders like
one vast obituary.

Has the birch wood ceased to fade and to come out in stains, to
lower its watery shade and to grow sparse? This one is still com-
plaining, and you're fifteen again, and again, my child, what shall
we do with them?

They're so many already that it's time to give up pranks; there
are as many of them as there are birds in the bushes and mushrooms beyond the boundary. . . . . . .

Ими свой кругозор уж случалось завесить,
Их туманом случалось застлать и чужой.

В ночь кончины от тифа сгорающий комик
Слышит гул: гомерический хохот райка.
Ныпⁱе в Спасском с дороги бревенчатый
домик
Видит, галлюцинируя, та же тоска.

Гамлет

Гул затих. Я вышел на подмостки.
Прислонясь к дверному косяку,
Я ловлю в далёком отголоске,
Что случится на моём веку.

На меня наставлен сумрак ночи
Тысячью биноклей на оси.
Если только можно, Авва Отче,
Чашу эту мимо пронеси.

Я люблю Твой замысел упрямый
И играть согласен эту роль.

We've already had occasion to curtain our horizon with them and
to veil another's vista with their mist.

On the night of his death the comedian burning with typhus
hears a rumble: it's the Homeric laughter from the 'gods'. Today
in Spasskoe the same anguish sees in hallucination the timbered
cottage from the road.

Hamlet

THE hum has died down. I have come out on to the stage. Leaning
against the door-frame, I seek to grasp in the distant echo what will
happen during my life.

The penumbra of night is focused upon me through a thousand
opera-glasses. If only it be possible, Abba, Father, take away this
cup from me.

I love your stubborn design, and am content to play this part.

Но сейчас идёт другая драма,
И на этот раз меня уволь.

Но продуман распорядок действий,
И неотвратим конец пути.
Я один, всё тонет в фарисействе.
Жизнь прожить - не поле перейти.

Зимняя ночь

Мело, мело по всей земле
Во все пределы.
Свеча горела на столе,
Свеча горела.

Как летом роем мошкара
Летит на пламя,
Слетались хлопья со двора
К оконной раме.

Метель лепила на стекле
Кружки и стрелы.
Свеча горела на столе,
Свеча горела.

But now another drama is being acted, so this time let me be.

But the order of the acts has been thought out, and the end of the road is inevitable. I am alone, everything is sinking in Pharisaism. To go through life is not the same as to walk across a field.*

Winter Night

SNOW swept over the whole earth, swept it from end to end. The candle burned on the table, the candle burned.

Like a swarm of midges in summer flying towards a flame, the snowflakes outside flew in swarms to the window.

The snow-storm modelled circles and arrows on the windowpane. The candle burned on the table, the candle burned.

* The last sentence is a Russian proverb.

BORIS PASTERNAK

На озарённый потолок
Ложились тени,
Скрещенья рук, скрещенья ног,
Судьбы скрещенья.

И падали два башмачка
Со стуком на пол.
И воск слезами с ночника
На платье капал.

И всё терялось в снежной мгле
Седой и белой.
Свеча горела на столе,
Свеча горела.

На свечку дуло из угла,
И жар соблазна
Вздымал, как ангел, два крыла
Крестообразно.

Мело весь месяц в феврале,
И то и дело
Свеча горела на столе,
Свеча горела.

Shadows fell on the brightly lit ceiling: crossed hands, crossed legs, crossed destinies.

Two shoes fell to the floor with a thud, and wax dripped like tear-drops from the night-light on to the dress.

And everything was lost in a grey-white snowy mist. The candle burned on the table, the candle burned.

A draught from the corner blew at the candle's flame, and, like an angel, the heat of temptation raised two wings in the form of a cross.

The snow swept all through February, and many a time the candle burned on the table, the candle burned.

Земля

В московские особняки
Врывается весна нахрапом.
Выпархивает моль за шкапом
И ползает по летним шляпам,
И прячут шубы в сундуки.

По деревянным антресолям
Стоят цветочные горшки
С левкоем и желтофиолем,
И дышат комнаты привольем,
И пахнут пылью чердаки.

И улица запанибрата
С оконницей подслеповатой,
И белой ночи и закату
Не разминуться у реки.

И можно слышать в коридоре,
Что происходит на просторе,
О чём в случайном разговоре
С капелью говорит апрель.
Он знает тысячи историй
Про человеческое горе,

The Earth

VIOLENTLY the spring bursts into Moscow houses. Moths flutter
out from behind wardrobes and crawl on summer hats, and fur
coats are put away in trunks.

In the wooden mezzanines pots of stock and wallflower are
standing, the rooms breathe an air of freedom, and the attics smell
of dust.

The street is on familiar terms with the bleary window, and the
sunset will not fail to meet the 'white night' by the river.

In the passage you can hear what's going on outdoors, and
April's casual gossip with the falling drops of thawing snow. April
knows a thousand stories of human sorrow; . . . .

И по заборам стынут зори,
И тянут эту канитель.

И та же смесь огня и жути
На воле и в жилом уюте,
И всюду воздух сам не свой.
И тех же верб сквозные прутья,
И тех же белых почек вздутья
И на окне, и на распутье,
На улице и в мастерской.

Зачем же плачет даль в тумане,
И горько пахнет перегной?
На то ведь и моё призванье,
Чтоб не скучали расстоянья,
Чтобы за городскою гранью
Земле не тосковать одной.

Для этого весною ранней
Со мною сходятся друзья,
И наши вечера – прощанья,
Пирушки наши – завещанья,
Чтоб тайная струя страданья
Согрела холод бытия.

and along the fences the afterglow grows chill and spins out the yarn.

In the open air and in the comfort of the home there is the same mixture of fire and trepidation, and everywhere the air is beside itself. The same openwork of willow twigs, the same swelling of white buds on the window-sill and at the crossroad, in street and workshop.

Then why does the distant horizon weep in mist, and the humus smell bitter? It is my calling, after all, to see that distances do not feel lonely and that beyond the town boundary the earth does not pine in solitude.

That is why in early spring my friends and I gather together, and our evenings are farewells and our parties are testaments – so that the secret stream of suffering may warm the cold of life.

Гефсиманский Сад

Мерцаньем звёзд далёких безразлично
Был поворот дороги озарён.
Дорога шла вокруг горы Масличной,
Внизу под нею протекал Кедрон.

Лужайка обрывалась с половины.
За нею начинался Млечный путь.
Седые серебристые маслины
Пытались вдаль по воздуху шагнуть.

В конце был чей-то сад, надел земельный.
Учеников оставив за стеной,
Он им сказал: «Душа скорбит смертельно,
Побудьте здесь и бодрствуйте со Мной».

Он отказался без противоборства,
Как от вещей, полученных взаймы,
От всемогущества и чудотворства,
И был теперь, как смертные, как мы.

The Garden of Gethsemane

THE bend of the road was lit by the twinkling of distant and indifferent stars. The road circled the Mount of Olives, beneath it flowed the Cedron.

The meadow broke off in the middle; beyond it began the Milky Way. The silver-haired olives were trying to stride into the distance through the air.

At the far end was someone's garden, a plot of earth. Leaving His disciples outside the wall, He said to them: 'My soul is exceeding sorrowful, even unto death: tarry ye here, and watch with Me.'

Unresisting, he renounced omnipotence and the power to work miracles, as though they were things received on loan; and He was now like mortal men, like ourselves.

Ночная даль теперь казалась краем
Уничтоженья и небытия.
Простор вселенной был необитаем,
И только сад был местом для житья.

И, глядя в эти чёрные провалы,
Пустые, без начала и конца,
Чтоб эта чаша смерти миновала,
В поту кровавом Он молил Отца.

Смягчив молитвой смертную истому,
Он вышел за ограду. На земле
Ученики, осиленные дрёмой,
Валялись в придорожном ковыле.

Он разбудил их: «Вас Господь сподобил
Жить в дни Мои, вы ж разлеглись, как пласт.
Час Сына Человеческого пробил.
Он в руки грешников Себя предаст».

И лишь сказал, неведомо откуда
Толпа рабов и скопище бродяг,
Огни, мечи и впереди – Иуда
С предательским лобзаньем на устах.

The far reaches of the night now seemed to be the brink of anni-
hilation and non-being. The vastness of the universe was uninhab-
ited, and only the garden was a place of life.

And, gazing into this black abyss, empty, without beginning or
end, in bloody sweat He prayed to His Father that this cup of
death should pass away from Him.

His mortal agony assuaged by prayer, He came out of the en-
closure. On the ground, the disciples, overcome by drowsiness, lay
about in the grass by the roadside.

He woke them: 'The Lord has granted you to live in my time,
yet you are lying flat on the ground. The hour of the Son of Man
has struck. He will betray Himself into the hands of sinners.'

No sooner had He spoken when there appeared – no one knew
from where – a crowd of slaves and a rabble of knaves, with lights
and swords and, leading them, Judas with a traitor's kiss on his
lips.

Пётр дал мечом отпор головорезам
И ухо одному из них отсек.
Но слышит: «Спор нельзя решать железом,
Вложи свой меч на место, человек.

Неужто тьмы крылатых легионов
Отец не снарядил бы Мне сюда?
И, волоска тогда на Мне не тронув,
Враги рассеялись бы без следа.

Но книга жизни подошла к странице,
Которая дороже всех святынь.
Сейчас должно написанное сбыться,
Пускай же сбудется оно. Аминь.

Ты видишь, ход веков подобен притче
И может загореться на ходу.
Во имя страшного её величья
Я в добровольных муках в гроб сойду.

Я в гроб сойду и в третий день восстану,
И, как сплавляют по реке плоты,
Ко Мне на суд, как баржи каравана,
Столетья поплывут из темноты».

Peter repulsed the ruffians with his sword, and cut off the ear of one of them. But he heard: 'You cannot decide a dispute with weapons; put your sword into its place, O man.

'Could not my Father equip hosts of winged legions to defend me here? Then my enemies would scatter without trace, touching not a hair of my head.

'But the Book of Life has reached the page more precious than all things holy. What is written must now be fulfilled; so let it be. Amen.

'You see, the course of ages is like a parable, and may burst into flames on the way. For the sake of the parable's awesome grandeur I shall descend into the tomb in voluntary suffering.

'I shall descend into the tomb and shall rise again on the third day; and, as rafts drift down a river, so the centuries, like barges in a convoy, shall come floating to me out of the darkness to be judged.'

BORIS PASTERNAK

Ветер

(Четыре отрывка о Блоке)

Кому быть живым и хвалимым,
Кто должен быть мёртв и хулим
Известно у нас подхалимам
Влиятельным только одним.

Не знал бы никто, может статься,
В почёте ли Пушкин иль нет,
Без докторских их диссертаций,
На всё проливающих свет.

Но Блок, слава Богу, иная,
Иная, по счастью, статья.
Он к нам не спускался с Синая,
Нас не принимал в сыновья.

Прославленный не по программе
И вечный вне школ и систем,
Он не изготовлен руками
И нам не навязан никем.

The Wind

(Four Fragments about Blok)

WHO is to live and be lauded, who is to be [reckoned] dead and be abused – this is known only to our influential sycophants.

Perhaps no one would know whether Pushkin is honoured or not, were it not for their doctoral dissertations which shed light on all things.

But Blok, fortunately, is quite another matter: he did not come down to us from Sinai, nor adopt us as his sons.

Renowned independently of any programme and eternal outside all schools and systems, he has not been manufactured, nor has anyone thrust him down our throats.

343

*

Он ветрен, как ветер. Как ветер,
Шумевший в имении в дни,
Как там ещё Филька – фалетер
Скакал во главе шестерни.

И жил ещё дед якобинец,
Кристальной души радикал,
От коего ни на мизинец
И ветреник внук не отстал.

Тот ветер, проникший под рёбра
И в душу, в течение лет
Недоброю славой и доброй
Помянут в стихах и воспет.

Тот ветер повсюду. Он – дома,
В деревьях, в деревне, в дожде,
В поэзии третьего тома,
В «Двенадцати», в смерти, везде.

He is gusty as the wind; as the wind that whistled on the estate in the days when Fil'ka the postilion* still galloped in the lead of a team of six horses.

The Jacobin grandfather was still alive – a radical with a soul as pure as crystal, whose gusty grandson did not lag behind him by a finger's breadth.

That wind, which penetrated beneath the ribs and into his soul, was in the course of years mentioned and celebrated in his verses both in ill and good repute.

That wind is everywhere. It's in the house, in the trees, in the country, in the rain, in the poetry of his third volume, in *The Twelve*, in death, everywhere.

* фалетер is a popular distortion of форейтор.

★

Широко, широко, широко
Раскинулись речка и луг.
Пора сенокоса, толóка,
Страда, суматоха вокруг.
Косцам у речного протока
Заглядываться недосуг.
Косьба разохотила Блока.
Схватил косовище барчук.
Ежа чуть не ранил с наскоку,
Косой полоснул двух гадюк.

Но он не доделал урока.
Упрёки: лентяй, лежебока.
О детство! О школы морока!
О песни пололок и слуг!

А к вечеру тучи с востока.
Обложены север и юг.
И ветер жестокий не к сроку
Влетает и режется вдруг
О косы косцов, об осоку,
Резучую гущу излук.

The river and the meadow are spread out far and wide. It's hay-making time, the time of communal labour, all around everyone is hard at work and bustling. The mowers have no time to loiter and gaze by the arm of the river. The mowing made Blok want to try his own hand: the young squire seized the haft of a scythe; with a swipe he nearly wounded a hedgehog and then slashed two adders with his scythe.

But he did not finish his lesson; rebukes [pour in]: 'Idler, lazy-bones!' Oh, childhood! Oh, the tedium of school! Oh, the songs of the weeders and the servants!

But towards evening clouds approach from the east; the horizon is overcast to the north and south. And a fierce and unseasonable wind suddenly blows in and slashes at the mowers' scythes, at the sedge, at the prickly thicket by the river-bends.

О детство! О школы морока!
О песни пололок и слуг!
Широко, широко, широко
Раскинулись речка и луг.

★

Зловещ горизонт и внезапен
И в кровоподтёках заря,
Как след незаживших царапин
И кровь на ногах косаря.

Нет счёта небесным порезам,
Предвестникам бурь и невзгод,
И пахнет водой и железом
И ржавчиной воздух болот.

В лесу, на дороге, в овраге,
В деревне или на селе
На тучах такие зигзаги
Сулят непогоду земле.

Oh, childhood! Oh, the tedium of school! Oh, the songs of the weeders and the servants! The river and the meadow are spread out far and wide.

★

The horizon is sinister and sudden, and the dawn is streaked with blood like the marks of unhealed scratches, like blood on a reaper's legs.

There's no counting the gashes in the sky, those portents of storms and bad weather, and the air of the swamps smells of water, iron, and rust.

In the forest, on the road, in the ravine, in hamlet or village such zigzags in the clouds portend bad weather to the earth!

Когда ж над большою столицей
Край неба так ржав и багрян,
С державою что-то случится,
Постигнет страну ураган.

Блок на небе видел разводы.
Ему предвещал небосклон
Большую грозу, непогоду,
Великую бурю, циклон.

Блок ждал этой бури и встряски.
Её огневые штрихи
Боязнью и жаждой развязки
Легли в его жизнь и стихи.

В больнице

Стояли, как перед витриной,
Почти запрудив тротуар.
Носилки втолкнули в машину,
В кабину вскочил санитар.

И скорая помощь, минуя
Панели, подъезды, зевак,

But when over the great capital the edge of the sky is so purple and rusty, [it means that] something will happen to the State, and a hurricane will strike the land.

Blok saw tracery in the sky. To him the firmament presaged a violent thunder-storm, bad weather, a great tempest, a cyclone.

Blok expected that storm, that upheaval. Its fiery features marked his life and his verse with a fear of and a longing for its dénouement.

In Hospital

THEY stood, almost blocking the pavement, as though before a shop window. The stretcher was pushed into the car, the hospital attendant jumped into the seat beside the driver.

And the ambulance, driving past pavements, doorways, gaping loiterers, ...

Сумятицу улиц ночную,
Нырнула огнями во мрак.

Милиция, улицы, лица
Мелькали в свету фонаря.
Покачивалась фельдшерица
Со склянкою нашатыря.

Шёл дождь, и в приёмном покое
Уныло шумел водосток,
Меж тем как строка за строкою
Марали опросный листок.

Его положили у входа.
Всё в корпусе было полно.
Разило парами иода,
И с улицы дуло в окно.

Окно обнимало квадратом
Часть сада и неба клочок.
К палатам, полам и халатам
Присматривался новичок.

and the bustle of the streets at night, plunged with its headlights into the darkness.

Policemen, streets, and faces were momentarily lit up by the car's headlights. The nurse was swaying with a bottle of smelling-salts in her hand.

It was raining, and the dreary sound of water running down the waste-pipe could be heard in the casualty ward, while the case-sheet was filled in with line after line of scribbling.

They gave him a bed by the entrance. The wing was quite full. The place reeked of iodine and there was a draught from the window.

Part of the garden and a piece of sky were framed in the square window. The new arrival was studying the wards, the floors, and the white coats;

Как вдруг из расспросов сиделки,
Покачивавшей головой,
Он понял, что из переделки
Едва ли он выйдет живой.

Тогда он взглянул благодарно
В окно, за которым стена
Была точно искрой пожарной
Из города озарена.

Там в зареве рдела застава
И, в отсвете города, клён
Отвешивал веткой корявой
Больному прощальный поклон.

«О, Господи, как совершенны
Дела Твои», – думал больной,
«Постели и люди и стены,
Ночь смерти и город ночной.

Я принял снотворного дозу
И плачу, платок теребя.
О, Боже, волнения слёзы
Мешают мне видеть Тебя.

when suddenly, from the questions the nurse was asking while shaking her head, he realized that he was unlikely to come out of this predicament alive.

Then, full of gratitude, he looked through the window, beyond which a wall was lit up by the glare of the city as though by the sparks of a fire.

Over there the town boundary glowed red, and in the light reflected from the city a maple-tree was making a low bow to the patient with its crooked branch, as a gesture of farewell.

'O Lord,' the patient was thinking, 'how perfect are Your works: the beds, and the people, and the walls, my death-night and the city at night.

'I have taken a sleeping draught and I weep as I pluck at my handkerchief. O God, tears of emotion prevent me from seeing You.

Мне сладко при свете неярком,
Чуть падающем на кровать,
Себя и свой жребий подарком
Бесценным Твоим сознавать.

Кончаясь в больничной постели,
Я чувствую рук Твоих жар.
Ты держишь меня, как изделье,
И прячешь, как перстень в футляр».

'It gives me such comfort, as the dim light falls faintly upon my bed, to know that I and my destiny are Your priceless gift.

'Dying in a hospital bed, I feel the warmth of Your hands. You are holding me as a work You have fashioned, and hiding me away like a ring in a jeweller's case.'

OSIP MANDEL'SHTAM

Айя-София

Айя-София – здесь остановиться
Судил Господь народам и царям!
Ведь купол твой, по слову очевидца,
Как на цепи, подвешен к небесам.

И всем векам – пример Юстиниана,
Когда похитить для чужих богов
Позволила Эфесская Диана
Сто семь зелёных мраморных столбов.

Но что же думал твой строитель щедрый,
Когда, душой и помыслом высок,
Расположил апсиды и экседры,
Им указав на запад и восток?

Прекрасен храм, купающийся в мире,
И сорок окон – света торжество;
На парусах, под куполом, четыре
Архангела прекраснее всего.

Hagia Sophia

HAGIA SOPHIA – the Lord ordained that nations and emperors should halt here! For, in the words of an eye-witness, your dome, as on a chain, is suspended from the heavens.

And Justinian set an example for all ages, when Diana of Ephesus permitted one hundred and seven green marble columns to be stolen for alien gods.

But what was in the mind of your bountiful builder when, exalted in soul and thought, he disposed the apses and the exedrae, pointing them west and east?

The temple, bathing in the world, is beautiful, and the forty windows are a triumph of light; finest of all are the four archangels in the pendentives beneath the dome.

И мудрое сферическое зданье
Народы и века переживёт,
И серафимов гулкое рыданье
Не покоробит тёмных позолот.

★

Есть иволги в лесах, и гласных долгота
В тонических стихах единственная мера.
Но только раз в году бывает разлита
В природе длительность, как в метрике Гомера.

Как бы цезурою зияет этот день:
Уже с утра покой и трудные длинноты;
Волы на пастбище, и золотая лень
Из тростника извлечь богатство целой ноты.

★

Бессонница. Гомер. Тугие паруса.
Я список кораблей прочёл до середины:
Сей длинный выводок, сей поезд журавлиный,
Что над Элладою когда-то поднялся.

And the wise, spherical building will outlive nations and centuries, and the resonant sobbing of the seraphim will not warp the dark gilded surfaces.

★

THERE are orioles in the woods, and in metrical verse the length of the vowels is the only measure. But only once a year is quantity diffused in nature, as in Homer's metre.

That day yawns like a caesura: from the very morning there is peace and a laborious protraction; the oxen are at pasture, and golden languor makes one too lazy to extract from a reed the richness of a whole note.

★

SLEEPLESSNESS. Homer. Taut sails. I have read the catalogue of ships down to half its length: that long-extended flock, that flight of cranes which once rose up above Hellas.

Как журавлиный клин в чужие рубежи –
На головах царей божественная пена –
Куда плывёте вы? Когда бы не Елена,
Что Троя вам одна, ахейские мужи?

И море, и Гомер – всё движется любовью.
Кого же слушать мне? И вот Гомер молчит,
И море чёрное, витийствуя, шумит
И с тяжким грохотом подходит к изголовью.

*

В разноголосице девического хора
Все церкви нежные поют на голос свой,
И в дугах каменных Успенского собора
Мне брови чудятся, высокие, дугой.

И с укреплённого архангелами вала
Я город озирал на чудной высоте.
В стенах Акрополя печаль меня снедала
По русском имени и русской красоте.

It is like a wedge of cranes flying off to distant lands. The heads of the kings are covered with the foam of the gods. Where are you sailing to? Were it not for Helen, what would Troy be to you, O Achaeans?

The sea, and Homer – all is moved by love. To which of the two, then, shall I listen? And now Homer is silent, and the black sea, declaiming, roars and draws near to my pillow with thunderous crashing.

*

IN the polyphony of a girls' choir every tender church sings its own melody; and the stone arches of the Cathedral of the Assumption call up in my mind a vision of rising, arch-shaped eyebrows.

And, standing on the marvellous eminence, I surveyed the city from the rampart fortified by archangels. Within the walls of the acropolis I was consumed by sorrow for the Russian name and for Russian beauty.

Не диво ль дивное, что вертоград нам снится,
Где реют голуби в горячей синеве,
Что православные крюки поёт черница:
Успенье нежное – Флоренция в Москве.

И пятиглавые московские соборы
С их итальянскою и русскою душой
Напоминают мне явление Авроры,
Но с русским именем и в шубке меховой.

★

На страшной высоте блуждающий огонь,
Но разве так звезда мерцает?
Прозрачная звезда, блуждающий огонь,
Твой брат, Петрополь, умирает.

На страшной высоте земные сны горят,
Зелёная звезда мерцает.
О если ты звезда – воды и неба брат,
Твой брат, Петрополь, умирает.

Is it not strange and wonderful that the hot blue sky, where the pigeons are soaring, makes us dream of a garden, and that a nun is singing the ancient chants of the Orthodox Church? The tender Cathedral of the Assumption – Florence in Moscow.

And the five-domed cathedrals of Moscow, with their Italian and Russian soul, remind me of the rise of Aurora, but with a Russian name and clothed in a fur-coat.

★

A WANDERING fire at a fearful height ... But does a star twinkle like this? O transparent star, wandering fire, your brother, Petropolis, is dying.

At a fearful height earthly dreams are burning and a green star is twinkling. Oh, if you, O star, are the brother of water and sky, your brother, Petropolis, is dying.

Чудовищный корабль на страшной высоте
Несётся, крылья расправляет –
Зелёная звезда, в прекрасной нищете
Твой брат, Петрополь, умирает.

Прозрачная весна над чёрною Невой
Сломалась, воск бессмертья тает.
О если ты звезда – Петрополь, город твой,
Твой брат, Петрополь, умирает.

★

Прославим, братья, сумерки свободы, –
Великий сумеречный год.
В кипящие ночные воды
Опущен грузный лес тенёт.
Восходишь ты в глухие годы,
О солнце, судия, народ.

Прославим роковое бремя,
Которое в слезах народный вождь берёт.

A monstrous ship, spreading its wings, is speeding at a fearful
height – O green star, your brother, Petropolis, is dying in beautiful
poverty.
Above the black Neva the transparent spring has been shattered,
and the wax of immortality is melting. Oh, if you, O star, are
Petropolis, your city, your brother, Petropolis, is dying.

★

BROTHERS, let us glorify the twilight of freedom – the great
crepuscular year. A heavy forest of nets has been lowered into the
seething waters of the night. You are rising during sombre years,
O sun – judge and people.
Let us glorify the fateful burden which the people's leader tear-
fully assumes. . . . . . .

Прославим власти сумрачное бремя,
Её невыносимый гнёт.
В ком сердце есть, тот должен слышать, время,
Как твой корабль ко дну идёт.

Мы в легионы боевые
Связали ласточек – и вот
Не видно солнца; вся стихия
Щебечет, движется, живёт;
Сквозь сети – сумерки густые –
Не видно солнца и земля плывёт.

Ну что ж, попробуем: огромный, неуклюжий,
Скрипучий поворот руля.
Земля плывёт. Мужайтесь, мужи.
Как плугом, океан деля,
Мы будем помнить и в летейской стуже,
Что десяти небес нам стоила земля.

Tristia

Я изучил науку расставанья
В простоволосых жалобах ночных.

Let us glorify the sombre burden of power, its unbearable yoke.
He who has a heart must hear your ship sinking, O time.

We have bound swallows into battle legions, and now we cannot
see the sun; the whole of nature is twittering, stirring, and alive;
through the nets – the dense twilight – the sun cannot be seen,
and the earth is afloat.

Well, let's try: a vast, clumsy, and creaking turn of the helm.
The earth is afloat. Take heart, men. Cleaving the ocean as with a
plough, we shall remember even in Lethe's cold that for us the
earth has been worth a dozen heavens.

Tristia

I HAVE studied the science of parting in the laments of the night,
when a woman's hair flows loose. . . . . . .

Жуют волы, и длится ожиданье,
Последний час вигилий городских,
И чту обряд той петушиной ночи,
Когда, подняв дорожной скорби груз,
Глядели в даль заплаканные очи,
И женский плач мешался с пеньем муз.

Кто может знать при слове – расставанье,
Какая нам разлука предстоит,
Что нам сулит петушье восклицанье,
Когда огонь в акрополе горит,
И на заре какой-то новой жизни,
Когда в сенях лениво вол жуёт,
Зачем петух, глашатай новой жизни,
На городской стене крылами бьёт?

И я люблю обыкновенье пряжи:
Снуёт челнок, веретено жужжит.
Смотри, навстречу, словно пух лебяжий,
Уже босая Делия летит!
О, нашей жизни скудная основа,
Куда как беден радости язык!

The oxen chew, and expectation lingers – the last hour of the town's vigil; and I revere the rites of that night when the cock was crowing, and when eyes red with crying, lifting their load of itinerant sorrow, gazed into the distance, and a woman's weeping mingled with the Muses' singing.

Who knows, when the word 'parting' is spoken, what kind of separation lies in store for us, what the cock's crowing augurs for us when the fire burns on the acropolis, and why at the dawn of some new life, when the ox is chewing lazily in the shed, the cock, herald of the new life, flaps its wings on the town wall?

I like the routine of spinning: the shuttle moves to and fro, the spindle hums. Look, barefooted Delia, like swansdown, is already flying to meet you. Oh, how scanty is the language of joy, that meagre foundation of our life! . . . . . .

Всё было встарь, всё повторится снова,
И сладок нам лишь узнаванья миг.

Да будет так: прозрачная фигурка
На чистом блюде глиняном лежит,
Как беличья распластанная шкурка,
Склонясь над воском, девушка глядит.
Не нам гадать о греческом Эребе,
Для женщин воск, что для мужчины медь.
Нам только в битвах выпадает жребий,
А им дано гадая умереть.

*

Сёстры – тяжесть и нежность – одинаковы ваши
приметы.
Медуницы и осы тяжёлую розу сосут.
Человек умирает, песок остывает согретый
И вчерашнее солнце на чёрных носилках несут.

Ах, тяжёлые соты и нежные сети,
Легче камень поднять, чем имя твоё повторить!

All was before, all will be repeated again, and only the moment of recognition brings us delight.

So let it be: a small transparent figures lies, like a stretched out squirrel-skin, on a clean earthenware dish; a girl is gazing, bending down over the wax. It is not for us to tell fortunes about the Greek Erebus; wax is for women what bronze is for men. It is only in battle that the lot falls upon us; but to them it is given to die while telling fortunes.

*

SISTERS – heaviness and tenderness – your distinguishing marks are the same. Bees and wasps suck the heavy rose. Man dies, the hot sand cools, and yesterday's sun is carried on a black stretcher.*

Oh, the heavy honeycombs and the tender meshes – it is easier to lift a stone than to repeat your name! . . . . . .

* A reference to Pushkin's death.

У меня остаётся одна забота на свете:
Золотая забота, как времени бремя избыть.

Словно тёмную воду я пью помутившийся воздух.
Время вспахано плугом, и роза землёю была.
В медленном водовороте тяжёлые нежные розы,
Розы тяжесть и нежность в двойные венки
                                        заплела!

*

В Петербурге мы сойдёмся снова,
Словно солнце мы похоронили в нём,
И блаженное бессмысленное слово
В первый раз произнесём.
В чёрном бархате советской ночи,
В бархате всемирной пустоты
Всё поют блаженных жён родные очи,
Всё цветут бессмертные цветы.

Дикой кошкой горбится столица,
На мосту патруль стоит,

I have one purpose left in the world, a golden purpose – how to free
myself from the burden of time.
   I drink the turbid air as though it were dark water. Time has
been ploughed up, and the rose was earth. In a slow vortex [love]
has woven the heavy and tender roses, the heaviness and tenderness of the rose, into double wreaths.

*

WE shall meet again in Petersburg, as though we had buried the
sun there, and utter for the first time the blessed and meaningless
word. In the black velvet of the Soviet night, in the velvet of the
world's emptiness, beloved eyes of blessed women are still singing,
everlasting flowers are still in bloom.
   The capital is arched like a wild cat; a patrol is standing on the
bridge; . . . . . .

Только злой мотор во мгле промчится
И кукушкой прокричит.
Мне не надо пропуска ночного,
Часовых я не боюсь:
За блаженное бессмысленное слово
Я в ночи советской помолюсь.

Слышу лёгкий театральный шорох
И девическое «ах» –
И бессмертных роз огромный ворох
У Киприды на руках.
У костра мы греемся от скуки,
Может быть века пройдут,
И блаженных жён родные руки
Лёгкий пепел соберут.

Где-то хоры сладкие Орфея,
И родные тёмные зрачки,
И на грядки кресел с галлереи
Падают афиши голубки.
Что ж, гаси, пожалуй, наши свечи,
В чёрном бархате всемирной пустоты
Всё поют блаженных жён крутые плечи,
А ночного солнца не заметишь ты.

only an angry motor speeds through the gloom and cries out like a cuckoo. I do not need a pass for the night, I do not fear the sentries: for the sake of the blessed and meaningless word I shall pray in the Soviet night.

I hear a gentle rustling in the theatre, and a girl's startled exclamation; and Cypris holds a huge bunch of everlasting roses in her arms. We warm ourselves from boredom by a bonfire; ages will pass, perhaps, and the beloved hands of blessed women will gather the light ashes.

Somewhere are the sweet-sounding choirs of Orpheus, and the beloved, dark pupils of their eyes; and programmes are fluttering down like doves from the gallery on to the rows of stalls. Well, you may as well blow out our candles; in the black velvet of the world's emptiness the rounded shoulders of blessed women are still singing; but you will not notice the night sun.

Век

Век мой, зверь мой, кто сумеет
Заглянуть в твои зрачки
И своею кровью склеит
Двух столетий позвонки?
Кровь-строительница хлещет
Горлом из земных вещей,
Захребетник лишь трепещет
На пороге новых дней.

Тварь, покуда жизнь хватает,
Донести хребет должна,
И невидимым играет
Позвоночником волна.
Словно нежный хрящ ребёнка –
Век младенческой земли,
Снова в жертву, как ягнёнка,
Темя жизни принесли.

Чтобы вырвать жизнь из плена,
Чтобы новый мир начать,
Узловатых дней колена
Нужно флейтою связать.

The Age

MY age, my beast, who will be able to look into the pupils of your eyes and stick together the vertebrae of two centuries with his blood? The blood that builds gushes out of earthly things; the parasite only trembles on the threshold of the new days.

The creature, so long as it has enough life left, must carry the backbone to the end; and a wave plays upon the invisible spine. Once again life's vertex has been sacrificed like a lamb, as though it were a child's tender cartilage – the age of the earth's infancy.

In order to wrest life from captivity and start a new world, the figures of knotty days must be linked together by means of a flute.

OSIP MANDEL'SHTAM

Это век волну колышет
Человеческой тоской,
И в траве гадюка дышит
Мерой века золотой.

И ещё набухнут почки,
Брызнет зелени побег,
Но разбит твой позвоночник,
Мой прекрасный жалкий век.
И с бессмысленной улыбкой
Вспять глядишь, жесток и слаб,
Словно зверь, когда-то гибкий,
На следы своих же лап.

It's the age rocking the wave with man's anguish; and a viper in the
grass breathes the golden measure of the age.

And the buds will swell again, and the green shoots will sprout.
But your spine has been smashed, my beautiful, pitiful age. And
you look back, cruel and weak, with an inane smile, like a beast that
has once been supple, at the tracks left by your own paws.

MARINA TSVETAEVA

Из строгого, стройного храма
Ты вышла на визг площадей . . .
– Свобода! – Прекрасная Дама
Маркизов и русских князей.

Свершается страшная спевка, –
Обедня ещё впереди!
– Свобода! – Гулящая девка
На шалой солдатской груди!

[*Из «Стихов о Сонечке»*]

В моё окошко дождь стучится,
Скрипит рабочий над станком.
Была я уличной певицей,
А ты был княжеским сынком.

Я пела про судьбу-злодейку,
И с раззолоченных перил
Ты мне не рупь и не копейку,
Ты мне улыбку подарил.

You came out of a severe, well-proportioned church into the
screaming public squares . . . Freedom! The Fair Lady of mar-
quises and Russian princes.

The fearful choir-practice is coming to an end – the Liturgy is
yet to come. Freedom! A wanton slut on a profligate soldier's
breast!

[*From 'Verses about Sonechka'*]

The rain is beating against my window, the workman is creaking
over his machine-tool. I was a street-singer, and you were a prince's
son.

I sang about cruel fate, and over the gilded balustrade you gave
me not a rouble nor a copeck, but a smile.

Но старый князь узнал затею:
Сорвал он с сына ордена
И повелел слуге-лакею
Прогнать девчонку со двора.

И напилась же я в ту ночку!
Зато, в блаженном мире – том –
Была я – княжескою дочкой,
А ты – был уличным певцом!

*

Есть в стане моём – офицерская прямость,
Есть в рёбрах моих – офицерская честь.
На всякую му́ку иду не упрямясь:
Терпенье солдатское есть!

Как будто когда-то прикладом и сталью
Мне выправили этот шаг.
Недаром, недаром черкесская талья
И тесный ременный кушак.

But the old prince found out about this fancy: he tore off his son's decorations and bade a footman drive the wench off the premises.

How gloriously drunk I got that night! But, to make up for it, in that other, blissful, world I was a prince's daughter, and you were a street-singer!

*

THERE is an officer's uprightness in my figure, there is an officer's honour in my ribs. I accept any suffering without self-will: there is [in me] a soldier's patience!

It's as though this marching step of mine had been straightened one day with a rifle butt and with steel. Not in vain, not in vain have I a Circassian's waist and a tightly-drawn leather belt.

А зо́рю заслышу – Отец ты мой ро́дный! –
Хоть райские – штурмом – врата!
Как будто нарочно для сумки походной –
Раскинутых плеч широта.

Всё может – какой инвалид ошалелый
Над люлькой мне песенку спел . . .
И что-то от этого дня уцелело:
Я слово беру – на прицел!

И так моё сердце над Рэ-сэ-фэ-сэром
Скрежещет – корми – не корми! –
Как будто сама я была офицером
В Октябрьские смертные дни.

Попытка ревности

Как живётся вам с другою, –
Проще ведь? – Удар весла! –
Линией береговою
Скоро ль память отошла

Обо мне, пловучем острове
(По́ небу – не по водам!)

And when I hear the retreat being sounded – Good Lord! – I could storm the very gates of paradise! It's as though the breadth of my wide shoulders were made on purpose for a field kit-bag.

Anything is possible – [perhaps] some frenzied war invalid sang me a song over my cradle . . . And something has remained from that day: I take aim at the word!

And so in my heart I gnash over the RSFSR [Russian Soviet Federal Socialist Republic] – feed me – feed me not! As though I had myself been an officer in the deadly days of October.

An Attempt at Jealousy

What is your life like with another woman? Simpler, isn't it? A stroke of the oar! Did the memory of me,

a floating island (in the sky, not on the waters), soon recede, like a coastline? . . . . . .

Души, души! быть вам сёстрами,
Не любовницами – вам!

Как живётся вам с *простою*
Женщиною? *Без* божеств?
Государыню с престола
Свергши (с оного сошед),

Как живётся вам – хлопочется –
Ёжится? Встаётся – как?
С пошлиной бессмертной пошлости
Как справляетесь, бедняк?

«Судорог да перебоев –
Хватит! Дом себе найму».
Как живётся вам с любою –
Избранному моему!

Свойственнее и съедобнее –
Снедь? Приестся – не пеняй . . .
Как живётся вам с подобием –
Вам, поправшему Синай!

Souls, O souls, you will be sisters, not lovers!

What is your life like with an *ordinary* woman? *Without* the divine? Now that you have dethroned your queen and have yourself renounced the throne,

what is your life like? How do you busy yourself? How are you shivering? How do you get up [from your bed]? How do you manage to pay the price for immortal triviality, poor fellow?

'I've had enough of convulsions and palpitations – I'll rent a house!' What is your life like with a woman like any other, you, my chosen one?

Is the food more congenial and eatable? Don't complain if you get sick of it! What is your life like with a semblance – you who have trodden upon Sinai?

Как живётся вам с чужою,
Здешнею? Ребром – люба?
Стыд Зевесовой вожжою
Не охлёстывает лба?

Как живётся вам – здоровится –
Можется? Поётся – как?
С язвою бессмертной совести
Как справляетесь, бедняк?

Как живётся вам с товаром
Рыночным? Оброк – крутой?
После мраморов Каррары
Как живётся вам с трухой

Гипсовой? (Из глыбы высечен
Бог – и начисто разбит!)
Как живётся вам с стотысячной –
Вам, познавшему Лилит!

Рыночною новизною
Сыты ли? К волшбам остыв,

What is your life like with a stranger, a woman of this world?
Tell me point-blank: do you love her? Does shame, like Zeus's
reins, not lash your brow?

What is your life like? How is your health? How do you sing?
How do you cope with the festering wound of immortal conscience,
poor fellow?

What is your life like with a market commodity? The price is
steep, isn't it! After the marble of Carrara what is your life like with
a piece of crumbling plaster of Paris?

(God was hewn out of a block, and has been smashed to bits!)
What is your life like with one of a hundred thousand women – you
who have known Lilith*?

Have you satisfied your hunger with the new market commodity? Now that magic has lost its power over you, ...

* In Rabbinical literature, the first wife of Adam.

Как живётся вам с земною
Женщиною, без шестых

Чувств? Ну, за голову: счастливы?
Нет? В провале без глубин —
Как живётся, милый? Тяжче ли,
Так же ли как мне с другим?

what is your life like with a woman of this earth, without either of you using a sixth sense?

Well, cross your heart: are you happy? No? In a pit without depth what is your life like, my beloved? Harder than my life with another man, or just the same?

VLADIMIR MAYAKOVSKY

Лиличка!

Вместо письма

Дым табачный воздух выел.
Комната –
глава в кручёныховском аде.
Вспомни –
за этим окном
впервые
руки твои, исступлённый, гладил.
Сегодня сидишь вот,
сердце в железе.
День ещё –
выгонишь,
может быть, изругав.
В мутной передней долго не влезет
сломанная дрожью рука в рукав.
Выбегу,
тело в улицу брошу я.
Дикий,
обезумлюсь,
отчаяньем иссечась.

Lilichka!

Instead of a letter

TOBACCO smoke has corroded the air. The room is a chapter in Kruchenykh's* hell. Remember – behind this window I first stroked your hands in a frenzy. Here you sit today, your heart encased in iron. Another day, and you will throw me out, perhaps, after reviling me. In your dim entrance-hall my arm, convulsed with tremor, will take a long time to insert itself into my sleeve. I'll run out, I'll hurl my body into the street. I'll become frantic and demented, lashed by despair. . . . . . .

* A. Kruchenykh (1886–1970), a Russian Futurist poet.

Не надо этого,
дорогая,
хорошая,
дай простимся сейчас.
Всё равно
любовь моя –
тяжкая гиря ведь –
висит на тебе,
куда ни бежала б.
Дай в последнем крике выреветь
горечь обиженных жалоб.
Если быка трудом уморят –
он уйдёт,
разляжется в холодных водах.
Кроме любви твоей,
мне
нету моря,
а у любви твоей и плачем не вымолишь
отдых.
Захочет покоя уставший слон –
царственный ляжет в опожаренном песке.
Кроме любви твоей,
мне
нету солнца,
а я и не знаю, где ты и с кем.

Don't let this happen, dearest, beloved: let's say goodbye now.
Whatever happens, my love – it's a heavy burden, you know –
weighs you down wherever you may run away. Let me bellow out
my bitter and wounded resentment in one last cry. When an ox
is exhausted by hard work it goes off and lies down in cool waters.
Apart from your love there is no sea for me – yet I cannot even
through tears obtain respite from your love. When a tired elephant
craves for rest it lies down like a king in the scorched sand. Apart
from your love there is no sun for me – yet I don't know where and
with whom you are. . . . . . .

Если б так поэта измучила,
он
любимую на деньги б и славу выменял,
а мне
ни один не радостен звон,
кроме звона твоего любимого имени.
И в пролёт не брошусь,
и не выпью яда,
и курок не смогу над виском нажать.
Надо мною,
кроме твоего взгляда,
не властно лезвие ни одного ножа.
Завтра забудешь,
что тебя короновал,
что душу цветущую любовью выжег,
и суетных дней взметённый карнавал
растреплет страницы моих книжек . . .
Слов моих сухие листья ли
заставят остановиться,
жадно дыша?

Дай хоть
последней нежностью выстелить
твой уходящий шаг.

If she had so tormented a poet to the point of exhaustion, he would have bartered his beloved for money and glory; but to me not one resonant sound brings joy except that of your beloved name. And I won't throw myself downstairs, nor drink poison, nor will I be able to press the trigger above my temple. Except for your gaze, no knife's blade has any power over me. To-morrow you will have forgotten that I crowned you, that I burnt out a blossoming soul with my love, and the whirling carnival of vainly spent days will ruffle the pages of my books . . . Will the dry leaves of my words make you pause, gasping for breath?

Let me at least strew the path of your departing steps with one last surge of tenderness.

Наш марш

Бейте в площади бунтов топот!
Выше, гордых голов гряда!
Мы разливом второго потопа
перемоем миров города.

Дней бык пег.
Медленна лет арба.
Наш бог бег.
Сердце наш барабан.

Есть ли наших золот небесней?
Нас ли сжалит пули оса?
Наше оружие – наши песни.
Наше золото – звенящие голоса.

Зеленью ляг, луг,
выстели дно дням.
Радуга, дай дуг
лет быстролётным коням.

Видите, скушно звёзд небу!
Без него наши песни вьём.

Our March

BEAT the tramp of revolt in the square! Up, row of proud heads! We will wash every city in the world with the surging waters of a second Flood.

The bull of the days is skewbald. The cart of the years is slow. Our god is speed. The heart is our drum.

Is there a gold more heavenly than ours? Can the wasp of a bullet sting us? Our songs are our weapons; ringing voices – our gold.

Meadows, be covered with grass, spread out a ground for the days. Rainbow, harness the fast-flying horses of the years.

See, the starry heaven is bored! We weave our songs without its help. . . . . . .

Эй, Большая Медведица! требуй,
чтоб на небо нас взяли живьём.

Радости пей! Пой!
В жилах весна разлита.
Сердце, бей бой!
Грудь наша – медь литавр.

Хорошее отношение к лошадям

Били копыта.
Пели будто:
– Гриб.
Грабь.
Гроб.
Груб. –

Ветром опита,
льдом обута,
улица скользила.
Лошадь на круп
грохнулась,
и сразу

Hey, you, Great Bear, demand that they take us up to heaven alive!
　　Drink joys! Sing! Spring flows in our veins. Beat to battle, heart!
Our breast is a copper kettledrum.

Kindness to Horses

THE hooves struck. It sounded as though they were singing:
'Grib, grab, grob, grub'.
Stripped by the wind, shod with ice, the street skidded. The horse
crashed down on its rump; and at once . . . .

за зевакой зевака,
штаны пришедшие Кузнецким
клёшить,
сгрудились,
смех зазвенел и зазвякал:
– Лошадь упала! –
– Упала лошадь! –
Смеялся Кузнецкий.
Лишь один я
голос свой не вмешивал в вой ему.
Подошёл
и вижу
глаза лошадиные . . .

Улица опрокинулась,
течёт по-своему . . .
Подошёл и вижу –
за каплищей каплища
по морде катится,
прячется в шёрсти . . .

И какая-то общая
звериная тоска
плеща вылилась из меня
и расплылась в шелесте.

there assembled a crowd of gaping loafers who had come to display
their bell-bottomed trousers along the Kuznetsky Most*; a chorus
of jingling laughter rang out: 'A horse has fallen, a horse has fallen!'
The Kuznetsky Most resounded with laughter. I alone did not merge
my voice in its howling. I walked up and saw the horse's eyes . . .

The street toppled over and was flowing in its own peculiar
way . . . I walked up and saw: large drops were rolling down its
face and burying themselves in its hair.

And an undefinable anguish, common to all animals, surged and
poured out of me, and dissolved in a rustle. . . . . . .

* A street in Moscow

«Лошадь, не надо.
Лошадь, слушайте –
чего вы думаете, что вы их плоше?
Деточка,
все мы немножко лошади,
каждый из нас по-своему лошадь.»
Может быть
– старая –
и не нуждалась в няньке,
может быть, и мысль ей моя показалась
                                        пошла́,
только
лошадь
рванулась,
встала на́ ноги,
ржанула
и пошла.
Хвостом помахивала.
Рыжий ребёнок.
Пришла весёлая,
стала в стойло.
И всё ей казалось –
она жеребёнок,
и стоило жить,
и работать стоило.

'Horse, you mustn't. Listen, horse; why do you think you're any worse than they? My little one, all of us are horses to some extent, every one of us is a horse in his own way.' Perhaps the old creature had no need of a nurse, perhaps, too, this thought of mine seemed trite to it, yet the horse gave a jerk, got on to its feet, neighed, and was off, flicking its tail. Chestnut and childlike. Cheerfully it returned and stood in its stall. And all the time it felt it was a colt, and that life was worth living, and work worth while.

Атлантический океан

Испанский камень° слепящ и бел,
а стены –° зубьями пил.
Пароход° до двенадцати° уголь ел
и пресную воду пил.
Повёл° пароход° окованным носом
и в час,
сопя,° вобрал якоря° и понёсся.
Европа° скрылась, мельчась.
Бегут° по бортам° водяные глыбы,
огромные,° как года́.
Надо мною птицы,° подо мною рыбы,
а кругом –° вода.
Недели° грудью своей атлетической –
то работяга,° то в стельку пьян –
вздыхает° и гремит° Атлантический
океан.
«Мне бы, братцы,
к Сахаре подобраться . . .
Развернись и плюнь –
пароход внизу.
Хочу топлю,
хочу везу.

The Atlantic Ocean

THE Spanish stone is blinding and white and the walls are like the teeth of a saw. Until twelve o'clock the steamer ate coal and drank fresh water. The steamer moved its iron-clad bow, and at one o'clock, breathing heavily, it weighed anchor and was off at full speed. Europe grew smaller, and vanished. Masses of water, huge as the years, run alongside. Above me are birds, below me – fishes, and all around is water. For weeks on end, now a hard-working fellow, now blind-drunk, the Atlantic Ocean sighs and thunders from its athletic chest. 'What I should like to do, lads, is to creep up to the Sahara . . . Let yourself go and spit: there's a steamer down below. I can sink it or carry it along, just as I like.'

Выходи сухой –
сварю ухой.
Людей не надо нам –
малы к обеду.
Не трону . . .°ладно . . .
пускай едут . . .»
Волны°будоражить мастера́:
детство выплеснут;°другому –°голос
        милой.
Ну, а мне б°опять°знамёна простирать!
Вон –°пошло́,°затарахте́ло,°загромило!
И снова°вода°присмирела сквозная,
и нет°никаких сомнений ни в ком.
И вдруг,°откуда-то –°чёрт его знает! –
встаёт°из глубин°воднячий Ревком.
И гвардия капель –°воды партизаны –
взбираются°ввысь°с океанского рва,
до неба метнутся°и падают заново,
порфиру пены в клочки изодрав.
И снова°спаялись во́ды в одно,
волне°повелев°разбурлиться вождём.

‘Come out dry – I'll boil you in a fish-soup. We've no use for
people – they're small fry for our supper. All right . . . I won't
touch them . . . Let them go on.' Waves are experts at exciting:
their splashes can throw up [a man's] childhood; to another [they
will bring back] the voice of his beloved. Well, as far as I am
concerned, [they make me want] to hoist banners! There – it's
started up, it's begun to rattle and thunder. And again the translucent water has quietened down, and there are no doubts about
anyone. And suddenly, from somewhere – the devil knows from
where – a watery Revolutionary Committee rises from the depths.
And a guard of drops – water-partisans – clamber up from the deep
of the ocean, fling themselves up to the sky and fall back, tearing
the imperial robe of foam to fragments. And once again the waters
have merged, commanding the wave to surge like a leader. . . .

И прёт волнища°с под тучи°на дно –
приказы°и лозунги°сыплет дождём.
И волны°клянутся°всеводному Цику
оружие бурь°до победы не класть.
И вот победили –°экватору в циркуль
Советов-капель бескрайняя власть.
Последних волн небольшие митинги
шумят°о чём-то°в возвышенном стиле.
И вот°океан°улыбнулся умытенький
и замер°на время°в покое и в штиле.
Смотрю за перила.°Старайтесь, приятели!
Под трапом,°нависшим°ажурным мостком,
при океанском предприятии
потеет°над чем-то°волновий местком.
И под водой°деловито и тихо
дворцом°растёт°кораллов плетёнка,
чтоб легше жилось°трудовой китихе
с рабочим китом°и дошкольным китёнком.
Уже°и луну°положили дорожкой.
Хоть прямо°на пузе,°как пò суху, лазь.

And a huge wave crashes from beneath a cloud down to the bottom, and rains down orders and slogans. And the waves swear to the all-watery Central Executive Committee that they will not lay down the weapon of storms till victory [comes]. And now victory is theirs: the unlimited power of the Soviets – the drops – circles the equator. Small meetings of final waves are clamouring about something in a high-flown style. And now the ocean, nicely washed and scrubbed, has smiled and become still for a time, calm and at peace. I look over the rail. Do your best, friends! Beneath the ship's ladder which is over-hanging like an open-work bridge, a local committee of waves, [intent] on the ocean's business, is sweating over something; while below the surface, in a quiet and business-like manner, a woven fabric of coral is growing like a palace, so that life may be easier for the working she-whale, the toiling whale, and the baby whale under school age. Already they've laid the moon down like a path. You could almost crawl along it on your belly, like over dry land.

Но враг не сунется – в небо сторожко
глядит, не сморгнув, Атлантический глаз.
То стынешь в блеске лунного лака,
То стонешь, облитый пеною ран.
Смотрю, смотрю – и всегда одинаков,
любим, близок мне океан.
Вовек твой грохот удержит ухо.
В глаза тебя опрокинуть рад.
По шири, по делу, по крови, по духу –
моей революции старший брат.

Разговор с фининспектором о поэзии

Гражданин фининспектор! Простите за
                                    беспокойство.
Спасибо . . . не тревожьтесь . . . я постою . . .
У меня к вам дело деликатного свойства:
о месте поэта в рабочем строю.
В ряду имеющих лабазы и угодья
и я обложен и должен караться.
Вы требуете с меня пятьсот в полугодие
и двадцать пять за неподачу деклараций.

But the enemy won't poke his nose [there]: watchfully, without
batting a lid, the Atlantic eye gazes into the sky. Now you grow
chilly in the radiance of the moon's varnish, now you moan,
drenched in the foam of wounds. I look and look – and the ocean
is always the same, dear and close to my heart. My ear will forever
retain your thunder. Gladly would I empty you into my eyes. In
your vast expanse, in your work and blood and spirit – elder brother
of my revolution.

Conversation with an Inspector of Taxes about Poetry

Citizen Inspector of Taxes! Forgive my bothering you. Thank
you . . . don't trouble . . . I'll stand . . . My business is of a
delicate nature: about the place of a poet in a workers' society.
Along with owners of stores and agricultural property, I'm also
subject to tax and penalties. You are claiming from me five hundred
for the half year and twenty-five for failing to send in my returns.

Труд мой°любому°труду°родствен.
Взгляните –°сколько я потерял,
какие°издержки°в моём производстве
и сколько тратится°на материал.
Вам,°конечно, известно°явление «рифмы».
Скажем,°строчка°окончилась словом°«отца»,
и тогда°через строчку,°слога повторив, мы
ставим°какое-нибудь°: «ламцадрица-ца́».
Говоря по-вашему,°рифма –°вексель.
Учесть через строчку! –°вот распоряжение.
И ищешь°мелочишку суффиксов и флексий
в пустующей кассе°склонений°и спряжений.
Начнёшь это°слово°в строчку всовывать,
а оно не лезет –°нажал и сломал.
Гражданин фининспектор,°честное слово,
поэту°в копеечку влетают слова.
Говоря по-нашему,°рифма –°бочка.
Бочка с динамитом.°Строчка –°фитиль.
Строка додымит,°взрывается строчка, –
и город°на воздух°строфой летит.

My work is like any other work. Look – see how much I've lost, what expenses I have in my production, and how much is spent on materials. You know, of course, about the phenomenon called 'rhyme'. Suppose a line ends with the word 'ottsa'*, and then, in the next line but one, repeating the syllables, we put something like 'lamtsadritsa-tsa'.* In your language rhyme is a promissory note: to be honoured in the next line but one – that's the regulation. And you hunt for the small change of suffixes and inflexions in the depleted cashbox of declensions and conjugations. You start shoving a word into a line, but it doesn't fit – you force it and it breaks. Citizen Inspector of Taxes, I give you my word of honour, words cost the poet a pretty penny. In our language rhyme is a barrel. A barrel of dynamite. The line is a fuse. The line smoulders to the end and explodes; and the town is blown sky-high in a stanza. . . . . . .

*A rough English equivalent of this rhyme would be 'day' and 'tarara-boom-de-ay'.

Где найдёшь,°на какой тариф,
рифмы,°чтоб враз убивали, нацелясь?
Может,°пяток°небывалых рифм
только и остался°что в Венецуэле.
И тянет°мεня°в холода и в зной.
Бросаюсь,°опутан в авансы и в займы я.
Гражданин,°учтите билет проездной!
– Поэзия°– вся! –°езда в незнаемое.
Поэзия –°та же добыча радия.
В грамм добыча,°в год труды.
Изводишь,°единого слова ради,
тысячи тонн°словесной руды.
Но как°испепеляюще°слов этих жжение
рядом°с тлением°слова-сырца.
Эти слова°приводят в движение
тысячи лет°миллионов сердца.
Конечно,°различны поэтов сорта.
У скольких поэтов°лёгкость руки!
Тянет,°как фокусник,°строчку изо рта
и у себя°и у других.
Что говорить°о лирических кастратах?!
Строчку°чужую°вставит – и рад.

Where will you find, and at what rate of assessment, rhymes that take aim and kill at one shot? It may be that five or six unused rhymes remain only in some place like Venezuela. And so I'm drawn to visit lands cold and hot. I rush there, entangled in payments on account and loans. Citizen! Allow me my travelling expenses. Poetry – all of it! – is a journey into the unknown. Poetry is like mining radium. For every gramme you work a year. For the sake of a single word you expend thousands of tons of verbal ore. But how much more heat arises from the combustion of these words than from the smouldering of raw verbal material! These words set in motion millions of hearts for thousands of years. Of course, there are different kinds of poets. So many poets have a nimble touch! Like conjurers, they pull lines out of their mouths – their own and other people's. Not to speak of the lyrical eunuchs! They slip in a borrowed line and feel happy. . . . . . .

Это°обычное°воровство и растрата
среди охвативших страну растрат.
Эти°сегодня°стихи и оды,
в аплодисментах°ревомые ревмя,
войдут°в историю°как накладные расходы
на сделанное нами —°двумя или тремя.
Пуд,˘как говорится,˘соли столовой
съешь°и сотней папирос клуби,
чтобы°добыть°драгоценное слово
из артезианских°людских глубин.
И сразу°ниже°налога рост.
Скиньте°с обложенья°нуля колесо!
Рубль девяносто°сотня папирос,
рубль шестьдесят°столовая соль.
В вашей анкете°вопросов масса:
– Были выезды?°Или выездов нет? –
А что,°если я°десяток пегасов
загнал°за последние°15 лет?!
У вас –°в моё положение войдите –
про слуг°и имущество°с этого угла.

This is a normal kind of robbery and embezzlement, one of the forms of speculation prevalent in the country. These verses and odes, bawled and sobbed out today amidst applause, will go down in history as the overhead expenses of what two or three of us have achieved. You eat forty pounds of table salt (as the saying goes)* and smoke a hundred cigarettes in order to extract one precious word from men's artesian depths. And at once my tax assessment is reduced. Strike off one wheel-like nought from the tax due! One rouble ninety for a hundred cigarettes; one rouble sixty for table salt. Your form has a mass of questions: 'Have you travelled on business? Or not?' But what if I have ridden ten Pegasuses to exhaustion in the last fifteen years? And here in this section – put yourself in my place – you have something about servants and property.

* The Russian saying is: 'To know a man, you must eat forty pounds (one *pud*) of salt with him.'

А что,°если я°народа водитель
и одновреме́нно –°народный слуга?
Класс°гласит°из слова из нашего,
а мы,°пролетарии,°двигатели пера.
Машину°души°с годами изнашиваешь.
Говорят:°– в архив,°исписался,°пора! –
Всё меньше любится,°всё меньше дерзается,
и лоб мой°время°с разбега круши́т.
Приходит°страшнейшая из амортизаций –
амортизация°сердца и души.
И когда°это солнце°разжиревшим боровом
взойдёт°над грядущим°без нищих и калек, –
я°уже°сгнию,°умерший под забором,
рядом°с десятком°моих коллег.
Подведите°мой°посмертный баланс!
Я утверждаю°и – знаю – не налгу:
на фоне°сегодняшних°дельцов и пролаз
я буду°– один! –°в непролазном долгу.
Долг наш –°реветь°медногорлой сиреной
в тумане мещанья,°у бурь в кипеньи.
Поэт°всегда°должник вселенной,
платящий°на го́ре°проценты°и пени.

But what if I am a leader of the people and at the same time the people's servant? The working class speaks through our mouths, and we, proletarians, are drivers of the pen. As the years pass, you wear out the machine of your soul. People say: 'He must be put on the shelf, he's written himself out, it's high time!' There's less and less love, less and less daring, and time is crashing into my forehead. The time comes for the most terrible of amortizations – that of the heart and of the soul. And when the sun like a fattened hog rises over a future without beggars or cripples, I shall already have rotted after dying under a fence, alongside a dozen of my colleagues. Draw up my posthumous balance-sheet! I hereby declare – and I know for certain, I'm telling no lies: compared with today's traffickers and sharpers, I alone shall be up to the neck in debt. Our duty is to blare like brazen-throated horns in the fog of philistinism and in seething storms. The poet is always indebted to the universe, paying interest and fines on sorrow. .   .   .   .   .   .

Я°в долгу°перед Бродвейской лампионией,
перед вами,°багдадские небеса,
перед Красной Армией,°перед вишнями
                         Японии -
перед всем,°про что°не успел написать.
А зачем°вообще°эта шапка Сене?
Чтобы – целься рифмой°и ритмом ярись?
Слово поэта –°ваше воскресение,
ваше бессмертие,°гражданин канцелярист.
Через столетья°в бумажной раме
возьми строку°и время верни!
И встанет°день этот°с фининспекторами,
с блеском чудес°и с вонью чернил.
Сегодняшних дней убеждённый житель,
выправьте°в энкапеэс°на бессмертье билет
и, высчитав°действие стихов,°разложите
заработок мой°на триста лет!
Но сила поэта°не только в этом,
что, вас°вспоминая,°в грядущем икнут.
Нет!°И сегодня°рифма поэта –
ласка°и лозунг,°и штык,°и кнут.

I am indebted to the lights of Broadway, to you, skies of Bagdadi,*
to the Red Army, to the cherry-trees of Japan – to all those things
about which I have not had time to write. But, after all, what is
the point of all this stuff? To aim with rhyme and to rage in rhythm?
The poet's word is your resurrection, your immortality, citizen
bureaucrat. Centuries hence, take a line of verse in its paper frame
and bring back time! And this day with its inspectors of taxes, its
lustre of miracles, and its stench of ink, will dawn again. Inveterate
dweller in the present day, get yourself a ticket to immortality in
the N.K.P.S. [People's Commissariat of Communications] and,
after computing the effect of verse, spread out my earnings over
three hundred years! But the poet is strong not only because,
remembering you, people in the future will hiccup. No! Today, too,
the poet's rhyme is a caress, and a slogan, and a bayonet, and a whip.

* Mayakovsky's birthplace in Georgia.

Гражданин фининспектор, я выплачу пять,
все°нули°у цифры скрестя!
Я°по праву°требую пядь
в ряду°беднейших°рабочих и крестьян.
А если°вам кажется,°что всего делóв –
это пользоваться°чужими словесами,
то вот вам,°товарищи,°моё стилó,
и можсте°писать°сами!

[Неоконченное]

I

Любит? не любит? Я руки ломаю
и пальцы
             разбрасываю разломавши
так рвут загадав и пускают
                     по маю
венчики встречных ромашек
пускай седины обнаруживает стрижка и бритьё
Пусть серебро годов вызванивает
                       уймою
надеюсь верую вовеки не придёт
ко мне позорное благоразумие

Citizen Inspector of Taxes, I'll cross out all the noughts on your figures and pay five. I demand as my right an inch of ground in the ranks of the poorest workers and peasants. And if you think that all I do is to make use of other people's words, then, comrades, here's my fountain pen – you can write with it yourselves!

[Unfinished]

I

She loves me? She loves me not? I wring my hands and then scatter my fingers when they are broken off. So, when telling fortunes you tear off the petals of wayside daisies, and let them drift away in the May [breeze]. Though streaks of grey are uncovered when I have my hair cut or when I shave, though the years' silvery hue proclaims itself in abundance, I hope and believe that shameful circumspection will never come to me.

385

2

Уже второй

        должно быть ты легла

А может быть

         и у тебя такое

Я не спешу

        И молниями телеграмм

мне незачем

     тебя

        будить и беспокоить

3

море уходит вспять

море уходит спать

Как говорят инцидент исперчен

любовная лодка разбилась о быт

С тобой мы в расчёте

И не к чему перечень

взаимных болей бед и обид

4

Уже второй должно быть ты легла

В ночи Млечпуть серебряной Окою

Я не спешу и молниями телеграмм

Мне незачем тебя будить и беспокоить

2

It's past one o'clock. You must have gone to bed. Or, perhaps, you feel the same as I . . . I'm in no hurry. And there's no point in my waking and disturbing you with express telegrams.

3

The sea is ebbing, the sea is retiring to sleep; as they say, the incident is closed.* Love's boat has been shattered against the life of everyday. You and I are quits, and it's useless to draw up a list of mutual hurts, sorrows, and pains.

4

It's past one o'clock. You must have gone to bed. In the night the Milky Way streams like a silvery Oka. I'm in no hurry. And there's no point in my waking and disturbing you with express telegrams.

   * A pun: literally 'the incident is too peppered'.

VLADIMIR MAYAKOVSKY

как говорят инцидент исперчен
любовная лодка разбилась о быт
С тобой мы в расчёте и не к чему перечень
взаимных болей бед и обид
Ты посмотри какая в мире тишь
Ночь обложила небо звёздной данью
в такие вот часы встаёшь и говоришь
векам истории и мирозданию

5

Я знаю силу слов я знаю слов набат
Они не те которым рукоплещут ложи
От слов таких срываются гроба
шагать четвёркою своих дубовых ножек
Бывает выбросят не напечатав не издав
Но слово мчится подтянув подпруги
звенит века и подползают поезда
лизать поэзии мозолистые руки
Я знаю силу слов Глядится пустяком
Опавшим лепестком под каблуками танца
Но человек душой губами костяком . . .

As they say, the incident is closed. Love's boat has been shattered
against the life of everyday. You and I are quits, and it's useless to
draw up a list of mutual hurts, sorrows, and pains. Look – what
stillness there is in the world! The night has laid the sky under a
tribute of stars. In hours like these one rises to address the ages,
history, and the universe.

5

I know the power of words, I know the tocsin of words – not the
words that are applauded in theatre-boxes, but those which make
coffins break loose and walk off on their four oaken legs. At times
they discard you, unprinted, unpublished, but the word gallops on,
tightening the saddle-girth, it rings for centuries, and railway-
trains creep up to lick poetry's calloused hands. I know the power of
words. It looks a trifle, like a fallen petal beneath a dancer's heel.
But man in his soul, his lips, his bones . . .

GEORGY IVANOV

С бесчеловечною судьбой
Какой же спор? Какой же бой?
Всё это наважденье.

Но этот вечер голубой
Ещё моё владенье.

И небо. Красно меж ветвей,
А по краям жемчужно . . .
Свистит в сирени соловей,
Ползёт по травке муравей –
Кому-то это нужно.

Пожалуй, нужно даже то,
Что я вдыхаю воздух,
Что старое моё пальто
Закатом слева залито,
А справа тонет в звёздах.

*

WHAT argument can there be with inhuman fate? What battle?
All this is delusion.

But this pale blue evening is still my domain.

And the sky: red between the branches, and pearl-coloured at
the edges . . . A nightingale is singing in the lilac bush, an ant is
crawling on the grass: This is of use to someone.

Perhaps even there is some use in the fact that I breathe in the
air, and that my old overcoat is bathed in the sunset on its left side
and, on its right, sinks into the stars.

Имя тебе непонятное дали,
Ты забытьё.
Или – точнее – цианистый
                      калий
Имя твоё.

Георгий Адамович

Как вы когда-то разборчивы были,
О, дорогие мои.
Водки не пили, её не любили,
Предпочитали Нюи.

Стал нашим хлебом – цианистый калий,
Нашей водой – сулема.
Что ж? Притерпелись и попривыкали,
Не посходили с ума.

Даже, напротив – в бессмысленно-
                                злобном
Мире – противимся злу:
Ласково кружимся в вальсе загробном
На эмигрантском балу.

---

*

They have given you an incomprehensible name: you are unconscious-
ness; or – more exactly – cyanide of
potassium is your name.

Georgy Adamovich

How fastidious you once were, my friends! You did not drink
vodka, you didn't like it: you preferred Burgundy.

Cyanide of potassium has become our bread, mercuric chloride
our water. Well, we've grown accustomed and inured, we haven't
gone off our heads.

On the contrary, in a senseless and evil world we are resisting
evil: tenderly we circle in a dead men's waltz at an *émigré* ball.

GEORGY IVANOV

> В Петербурге мы сойдёмся
> снова,
> Словно солнце мы похоро-
> нили в нём.
>
> *О. Мандельштам*

Четверть века прошло заграницей
И надеяться стало смешным.
Лучезарное небо над Ниццей
Навсегда стало небом родным.

Тишина благодатного юга,
Шорох волн, золотое вино . . .

Но поёт петербургская вьюга
В занесённое снегом окно,
Что пророчество мёртвого друга
Обязательно сбыться должно.

*

> We shall meet again in Petersburg,
> as though we had buried the sun
> there.
>
> *O. Mandel'shtam*

A QUARTER of a century has passed abroad, and it is now ludicrous to hope. The radiant sky above Nice has forever become the sky of home.

The stillness of the blissful South, the murmur of the waves, the golden wine . . .

But a Petersburg snow-storm is singing through the snow-plastered window that a dead friend's prophecy will surely come true.

SERGEY ESENIN

Песнь о собаке

Утром в ржаном закуте,
Где златятся рогожи в ряд,
Семерых ощенила сука,
Рыжих семерых щенят.

До вечера она их ласкала,
Причёсывая языком,
И струился снежок подталый
Под тёплым её животом.

А вечером, когда куры
Обсиживают шесток,
Вышел хозяин хмурый,
Семерых всех поклал в мешок.

По сугробам она бежала,
Поспевая за ним бежать.
И так долго, долго дрожала
Воды незамёрзшей гладь.

Song about a Bitch

IN the morning, in a barn for storing rye, where bast mats gleam golden in a row, a bitch gave birth to seven red-brown puppies.

She fondled them until the evening, licking them smooth with her tongue, while the melting snow flowed beneath her warm belly.

But in the evening, when the hens bespatter their perch with their droppings, the grim-faced master came out and bundled all seven into a sack.

She raced over the snowdrifts, keeping pace with him; and for a long, long time shudders ran across the smooth surface of the unfrozen water.

А когда чуть плелась обратно,
Слизывая пот с боков,
Показался ей месяц над хатой
Одним из её щенков.

В синюю высь звонко
Глядела она, скуля,
А месяц скользил тонкий
И скрылся за холм в полях.

И глухо, как от подачки,
Когда бросят ей камень в смех,
Покатились глаза собачьи
Золотыми звёздами в снег.

*

О пашни, пашни, пашни,
Коломенская грусть,
На сердце день вчерашний,
А в сердце светит Русь.

But when she dragged herself wearily back, licking the sweat from her sides, she thought the moon above the cottage was one of her puppies.

She gazed up into the dark blue sky, whining loudly, but the slender moon slid on and disappeared in the fields behind the hill.

And softly, as though someone had thrown her a stone in jest, tears rolled from the bitch's eyes like golden stars into the snow.

*

O PLOUGHED fields, ploughed fields, the sadness of provincial Russia*; on my heart is yesterday, and inside my heart Russia shines.

* Literally, 'the sadness of Kolomna' (a provincial town in Central Russia).

SERGEY ESENIN

Как птицы, свищут вёрсты
Из-под копыт коня.
И брызжет солнце горстью
Свой дождик на меня.

О край разливов грозных
И тихих вешних сил,
Здесь по заре и звёздам
Я школу проходил.

И мыслил, и читал я
По Библии ветров,
И пас со мной Исайя
Моих златых коров.

[*Жеребёнок и поезд из «Сорокоуста»*]

Видели ли вы,
Как бежит по степям,
В туманах озёрных кроясь,
Железной ноздрёй храпя
На лапах чугунных поезд?

Like birds, the miles whistle from under my horse's hooves. And
the sun sprinkles its rain in handfuls over me.

O land of dreaded floods and of the gentle forces of spring! Here
I received my schooling from the dawn and the stars.

And I thought, and read from the Bible of the winds; and Isaiah
tended my golden cows with me.

[*The Colt and the Train from 'Prayers for the Dead'*]

DID you see the train on its cast-iron feet rushing through the
steppes, hiding in the mists of the lakes, snorting through its iron
nostril?

393

А за ним
По большой траве,
Как на празднике отчаянных гонок,
Тонкие ноги закидывая к голове,
Скачет красногривый жеребёнок?

Милый, милый, смешной дуралей,
Ну куда он, куда он гонится?
Неужель он не знает, что живых коней
Победила стальная конница?
Неужель он не знает, что в полях бессиян-
ных
Той поры не вернёт его бег,
Когда пару красивых степных россиянок
Отдавал за коня печенег?
По-иному судьба на торгах перекрасила
Наш разбуженный скрежетом плёс,
И за тысчи пудов конской кожи и мяса
Покупают теперь паровоз.

Письмо к матери

Ты жива ещё, моя старушка?
Жив и я. Привет тебе, привет!

And in its wake, as though in a desperate race at a gymkhana, a red-maned colt is galloping over the high-growing grass, flinging its slender legs as high as its head.

The dear, dear, funny little fool! Where, oh where, is he racing to like this? Doesn't he know that live horses have been vanquished by steel cavalry? Doesn't he know that his gallop in the sombre plain will not bring back the days when the Pecheneg would give a couple of beautiful Russian girls of the steppe in exchange for a horse? Fate in the markets has altered the face of our deep and quiet waters, awakened by the grinding noise [of trains], and you now buy a railway-engine for tons of horses' flesh and skin.

Letter to my Mother

Are you still alive, my old lady? I, too, am alive. Greetings, greetings to you. . . . . . .

Пусть струится над твоей избушкой
Тот вечерний несказанный свет.

Пишут мне, что ты, тая тревогу,
Загрустила шибко обо мне,
Что ты часто ходишь на дорогу
В старомодном ветхом шушуне.

И тебе в вечернем синем мраке
Часто видится одно и то ж –
Будто кто-то мне в кабацкой драке
Саданул под сердце финский нож.

Ничего, родная! Успокойся.
Это только тягостная бредь.
Не такой уж горький я пропойца,
Чтоб, тебя не видя, умереть.

Я попрежнему такой же нежный
И мечтаю только лишь о том,
Чтоб скорее от тоски мятежной
Воротиться в низенький наш дом.

May that ineffable evening light flow over your little house.

They write to tell me that, though you hide your anxiety, you're pining for me ever so much, and that you often come out on to the road in your worn old-fashioned coat;

and that in the blue darkness of evening you often imagine the same thing: someone, you fancy, has stuck a sheath-knife into me beneath the heart during a tavern brawl.

It's nothing, my dearest, calm yourself: this is only a harassing play of fancy. I'm not such a confirmed drunkard that I should die without seeing you first.

I'm just as loving as before, and my only dream is to escape from my restless misery and return to our little house.

Я вернусь, когда раскинет ветви
По-весеннему наш белый сад.
Только ты меня уж на рассвете
Не буди, как восемь лет назад.

Не буди того, что отмечталось,
Не волнуй того, что не сбылось, –
Слишком раннюю утрату и усталость
Испытать мне в жизни привелось.

И молиться не учи меня. Не надо!
К старому возврата больше нет.
Ты одна мне помощь и отрада,
Ты одна мне несказанный свет.

Так забудь же про свою тревогу,
Не грусти так шибко обо мне.
Не ходи так часто на дорогу
В старомодном ветхом шушуне.

★

Мы теперь уходим понемногу
В ту страну, где тишь и благодать.

I'll return when our white garden spreads its branches in spring-time fashion. But you mustn't wake me at dawn, as you did eight years ago.

Don't awaken the dreams that have vanished, don't disturb that which did not come true: too early in life it fell to my lot to suffer weariness and bereavement.

And don't teach me to pray. Don't do that. There's no returning to the past. You alone are my help and my comfort, you alone are my ineffable light.

So forget your anxiety, don't pine for me so much. Don't come out on to the road so often in your worn old-fashioned coat.

★

LITTLE by little we are now departing to the land where there is peace and happiness. . . . . . .

Может быть, и скоро мне в дорогу
Бренные пожитки собирать.

Милые берёзовые чащи!
Ты, земля! И вы, равнин пески!
Перед этим сонмом уходящих
Я не в силах скрыть моей тоски.

Слишком я любил на этом свете
Всё, что душу облекает в плоть.
Мир осинам, что, раскинув ветви,
Загляделись в розовую водь!

Много дум я в тишине продумал,
Много песен про себя сложил,
И на этой на земле угрюмой
Счастлив тем, что я дышал и жил.

Счастлив тем, что целовал я женщин,
Мял цветы, валялся на траве
И зверьё, как братьев наших меньших,
Никогда не бил по голове.

Perhaps for me, too, it will soon be time to pack my perishable belongings for the journey.

Dear birch woods, you, earth, and you, sands of the plains! I cannot hide my anguish at this crowd of departing fellow-men.

In this world I have loved too much everything that clothes the soul with flesh. Peace be to the aspens which have spread their branches and are gazing into the pink waters.

I have cherished many thoughts in silence, I have composed many songs in my mind, and I am happy to have breathed and lived upon this gloomy earth.

I am happy at the thought that I have kissed women, crumpled flowers, lain about on the grass, and have never struck animals, our lesser brethren, on the head.

Знаю я, что не цветут там чащи,
Не звенит лебяжьей шеей рожь.
Оттого пред сонмом уходящих
Я всегда испытываю дрожь.

Знаю я, что в той стране не будет
Этих нив, златящихся во мгле.
Оттого и дороги мне люди,
Что живут со мною на земле.

★

Отговорила роща золотая
Берёзовым, весёлым языком,
И журавли, печально пролетая,
Уж не жалеют больше ни о ком.

Кого жалеть? Ведь каждый в мире странник-
Пройдёт, зайдёт и вновь оставит дом.
О всех ушедших грезит конопляник
С широким месяцем над голубым прудом.

I know that thickets do not flower there, nor do the rye-stalks
jingle their swan-like necks. That is why I always tremble at the
crowd of departing fellow-men.

I know that in that land there will not be these cornfields, gleaming golden in the haze. It is because they live with me upon the
earth that men are dear to me.

★

THE golden grove has ceased to speak in the gay language of
birches, and the cranes, sadly flying past, no longer regret anyone.

Who is there to regret? Is not every man in this world a wanderer? He passes by, he pays a visit, and again he leaves the house.
The hemp-field, together with the broad moon over the pale blue
pond, dreams of all those who have gone away.

Стою один среди равнины голой,
А журавлей относит ветер вдаль.
Я полон дум о юности весёлой,
Но ничего в прошедшем мне не жаль.

Не жаль мне лет, растраченных напрасно,
Не жаль души сиреневую цветь.
В саду горит костёр рябины красной,
Но никого не может он согреть.

Не обгорят рябиновые кисти,
От желтизны не пропадёт трава.
Как дерево роняет тихо листья,
Так я роняю грустные слова.

И если время, ветром разметая,
Сгребёт их все в один ненужный ком . . .
Скажите так . . . что роща золотая
Отговорила милым языком.

*

До свиданья, друг мой, до свиданья.
Милый мой, ты у меня в груди.

I am standing alone in the bare plain, while the cranes are carried far away by the wind; I am full of thoughts about my gay youth, but I regret nothing in the past.

I do not regret the years I squandered in vain, I do not regret the lilac blossom of my soul. A fire of rowan-tree branches is burning in the garden, but it cannot warm anyone.

The clusters of rowan-berries will not be scorched, the grass will not grow yellow and perish. As a tree gently lets fall its leaves, so I let fall sad words.

And if time, after scattering them in the wind, should rake them all into one useless heap . . . just say that the golden grove has ceased to speak in the language I love.

*

GOOD-BYE, my friend, good-bye. Dear friend, you are in my heart. . . . . . .

Предназначенное расставанье
Обещает встречу впереди.

До свиданья, друг мой, без руки и слова,
Не грусти и не печаль бровей, –
В этой жизни умирать не ново,
Но и жить, конечно, не новей.

Our predestined parting holds a promise of a future meeting.
   Good-bye, my friend, no hand clasped, no word spoken. Don't be sad, and don't knit your brows in sorrow. In this life to die is nothing new, but, of course, there is as little novelty in living.

EDUARD BAGRITSKY

Я сладко изнемог
               От тишины и снов,
От скуки медленной
                  И песен неумелых,
Мне любы петухи на полотенцах белых
И копоть древняя суровых образов.

Под жаркий шорох мух
                  Проходит день за днём,
Благочестивейшим исполненный смиреньем,
Бормочет перепел
               Под низким потолком,
Да пахнет в праздники малиновым вареньем.

А по ночам томит гусиный нежный пух,
Лампада душная мучительно мигает,
И, шею вытянув,
                Протяжно запевает
На полотенце вышитый петух.

Там мне, о Господи, ты скромный дал
                        приют,
Под кровом благостным,
                Не знающим волненья,

I AM pleasantly exhausted by silence and dreams, by creeping boredom and inexpert singing; I like the cocks on the white towels and the ancient soot on the austere icons.

To the hot rustling of flies days succeed each other, each filled with most devout humility, a quail mutters beneath the low ceiling, and on feast days there is a smell of raspberry jam.

And at night the tender goose-down is oppressive, the stuffy iconlamp flickers harassingly, and a cock embroidered on the towel, stretching out its neck, starts to crow in a long-drawn-out manner.

There, O Lord, you have given me a modest retreat beneath a kindly roof that knows no agitation, ...

Где дни тяжёлые,
            Как с ложечки варенье,
Густыми каплями текут, текут, текут.

Арбуз

Свежак надрывается. Прёт на рожон
Азовского моря корыто.
Арбуз на арбузе – и трюм нагружён,
Арбузами пристань покрыта.

Не пить первача в дорассветную стыдь,
На скучном зевать карауле,
Три дня и три ночи придётся проплыть –
И мы паруса развернули . . .

В густой бородач ударяет бурун,
Чтоб брызгами вдрызг разлететься;
Я выберу звонкий, как бубен, кавун –
И ножиком вырежу сердце . . .

where hard days fall endlessly in thick drops, like jam from a spoon.

The Water-melon

THE gale is straining itself. The ramshackle old boat is running the gauntlet of the Sea of Azov. Water-melons are piled up – the hold is loaded to the full, and the quay is covered with water-melons.

Instead of drinking a choice home-brew in the cold that precedes the dawn we shall be yawning on a tedious watch; we shall have to be at sea for three days and three nights; we have unfurled the sails.

A breaker dashes against a shaggy white-cap and scatters in fragments of spray; I shall choose a water-melon resonant as a tambourine, and carve out a heart with a knife . . .

Пустынное солнце садится в рассол,
И выпихнут месяц волнами . . .
Свежак задувает!
Наотмашь!
Пошёл!
Дубок, шевели парусами!

Густыми барашками море полно,
И трутся арбузы, и в трюме темно . . .

В два пальца, по-боцмански, ветер свистит,
И тучи сколочены плотно.
И ёрзает руль, и обшивка трещит,
И забраны в рифы полотна.

Сквозь волны – навылет!
Сквозь дождь – наугад!
В свистящем гонимые мыле,
Мы рыщем на ощупь . . .
Навзрыд и не в лад
Храпят полотняные крылья.

Мы втянуты в дикую карусель.
И море топочет, как рынок,

A lonely sun sets in the brine, and the moon is ousted by the waves . . . The gale is blowing; it buffets [the boat]; get under way, little boat, spread canvas!

The sea is covered with shaggy white-caps, the water-melons rub against each other, and it's dark in the hold.

The wind whistles through two fingers, like a boatswain, the clouds are thickly clustered; the rudder shifts about, the planking creaks, and the sails are reefed.

Straight through the waves! A random course through the rain! Driven through the whistling foam, blindly we roam the sea . . . The canvas wings sob and snort discordantly.

We are sucked into a wild merry-go-round. The sea stamps like a market-place; . . . . . .

На мель нас кидает,
Нас гонит на мель,
Последняя наша путина!

Козлами кудлатыми море полно,
И трутся арбузы, и в трюме темно . . .

Я песни последней ещё не сложил,
А смертную чую прохладу . . .
Я в карты играл, я бродягою жил,
И море приносит награду, –

Мне жизни весёлой теперь не сберечь, –
И руль оторвало, и в кузове течь! . . .

Пустынное солнце над морем встаёт,
Чтоб воздуху таять и греться;
Не видно дубка, и по волнам плывёт
Кавун с нарисованным сердцем . . .

В густой бородач ударяет бурун,
Скумбрийная стая играет,
Низовый на зыби качает кавун,
И к берегу он подплывает . . .

we are being driven and dashed aground: this is our last voyage!
   The sea is covered with shaggy white-caps, the water-melons rub
against each other, and it's dark in the hold. I have not yet composed my last song, yet I feel the chill of death . . . I've played
cards, and lived like a tramp . . . And the sea brings retribution.
   I shall not now save my gay life . . . The rudder has been torn
off, and the hull has sprung a leak! . . .
A lonely sun rises over the sea, so that the air may thaw and
become warmer. The boat has vanished, and a water-melon with a
heart engraved upon it floats upon the waves . . .
A breaker dashes against a shaggy white-cap, a shoal of mackerel
glides through the water, the south-east wind rocks the water-
melon on the surge, and it comes floating to the shore.

Конец путешествию здесь он найдёт,
Окончены ветер и качка, –
Кавун с нарисованным сердцем берёт
Любимая мною казачка . . .

И некому здесь надоумить её,
Что в руки взяла она сердце моё! . . .

Here it will reach the end of its voyage; the wind and the tossing are over. The Cossack girl whom I love picks up the water-melon with the heart engraved upon it.

And there is no one here to tell her that she has taken my heart in her hands . . .

NIKOLAY TIKHONOV

Праздничный, весёлый, бесноватый,
С марсианской жаждою творить,
Вижу я, что небо небогато,
Но про землю стоит говорить.

Даже породниться с нею стоит,
Снова глину замешать огнём,
Каждое желание простое
Осветить неповторимым днём.

Так живу, а если жить устану,
И запросится душа в траву,
И глаза, не видя, в небо взглянут, –
Адвокатов рыжих позову.

Пусть найдут в законах трибуналов
Те параграфы и те года,
Что в земной дороге растоптала
Дней моих разгульная орда.

FESTIVE, gay, and frenzied, with a Martian's craving to create, I
see that heaven holds few riches, but that the earth is worth
speaking about.

It's even worth becoming kin with her – worth kneading clay
with fire once again, and illuminating every simple desire with the
light of a day that is unique.

That's how I live; and if I grow tired of living, and my soul
starts begging to go beneath the grass, and if my eyes, unseeing,
look up to the sky, I'll summon the red-haired lawyers.

Let them find in the laws of the courts those clauses and those
years which the turbulent horde of my days has trampled under
foot on the earth's road.

*

Мы разучились нищим подавать,
Дышать над морем высотой солёной,
Встречать зарю и в лавках покупать
За медный мусор – золото лимонов.

Случайно к нам заходят корабли,
И рельсы груз проносят по привычке;
Пересчитай людей моей земли –
И сколько мёртвых встанет в перекличке.

Но всем торжественно пренебрежём.
Нож сломанный в работе не годится,
Но этим чёрным, сломанным ножом
Разрезаны бессмертные страницы.

Ветер

Вперебежку, вприпрыжку, по перекрытым
Проходам рынка, хромая влёт
Стеной, бульваром, газетой рваной,
Ещё не дочитанной, не дораскрытой,
Вчера родилась – сейчас умрёт,

WE have forgotten how to give alms to beggars, how to breathe the salt air high above the sea, how to greet the sunrise and buy in shops the gold of lemons with our copper trash.

By accident ships call at our ports, and the rails carry the goods by force of habit. Count up the people of my land: how many dead will rise at the roll-call!

But solemnly we will ignore all this. A broken knife is no good for work, but with this black and broken knife immortal pages have been cut.

The Wind

RACING, hopping along the covered passage-ways of the market, limping in his flight along the wall and the avenue, through the torn newspaper not yet read to the end nor properly unfolded which was born yesterday and will presently die,

Над старой стеною часы проверив,
У моря отрезал углы, как раз –
Ты помнишь ветер над зимним рассветом,
Что прыгал, что все перепутывал сети,
Что выкуп просил за себя и за нас?

Сегодня он тот же в трубе и, редея,
Рассыпался в цепь, как стрелки, холодея,
И грудью ударив, растаял, как залп.
Но что б он сказал, залетев в наши стены,
Мы квиты с ним, правда, но что б он сказал?

*

Как след весла, от берега ушедший,
Как телеграфной рокоты струны,
Как птичий крик, гортанный, сумасшедший,
Прощающийся с нами до весны,

Как радио, которых не услышат,
Как дальний путь почтовых голубей,
Как этот стих, что, задыхаясь, дышит,
Как я – в бессонных думах о тебе.

he checked the time on the clock above the old wall and lopped off the sea's corners in a trice. Do you remember the wind above the winter dawn that was leaping, entangling all the nets, and holding himself and us to ransom?

He is the same today in the chimney; as he slackened and grew colder, he spread out, like skirmishers, in an extended line, and, after a headlong attack, melted away like a salvo. But what would he say if he were to fly into our house? We are quits with him, it is true, but what would he say?

*

LIKE the trace left by an oar that has rowed away from the bank, like the quavering sounds of a telegraph wire, like a bird's cry, guttural and frenzied, that bids us farewell till the spring,

like radio broadcasts that will not be heard, like the distant flight of carrier-pigeons, like this line of verse which is gasping for breath – yet breathes just as I do – in sleepless thoughts of you;

Но это всё одной печали росчерк,
С которой я поистине дружу,
Попросишь ты: скажи ещё попроще,
И я ещё попроще расскажу.

Я говорю о мужестве разлуки,
Чтобы слезам свободы не давать,
Не будешь ты, заламывая руки,
Белее мела, падать на кровать.

Но ты, моя чудесная тревога,
Взглянув на небо, скажешь иногда:
Он видит ту же лунную дорогу
И те же звёзды, словно изо льда!

but all this is but a flourish of sorrow with which I am truly on
friendly terms; if you ask me to say it still more simply I shall tell
you more simply still.

I speak of the courage of parting, of the need to keep back one's
tears; you will not wring your hands and fall onto your bed, whiter
than chalk.

But you, my wonderful turmoil, you will sometimes say, looking
up at the sky: 'He sees the same path of the moon and the same
stars, as though made of ice!'

PAVEL ANTOKOL'SKY

Портрет Инфанты

Художник был горяч, приветлив, чист, умён.
Он знал, что розовый застенчивый ребёнок
Давно уж сух и жёлт, как выжатый лимон;
Что в пульсе этих вен – сны многих погребённых;
Что не брабантские бесценны кружева, –
А, верно, ни в каких Болоньях иль Сорбоннах
Не сосчитать смертей, которыми жива
Десятилетняя.

        Тлел перед ним осколок
Издёрганной семьи. Ублюдок божества.
Тихоня. Лакомка. Страсть карликов бесполых
И бич духовников. Он видел в ней итог
Истории страны. Пред ним метался полог
Безжизненной души. Был пуст её чертог.

Дуэньи шли гурьбой, как овцы. И смотрелись
В портрет, как в зеркало. Он услыхал поток

Portrait of an Infanta

THE painter was ardent, friendly, pure, intelligent. He knew that the shy, rosy child had long been desiccated and yellow, like a squeezed lemon; that in the pulse which beat in those veins were the dreams of many who lie buried; that what is priceless is not the lace of Brabant: and that doubtless in none of the Bolognas or the Sorbonnes would they be able to calculate the number of deaths by which the ten-year-old girl was alive.

A chip of an effete family was mouldering before his eyes; an abortion of divinity, demure, sweet-toothed; the passion of sexless dwarfs and the scourge of confessors. He saw in her the outcome of her country's history. The drapery of a lifeless soul fluttered before him. Its palace was empty.

The duennas came trooping in like sheep. And they looked at themselves in the portrait, as in a mirror. He heard a torrent . .

Витиеватых фраз. Тонуло слово «прелесть»
Под длинным титулом в двенадцать ступеней.
У короля-отца отваливалась челюсть.
Оскалив чёрный рот и став ещё бледней,
Он проскрипел: «Внизу накормят вас, Веласкец».
И тот, откланявшись, пошёл мечтать о ней.

Дни и года его летели в адской пляске.
Всё было. Золото. Забвение. Запой
Бессонного труда. Не подлежит огласке
Душа художника. Она была *собой*.
Ей мало юности. Но быстро постареть ей.
Ей мало зоркости. И всё же стать слепой.

Потом прошли века. Один. Другой. И третий.
И смотрит мимо глаз, как он ей приказал,
Инфанта-девочка на пасмурном портрете.
Пред ней пустынный Лувр. Седой музейный зал.
Паркетный лоск. И тишь, как в дни Эскуриала.

of florid phrases. The word 'charming' was drowned beneath a
long, twelve-fold title. The jaw of the king, her father, was sagging.
Opening his black mouth, his face paler than ever, he croaked:
'They'll give you to eat below stairs, Velazquez.' And he, making
his bow, went off to dream of her.

His days and years flew by in an infernal dance. There was
everything. Gold. Oblivion. The intoxication of sleepless toil. The
artist's soul may not be disclosed. It was *itself*. It needs more youth
than is given to it; yet it will age swiftly. It needs a sharper vision
than it possesses; and yet it will grow blind.

Then centuries passed. One. Another. And a third. And the
child Infanta in the sombre portrait looks past the [spectator's]
eyes, as he commanded her to do. Before her is the deserted Louvre.
The hoary museum-gallery. The sheen of the parquet. And
silence, as in the Escorial days.

И ясно девочке по всем людским глазам,
Что ничего с тех пор она не потеряла –
Ни карликов, ни царств, ни кукол, ни святых;
Что сделан целый мир из тех же матерьялов,
От века данных ей. Мир отсветов златых,
В зазубринах резьбы, в подобье звона где-то
На бронзовых часах. И снова – звон затих.

И в тот же тяжкий шёлк безжалостно одета,
Безмозгла, как божок, бесспорна, как трава
Во рвах кладбищенских, старей отца и деда, –
Смеётся девочка. Сильна тем, что мертва.

Полёт светляков

Сон Летней Ночи! Факелов пыланье
В листве ночного парка. Словно там
Шекспир за нежной и строптивой ланью
Со сворой гончих рыщет по пятам.

And the little girl sees clearly from the eyes of all the people that she has lost nothing since those days – neither dwarfs, nor kingdoms, nor dolls, nor saints; that the whole world is made of the very same materials which she was given from the beginning. The world of golden reflections, in the notches of the carvings, like the chime of a bronze clock somewhere. And, once more, the chime has died away into silence.

And, pitilessly dressed in the same heavy silk, brainless as an idol, incontrovertible as the grass on the cemetery graves, older than her father and her grandfather, the little girl is laughing. She is strong because she is dead.

The Flight of Fire-flies

A MIDSUMMER Night's Dream! The blaze of torches in the leaves of a park at night. It is as if Shakespeare were ranging with a pack of hounds in close pursuit of a tender and unyielding doe.

Трубят рога метафор. Это снова,
Вся в изумруде стрекозиных крыл,
Титания влюбляется в Основу,
Едва Шекспир о нём заговорил.

Вот, вот она – запенилась в стакане!
Вот, вот она – в полёте светляков,
В полёте брачном! Вот её мельканье!
Весь звёздный танец, может быть, таков.

Но разве не мохнаты ели в чащах,
Полнеба не луною залито,
И флейт ночных, заливисто звучащих,
По всей земле не слушает никто?

Ни флейт, ни нежных скрипок, ни гобоя?..
Сон Летней Ночи! Для чего же ты
Вторгаешься под гулкий марш прибоя
В теснину человеческой мечты?

Ещё тебя сырым дождём прохватит
И скрючит в три погибели заря.

The hunting-horns of metaphors sound. It's Titania, covered with the emerald of dragon-flies' wings, once again falling in love with Bottom, as soon as Shakespeare mentioned him.

There, there she is – foaming in a glass! There, there she is – in the flight of fire-flies! In a nuptial flight! There she flashes! Perhaps the dance of the stars is like this.

But are not the fir-trees shaggy in the thickets, is not half the sky bathed in moonlight, and is no one on the whole earth listening to the warbling sounds of the flutes at night?

Not to the flutes, nor to the tender violins, nor to the oboe? O Midsummer Night's Dream! Why do you break into the narrow confines of human dreams to the resonant and marching rhythm of the surf?

The cold rain may yet chill you to the marrow, and the dawn bend you crooked. . . . . . .

Ещё тебе и денег не заплатят
И скажут, что привиделся ты зря.

Уйдёт Шекспир с открытой летней сцены.
Потом, когда шаги его замрут,
В траве погаснет маленький, бесценный
И никому не нужный изумруд.

They may yet pay you no money and say that you might as well
not have been dreamed.

Shakespeare will walk off the open-air summer stage. Then,
when his footsteps have died away, a tiny, priceless, and unwanted
emerald will fade into darkness in the grass.

NIKOLAY ZABOLOTSKY

Ивановы

Стоят чиновные деревья,
почти влсэая в каждый дом;
давно их кончено кочевье –
они в решётках, под замком.
Шумит бульваров теснота,
домами плотно заперта.

Но вот – все двери растворились,
повсюду шопот пробежал:
на службу вышли Ивановы
в своих штанах и башмаках.
Пустые гладкие трамваи
им подают свои скамейки;
герои входят, покупают
билетов хрупкие дощечки,
сидят и держат их перед собой,
не увлекаясь быстрою ездой.

А мир, зажатый плоскими домами,
стоит, как море, перед нами,

The Ivanovs

TREES stand like officials, almost growing into every house; their
nomadic existence ended long ago: they are behind railings, under
lock and key. The narrow boulevards, closely hemmed in by the
houses, are noisy.

But suddenly all the doors are flung open; a whisper has passed
far and wide: the Ivanovs, in their trousers and shoes, have gone
out to work. The smooth empty trams offer them their benches; our
heroes enter, buy their brittle pasteboard tickets, sit and hold them
out in front of them, feeling no excitement at the fast movement.

And the world, hemmed in by the flat houses, stands before us
like a sea; . . . . . .

грохочут волны мостовые,
и через лопасти колёс –
сирены мечутся простые
в клубках оранжевых волос.
Иные – дуньками одеты,
сидеть не могут взаперти:
ногами делая балеты,
они идут.

Куда итти,
кому нести кровавый ротик,
кому сказать сегодня «котик»,
у чьей постели бросить ботик
и дёрнуть кнопку на груди?
Неужто некуда итти?!

О мир, свинцовый идол мой,
хлещи широкими волнами
и этих девок упокой
на перекрёстке вверх ногами!
Он спит сегодня – грозный мир,
в домах – спокойствие и мир.

Ужели там найти мне место,
где ждёт меня моя невеста,

the waves of the roadway clatter, and through the broad, paddle-like wheels plain sirens glide hurriedly in tangles of orange-coloured hair. Others, dressed like country wenches, cannot sit indoors: they walk along, their feet tracing ballet figures.

Where shall I go? To whom shall I bring my blood-red mouth? To whom shall I say 'dearie' today? By whose bed shall I throw off my bootees and tug at a press-button on my breast? Is there really nowhere to go?

O world, my leaden idol, beat with your wide waves and give rest to these strumpets at the crossroads, upside down! It sleeps today, my terrible world; peace and quiet reign in the houses.

Shall I really find my place where my betrothed is waiting for me,

где стулья выстроились в ряд,
где горка – словно Арарат,
повитый кружевцем бумажным,
где стол стоит и трёхэтажный
в железных латах самовар
шумит домашним генералом?

О мир, свернись одним кварталом,
одной разбитой мостовой,
одним проплёванным амбаром,
одной мышиною норой,
но будь к оружию готов:
целует девку – Иванов!

Обводный канал

В моём окне – на весь квартал
Обводный царствует канал.

Ломовики как падишахи,
коня запутав медью блях,
идут закутаны в рубахи,
с нелепой важностью нерях.

---

where the chairs are lined up in a row, where the cabinet is like Mount Ararat,* trimmed with paper lace, where there is a table, and a three-storied samovar in iron armour makes a noise like a household general?

O world, curl up into one block of buildings, one broken roadway, one bespattered barn, one mouse-hole – but be ready to take up arms: Ivanov is kissing a strumpet!

The Loop Canal

THROUGH my window the loop canal dominates the whole neighbourhood.

Draymen, having entangled their horses in their harness adorned with copper plates, are walking like padishahs, wrapped in their jackets, with the absurd lordliness of slovens . . . . . .

* A pun: горка means both 'hill' and 'cabinet'.

Вокруг – пивные стали в ряд,
ломовики в пивных сидят
и в окна конских морд собор
глядит, поставленный в упор.
А там за ним, за морд собором,
течёт толпа на полверсты,
кричат слепцы блестящим хором,
стальные вытянув персты.
Маклак штаны на воздух мечет,
ладонью бьёт, поёт как кречет:
маклак – владыка всех штанов,
ему подвластен ход миров,
ему подвластно толп движенье,
толпу томит штанов круженье,
и вот – она, забывши честь,
стоит, не в силах глаз отвесть,
вся – прелесть и изнеможенье!

Кричи, маклак, свисти уродом,
мечи штаны под облака!
Но перед сомкнутым народом
иная движется река:

All around beer-houses stand in a row; the draymen are sitting in beer-houses, and a conclave of horses' faces stares at close range through the windows. And there, beyond the conclave of faces, the crowd is moving along for half a verst: blind men, stretching out their fingers like steel [antennae], cry out in a shining chorus. A hawker is throwing a pair of trousers up in the air, clapping his hands, and screeching like a falcon: the hawker is the lord of all trousers, the course of the planets and the movement of crowds are obedient to him; the whirl of the trousers holds the crowd in suspense, and there it stands, forgetting its self-respect, unable to take its eyes off the spectacle, all rapture and exhaustion!

Cry out, hawker, whistle like a buffoon, hurl the trousers up to the sky! But another stream is moving in front of the closely packed crowd: . . . . . .

один – сапог несёт на блюде,
другой – поёт собачку-пудель,
а третий, грозен и румян,
в кастрюлю бьёт, как в барабан.
И нету сил держаться боле:
толпа в плену, толпа в неволе,
толпа лунатиком идёт,
ладони вытянув вперёд.

А вкруг – черны заводов замки,
высок под облаком гудок,
и вот опять идут мустанги
на колоннаде пышных ног.
И воют жалобно телеги,
и плещет взорванная грязь,
и над каналом спят калеки,
к пустым бутылкам прислонясь.

*

Уступи мне, скворец, уголок,
Посели меня в старом скворешнике.
Отдаю тебе душу в залог
За твои голубые подснежники.

one [character] is carrying a boot on a dish, another is chanting the praises of a poodle [he is selling], a third, fierce and rubicund, is beating a saucepan like a drum. And there is no resistance left: the crowd is held captive, the crowd is enslaved, the crowd moves like a sleep-walker, with hands outstretched.

And all around, the black factories stand like castles, and the sound of the hooter is high in the sky; and once more the mustangs are walking past on a colonnade of splendid legs. And carts are wailing plaintively, the ploughed-up mud is splashed about, and cripples are asleep above the canal, reclining against empty bottles.

*

STARLING, let me have a little corner, lodge me in your old starling-cote. I pledge you my soul for your pale blue snowdrops.

И свистит и бормочет весна.
По колено затоплены тополи.
Пробуждаются клёны от сна,
Чтоб, как бабочки, листья захлопали.

И такой на полях кавардак
И такая ручьёв околёсица,
Что попробуй, покинув чердак,
Сломя голову в рощу не броситься!

Начинай серенаду, скворец!
Сквозь литавры и бубны истории
Ты – наш первый весенний певец
Из берёзовой консерватории.

Открывай представленье, свистун!
Запрокинься головкою розовой,
Разрывая сияние струн
В самом горле у рощи берёзовой.

Я и сам бы стараться горазд,
Да шепнула мне бабочка-странница:

The spring is whistling and muttering. The poplars are submerged up to their knees. The maples are awakening from sleep, so that the leaves may flap as butterflies their wings.

And there is such a hurly-burly in the fields, and such a babbling of streams: just you try not to rush headlong out of your garret into the grove!

Start up the serenade, starling! Through the kettledrums and the tambourines of history, you are our first spring-time singer from the birch tree conservatoire.

Begin the performance, whistler! Throw back your little pink head, and tear apart the radiant chords in the very throat of the birch grove.

I wouldn't mind trying out my own skill, but the wandering butterfly whispered to me: . . . . . .

— Кто бывает весною горласт,
Тот без голоса к лету останется.

А весна хороша, хороша!
Охватило всю душу сиренями.
Поднимай же скворечню, душа,
Над твоими садами весенними.

Поселись на высоком шесте,
Полыхая по небу восторгами,
Прилепись паутинкой к звезде
Вместе с птичьими скороговорками.

Повернись к мирозданью лицом,
Голубые подснежники чествуя,
С потерявшим сознанье скворцом
По весенним полям путешествуя.

Детство

Огромные глаза, как у нарядной куклы,
Раскрыты широко. Под стрелами ресниц,

he who is vociferous in the spring will be left without voice by
the summer.

And the spring is beautiful, beautiful! My whole soul is lapped
in lilac blossom. Lift the starling-cote above your spring gardens,
O my soul!

Lodge yourself on the top of a high pole, blazing with rapture
through the sky; cling like gossamer to a star, together with the
birds' chatter.

Turn your face to the universe, paying honour to the pale blue
snowdrops and journeying over the spring fields with a starling
that has swooned.

Childhood

HER huge eyes, like those of an elegant doll, are wide open.
Beneath the arrows of her eye-lashes, . . ⚬ ● ◠ ◡

Доверчиво ясны и правильно округлы,
Мерцают ободки младенческих зениц.
На что она глядит? И чем необычаен
И сельский этот дом, и сад, и огород,
Где, наклонясь к кустам, хлопочет их хозяин,
И что-то вяжет там, и режет, и поёт?
Два тощих петуха дерутся на заборе,
Шершавый хмель ползёт по столбику крыльца.
А девочка глядит. И в этом чистом взоре
Отображён весь мир до самого конца.
Он, этот дивный мир, поистине впервые
Очаровал её, как чудо из чудес,
И в глубь души её, как спутники живые,
Вошли и этот дом, и этот сад, и лес.
И много минет дней. И боль сердечной смуты
И счастье к ней придёт. Но и жена, и мать,
Она блаженный смысл короткой той минуты
Вплоть до седых волос всё будет вспоминать.

her round and childish pupils twinkle, trusting, regular, and clear. What is she gazing at? And what is unusual about this house in the country, this garden, and this kitchen garden, where the owner, bending over some bushes, is busy tying and cutting something, and is singing? Two scraggy cocks are fighting on a fence; a rough hop-vine is creeping up the post of the porch. And the little girl gazes. And in these pure eyes the whole world is reflected to the very end. This world, this marvellous world, seems to her the wonder of wonders and has truly enchanted her for the first time; and this house, this garden, and the wood have entered the depths of her soul like living fellow travellers. And many days will pass. The pain of the heart's turmoil, and happiness, will come to her. But, both as a wife and as a mother, she will always remember till her hair grows grey the blessed meaning of that brief moment.

ALEKSANDR TVARDOVSKY

Нет, жизнь меня не обделила,
Добром своим не обошла,
Всего с лихвой дано мне было
В дорогу – света и тепла.

И сказок в трепетную память,
И песен стороны родной,
И старых праздников с попами,
И новых с музыкой иной.

И в захолустье, потрясённом
Всемирным чудом новых дней,
Старинных зим с певучим стоном
Далёких – за лесом – саней.

И вёсен в дружном развороте,
Морей и речек на дворе,
Икры лягушечьей в болоте,
Смолы у сосен на коре.

И летних гроз, грибов и ягод,
Росистых троп в траве глухой,

No, life has not denied me my share, nor begrudged me its bounty;
I have been allotted everything in abundance for the journey –
light and warmth;
  stories to remember with a thrill of emotion, songs of my native
land, the old festivals with priests and the new ones with another
music;
  ancient winters in a remote spot which was deeply stirred by the
world-wide miracle of the new days, with the melodious plaint of a
distant sleigh beyond the wood;
  the sudden burst of spring, seas and rivers out of doors, frog-
spawn in the swamp, resin on the bark of the pines;
  summer thunder-storms, mushrooms, and berries, dew-sprinkled
paths in the overgrown grass, ...

Пастушьих радостей и тягот,
И слёз над книгой дорогой.

И ранней горечи и боли,
И детской мстительной мечты,
И дней не высиженных в школе,
И босоты, и наготы.

Всего – и скудости унылой
В потёмках отчего угла . . .

Нет, жизнь меня не обделила,
Ничем в ряду не обошла.

Ни щедрой выдачей здоровья
И сил надолго про запас.
Ни первой дружбой и любовью,
Что во второй не встретишь раз.

Ни славы замыслом зелёным –
Отравой сладкой строк и слов,
Ни кружкой с дымным самогоном
В кругу певцов и мудрецов,

the shepherd's joys and trials, tears shed over a favourite book;
    pain and bitterness early in life, childish dreams of revenge, days
of truancy from school, running about barefoot and clad in rags;
    a lot of everything, including dismal poverty in the darkness of
my father's home . . .
No, life has not denied me my share, nor begrudged me anything in turn:
    it has given me a generous supply of health, reserves of strength
for a long time, a first friendship and love such as one does not
experience a second time;
    a greenhorn's designs of glory – the sweet poison of lines and
words – a tankard with steaming home-brew, drained in a circle of
singers and wise men,

Тихонь и спорщиков до страсти,
Чей толк не прост и речь остра
Насчёт былой и новой власти,
Насчёт добра и недобра . . .

Чтоб жил и был всегда с народом,
Чтоб ведал всё, что станет с ним,
Не обошла тридцатым годом,
И сорок первым, и иным . . .

И столько в сердце поместила,
Что диву даться до поры,
Какие резкие под силу
Ему ознобы и жары.

И что мне малые напасти
И незадачи на пути,
Когда я знаю, это счастье –
Не мимоходом жизнь пройти,

Не мимоездом стороною
Её увидеть без хлопот,
Но знать горбом и всей спиною
Её крутой и жёсткий пот.

placid or passionate in argument, who talk subtly and discourse
acutely about the past and the present forms of government, about
good and evil . . .
To enable me always to be and remain with the people and to
know everything that befalls them, it has not begrudged me the
year 1930, nor 1941, nor another year . . .
And it has stored so much in my heart that I still marvel at the
extremes of cold and heat that I am able to bear.
What do minor misfortunes and setbacks on the way matter to
me when I know that to be happy is not to pass life by,
nor to see it without effort while journeying past it at a distance,
but to experience on your own back and by dint of your own hard
toil its severe and harsh sweat;

И будто дело молодое –
Всё, что затеял и слепил,
Считать одной ничтожной долей
Того, что людям должен был.

Зато порукой обоюдной
Любая скрашена страда.

Ещё и впредь мне будет трудно,
Но чтобы страшно – никогда.

and to regard everything you have undertaken and shaped as an insignificant fragment of your debt to men, as though it were the work of youth ?

To make up for it all, hard work is enlivened by a mutual guarantee.

There are still hard times ahead for me, but never shall I be frightened.

PAVEL VASILIEV

Стихи в честь Натальи

В наши окна, щурясь, смотрит лето,
Только жалко – занавесок нету,
Ветреных, весёлых, кружевных.
Как бы они весело летали
В окнах приоткрытых у Натальи,
В окнах незатворенных твоих!

И ещё прошеньем прибалую –
Сшей ты, ради Бога, продувную
Кофту с рукавом по локоток,
Чтобы твоё яростное тело
С ядрами грудей позолотело,
Чтобы наглядеться я не мог.

Я люблю телесный твой избыток,
От бровей широких и сердитых
До ступни, до ноготков люблю,
За ночь обескрылевшие плечи,
Взор, и рассудительные речи,
И походку важную твою.

Verses in Praise of Natal'ya

SUMMER, screwing up its eyes, looks through our windows; but it's a pity that there are no curtains – volatile, gay, lace ones. How gaily they would flutter in Natal'ya's half-open windows, in your windows which are ajar!

And I will also indulge you with a request: for heaven's sake, make yourself a semi-transparent blouse with elbow-length sleeves, so that your fierce body, with the cannon-balls of your breasts, may become golden, and that I may never tire of gazing at you.

I love the exuberance of your body, from the wide and angry eyebrows down to the soles of your feet and to your nails, your shoulders which have lost their wings during the night, the expression in your eyes, your deliberate speech, and your stately gait.

А улыбка – ведь какая малость! –
Но хочу, чтоб вечно улыбалась –
До чего тогда ты хороша!
До чего доступна, недотрога,
Губ углы приподняты немного:
Вот где помещается душа.

Прогуляться ль выйдешь, дорогая,
Всё в тебе ценя и прославляя,
Смотрит долго умный наш народ.
Называет «прелестью» и «павой»
И шумит вослед за величавой:
«По стране красавица идёт».

Так идёт, что ветви зеленеют,
Так идёт, что соловьи чумеют,
Так идёт, что облака стоят.
Так идёт, пшеничная от света,
Больше всех любовью разогрета,
В солнце вся от макушки до пят.

As for your smile – such a faint one! Yet I would have you smile for ever: how beautiful you are then, how approachable – you, the touch-me-not! The corners of your mouth are slightly turned up: that's where your soul is.

When you go out for a walk, my beloved, our wise folk gaze at you for a long time, valuing and applauding everything about you. They call you 'a peach' and 'a swan', and exclaim in the wake of the stately creature: 'A beauty walks through the land.'

She walks, and the branches grow green, she walks, and the nightingales go crazy, she walks, and the clouds stand still. She walks, radiant with the colour of corn, warmed by love above all others, bathed in sunshine from top to toe.

Так идёт, земли едва касаясь,
И дают дорогу, расступаясь,
Шлюхи из фокстротных табунов,
У которых кудлы пахнут псиной,
Бёдра крыты кожею гусиной,
На ногах мозоли от обнов.

Лето пьёт в глазах её из брашен,
Нам пока Вертинский ваш не страшен –
Чёртова рогулька, волчья сыть.
Мы ещё Некрасова знавали,
Мы ещё «Калинушку» певали,
Мы ещё не начинали жить.

И в июне в первые недели
По стране весёлое веселье,
И стране нет дела до трухи.
Слышишь, звон прекрасный возникает?
Это петь невеста начинает,
Пробуют гитары женихи.

So she walks, barely touching the ground; and the tarts from the fox-trotting droves, their straggling hair smelling of dogs, their hips covered with goose-flesh and their feet with corns from their new shoes, step aside to make way for her.

Summer eats and drinks out of her eyes; we are not yet afraid of your Vertinsky* – that horn of the devil, that food fit only for wolves. We have known Nekrasov, we have sung 'Kalinushka',† we have not yet begun to live.

And during the first weeks in June, there is merry-making throughout the land, and the land has no use for trash. Do you hear that beautiful sound rising up? That's a girl starting to sing, and the young men tuning their guitars.

* A well-known Russian cabaret singer.
† A folk-song.

А гитары под вечер речисты,
Чем не парни наши трактористы?
Мыты, бриты, кепки набекрень.
Слава, слава счастью, жизни слава.
Ты кольцо из рук моих, забава,
Вместо обручального надень.

Восславляю светлую Наталью,
Славлю жизнь с улыбкой и печалью,
Убегаю от сомнений прочь,
Славлю все цветы на одеяле,
Долгий стон, короткий сон Натальи,
Восславляю свадебную ночь.

The guitars are garrulous towards the evening. Aren't our tractor-drivers fine fellows? Washed, shaven, their caps askew. Glory, glory to happiness, glory to life! Take a ring from my hand, O my beloved, and slip it on your finger instead of a wedding ring.

I sing the praises of the fair Natal'ya, I sing the praises of life with its smile and sorrow, I run away from doubts, I sing the praises of all the flowers on the blanket, of Natal'ya's long moan and short sleep, I sing the praises of the wedding night.

MARGARITA ALIGER

[Из «Весны в Ленинграде»]

В теченье этой медленной зимы,
круша её железные потёмки, –
«Мы не уступим. Каменные мы», –
ты говорила голосом негромким.

Всё ýже ядовитое кольцо.
Враг продолжает дальше продвигаться.
И вот в его угрюмое лицо
взглянули, как солдаты, ленинградцы.
О город без огня и без воды!
Сто двадцать пять блокадных граммов
                              хлеба . . .
Звериное урчание беды
с безжалостного, мёртвенного неба.
Стонали камни,
                    ахали торцы,
но люди жили, находили силы,
а те, что погибали, как бойцы
ложились тесно в братские могилы.

[From 'Spring in Leningrad']

DURING that slow winter, shattering its iron darkness, you used to say in a low voice: 'We will not give in. We are made of stone.'

The poisonous ring grows more narrow all the time, the enemy is still advancing; and at last the people of Leningrad looked, as soldiers, into his sullen face. O city without light or water! The blockade rations of one hundred and twenty-five grammes of bread, the animal-like growl of trouble from the pitiless, lifeless sky. The stones groaned, the pavement-blocks gasped, yet people found strength enough to live, while those who perished lay down like soldiers in crowded communal graves.

Но, наконец, изнемогла зима,
открылись заволоченные дали.
Чернеют разбомблённые дома, –
они мертвы, они не устояли.
А мы с тобой выходим на мосты,
и под крылом торжественного мая
волнуешься и радуешься ты,
причины до конца не понимая.
А мы с тобой на облачко глядим,
и ветер нам глаза и губы студит.
А мы с тобой негромко говорим
о том, что было, и о том, что будет.
Мы вырвались из этой длинной тьмы,
прошли через заслоны огневые.
Ты говорила: «Каменные мы».
Нет,
    мы сильнее камня,

            мы – живые.

*

Осень только взялась за работу,
только вынула кисть и резец,

But at last winter became exhausted; the clouded horizons cleared, and the bombed houses loom black: they are dead, they have not held out. And you and I walk out on to the bridges, and under the wing of stately May you are excited and happy, without quite knowing why. And you and I gaze at a little cloud, and the wind chills our eyes and lips. And you and I talk in a low voice of what happened and of what will happen. We have fought our way out of that long darkness, and passed through barrages of fire. You used to say: 'We are made of stone.' No, we are stronger than stone: we are alive.

*

AUTUMN has only started her work, only brought out her brush and chisel; . . . . . .

положила кой-где позолоту,
кое-где уронила багрец.
И замешкалась, будто решая,
приниматься ей этак иль так.

То раздумает, краски мешая,
и в смущенье отступит на шаг.
То зайдётся от злости и в клочья
всё порвёт беспощадной рукой . . .
И однажды, решительной ночью,
обретёт величавый покой.

И тогда уж, собрав воедино
все усилья, раздумья в пути,
нарисует такую картину,
что не сможем мы глаз отвести.
Залюбуемся ею невольно, –
что тут сделать и что тут сказать ?!

А она всё собой недовольна:
мол, не то получилось опять!
И сама уничтожит всё это,
ветром сдует, дождями зальёт,
чтоб отмаяться зиму и лето
и сначала начать через год.

here and there she has applied the gilding, and let fall some dabs of purple. And she lingers, as though uncertain whether to settle down to work in this manner or that.

Now she changes her mind as she mixes her colours, and recoils a step in perplexity; now she flies into a rage and tears everything to shreds with a merciless hand . . . And, one decisive night, she finds a majestic peace.

And then, collecting together all her preliminary efforts and meditations, she draws such a picture that we can't take our eyes off it. We can't help being lost in admiration – what can one do or say ?

But still she is dissatisfied with herself: again she says to herself – it's not what it should be. And she destroys it all, blows it away with the wind, floods it with rain, only to rest through the winter and summer and to begin anew in a year's time.

VLADIMIR SOLOUKHIN

Ветер

Ветер
Летит над морем.
Недавно он не был ветром,
А был неподвижным, тёплым воздухом над
землёй.
Он окружал ромашки.
Пах он зелёным летом,
Зыбко дрожал над рожью в жёлтый полдневный
зной
Потом,
Шевельнув песчинки,
Слегка пригибая травы,
Он начал своё движенье. Из воздуха ветром стал.
И вот
Он летит над морем.
Набрал он большую скорость,
Забрал он большую силу. Крылища распластал
Ходят
Морские волны.
С них он срывает пену.
Пена летит по ветру. Мечется над волной.

The Wind

THE Wind flies over the sea. Not so long ago he was not the Wind,
but calm, warm air above the ground. He floated all around the
daisies. He smelt of the green summer. He trembled and quivered
above the rye in the yellow noonday heat. Then, stirring the grains
of sand, lightly bending the grass, he started to move. From being
air, he became the Wind. And now he flies over the sea. He has
picked up great speed, gathered great power, spread his huge
wings. The waves of the sea are rolling. He whips the spray from
off them. The spray flies down the wind. It dances above the waves.

VLADIMIR SOLOUKHIN

Светлый
Упругий ветер
Не мёдом пахнет, а йодом,
Солью тревожно пахнет. Смутно пахнет бедой.

Руки мои как крылья. Сердце моё распахнуто.
Ветер в меня врывается. Он говорит со мной:
– Спал я
Над тихим лугом.
Спал над ромашкой в поле.
Меня золотые пчёлы пронизывали насквозь.
Но стал я
Крылатым ветром,
Лечу я над тёмным морем,
Цепи я рву на рейдах, шутки со мною – брось!
Я
Говорю открыто:
Должен ты выбрать долю,
Должен взглянуть на вещи под резким, прямым
углом:

Быть ли
Ромашкой тихой?

The clear, buoyant Wind smells not of honey but of ozone. He smells menacingly of salt. Obscurely he smells of trouble.

My arms are like wings. My heart is wide open. The Wind bursts into me. He speaks to me: 'I slumbered above a still meadow. I slumbered above the daisies in a field. Golden bees pierced me through and through. But I became the winged Wind, I fly over the dark sea, I tear the anchor-chains asunder in the roadsteads – you can't trifle with me! I speak plainly: You must choose your destiny, you must face things squarely, look at them in a sharply defined manner: which would you rather: be a humble daisy, ...

Мёдом ли пахнуть в поле?
Или лететь над миром, время круша крылом?
Что я
Ему отвечу?
– Сходны дороги наши.
Но опровергну, ветер,

главный я твой резон:

Если б
Ты не был тихим
Воздухом над ромашкой,
Где бы ты, ветер, взялся?

Где бы ты взял разгон?

and smell of honey in the field? Or fly above the earth, shattering time with your wing?' What shall I answer him? 'Our paths are similar; but I will refute your main proposition, O Wind: if you had not started as the still air above the daisies, where, O Wind, would you have come from? Where would you have found your impetus?'

EVGENY VINOKUROV

Весна

Ночь выла, кружила, трубила округой.
И каждому падающсму мертвецу
Так жизнь и запомнилась – белой вьюгой,
Наотмашь хлещущей их по лицу.

А утром всё стихло,
И мир открылся
Глазам в первозданной голубизне.
Я вылез на бруствер и удивился
Вновь – в восемнадцатый раз – весне.

Сырые холмы порыжели на склонах,
Весенние ветры сходили с ума.
И только у мёртвых в глазах оголённых,
В широких,
На веки застыла зима.

Spring

THE night howled, whirled, blared all around, and each dead man, as he fell, remembered life as a white blizzard, lashing his face with fury.

But in the morning all became still, and the world revealed itself in its pristine blue. I climbed out on to the breastwork and once again – for the eighteenth time – marvelled at the spring.

The damp hills had reddened on their slopes, the winds of spring were going crazy; and only in the naked, wide eyes of the dead was winter frozen for ever.

EVGENY VINOKUROV

Поэма о движении

Полы трёт полотёр.
Бредёт он полосой.
Так трогают,
            – хитёр! –
Ручей ногой босой.

Он тропку всё торит.
Его неверен шаг.
Но вот простор открыт
Он вышел на большак!

Полы трёт полотёр.
А ну смелее. Жарь!
И он вошёл в задор,
Как на косьбе косарь.

Вперёд он сделал крен.
Рубахи нет – штаны.
А ноги до колен
Его обнажены.

Poem about Movement

THE polisher is polishing the floors. He shuffles along, following the strips. He's a wily one! That's how one feels the water of a stream with a bare foot.

On and on he trails a path. His gait is unsteady. But there! A wide expanse opens up: he's come out on to the highway.

The polisher is polishing the floors. Come on, put a bit more life into it! More spirit! And he's let himself go, like a mower at mowing time.

He has lurched forward. He wears no shirt – only his trousers. And his legs are bared to the knees. . . . . .

Полы трёт полотёр.
Он с плешью. Он костист.
Он руки вдаль простёр,
Кружа, как фигурист.

Весёлую игру
Он воспринял всерьёз.
Чечётку бьёт в углу,
Как «Яблочко» матрос.

Полы трёт полотёр.
Как будто на пари,
Напористый мотор
Работает внутри.

Струится пот со щёк,
А пляска всё лютей.
Он маятник. Волчок.
Сплошной костёр страстей.

Полы трёт полотёр.
Паркет да будет чист!

The polisher is polishing the floors. There's a bald patch on his
head. He's bony. He's stretched out his arms, circling like a
figure-skater.
He's taken the light-hearted game seriously. He beats a tap-
dance in the corner, like a sailor dancing to 'Yablochko'*.
The polisher is polishing the floors. A tireless engine is working
inside him, as though for a wager.
Sweat pours from his cheeks, while the dance becomes ever
more frantic. He is a pendulum. A top. A sheer bonfire of passions.
The polisher is polishing the floors. Let the parquet be spotless!

* A popular song.

Он мчит –
                    пустынен взор! –
Как на раденье хлыст.

Ему не до красот.
Он поглощён трудом.
Ой-ёй, он разнесёт,
Того гляди, весь дом!

Полы трёт полотёр.
Его летит рука.
Он как тореадор,
Пронзающий быка!

Он мчит. Он там. Он тут.
Устал. Как поднял воз!
Он начертал этюд
Из жестов и из поз.

Полы трёт полотёр.
В нём порох. В нём запал.
Вот он нашёл упор.
От плоти валит пар.

He dashes along with a vacant gaze, like a *Khlyst** taking part in the ritual of his sect.

He's no time for beautiful things. He's absorbed in his work. Look out, he'll pull the house down any moment!

The polisher is polishing the floors. His arm flies through the air. He's like a toreador transfixing his bull.

He tears along. He's here. He's there. He's tired, as though he'd lifted a cartload. He's drawn a sketch of gestures and poses.

The polisher is polishing the floors. There's dash and fire in him. Now he's found his balance. Steam pours from his body. . .

* The *Khlysty* were Russian sectarians, noted for the ecstatic dances which formed part of their ritual.

Расплавил пыл его.
А ритм его слепил.
Ухваток торжество.
Телодвиженья пир.

Полы трёт полотёр,
А позы, как хорал!
Мимический актёр
Трагедию сыграл.

Он мчит, неумолим,
От окон до дверей.

Движенье правит им.
Оно его мудрей.

His ardour has melted him, but the rhythm has fused him to-
gether. A triumph of motion. A feast of bodily movement.
  The polisher is polishing the floors. His poses are like a chorale.
He is a mime, acting out a tragedy.
  He tears along, inexorably, from the windows to the doors.
Movement rules him. It is wiser than he.

EVGENY EVTUSHENKO

По ягоды

Три женщины,

             и две девчонки куцых,

да я . . .

       Летел набитый сеном кузов

среди полей, шумящих широко.

И, глядя на мелькание косилок,

коней,

     колосьев,

           кепок и косынок,

мы доставали булки из корзинок

и пили молодое молоко.

Из-под колёс взметались перепёлки,

трещали, оглушая перепонки.

Мир трепыхался,

       зеленел,

          галдел.

А я –

   я слушал,

     слушал и глядел.

Berry-picking

THREE women and two skimpy little girls and I. The lorry, crammed with hay, flew along amid the fields which rustled far and wide; and, while we glanced at the mowing-machines, the horses, the ears of corn, the caps, and the kerchiefs flashing past, we took out loaves of bread from the baskets and drank new milk.

Quails started up from under the wheels with ear-splitting cries. The world was a-flutter, green, clamorous. As for me, I listened, listened and watched.

EVGENY EVTUSHENKO

Мальчишки у ручья швыряли камни,
и солнце распалившееся жгло,
но облака накапливали капли,
ворочались,
                дышали тяжело.
Всё становилось мглистей, молчаливей.
Уже в стога народ колхозный лез.
И без оглядки мы влетели в ливень
и вместе с ним и с молниями –
                в лес!

Весь кузов перестраивая с толком,
мы разгребали сена вороха
и укрывались.
                Не укрылась только
попутчица одна, лет сорока.
Она глядела целый день устало,
молчала нелюдимо за едой,
и вдруг сейчас приподнялась, и встала,
и стала молодою-молодой.
Она сняла с волос платочек белый,
какой-то шалой лихости полна,
и повела плечами,
                и запела,
веселая и мокрая, она:

Boys were throwing stones by a stream, and the sun burned hot;
but the clouds, piling up the rain drops, rolled and breathed
heavily. It was getting ever dimmer and more silent. The people
from the collective farm were already scrambling into the hay-
ricks; and we crashed headlong into the downpour and – with it
and with the lightning – into the forest!

Rearranging the lorry sensibly, we raked up the piles of hay and
took shelter. One of our companions, however, a woman of about
forty, did not shelter. All day long she had looked tired and had
been silent and unsociable when we ate; and now all of a sudden
she raised herself, and stood up, and became the very picture of
youth. Filled with a kind of wild abandon, she took her white kerchief off her hair, swayed her shoulders, and, joyful and wet, began
to sing: . . . . . .

«Густым лесом босоногая
девчоночка идёт.
Мелку ягоду не трогает –
крупну ягоду берёт».

Она стояла с гордой головою,
и всё вперёд –

        и сердце

             и глаза,

а по лицу –

        хлестанье мокрой хвои,
и на ресницах –

        слёзы и гроза . . .
«Чего ты там –

        простудишься, дурило!» –
её тянула тётя, теребя,
но всю себя она дождю дарила,
и дождь за это ей дарил себя.
Откинув косы смуглою рукою,
глядела вдаль,

        как будто там,

           вдали,

поющая

        увидела такое,
что остальные видеть не могли.

'A little girl is walking barefoot through the thick forest; she won't touch the small berries – she picks the large ones.'

She stood, her head proudly raised, everything – heart and eyes – straining forward, the wet pine branches lashing her face, and tears and the storm on her eyelashes. 'What are you up to? You'll catch cold, you silly girl,' my aunt exclaimed, pulling and tugging at her; but she gave herself completely to the rain, and in return the rain gave itself to her. She threw back her plaits with her swarthy hand and gazed into the distance, as if, as she sang, she saw far away, over there, something the others could not see.

Казалось мне,

        нет ничего на свете –

лишь этот

        в мокром кузове полёт,

нет ничего –

        лишь бьёт навстречу ветер,

и ливень льёт,

        и женщина поёт . .

Мы ночевать устроились в амбаре.

Амбар был низкий.

        Душно пахло в нём

овчиною,

        сушёными грибами,

мочёною брусникой и зерном.

Листом зелёным веники дышали.

В скольжении лучей и темноты

огромными летучими мышами

под потолком чернели хомуты.

Мне не спалось.

        Едва белели лица,

и женский шёпот слышался во мгле.

Я вслушался в него.

        «Ах, Лиза, Лиза,

ты и не знаешь, как живётся мне!

It seemed to me that nothing existed in the whole world save this flight in the wet lorry – nothing but the head-wind beating, the rain pouring down, and the woman singing.

We settled down to spend the night in a barn. The barn was low-roofed. It had a stuffy smell of sheepskin, dried mushrooms, preserved cranberries, and grain. Brooms smelt of green leaves. In the shafts of light and the darkness, horse-collars loomed black under the roof, like gigantic bats. I couldn't sleep. Faces glimmered, faintly white; and a woman's whispering could be heard in the dark. I strained my ears to listen: 'Oh, Lisa, Lisa, you've no idea what a life I lead! . . . . . .

Ну, фикусы у нас, ну, печь-голландка,
ну, цинковая крыша хороша.
Всё вычищено,

        выскоблено,

                гладко . . .
Есть дети,

        муж . . .

                  Но есть ещё душа!
А в ней какой-то холод, лютый холод . . .
Вот говорит мне мать:

                    «Чем плох твой Пётр?
Он бить не бьёт, на сторону не ходит,
ну, пьёт, конечно, –

                ну, а кто не пьёт?»
Ах, Лиза, вот придёт он, пьяный, ночью,
рычит, неужто я ему навек . . .
и грубо повернёт и – молча, молча,
как будто вовсе я не человек.
Я раньше, помню, плакала бессонно.
Теперь уже умею засыпать.
Какой я стала!

              Все дают мне сорок,
а мне ведь, Лиза, только тридцать пять!
Как дальше буду?

Oh, we've got potted plants all right, and a tiled stove, and our zinc roof is fine; everything is swept and scrubbed and polished; I have my children, and my husband . . . But I have a soul as well! And somehow it's cold in my soul, bitterly cold . . . And mother says to me: "What's so wrong with your Peter? He doesn't beat you, he doesn't carry on with other women; he drinks, of course, but who doesn't drink?" Oh, Lisa, he comes home late at night, drunk, and he growls, just as if he owned me for ever . . . And roughly he turns me over and . . . without a word, without a word – as if I weren't a person at all. Before, I remember, I used to lie awake crying; now I've learnt to fall asleep. What's become of me! They all think I'm forty, but you know, Lisa, I'm only thirty-five. How can I carry on? . . . . . .

Больше нету силы . . .
Ах, если б у меня любимый был,
уж как бы я за ним тогда ходила, –
пускяй бы бил –

мне только бы любил!»

Да это ведь она сквозь дождь и ветер
летела с песней, жаркой и простой,
и я –

я ей завидовал,

я верил
раздольной незадумчивости той.
Стих разговор.

Донёсся скрип колодца
и плавно смолк.

Всё улеглось в селе.
И только сыто чавкали колёса
по втулку в придорожном киселе . . .

. . . Запомнил я отныне и навеки,
как сквозь тайгу летел наш грузовик,
разбрызгивая грязь,

сшибая ветки,
и в белом блеске молний грозовых.

I've no strength left. Oh, if only I had someone I really loved, how I'd look after him! I wouldn't care if he beat me, if only he loved me!'

So this was the one who, flying through the rain and wind, had sung that burning, simple song! And I . . . I had envied her, I had believed in that carefree spontaneity of hers. The conversation faded away. A creaking sound came from the well, and smoothly died away. Everything in the village had settled down for the night. And only the wheels [of some vehicle] were champing with a sated sound, axle-deep in the roadside mud . . .

. . . Never, as long as I live, shall I forget how our lorry flew through the forest, spattering mud, tearing off branches, and lit up by the storm's white lightning-flashes; . . . . . .

И пела женщина,

               и струйки,

                        струйки,

                                 пенясь,

по мокрому стеклу стекали вкось . . .
И я хочу,

             чтобы и мне так пелось,

как трудно бы мне в жизни ни жилось!
Чтоб шёл по свету с гордой головою,
чтоб всё вперёд –

                 и сердце

                         и глаза,

а по лицу –

               хлестанье мокрой хвои,

и на ресницах –

               слёзы и гроза!

Битница

Эта девочка из Нью-Йорка,
но ему не принадлежит.
Эта девочка вдоль неона
от самой же себя бежит.

and how the woman sang, and stream upon stream of foaming
water ran obliquely down the wet glass . . . And I, too, wish that I
could sing like that, no matter how hard my life might be; and walk
this earth, my head proudly raised, everything – heart and eyes –
straining forward, the wet pine branches lashing my face, and
tears and the storm on my eyelashes!

The Beatnik Girl

THIS girl lives in New York, yet she does not belong to it. This
girl is running past the neon lights, away from herself. . . . . .

Этой девочке ненавистен
мир – освистанный моралист.
Для неё не осталось в нём истин.
Заменяет ей истины «твист».

И с печёсаными волосами,
в грубом свитере и очках
пляшет худенькое отрицанье
на тонюсеньких каблучках.

Всё ей кажется ложью на свете,
всё – от Библии до газет.
Есть Монтекки и Капулетти.
Нет Ромео и нет Джульетт.

От раздумий деревья поникли,
и слоняется во хмелю
месяц, сумрачный, словно битник,
вдоль по млечному авеню.

Он бредёт, как от стойки к стойке,
созерцающий, нелюдим,
и прекрасный, но и жестокий
простирается город под ним.

The world, that moralist whistled off stage, is for this girl a
hateful thing. It no longer holds any truths for her. Her substitute
for truths is the 'twist'.

And, with her hair unbrushed, in a rough sweater and bespec-
tacled, this skinny little negation dances along on her stiletto heels.

Everything in the world, it seems to her, is a lie – everything from
the Bible to the newspapers. There are Montagues and Capulets,
but no Romeos and no Juliets.

The trees have hung their heads, deep in thought, and the moon,
sombre and tipsy, ambles along like a beatnik down the milky
avenue.

It wanders on as though from bar to bar, watchful and aloof, and
the beautiful but cruel city extends below. . . . . .

Всё жестоко – и крыши, и стены,
и над городом неспроста
телевизорные антенны
как распятия без Христа ...

Тайны

Тают отроческие тайны,
как туманы на берегах ...
Были тайнами – Тони, Тани,
даже с цыпками на ногах.

Были тайнами звёзды, звери,
под осинами стайки опят,
и скрипели таинственно двери –
только в детстве так двери скрипят.

Возникали загадки мира,
словно шарики изо рта
обольстительного факира,
обольщающего неспроста.

Everything is cruel – the roofs and the walls; and above the city the television aerials are – not for nothing – like crucifixes without Christ.

Mysteries

THE mysteries of adolescence melt like mists by the shore...
Tonyas and Tanyas were mysteries, even with chapped legs.
Stars and animals were mysteries, and so were clumps of mushrooms beneath the aspens; and doors creaked mysteriously: only in our childhood do they creak like this.
The riddles of the universe appeared like balls out of the mouth of a fascinating conjurer, who fascinates us to good effect ...

Оволшебленные снежинки
опускались в полях и лесах.
Оволшебленные смешинки
У девчонок плясали в глазах.

Мы таинственно что-то шептали
на таинственном льду катка,
и пугливо, как тайна к тайне,
прикасалась к руке рука . . .

Но пришла неожиданно взрослость.
Износивший свой фрак до дыр,
в чьё-то детство, как в дальнюю область,
гастролировать убыл факир.

Мы, как взрослые, им забыты.
Эх, факир, ты плохой человек.
Нетаинственно до обиды
нам на плечи падает снег.

Где вы, шарики колдовские?
Нетаинственно мы грустим.
Нетаинственны нам другие,
да и мы нетаинственны им.

Enchanted snowflakes descended on the fields and the woods;
enchanted sparks of laughter danced in the eyes of the girls.

Mysteriously we whispered things to each other on the mysterious ice of the skating-rink; and timidly, like mystery touching mystery, hand touched hand.

But suddenly adulthood came. The conjurer, his tail-coat worn to tatters, departed like a touring player to a far-away land, to perform in someone else's childhood.

We grown-ups are forgotten by him. Oh, conjurer, you're a bad man! Woefully unmysterious, the snow falls on our shoulders.

Where are you, magic balls? When we feel sad, it is unmysteriously. Other people are unmysterious for us, and we are unmysterious for them. . . . . .

Ну, а если рука случайно
прикасается, гладя слегка,
это только рука, а не тайна,
понимаете – только рука!

Дайте тайну простую-простую,
тайну – робость и тишину,
тайну худенькую, босую . . .
Дайте тайну – хотя бы одну!

    And if by chance one hand touches another, stroking it lightly,
it's only a hand, not a mystery, don't you see? – only a hand!
    Give me a mystery – just a plain and simple one – a mystery
which is diffidence and silence, a slim little, barefoot mystery: give
me a mystery – just one!

ANDREY VOZNESENSKY

Гойя

Я – Гойя!
Глазницы воронок мне выклевал ворог,
                    слетая на поле нагое.
Я – Горе.
Я – голос
Войны, городов головни
                    на снегу сорок первого года.
Я – голод.
Я горло
Повешенной бабы, чьё тело, как колокол,
                    било над площадью голой . . .
Я – Гойя!
О грозди
Возмездья!   Взвил залпом на Запад –
                    я пепел незваного гостя!
И в мемориальное небо вбил крепкие
                                звёзды –
Как гвозди.
Я – Гойя.

Goya

I AM Goya. Swooping down on the bare field, the enemy gouged
my eyes out of their crater-sockets. I am sorrow. I am the voice of
war, of the charred ruins of towns in the snow of '41. I am hunger.
I am the throat of the hanged woman, whose body, like a bell,
swung over the naked square. I am Goya. Oh, grapes of wrath!
I fired in a salvo towards the West the ashes of the unbidden
guest;* and hammered solid stars, like nails, into the memorial
sky. I am Goya.

* After the murder of 'the False Dimitri' by the Muscovites in 1606, his ashes
were said to have been fired from a cannon in the direction of Poland, whence
he had come.

Параболическая баллада

Судьба, как ракета, летит по параболе
Обычно – во мраке и реже – по радуге.

Жил огненно-рыжий художник Гоген,
Богема, а в прошлом торговый агент.
Чтоб в Лувр королевский попасть
                              из Монмартра,
Он
    дал
              кругаля через Яву с Суматрой!
Унёсся, забыв сумасшествие денег,
Кудахтанье жён, духоту академий.
Он преодолел
              тяготенье земное.
Жрецы гоготали за кружкой пивною:
«Прямая – короче, парабола – круче,
Не лучше ль скопировать райские кущи?»

А он уносился ракетой ревущей
Сквозь ветер, срывающий фалды и уши,
И в Лувр он попал не сквозь главный
                                    порог –

Parabolic Ballad

LIKE a rocket, fate describes a parabola, flying usually in darkness, and more rarely along the rainbow.

There lived a painter with fiery red hair, called Gauguin – a Bohemian, but in the past an exchange broker. To get from Montmartre into the royal Louvre he made a detour through Java and Sumatra. He took off, forgetting the madness of money, the cackling of women, the stuffiness of academies. He overcame the force of the earth's gravity. The high priests gaggled over their tankards of beer: 'The straight line is the shorter, the parabola the steeper: wouldn't it be better to copy the heavenly mansions?'

But he sped away like a roaring rocket through a gale that tore off coat-tails and ears; and he entered the Louvre not through the main entrance . . . . . .

Параболой
>   гневно
>   пробив потолок!
Идут к своим правдам, по-разному храбро.
Червяк – через щель, человек – по
>   параболе.

Жила-была девочка рядом в квартале.
Мы с нею учились, зачёты сдавали.
Куда ж я уехал!
>   И чёрт меня нёс
Меж грузных тбилисских двусмысленных
>   звёзд!
Прости мне дурацкую эту параболу.
Простывшие плечики в чёрном парадном . . .
О, как ты звенела во мраке Вселенной
Упруго и прямо, – как прутик антенны!
А я всё лечу,
>   приземляясь по ним –
Земным и озябшим твоим позывным.
Как трудно даётся нам эта парабола! . . .

but by angrily crashing through the ceiling on a parabola! Everyone moves towards his own truth, each one bravely in his own way: the worm through a chink, man along a parabola.

Once upon a time there was a girl who lived in my neighbourhood. We were fellow-students, and took our exams together. Why on earth did I go away? What devil possessed me to journey among the bulky, double-faced stars of Tiflis? Forgive me for this idiotic parabola. Frail shoulders numb with cold by the dark entrance ..
Oh, how you quavered in the darkness of the universe, pliant and straight, like an aerial wire! But I am still air-borne, and coming in to land, guided by your frozen ground signals. What an ordeal this parabola is for us! . . .

Сметая каноны, прогнозы, параграфы,
Несутся искусство, любовь и история –
По параболической траектории!

В Сибирь уезжает он нынешней ночью.

А может быть, всё же прямая – короче?

Последняя электричка

Мальчики с финками, девочки с «фиксами» . . .
Две проводницы дремотными сфинксами . . .

В вагоне спят рабочие,
Вагон во власти сна,
А в тамбуре бормочет
Нетрезвая струна . . .

Я еду в этом тамбуре,
Спасаясь от жары.
Кругом гудят, как в таборе,
Гитары и воры.

Sweeping away canons and predictions and paragraphs, art,
love, and history speed on, following a parabolic trajectory.
He leaves tonight for Siberia.
Perhaps, after all, the straight line is the shorter?

The Last Suburban Train

BOYS with their flick-knives, girls with gold crowns on their teeth,*
two conductresses like drowsy sphinxes.

Workers are asleep in the carriage, the carriage is in the grip of
sleep, while on the platform [of the carriage] a tipsy string is
strumming.

I am travelling on this platform, to escape from the heat. Around
me guitars and thieves are droning, like a gipsy camp. . . .

* A false gold crown placed on a healthy tooth is a fashionable adornment of
Soviet 'beatnik girls'.

И как-то получилось,
Что я читал стихи
Между теней плечистых,
Окурков, шелухи.

У них свои ремёсла.
А я читаю им,
Как девочка примёрзла
К окошкам ледяным.

Они сто раз судились,
Плевали на расстрел.
Сухими выходили
Из самых мокрых дел.

На черта им девчонка?
И рифм ассортимент?
Таким как эта – с чолкой
И пудрой в сантиметр?!

Стоишь – черты спитые.
На блузке видит взгляд
Всю дактилоскопию
Малаховских ребят . . .

And somehow it happened that I was reciting poetry among the broad-shouldered shadows, cigarette ends, and husks [of sunflower seeds].

These fellows have their own 'trades'; yet I am reciting a poem to them about a little girl who froze to an ice-covered window pane.

They've been in the dock dozens of times, not giving a damn for the firing squad; they've come dry out of the most blood-stained jobs.

What the hell do they care about a little girl, or a bunch of rhymes? Take this one, for instance, with a fringe, and her face inch-deep in powder.

You stand there, with jaded features. On your blouse one can see the whole finger-print range of the [suburban] lads from Malakhov-ka. . . . .

Чего ж ты плачешь бурно?
И, вся от слёз светла,
Мне шепчешь нецензурно –
Чистейшие слова? . . .

И вдруг из электрички,
Ошеломив вагон,
Ты
     чище
          Беатриче
Сбегаешь на перрон.

Кроны и корни

Несли не хоронить,
Несли короновать.

Седее, чем гранит,
Как бронза – красноват,
Дымясь локомотивом,
Художник жил,
          лохмат,
Ему лопаты были
Божественней лампад!

Why, then, do you cry so violently? And why, radiant with tears, do you coarsely whisper purest words to me?

And suddenly, dumbfounding the whole carriage and purer than Beatrice, you run down from the train on to the railway platform.

Leaves and Roots

THEY bore him not to his burial but to his coronation.

Greyer than granite, ruddy as bronze, steaming like a locomotive, the artist lived, shaggy-haired; spades were more sacred to him than icon-lamps. . . . . .

Его сирень томилась . .
Как звездопад,
               в поту
Его спина дымилась
Буханкой на поду! . . .

Зияет дом его.
Пустые этажи,
В столовой никого.
В России – ни души.

Художники уходят
Без шапок,
             будто в храм,
В гудящие угодья
К берёзам и дубам.

Побеги их – победы.
Уход их – как восход.
Полянам и планетам
От ложных позолот.

Леса роняют кроны.
Но мощно под землёй
Ворочаются корни
Корявой пятернёй.

His lilac languished . . . Like a cascade of falling stars, his back steamed with sweat – a loaf of bread on the oven-floor.

His house stands open wide. All its floors are empty. There is no one in the dining-room; not a soul in Russia.

The artists depart, heads bared, as though to church, to the resonant domains, to the birches and the oaks.

Their flights are victories. Their departure is like the sunrise; to the glades and the planets, away from false gilt.

The forests shed their crowns of leaves, but underground the roots powerfully move their gnarled fingers.

BELLA AKHMADULINA

Новая домна на КМК

Где вздымается новая домна,
так работа идёт наверху,
словно этому парню удобно
хохотать и висеть на ветру.

Он небрежно идёт по карнизу,
но, быть может, заметно едва
мимолётною завистью к низу
замутится его голова.

Он вздыхает привольно и сладко,
и ступени гудят невпопад,
и огнём осыпается сварка –
августовский её звездопад.

В нём, конечно, отвага без меры,
и задор, и мгновенный расчёт,
что девчонка высокие метры
между ним и землёю сочтёт.

The New Blast-Furnace in the Kemerovo Metallurgical Combine

UP there, where the new blast-furnace rises, work is going on – just as if that lad enjoyed laughing and balancing in the wind.

Carelessly he walks along the ledge, but perhaps for a fleeting instant and almost imperceptibly his head will swim with dizziness, yearning for the ground below.

He breathes freely and happily, his irregular footsteps echoing, while fire from the welding-burner scatters in sparks, like a cascade of falling stars in August.

Of course, there is boundless daring and ardour in him, and a sudden expectation that one of the girls will count the yards that stretch between him and the ground far below. . . . .

У девчонок иные привычки.
Поглядит, не поняв ничего.
Что-то нравится ей, что превыше
высоты, подымавшей его.

Но, бывавшая в цирке нечасто,
напряжённо подавшись вперёд,
побледнеет она за гимнаста,
если тот по канату пройдёт.

И, глубокой обиды не выдав,
на девчонок, забывших о нём,
он опять с независимым видом
смотрит сверху и брызжет огнём.

But girls behave differently. One of them will look up at him, understanding nothing. There is something she likes about it all, something far higher than the height on which he is standing.

But on her rare visits to the circus, anxiously straining forward, she turns pale with anxiety for the acrobat when he walks the tight-rope.

And without betraying how deeply he is piqued, he once again with an unconcerned air looks down from his height on the girls who have forgotten all about him, and scatters sparks of fire.

INDEX OF TITLES AND FIRST LINES

Айя-София 351
«Айя-София – здесь остановиться» 351
Аккорды 243
Ангел 154
Анчар 98
Арбуз 402
Атлантический океан 376
«Ах, зачем меня» 151
Ахиллес у алтаря 251

Баллада 304
Баллада о камергере Деларю 182
Бежецк 321
«Без отдыха пирует с дружиной удалой» 172
«Бейте в площади бунтов топот!» 372
«Берёзы севера мне милы» 191
«Бессонница. Гомер. Тугие паруса» 352
Бесы 101
«Били копыта» 373
Битница 448
«Блажен, кто мог на ложе ночи» 124
«Божья Матерь *Утоли мои печали*» 266
«Болящий дух врачует песнопенье» 120
Борис Годунов [отрывок] 88
«Буря мглою небо кроет» 90
«Буря на небе вечернем» 191
Бык 326
«Были святки кострами согреты» 323

«В аллею чёрные спустились небеса» 227
«В армяке с открытым воротом» 201
В больнице 347
«В глухую степь земной дороги» 143
В деревне [отрывок] 198
«В жаркое лето и в зиму метельную» 281
«В златотканые дни Сентября» 310
«В Испании Амур не чужестранец» 83
«В красоте музыкальности» 243

В лесу 332
«В моё окошко дождь стучится» 363
«В моём окне – на весь квартал» 417
«В московские особняки» 338
«В наши окна, щурясь, смотрит лето» 427
«В Петербурге мы сойдёмся снова» 359
«В полдневный жар, в долине Дагестана» 169
«В пустыне чахлой и скупой» 98
«В разноголосице девического хора» 353
«В своей бессовестной и жалкой низости» 245
«В святой Софии голуби летали» 248
«В течаенье этой медленной зимы» 431
«В тумане утреннем неверными шагами» 219
«В чащах. в болотах огромных» 295
Вальс 247
Век 361
«Век мой, зверь мой, кто сумеет» 361
«Весёлый день горит . . . Среди сомлевших трав» 222
«Весенний лепет не разнежит» 306
Весенняя гроза 129
Весна 437
Весна в Ленинграде [отрывок] 431
Ветер (Пастернак) 343
Ветер (Солоухин) 434
Ветер (Тихонов) 407
Вечер 79
Вечернее размышление о Божием величестве 52
Вечером 315
«Видели ли вы» 393
Видение 129
Виноград 84
Влас 201
Властителям и судиям 57
«Вновь арок древних верный пилигрим» 238
«Возьми, египтянка, гитару» 61
Воин Агамемнона 291
«Вонзил кинжал убийца нечестивый» 182
«Ворочая тяжёлыми белками» 326
Воспоминание 98
«Восстал Всевышний Бог, да судит» 57
«Вот бреду я вдоль большой дороги» 141
«Вперебежку, вприпрыжку, по перекрытым» 407
Врата рая 292

«Всё расхищено, предано, продано» 320
«Всё, что минутно, всё, что бренно» 274
Вступление к «Медному Всаднику» 111
«Вся ты закуталась шубой пушистой» 220
«Высока луна Господня» 231
«Выхожу один я на дорогу» 170

Гамлет 335
«Где вздымается новая домна» 460
Гефсиманский Сад 340
«Глубокий взор вперив на камень» 121
«Годовщину весёлую празднуй» 322
Гойя 453
Голоса 236
Горькая доля 150
«Гражданин фининспектор! Простите за беспокойство» 379
«Гул затих. Я вышел на подмостки» 335
Гуси 64

«Дало две доли Провидение» 116
Два стихотворения 324
Две доли 116
19-го марта 1823 г. 70
Decrescendo 228
Демон [отрывок] 156
День и ночь 135
Детство 421
«Для берегов отчизны дальной» 104
Дмитровская Суббота 46
«До свиданья, друг мой, до свиданья» 399
«Довольно: не жди, не надейся» 260
Дон-Кихот [отрывок] 234
«Дон-Кихот путей не выбирает» 234
«Духовной жаждою томим» 92
«Дым табачный воздух выел» 369

Евгений Онегин [отрывок] 84
«Еду ли ночью по улице тёмной» 196
«Если ты поэт, и хочешь быть могучим» 244
«Есть в близости людей заветная черта» 317
«Есть в напевах твоих сокровенных» 278
«Есть в стане моём – офицерская прямость» 364

«Есть иволги в лесах, и гласных долгота»   352
«Есть некий час, в ночи, всемирного молчанья»   129
«Есть тонкие властительные связи»   250
«Ещё весны душистой нега»   192
«Ещё одно, последнее сказанье»   88
«Ещё раз, ещё раз»   289

«Жив Бог! Умён, а не заумен»   307
«Жизнь наша в старости – изношенный халат»   80

«За вздохом утренним мороза»   194
За гробом   266
Заблудившийся трамвай   300
«Забыты вино и веселье»   233
«Зачем, о Просперо волшебный»   241
«Звенела музыка в саду»   315
«Здравствуй, родная.» – «Как можется, кумушка?»   198
Земля   338
«Зефир последний свеял сон»   77
Зимний вечер   90
Зимняя ночь   336
«Зловещ горизонт и внезапен»   346
«Знаю я, во вражьем стане»   251

«И море и буря качали наш чёлн»   130
«И скучно, и грустно, и некому руку подать»   163
«И цветы, и шмели, и трава, и колосья»   248
Ивановы   415
Ивы и берёзы   191
«Из строгого, стройного храма»   363
«Из тучи с тучей в безумном споре»   228
«Имя где для тебя?»   68
Иоанн Дамаскин [отрывок]   177
«Испанский камень слепящ и бел»   376
Июль 1914   318

К ***   89
К Музе   278
К ней   68
К Рейну   125

Казачья колыбельная песня — 161
«Как были те выходы в тишь хороши!» — 330
«Как ветер мокрый, ты бьёшься в ставни» — 246
«Как воды далёких озёр» — 286
«Как вы когда-то разборчивы были» — 389
«Как живётся вам с другою» — 365
«Как след весла, от берега ушедший» — 408
«Как хорош чуть мерцающим утром» — 193
«Как хорошо ты, о море ночное» — 139
«Как часто, пёстрою толпою окружён» — 159
«Какая сладость в жизни сей» — 177
«Какой тяжёлый, тёмный бред!» — 223
Капитаны [отрывок] — 293
Квартет — 65
«Клянусь я первым днём творенья» — 156
Князь Михайло Репнин — 172
«Когда волнуется желтеющая нива» — 155
«Когда для смертного умолкнет шумный день» — 98
«Когда, печалью вдохновенный» — 118
Колокольчик — 186
«Кому быть живым и хвалимым» — 343
«Кому повем печаль мою» — 43
Коробейники [отрывок] — 206
Кроны и корни — 458

Лебедь — 188
Лиличка! — 369
«Лице свое скрывает день» — 52
«Луга мутило жаром лиловатым» — 332
«Любви начало было летом» — 311
«Любит? не любит? Я руки ломаю» — 385
«Люблю глаза твои, мой друг» — 134
«Люблю грозу в начале мая» — 129
«Люблю отчизну я, но странною любовью» — 168
«Люблю я вас, богини пенья» — 122
Любовь (Баратынский) — 117
Любовь (В. Иванов) — 237
«Любовь, любовь – гласит преданье» — 135
Люцифер — 248

Маки — 222
«Мальчики с финками, девочки с «фиксами»» — 456

«Мати, мати, Мать Божия, Мария Пресвятая!»   49
Медный Всадник [отрывок]   111
«Меж тем, как Франция, среди рукоплесканий»   164
«Мело, мело по всей земле»   336
«Мерцаньем звёзд далёких безразлично»   340
«Минувших дней очарованье»   69
Мой гений   76
«Молчи, скрывайся и таи»   132
Монолог Пимена   88
Мороз, Красный Нос [отрывок]   208
Мужик   295
«Муз моих вещунья и подруга»   236
Муза   119
«Мчатся тучи, вьются тучи»   101
«Мы – два грозой зажжённые ствола»   237
«Мы едем поляною голой»   148
«Мы пьём в любви отраву сладкую»   117
«Мы разучились нищим подавать»   407
«Мы теперь уходим понемногу»   396

«На берегу пустынных волн»   111
«На кануне суботы Дмитровской»   46
«На мир таинственный духов»   135
На поле Куликовом   267
«На полярных морях и на южных»   293
На Сайме зимой   220
«На свою бессчетну золоту казну»   32
«На стоге сена ночью южной»   193
«На страшной высоте блуждающий огонь»   354
«На что вы, дни! Юдольный мир явленья»   120
«Над зыбкой рябью вод встаёт из глубины»   256
Накануне годовщины 4-го августа 1864 г.   141
Наш марш   372
«. . . Не ветер бушует над бором»   208
«Не лѣпо ли ны бяшетъ, братие, начяти старыми сло-
    весы»   1
«Не ослеплён я музою моею»   119
«Не семью печатями алмазными»   292
«Не стану я жалеть о розах»   84
«Не сырой дуб к земле клонится»   23
«Небо нас совсем свело с ума»   224
«Незабвенный сентябрь осыпается в Спасском»   333

Незнакомка — 262
Нелюбовь — 246
«Несли не хоронить» — 458
«Нет, жизнь меня не обделила» — 423
Новая домпа на КМК — 460
Ночь — 71
«Ночь выла, кружила, трубила округой» — 437
«Ночь, улица, фонарь, аптека» — 280

«О былом, о погибшем, о старом» — 147
«О, быть покинутым – какое счастье!» — 254
«О вещая душа моя!» — 138
«О, говори хоть ты со мной» — 214
«О доблестях, о подвигах, о славе» — 264
«О, как на склоне наших лет» — 137
«О память сердца! ты сильней» — 76
«О пашни, пашни, пашни» — 392
«О тебе вспоминаю я редко» — 316
«О чём ты воешь, ветр ночной?» — 133
Обводный канал — 417
Объяснение в любви — 259
«Огромные глаза, как у нарядной куклы» — 421
«Ой, полна, полна коробушка» — 206
«Окаменев под чарами журчанья» — 239
«Октябрь уж наступил – уж роща отряхает» — 105
«Он ветрен, как ветер. Как ветер» — 344
«Он стоит пред раскалённым горном» — 297
Она — 245
«Оратор римский говорил» — 131
Осень — 105
«Осень только взялась за работу» — 432
«Отговорила роща золотая» — 398
Отчизна — 168

«Падает снег на дорогу» — 312
Памятник — 58
Параболическая баллада — 454
«Пахнет гарью. Четыре недели» — 318
«Певучесть есть в морских волнах» — 140
«Пел смычок, – в садах горели» — 188

Первая поездка Ильи Муромца; Илья и Соловей-Разбойник 23
Первое января 159
Перед зеркалом 308
Песнь о собаке 391
Песня (Жуковский) 69
Песня (Кольцов) 151
Письмо к матери 394
Плач Иосифа 43
Плач о Есенине [отрывок] 312
«По вечерам над ресторанами» 262
«По гребле неровной и тряской» 175
«По небу полуночи ангел летел» 154
По ягоды 442
«Погасла последняя краска» 229
Подражателям 118
«Пока не требует поэта» 93
Полёт светляков 412
«Полы трёт полотёр» 438
Попытка ревности 365
«Пора, мой друг, пора! покоя сердце просит» 115
Портрет Инфанты 410
После казни в Женеве 216
После концерта 227
Последнее новоселье 164
Последняя любовь 137
Последняя электричка 456
«Похолодели лепестки» 247
Поэма без героя [отрывок] 323
Поэма о движении 438
Поэт 93
Поэту 252
«Праздничный, весёлый, бесноватый» 406
«Предлинной хворостиной» 64
Предопределение 135
«Прекрасно в нас влюблённое вино» 299
«Прелестный вечер! В сладком обаяньи» 79
«При долине, при долине» 44
Пробуждение 77
«Проказница-мартышка» 65
Пророк 92
«Прославим, братья, сумерки свободы» 355
«Пусть кто-то ещё отдыхает на юге» 325

Рабочий 297
Равенна 274
Разговор с фининспектором о поэзии 379
Разговор Татьяны с няней 84
«Раззолочённые, но чахлые сады» 222
«Река времён в своём стремленьи» 63
«Река раскинулась. Течёт, грустит лениво» 267
Рим 148
Римские сонеты I, IV, and VII 238
«Рождённые в года глухие» 284
Руслан и Людмила [отрывок] 96

«С бесчеловечною судьбой» 388
Садко и Морской Царь 32
«Свежак надрывается. Прёт на рожон» 402
Святая Русь 257
Сентябрь 222
Сентябрьская роза 194
«Сёстры – тяжесть и нежность – одинаковы ваши приметы» 358
«Сижу, освещаемый сверху» 304
Silentium 132
Sin miedo 244
«Сияет роса на листочках» 259
«Сквозь чайный пар я вижу гору Фузий» 254
Скульптор 121
Слово о плъку Игоревѣ 1
«Смутную душу мою тяготит» 291
Смычок и струны 223
Соловей во сне 60
Соловьём залётным 150
Сон 169
«Сон Летней Ночи! Факелов пыланье» 412
Сон на море 130
Сон Пресвятыя Богородицы 49
Сонет к форме 250
Сорокоуст [отрывок] 393
Спасское 333
«Спи, младенец мой прекрасный» 161
«Спит водоём осенний, окроплён» 240
«Спокойный взор, подобный взору лани» 247
«Стал мне реже сниться, слава Богу» 317

Стальная цикада 226
Старая шарманка 224
Степь 330
Стихи в честь Натальи 427
Стихи о Сонечке [отрывок] 363
«Стояли, как перед витриной» 347
«Стоят чиновные деревья» 415
«Судьба, как ракета, летит по параболе» 454
«Суздаль да Москва не для тебя ли» 257

«Таинственной невстречи» 324
Тайны 450
Талисман 94
«Там белые церкви и звонкий, светящийся лёд» 321
«Там, где море вечно плещет» 94
«Тают отроческие тайны» 450
Тень друга 74
«То было раннею весной» 181
«. . . Тоска любви Татьяну гонит» 84
Тоска миража 229
«Три женщины» 442
Три розы 143
Три сестры 286
Tristia 356
«Тщетно я скрываю сердца скорби люты» 55
«Ты должен быть гордым, как знамя» 252
«Ты жива ещё, моя старушка?» 394
«Ты помнишь? В нашей бухте сонной» 283
«Ты предо мною» 70
«Тяжёлый день . . . ты уходил так вяло» 216
«Тяжкий, плотный занавес у входа» 276

«У лукоморья дуб зелёный» 96
«У царицы моей есть высокий дворец» 218
«Уже утомившийся день» 71
«Улеглася метелица . . . путь озарён» 186
«Уступи мне, скворец, уголок» 419
«Утром в ржаном закуте» 391

Фузий в блюдечке 254

Хор вершин	328
Хорошее отношение к лошадям	373
Художник	281
«Художник был горяч, приветлив, чист, умён»	410
Царевич Иосаф, Пустынник	44
Цицерон	131
Цыганская пляска	61
«Четверть века прошло заграницей»	390
«Что селения наши убогие»	231
Шаги Командора	276
«Шёл я по улице незнакомой»	300
Шестое чувство	299
«Широкие плечи гор»	328
«Широко, широко, широко»	345
Элегия	124
«Эта девочка из Нью-Йорка»	448
Эти бедные селенья	138
«Я берег покидал туманный Альбиона»	74
«Я вас любил: любовь ещё, быть может»	100
«Я видел, как бегут твои зелёны волны»	125
«Я – Гойя»	453
«Я знал, что она вернётся»	226
«Я изучил науку расставанья»	356
«Я Музу юную, бывало»	71
«Я на холме спал высоком»	60
«Я очи знал – о, эти очи!»	136
«Я памятник себе воздвиг чудесный, вечный»	58
«Я помню чудное мгновенье»	89
«Я пришёл к тебе с приветом»	190
«Я сладко изнемог»	401
«Я чувствую, во мне горит»	144
«Я, я, я. Что за дикое слово!»	308

INDEX OF POETS

Akhmadulina, Bella 460
Akhmatova, Anna 315
Aliger, Margarita 431
Annensky, Innokenty 222
Antokol'sky, Pavel 410
Aseev, Nikolay 326

Bagritsky, Eduard 401
Bal'mont, Konstantin 243
Baratynsky, Evgeny 116
Batyushkov, Konstantin 74
Bely, Andrey 259
Blok, Aleksandr 262
Bryusov, Valery 250
Bunin, Ivan 247
Byliny 23

Del'vig, Baron Anton 83
Derzhavin, Gavriil 57
Dukhovnye Stikhi 43

Esenin, Sergey 391
Evtushenko, Evgeny 442

Fet, Afanasy 190

Gippius, Zinaida 245
Grigoriev, Apollon 214
Gumilev, Nikolay 291

Ivanov, Georgy 388
Ivanov, Vyacheslav 236

Khlebnikov, Velimir 286
Khodasevich, Vladislav 304
Klyuev, Nikolay 310
Kol'tsov, Aleksey 150
Krylov, Ivan 64
Kuzmin, Mikhail 254

Lermontov, Mikhail 154
Lomonosov, Mikhail 52

Mandel'shtam, Osip 351
Mayakovsky, Vladimir 369

Nekrasov, Nikolay 196

Pasternak, Boris 330
Pavlova, Karolina 147
Polonsky, Yakov 186
Pushkin, Aleksandr 84

Slovo o polku Igoreve 1
Sluchevsky, Konstantin 216
Sologub, Fedor 231
Soloukhin, Vladimir 434
Soloviev, Vladimir 218
Sumarokov, Aleksandr 55

Tikhonov, Nikolay 406
Tolstoy, Count Aleksey 172
Tsvetaeva, Marina 363
Tvardovsky, Aleksandr 423
Tyutchev, Fedor 129

Vasiliev, Pavel 427
Venevitinov, Dmitri 143
Vinokurov, Evgeny 437
Voloshin, Maksimilian 256
Voznesensky, Andrey 453
Vyazemsky, Prince Petr 79

Yazykov, Nikolay 124

Zabolotsky, Nikolay 415
Zhukovsky, Vasily 68